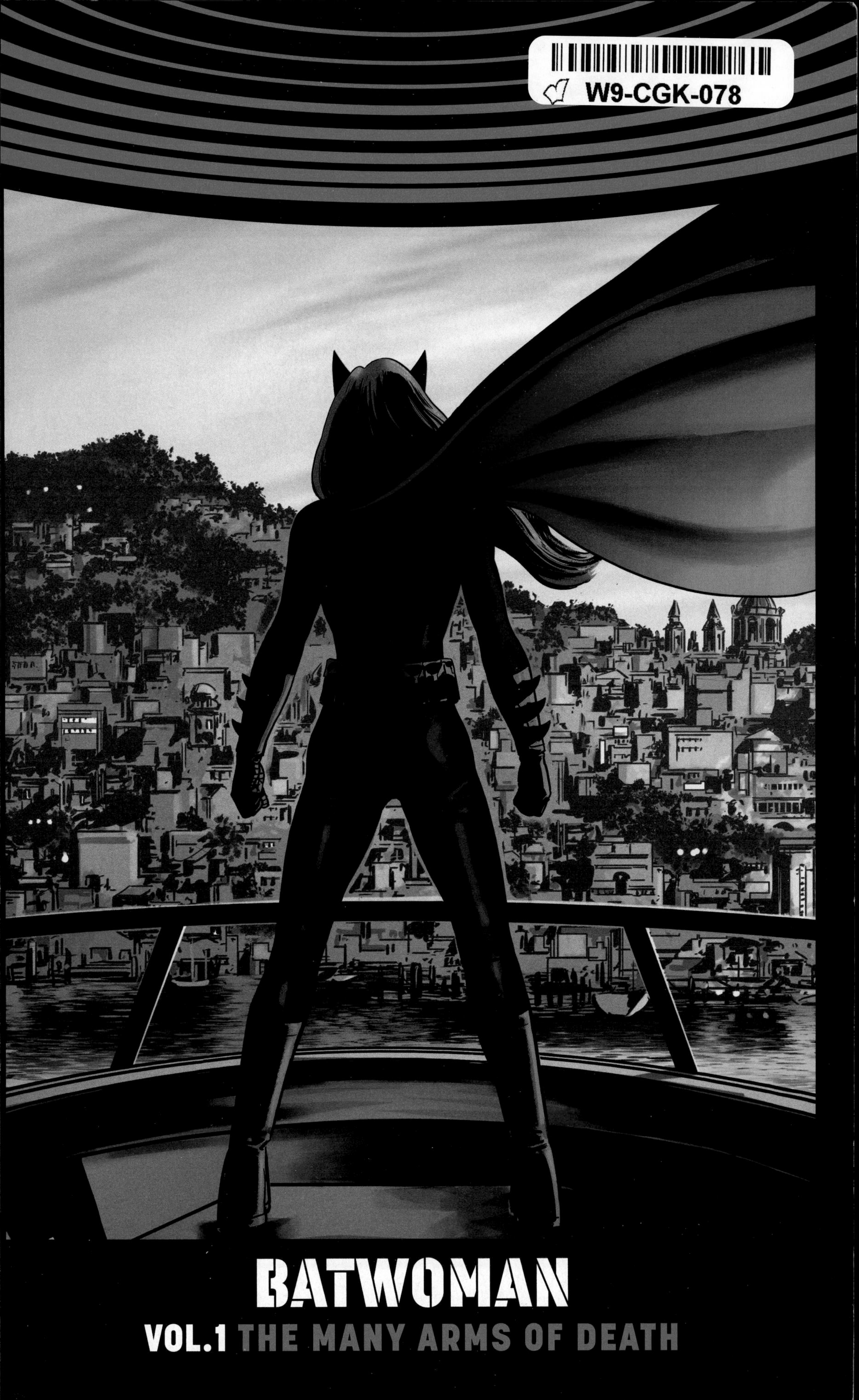

BATWOMAN

VOL.1 THE MANY ARMS OF DEATH

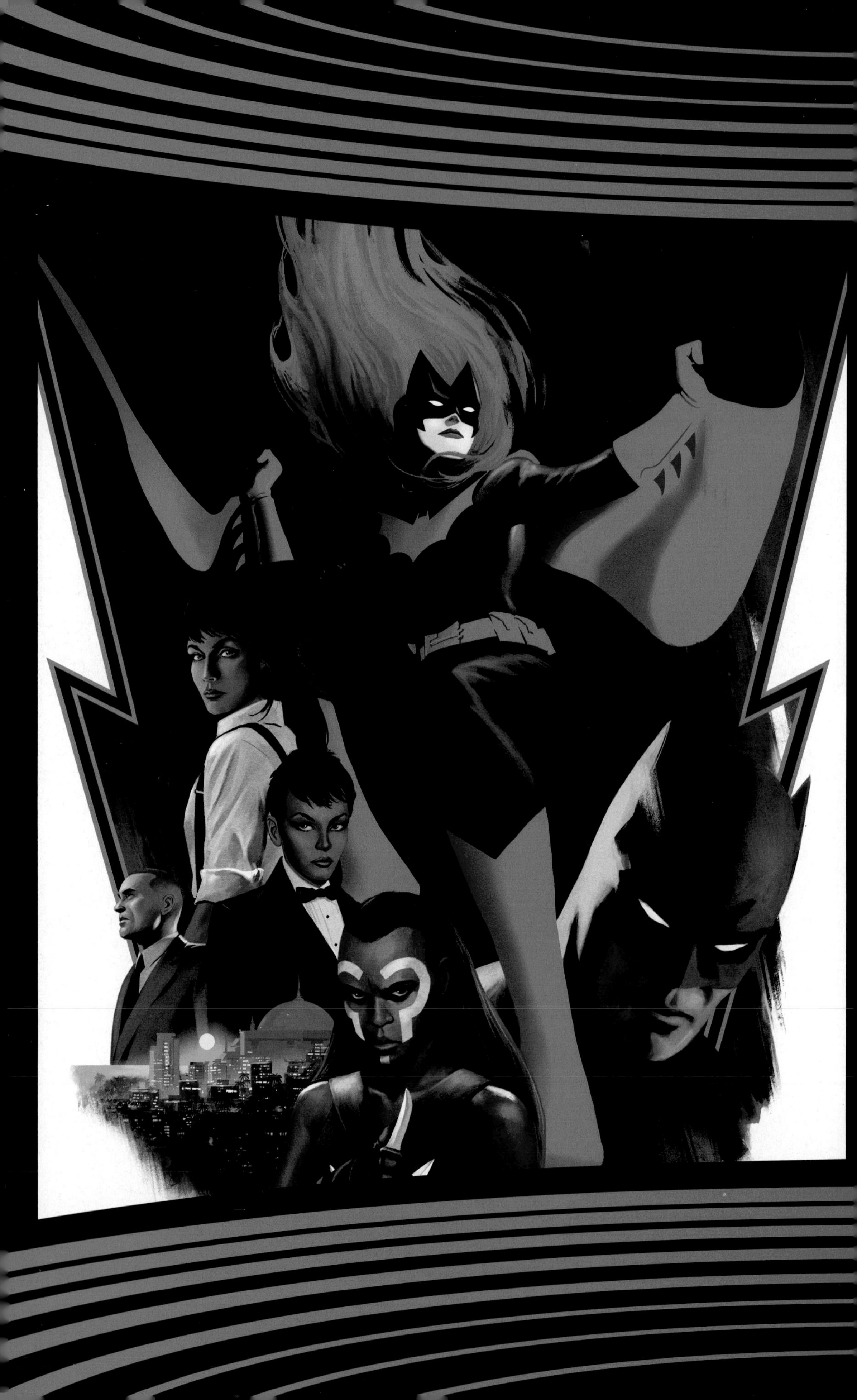

BATWOMAN

VOL.1 THE MANY ARMS OF DEATH

MARGUERITE BENNETT * **JAMES TYNION IV**
writers

STEVE EPTING * **STEPHANIE HANS** * **RENATO ARLEM**
artists

JEROMY COX * **ADRIANO LUCAS**
colorists

DERON BENNETT
letterer

STEVE EPTING
collection cover art

STEVE EPTING * **STEPHANIE HANS**
EDDY BARROWS, EBER FERREIRA and ADRIANO LUCAS
original series covers

CHRIS CONROY Editor - Original Series ✳ **DAVE WIELGOSZ** Assistant Editor - Original Series
JEB WOODARD Group Editor - Collected Editions ✳ **SCOTT NYBAKKEN** Editor - Collected Edition
STEVE COOK Design Director - Books ✳ **MONIQUE NARBONETA** Publication Design

BOB HARRAS Senior VP - Editor-in-Chief, DC Comics
PAT McCALLUM Executive Editor, DC Comics

DAN DiDIO Publisher ✳ **JIM LEE** Publisher & Chief Creative Officer
BOBBIE CHASE VP - New Publishing Initiatives & Talent Development ✳ **DON FALLETTI** VP - Manufacturing Operations & Workflow Management
LAWRENCE GANEM VP - Talent Services ✳ **ALISON GILL** Senior VP - Manufacturing & Operations
HANK KANALZ Senior VP - Publishing Strategy & Support Services ✳ **DAN MIRON** VP - Publishing Operations
NICK J. NAPOLITANO VP - Manufacturing Administration & Design ✳ **NANCY SPEARS** VP - Sales
MICHELE R. WELLS VP & Executive Editor, Young Reader

This book is dedicated to a girl in high school the week that DC Comics announced a queer superheroine
by the name of Batwoman. You went into the bathroom and cried because you couldn't believe it.
To that girl–it'll be okay. Keep working. Keep going. It's all gonna turn out right in the end.
–Marguerite Bennett

BATWOMAN VOL. 1: THE MANY ARMS OF DEATH

DC Comics, 2900 West Alameda Ave., Burbank, CA 91505
Printed by LSC Communications, Kendallville, IN, USA. 7/22/19. Second Printing.
ISBN: 978-1-4012-7430-6

Library of Congress Cataloging-in-Publication Data is available.

PEFC Certified

This product is from
sustainably managed
forests and controlled
sources

PEFC/29-31-337   www.pefc.org

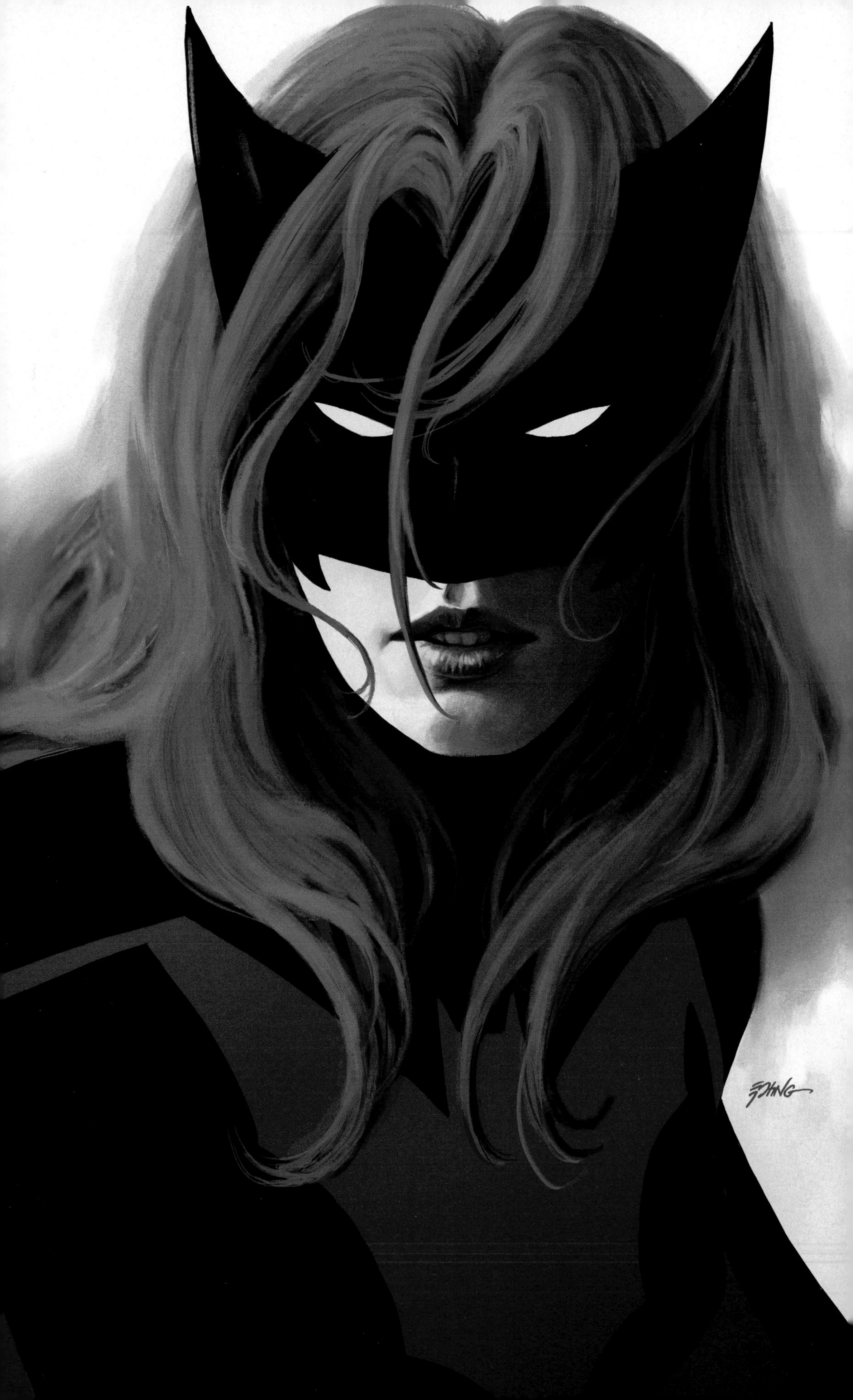

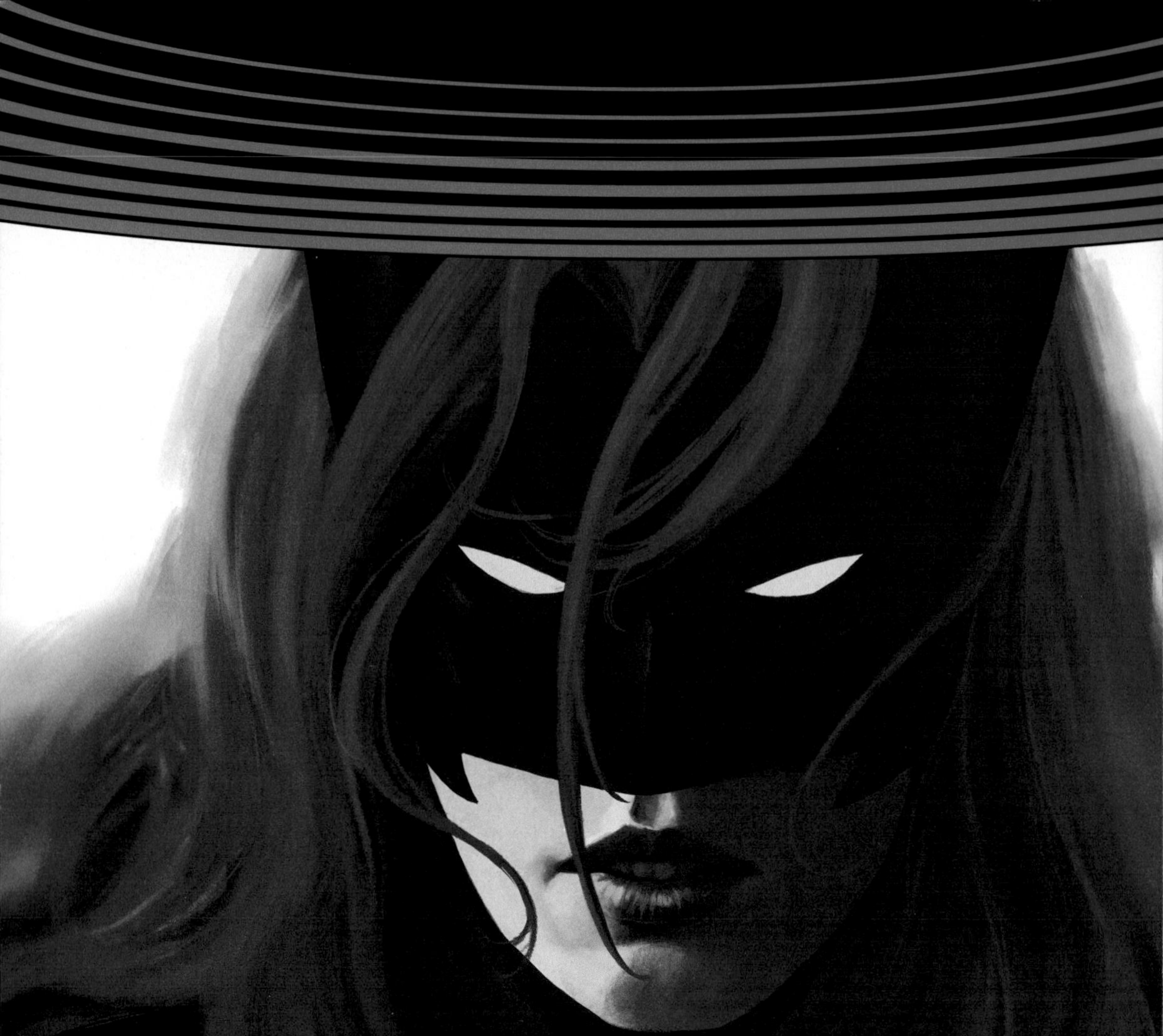

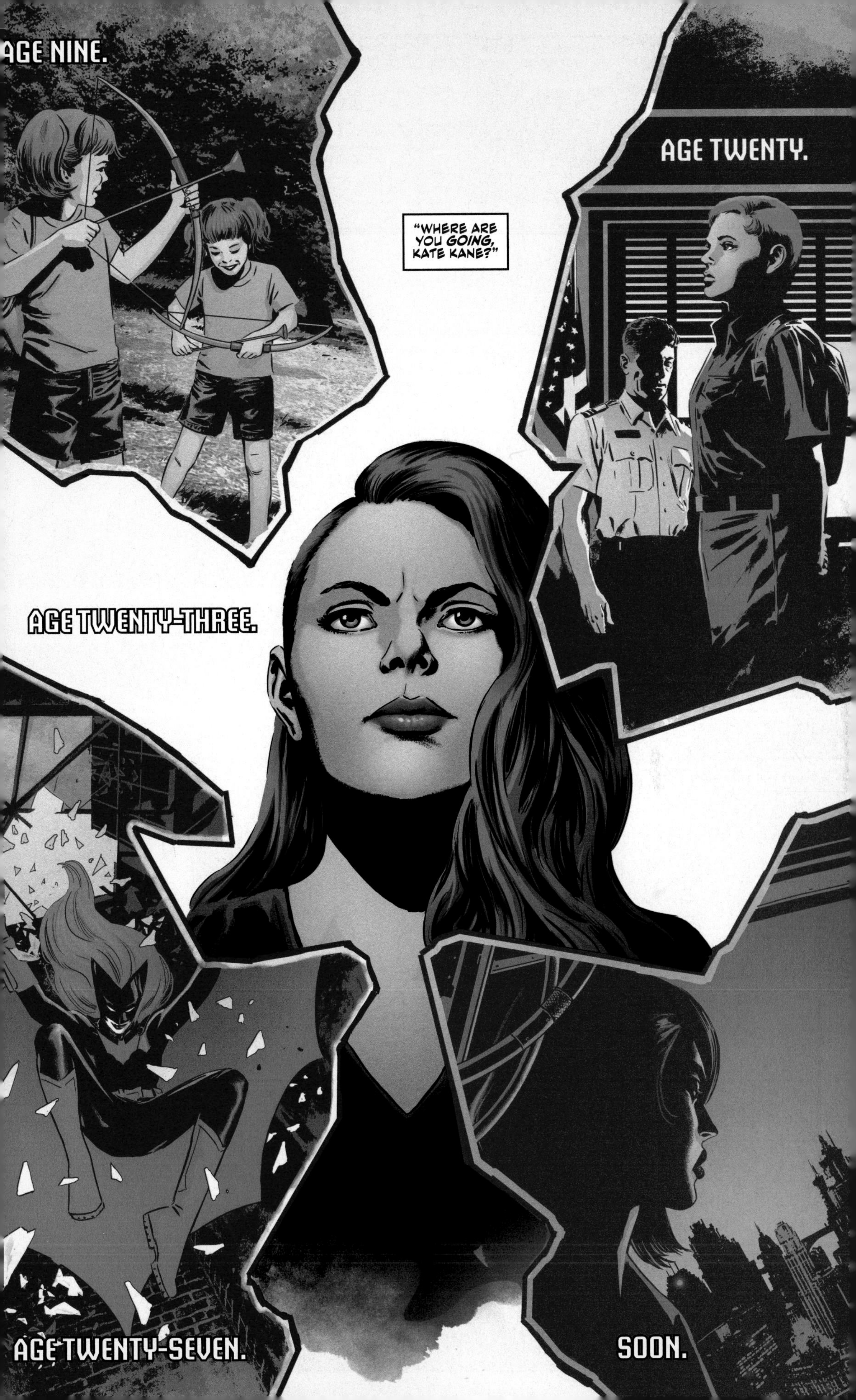
AGE NINE.
"WHERE ARE YOU GOING, KATE KANE?"
AGE TWENTY.
AGE TWENTY-THREE.
AGE TWENTY-SEVEN.
SOON.

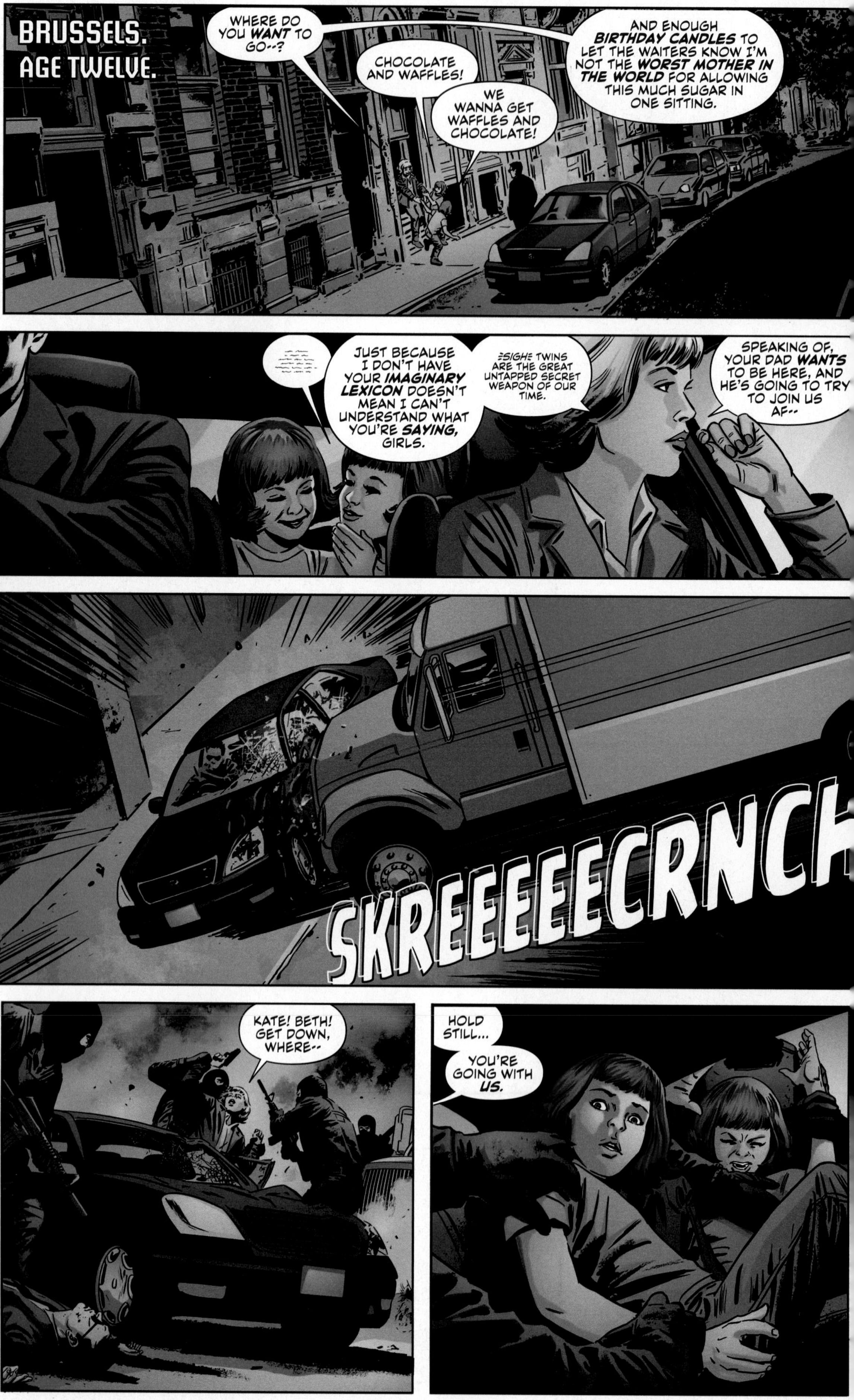
BRUSSELS. AGE TWELVE.
WHERE DO YOU WANT TO GO--?
CHOCOLATE AND WAFFLES!
WE WANNA GET WAFFLES AND CHOCOLATE!
AND ENOUGH BIRTHDAY CANDLES TO LET THE WAITERS KNOW I'M NOT THE WORST MOTHER IN THE WORLD FOR ALLOWING THIS MUCH SUGAR IN ONE SITTING.
JUST BECAUSE I DON'T HAVE YOUR IMAGINARY LEXICON DOESN'T MEAN I CAN'T UNDERSTAND WHAT YOU'RE SAYING, GIRLS.
=SIGH= TWINS ARE THE GREAT UNTAPPED SECRET WEAPON OF OUR TIME.
SPEAKING OF, YOUR DAD WANTS TO BE HERE, AND HE'S GOING TO TRY TO JOIN US AF--
SKREEEEEECRNCH
KATE! BETH! GET DOWN, WHERE--
HOLD STILL...
YOU'RE GOING WITH US.

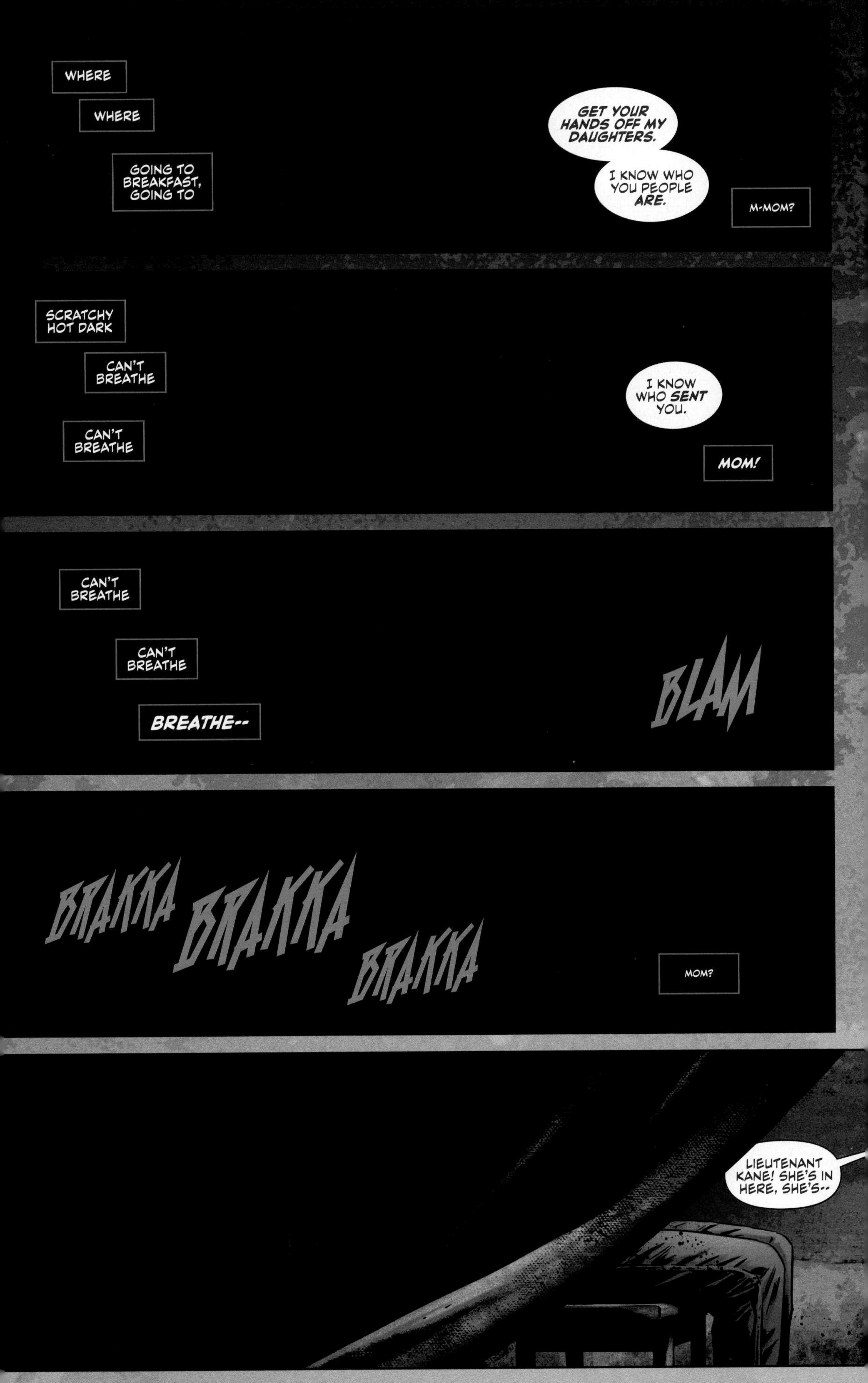
WHERE
WHERE
GOING TO BREAKFAST, GOING TO
GET YOUR HANDS OFF MY DAUGHTERS.
I KNOW WHO YOU PEOPLE ARE.
M-MOM?
SCRATCHY HOT DARK
CAN'T BREATHE
CAN'T BREATHE
I KNOW WHO SENT YOU.
MOM!
CAN'T BREATHE
CAN'T BREATHE
BREATHE--
BLAM
BRAKKA BRAKKA BRAKKA
MOM?
LIEUTENANT KANE! SHE'S IN HERE, SHE'S--

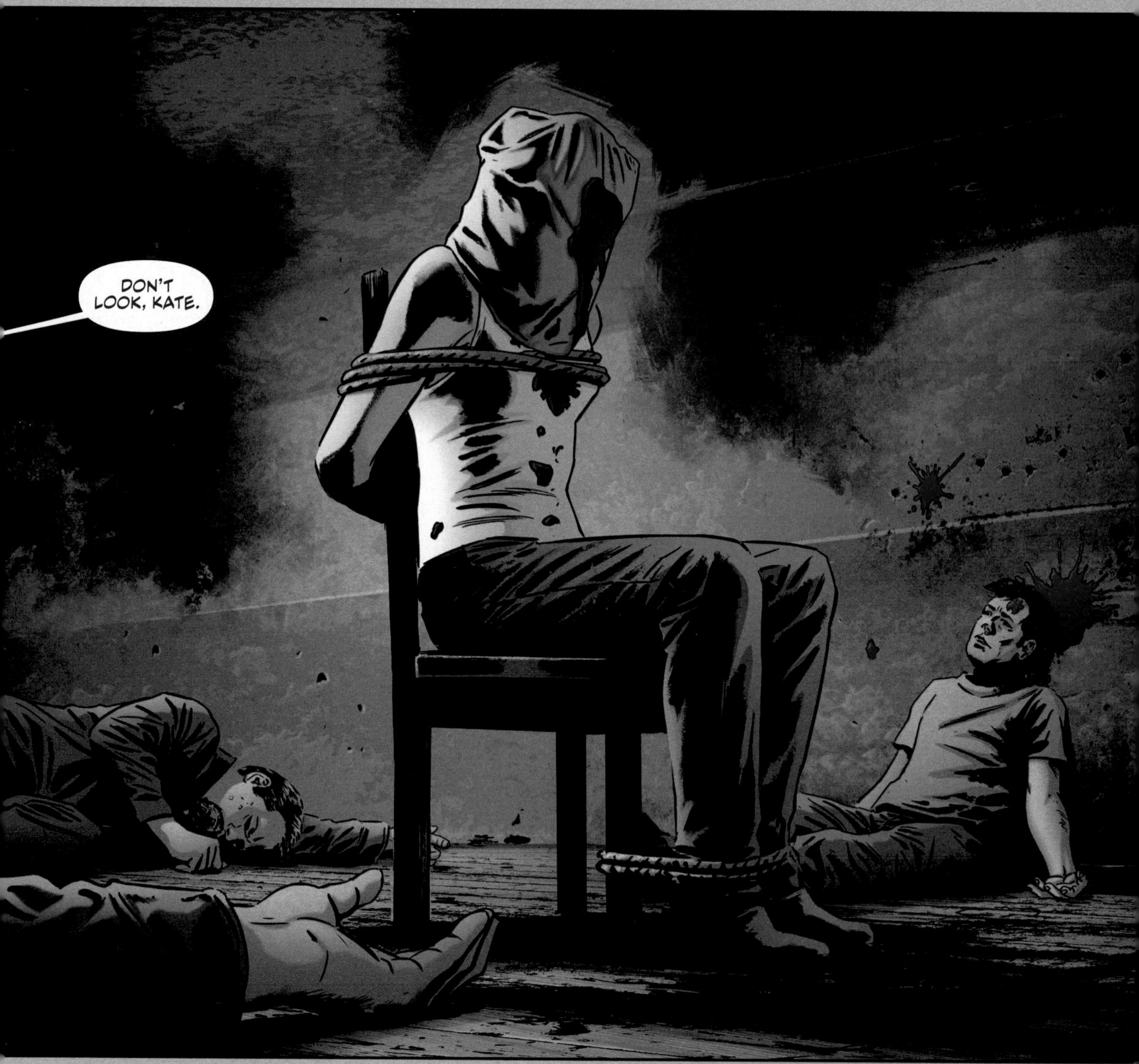
DON'T LOOK, KATE.

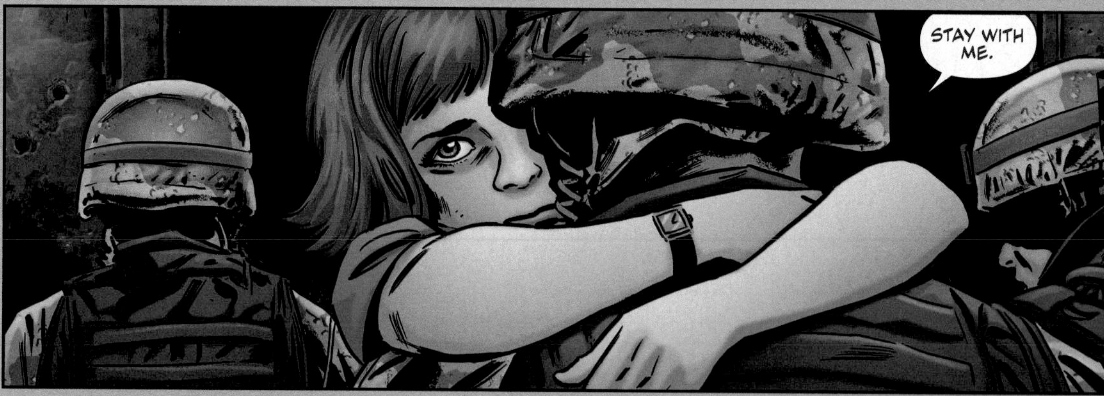
STAY WITH ME.

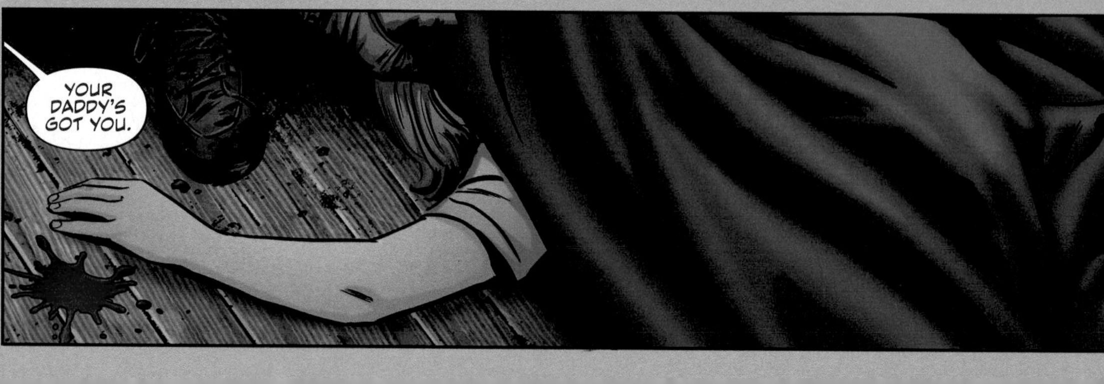
YOUR DADDY'S GOT YOU.

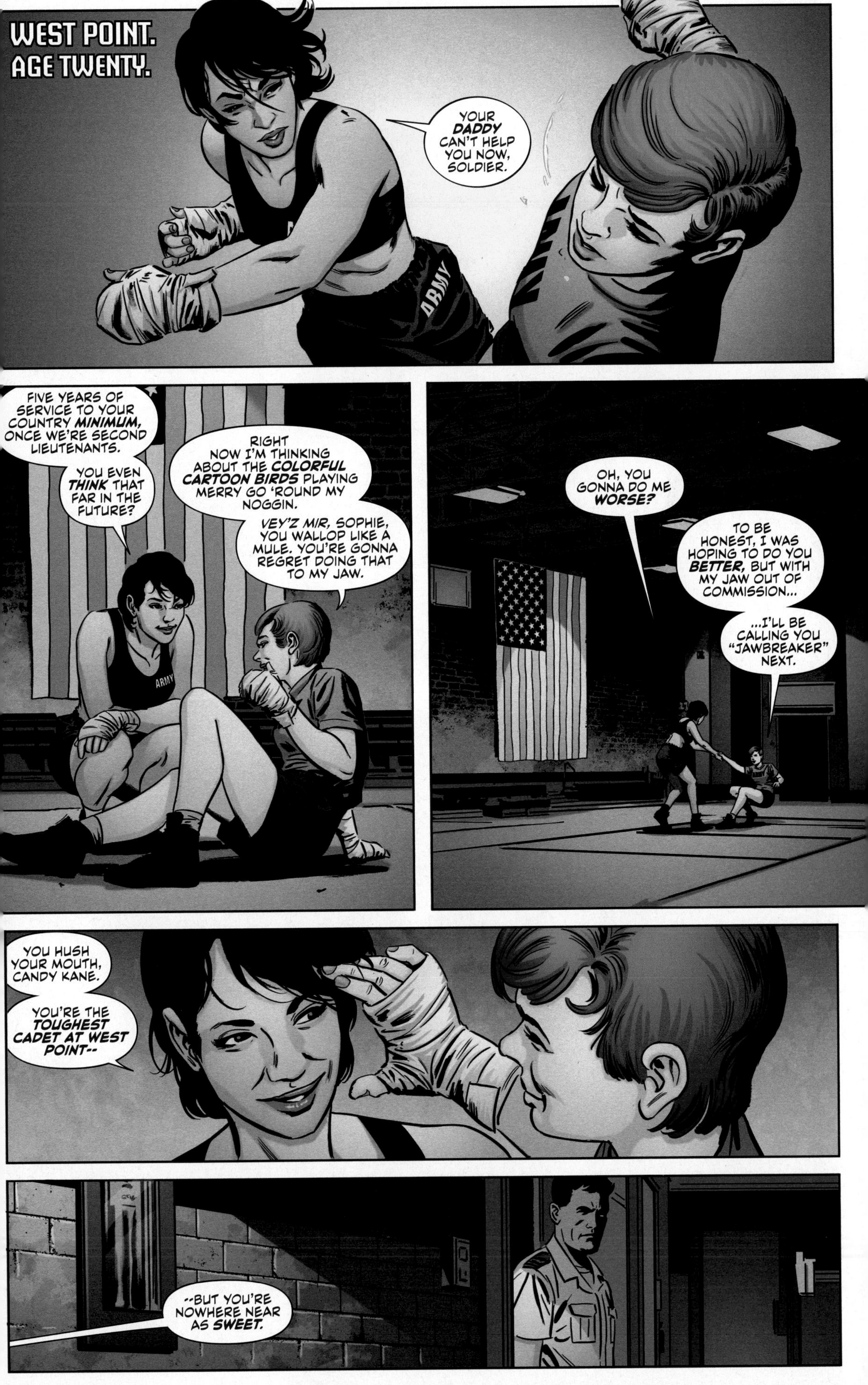
WEST POINT. AGE TWENTY.
YOUR DADDY CAN'T HELP YOU NOW, SOLDIER.
ARMY
FIVE YEARS OF SERVICE TO YOUR COUNTRY MINIMUM, ONCE WE'RE SECOND LIEUTENANTS.
YOU EVEN THINK THAT FAR IN THE FUTURE?
RIGHT NOW I'M THINKING ABOUT THE COLORFUL CARTOON BIRDS PLAYING MERRY GO 'ROUND MY NOGGIN.
VEY'Z MIR, SOPHIE, YOU WALLOP LIKE A MULE. YOU'RE GONNA REGRET DOING THAT TO MY JAW.
ARMY
OH, YOU GONNA DO ME WORSE?
TO BE HONEST, I WAS HOPING TO DO YOU BETTER, BUT WITH MY JAW OUT OF COMMISSION...
...I'LL BE CALLING YOU "JAWBREAKER" NEXT.
YOU HUSH YOUR MOUTH, CANDY KANE.
YOU'RE THE TOUGHEST CADET AT WEST POINT--
--BUT YOU'RE NOWHERE NEAR AS SWEET.

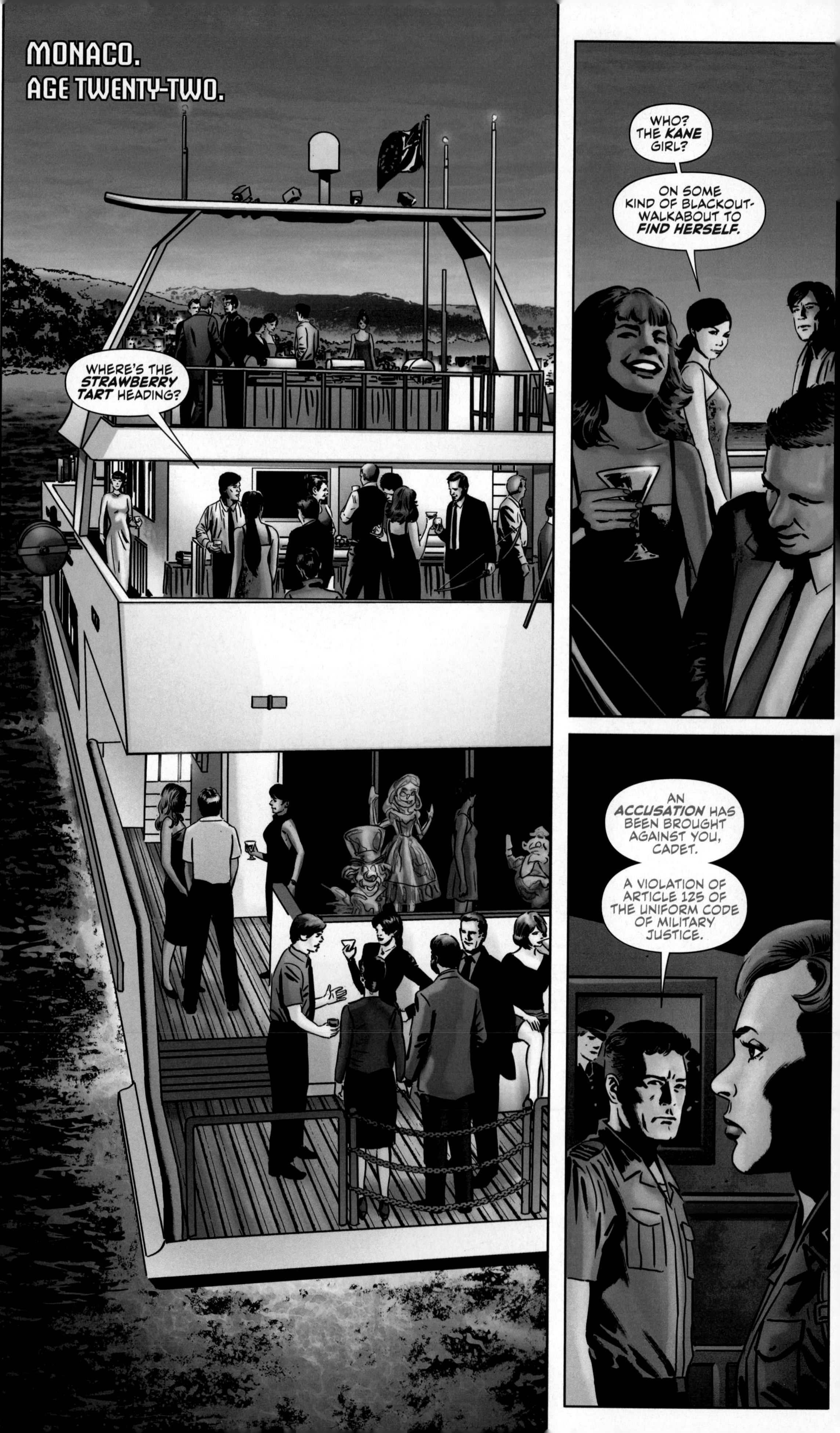
MONACO.
AGE TWENTY-TWO.
WHERE'S THE STRAWBERRY TART HEADING?
WHO? THE KANE GIRL?
ON SOME KIND OF BLACKOUT-WALKABOUT TO FIND HERSELF.
AN ACCUSATION HAS BEEN BROUGHT AGAINST YOU, CADET.
A VIOLATION OF ARTICLE 125 OF THE UNIFORM CODE OF MILITARY JUSTICE.

SPOILED HEIRESS WITH A LITTLE *KRAV MAGA*.

HEARD WEST POINT KICKED HER OUT OVER STICKING HER FINGERS IN THE *COOKIE JARHEAD*.

HAHA I'M GOOD

I CAN DO IT

YOU CAN *TELL* ME THIS IS A MISUNDERSTANDING, KANE.

AND THAT IT WILL *NEVER* HAPPEN AGAIN.

KANE

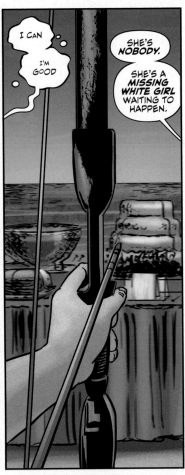

I CAN

I'M GOOD

SHE'S *NOBODY*.

SHE'S A *MISSING WHITE GIRL* WAITING TO HAPPEN.

"A CADET SHALL NOT LIE, CHEAT, OR STEAL, NOR SUFFER OTHERS TO DO SO."

KANE

"I'M SORRY, SIR."

"I CAN'T."

FWP

I CANT...

"I'M GAY."

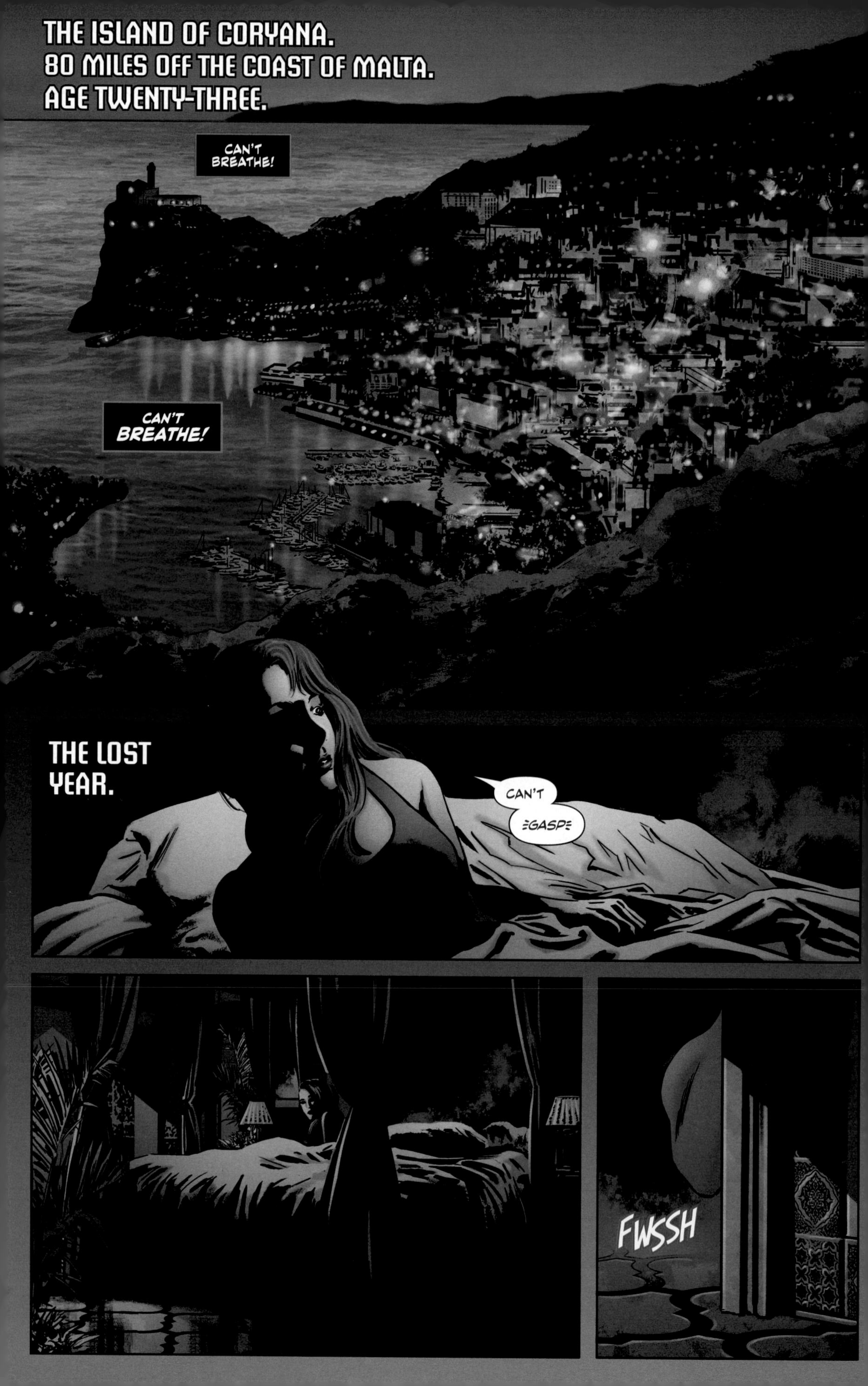
THE ISLAND OF CORYANA.
80 MILES OFF THE COAST OF MALTA.
AGE TWENTY-THREE.
CAN'T BREATHE!
CAN'T BREATHE!
THE LOST YEAR.
CAN'T
=GASP=
FWSSH

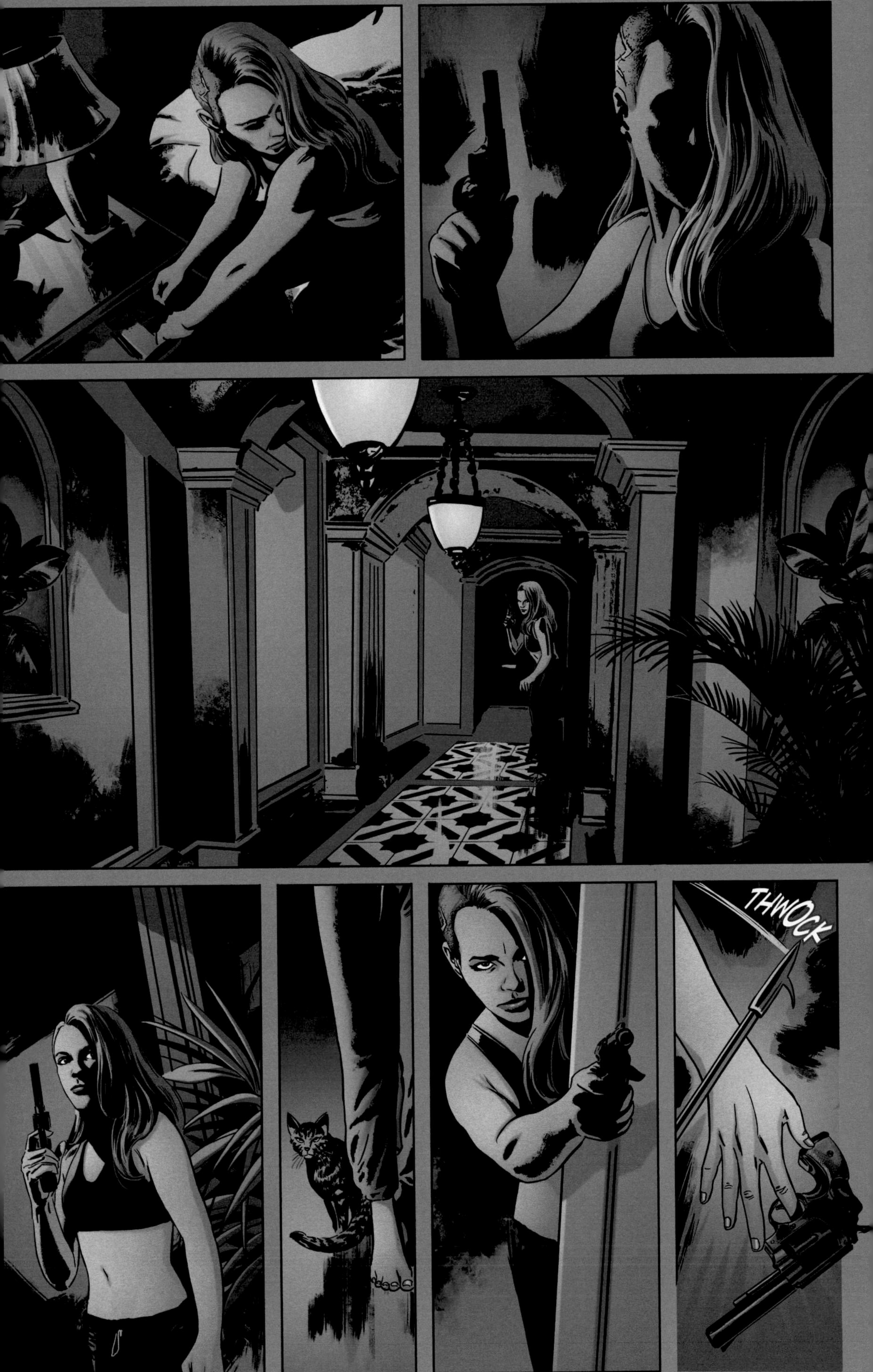
THWOCK

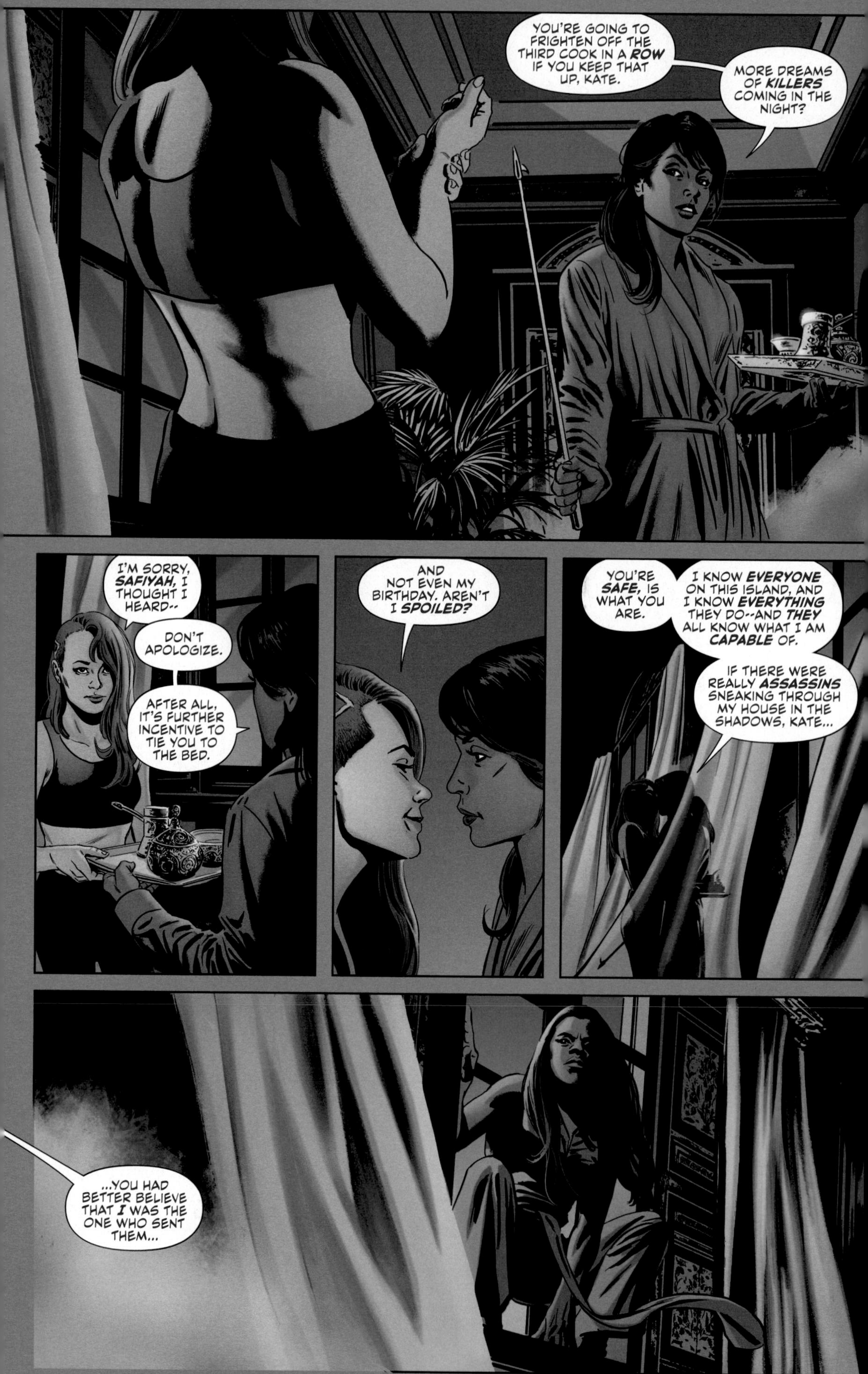

YOU'RE GOING TO FRIGHTEN OFF THE THIRD COOK IN A ROW IF YOU KEEP THAT UP, KATE.
MORE DREAMS OF KILLERS COMING IN THE NIGHT?
I'M SORRY, SAFIYAH, I THOUGHT I HEARD--
DON'T APOLOGIZE.
AFTER ALL, IT'S FURTHER INCENTIVE TO TIE YOU TO THE BED.
AND NOT EVEN MY BIRTHDAY. AREN'T I SPOILED?
YOU'RE SAFE, IS WHAT YOU ARE.
I KNOW EVERYONE ON THIS ISLAND, AND I KNOW EVERYTHING THEY DO--AND THEY ALL KNOW WHAT I AM CAPABLE OF.
IF THERE WERE REALLY ASSASSINS SNEAKING THROUGH MY HOUSE IN THE SHADOWS, KATE...
...YOU HAD BETTER BELIEVE THAT I WAS THE ONE WHO SENT THEM...

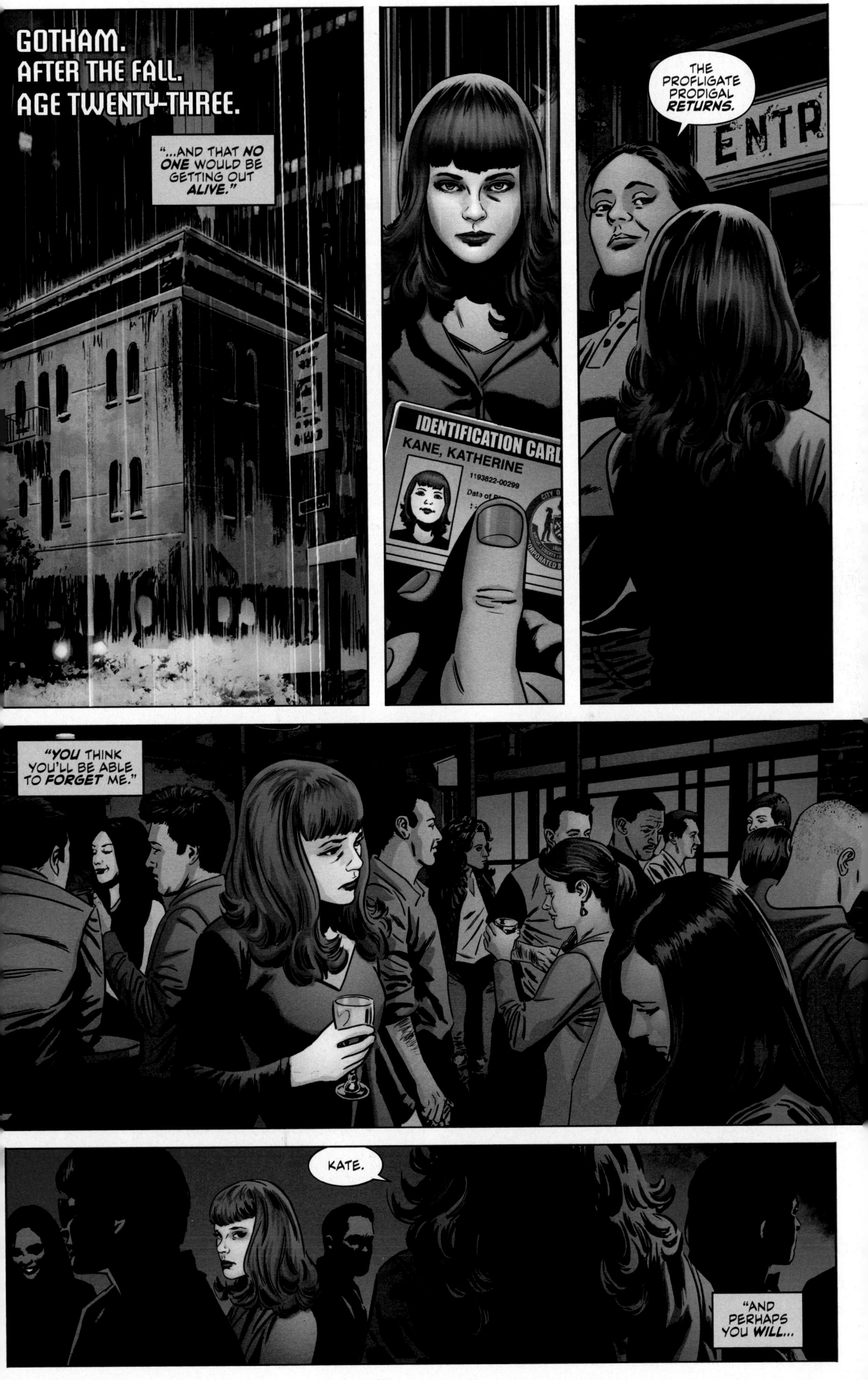
GOTHAM.
AFTER THE FALL.
AGE TWENTY-THREE.
"...AND THAT NO ONE WOULD BE GETTING OUT ALIVE."
KANE, KATHERINE
1193822-00299
THE PROFLIGATE PRODIGAL RETURNS.
"YOU THINK YOU'LL BE ABLE TO FORGET ME."
KATE.
"AND PERHAPS YOU WILL...

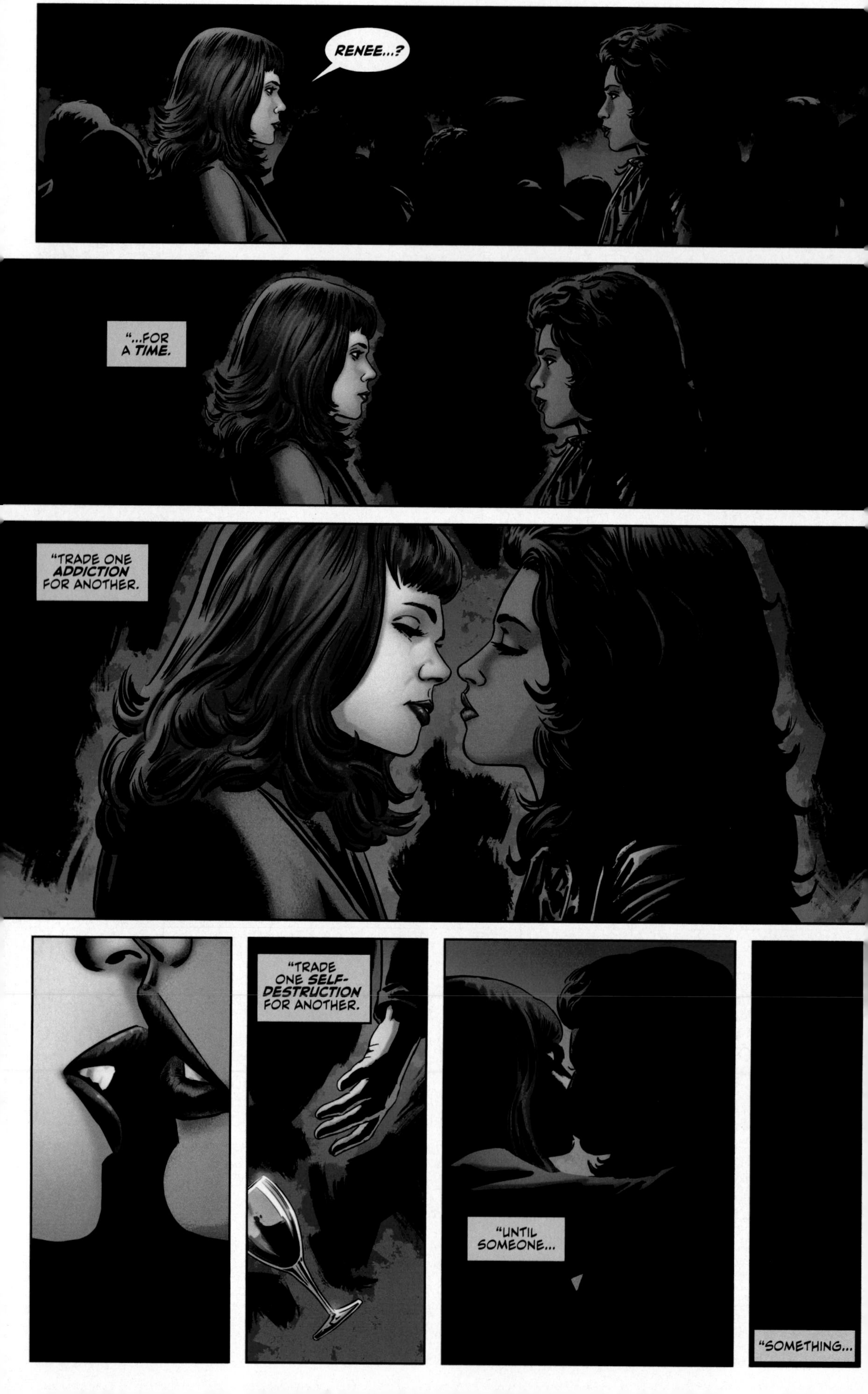
RENEE...?
"...FOR A TIME.
"TRADE ONE ADDICTION FOR ANOTHER.
"TRADE ONE SELF-DESTRUCTION FOR ANOTHER.
"UNTIL SOMEONE...
"SOMETHING...

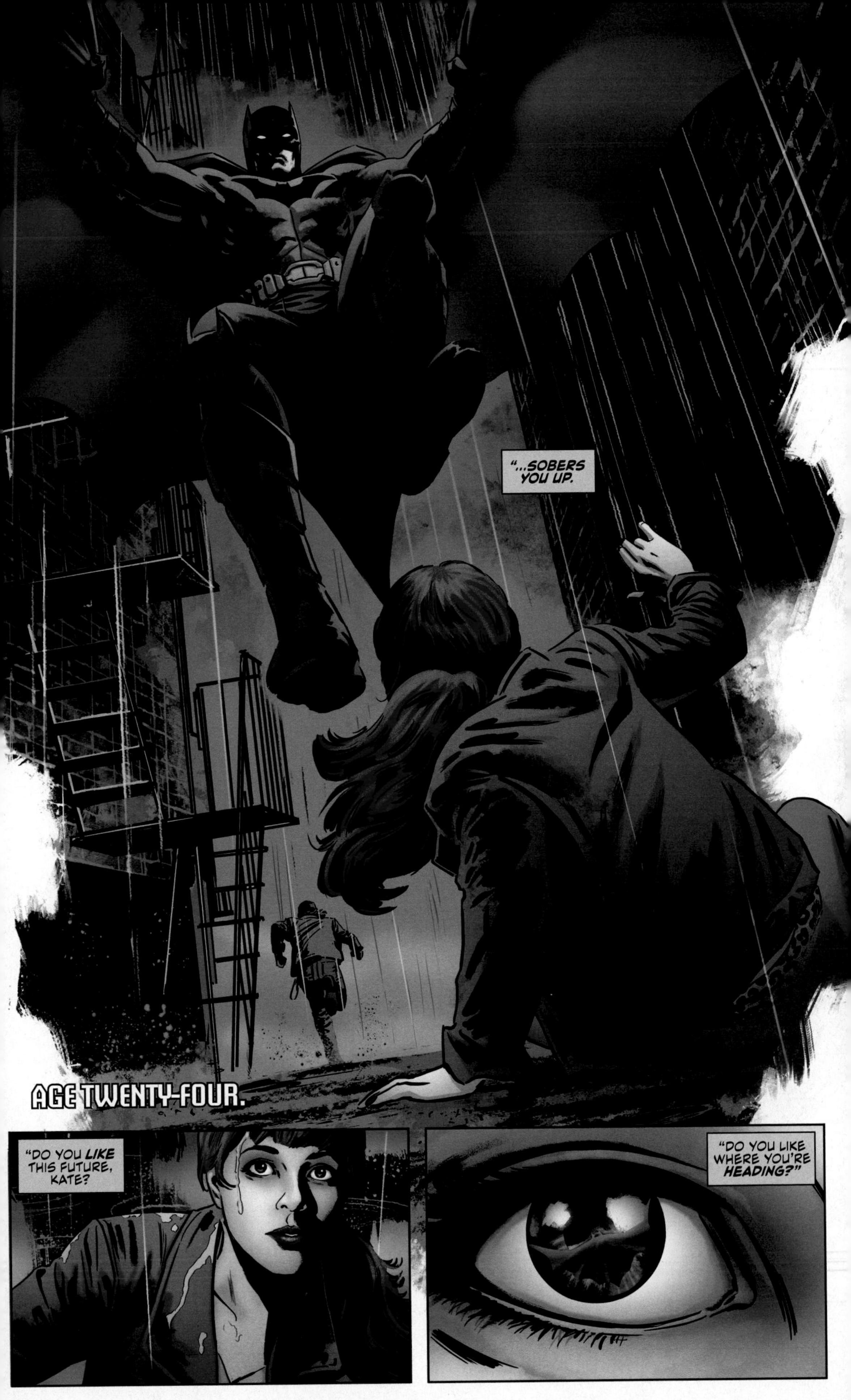
"...SOBERS YOU UP.
AGE TWENTY-FOUR.
"DO YOU *LIKE* THIS FUTURE, KATE?
"DO YOU LIKE WHERE YOU'RE *HEADING?*"

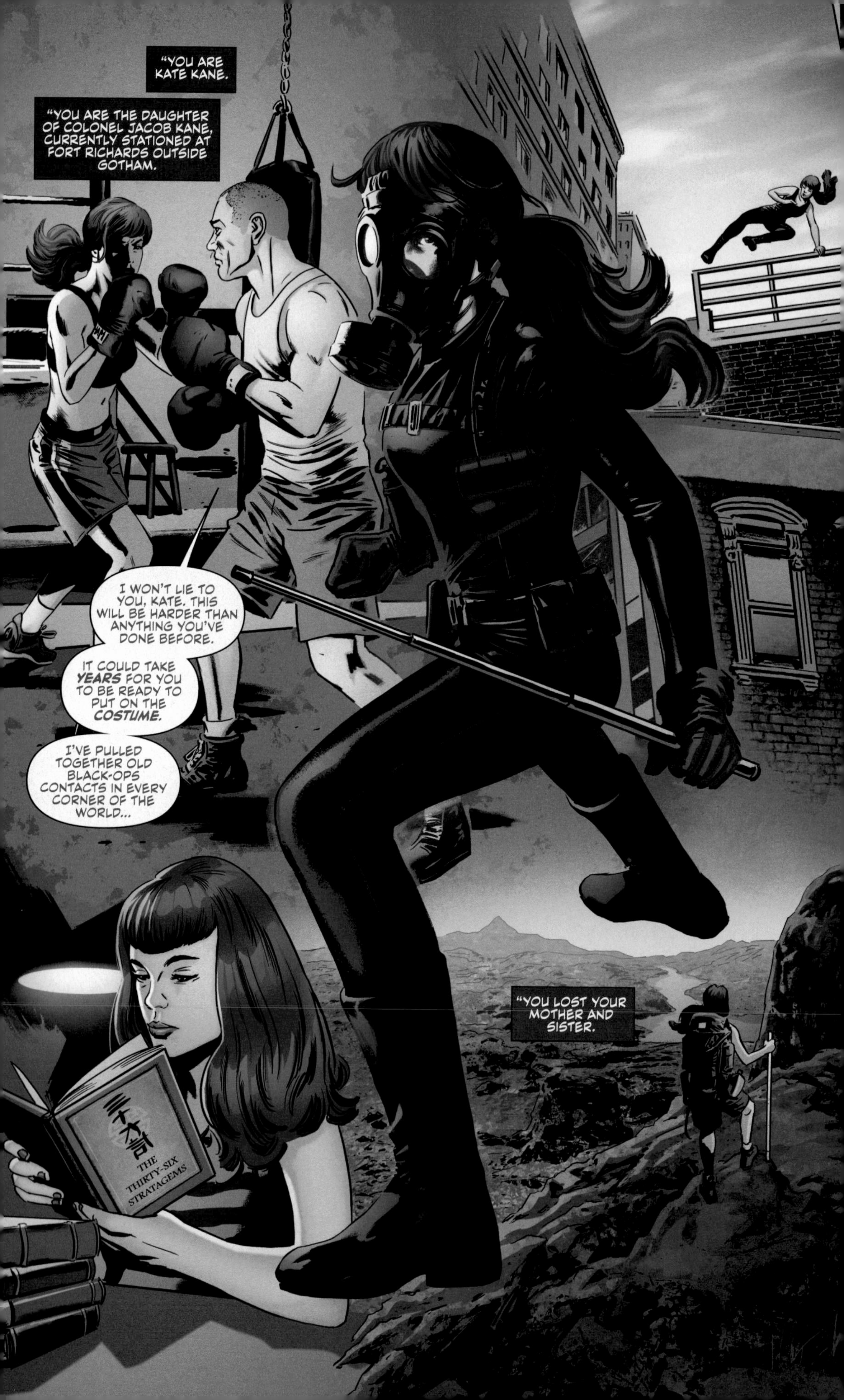
"YOU ARE KATE KANE.
"YOU ARE THE DAUGHTER OF COLONEL JACOB KANE, CURRENTLY STATIONED AT FORT RICHARDS OUTSIDE GOTHAM.
I WON'T LIE TO YOU, KATE. THIS WILL BE HARDER THAN ANYTHING YOU'VE DONE BEFORE.
IT COULD TAKE *YEARS* FOR YOU TO BE READY TO PUT ON THE *COSTUME.*
I'VE PULLED TOGETHER OLD BLACK-OPS CONTACTS IN EVERY CORNER OF THE WORLD...
THE THIRTY-SIX STRATAGEMS
"YOU LOST YOUR MOTHER AND SISTER.

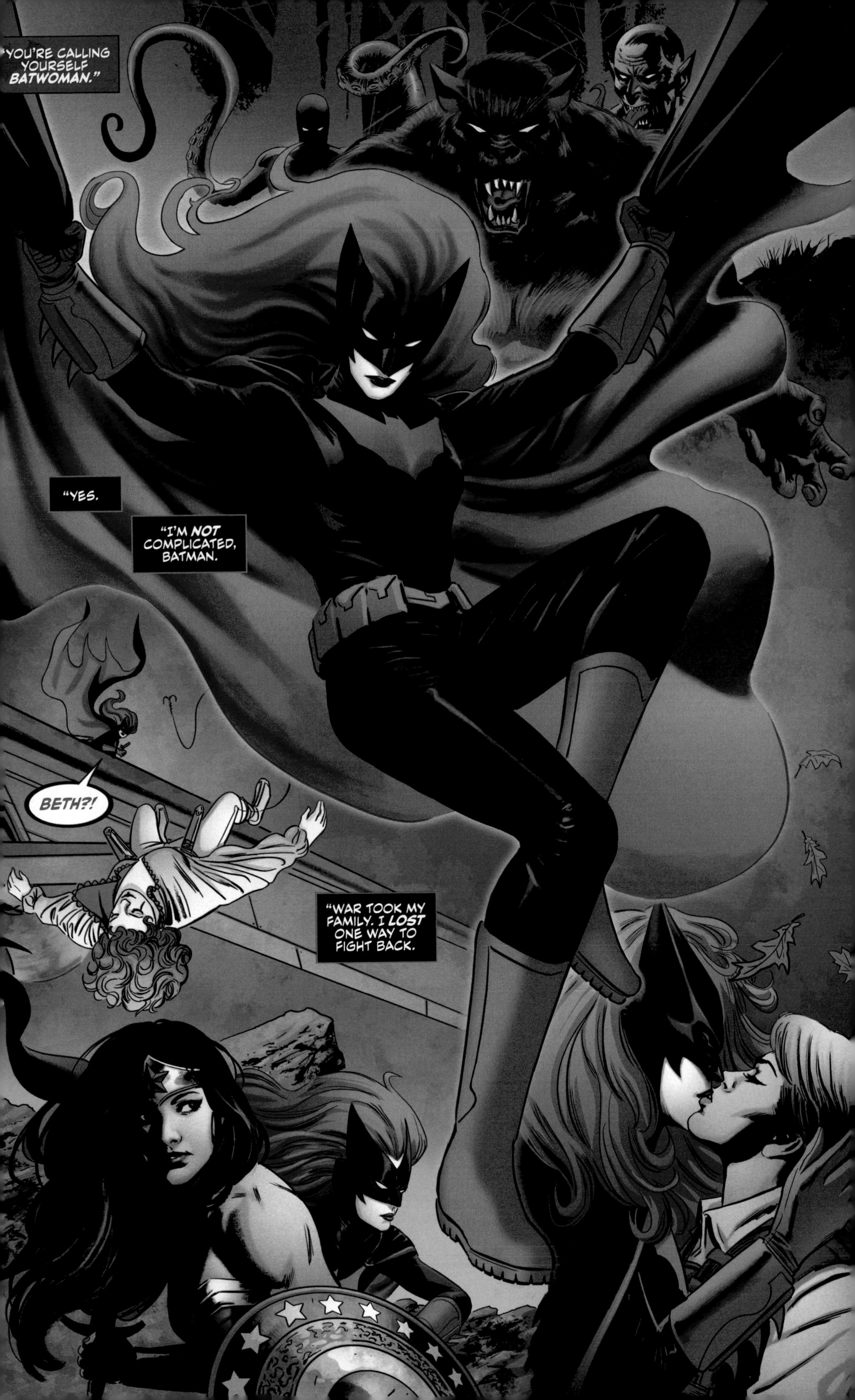
"YOU'RE CALLING YOURSELF **BATWOMAN.**"
"YES.
"I'M **NOT** COMPLICATED, BATMAN.
BETH?!
"WAR TOOK MY FAMILY. I **LOST** ONE WAY TO FIGHT BACK.

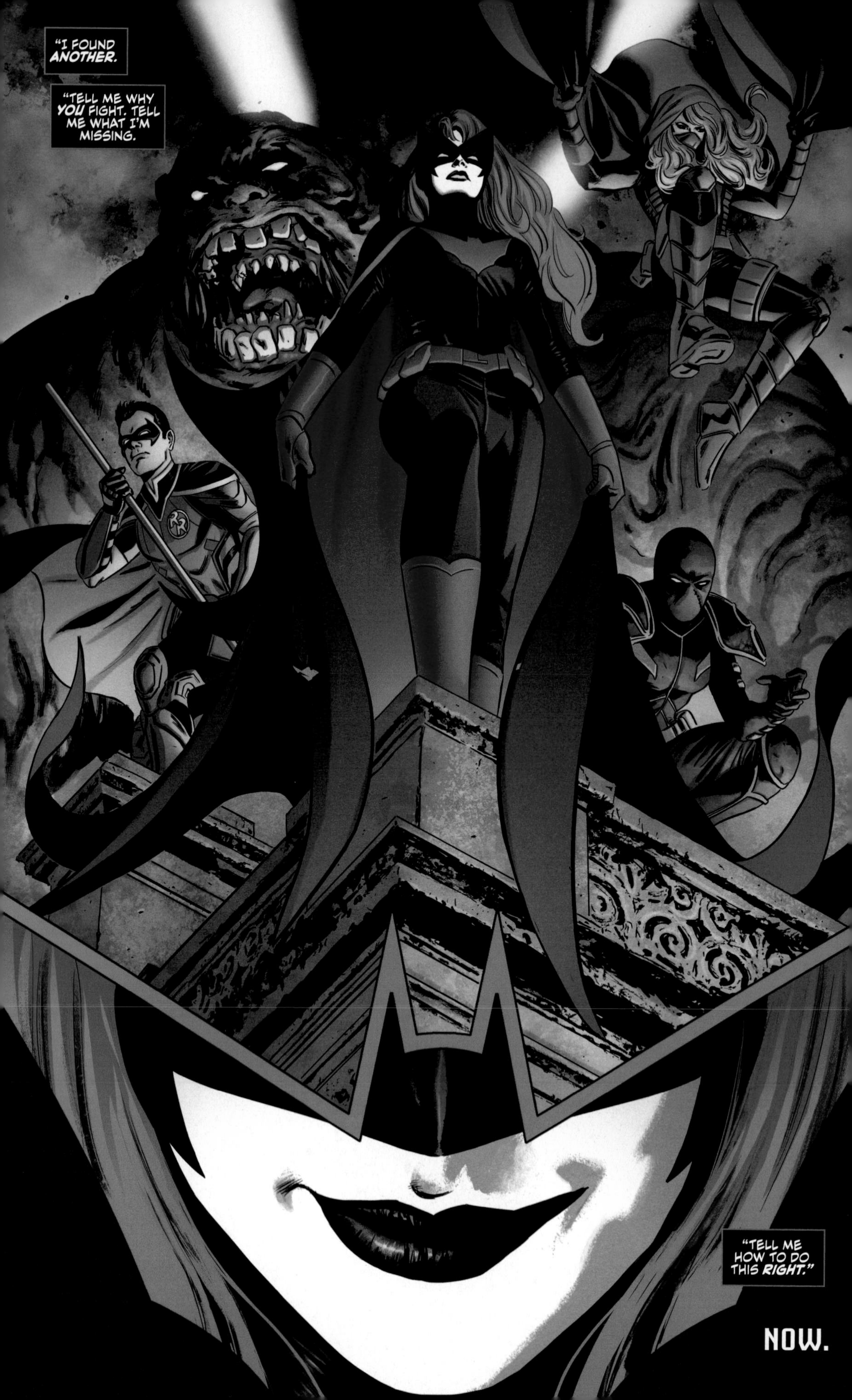
"I FOUND ANOTHER.
"TELL ME WHY YOU FIGHT. TELL ME WHAT I'M MISSING.
"TELL ME HOW TO DO THIS RIGHT."
NOW.

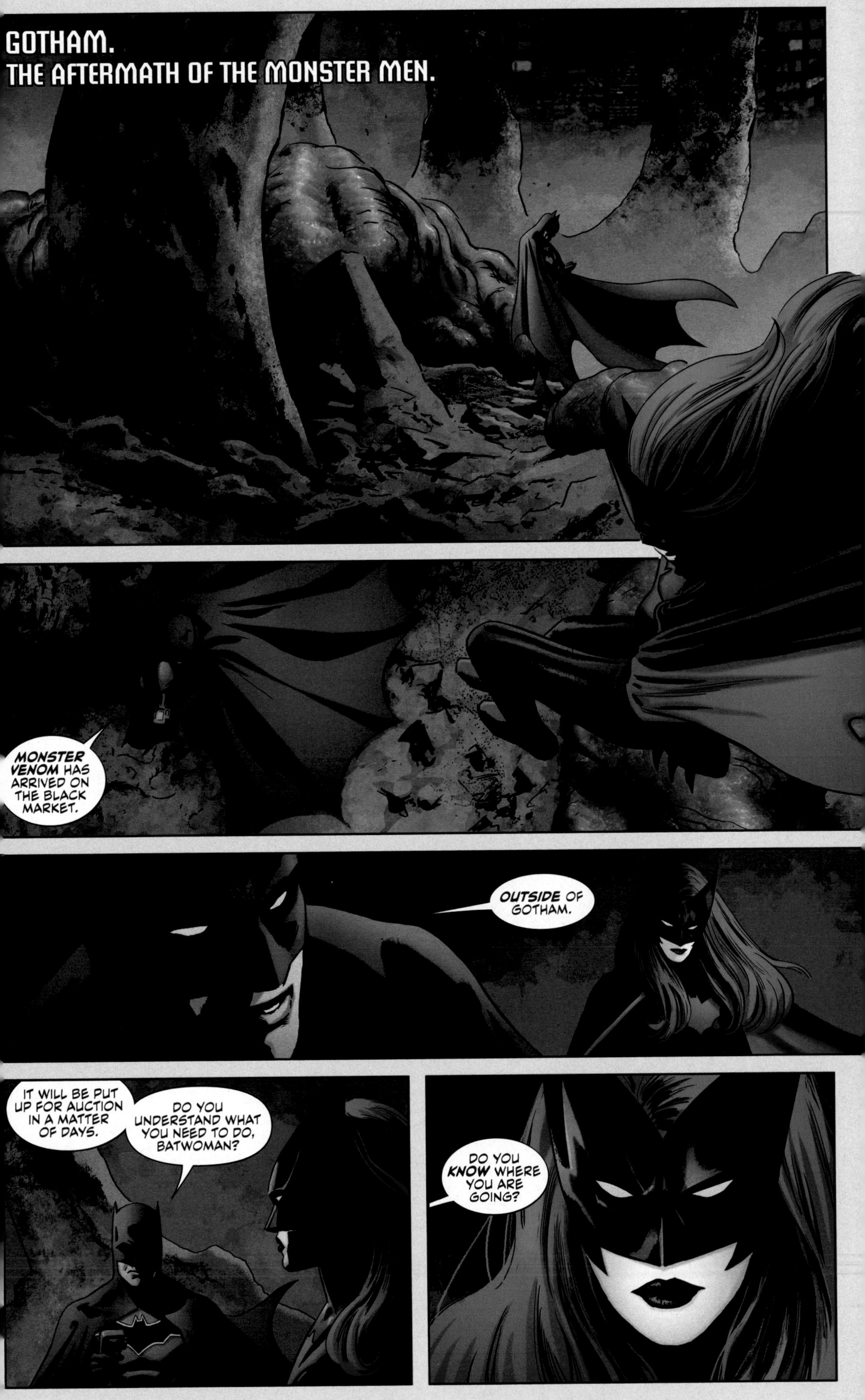
GOTHAM.
THE AFTERMATH OF THE MONSTER MEN.
MONSTER VENOM HAS ARRIVED ON THE BLACK MARKET.
OUTSIDE OF GOTHAM.
IT WILL BE PUT UP FOR AUCTION IN A MATTER OF DAYS.
DO YOU UNDERSTAND WHAT YOU NEED TO DO, BATWOMAN?
DO YOU KNOW WHERE YOU ARE GOING?

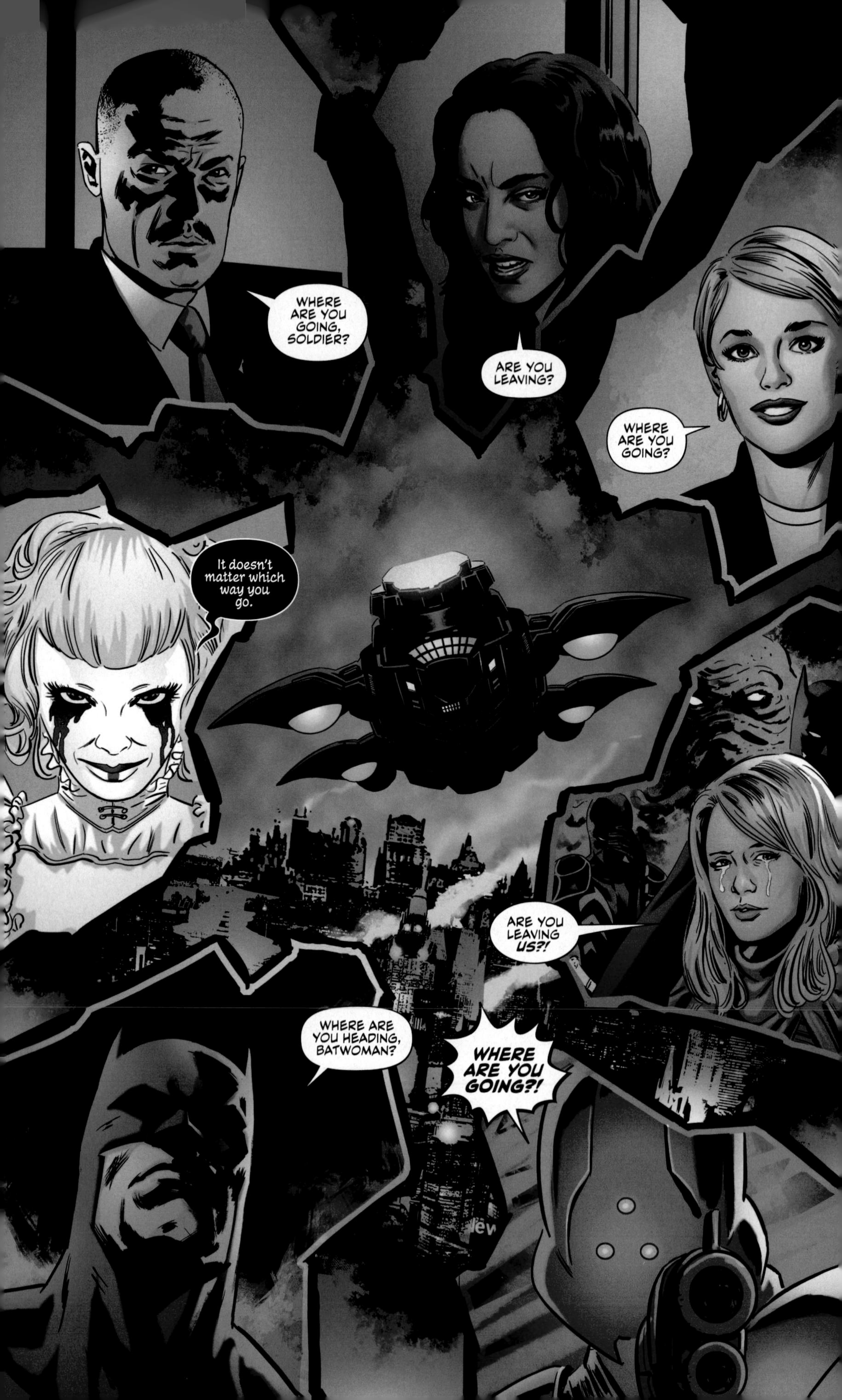

WHERE ARE YOU GOING, SOLDIER?
ARE YOU LEAVING?
WHERE ARE YOU GOING?
It doesn't matter which way you go.
ARE YOU LEAVING US?!
WHERE ARE YOU HEADING, BATWOMAN?
WHERE ARE YOU GOING?!

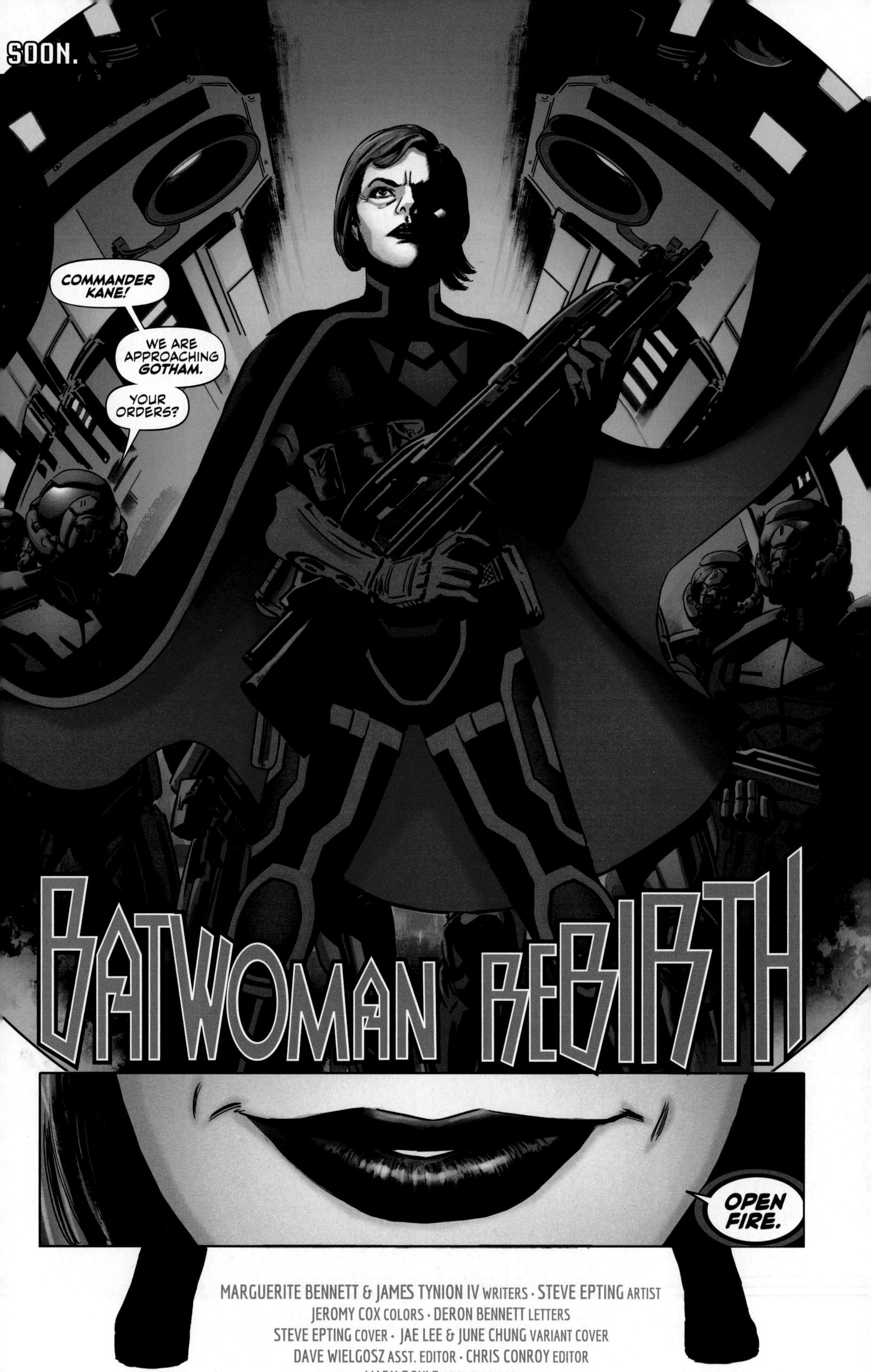
SOON.
COMMANDER KANE!
WE ARE APPROACHING GOTHAM.
YOUR ORDERS?
BATWOMAN REBIRTH
OPEN FIRE.

MARGUERITE BENNETT & JAMES TYNION IV WRITERS • STEVE EPTING ARTIST
JEROMY COX COLORS • DERON BENNETT LETTERS
STEVE EPTING COVER • JAE LEE & JUNE CHUNG VARIANT COVER
DAVE WIELGOSZ ASST. EDITOR • CHRIS CONROY EDITOR
MARK DOYLE GROUP EDITOR

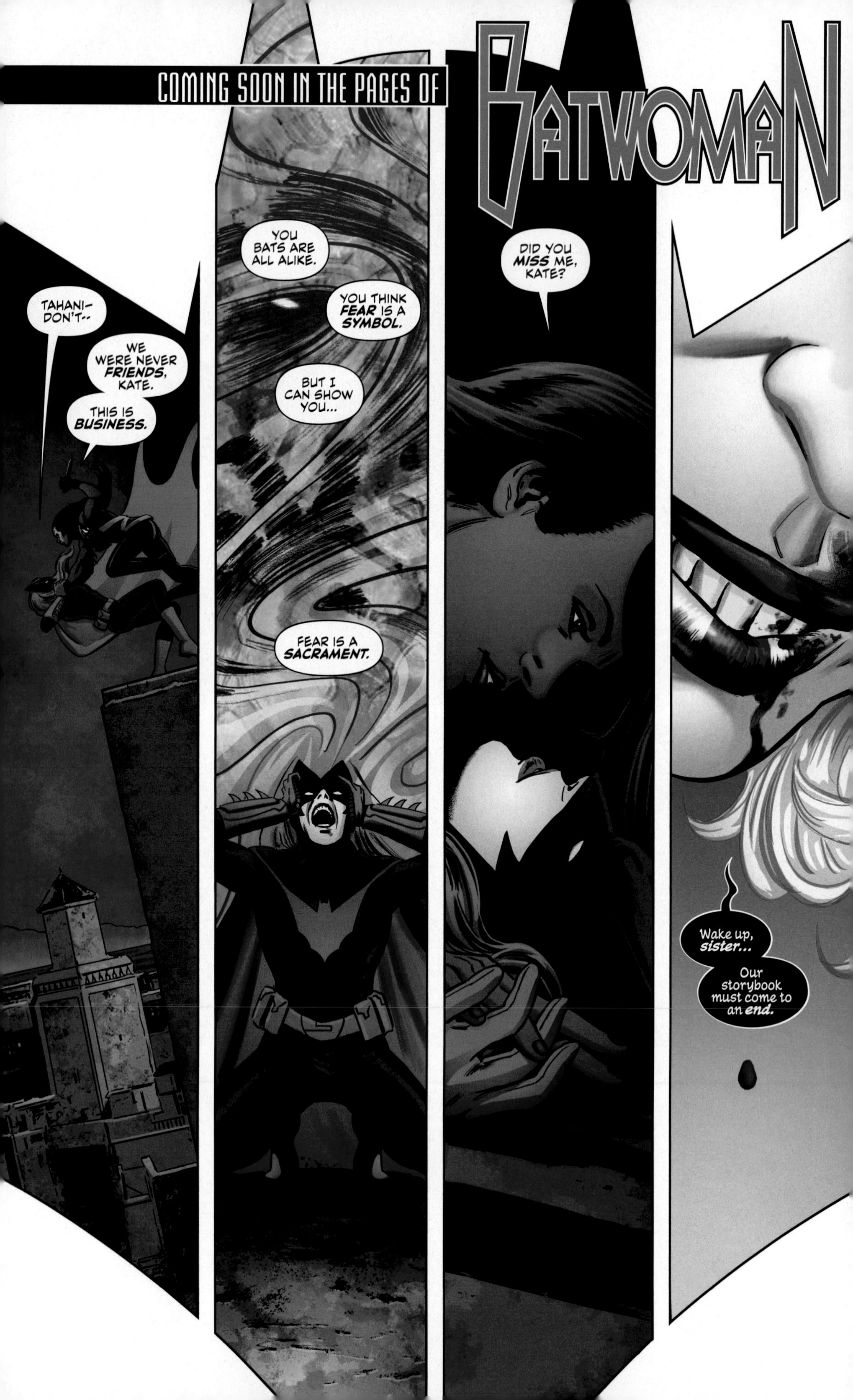

COMING SOON IN THE PAGES OF
BATWOMAN
TAHANI-- DON'T--
WE WERE NEVER FRIENDS, KATE.
THIS IS BUSINESS.
YOU BATS ARE ALL ALIKE.
YOU THINK FEAR IS A SYMBOL.
BUT I CAN SHOW YOU...
FEAR IS A SACRAMENT.
DID YOU MISS ME, KATE?
Wake up, sister...
Our storybook must come to an end.

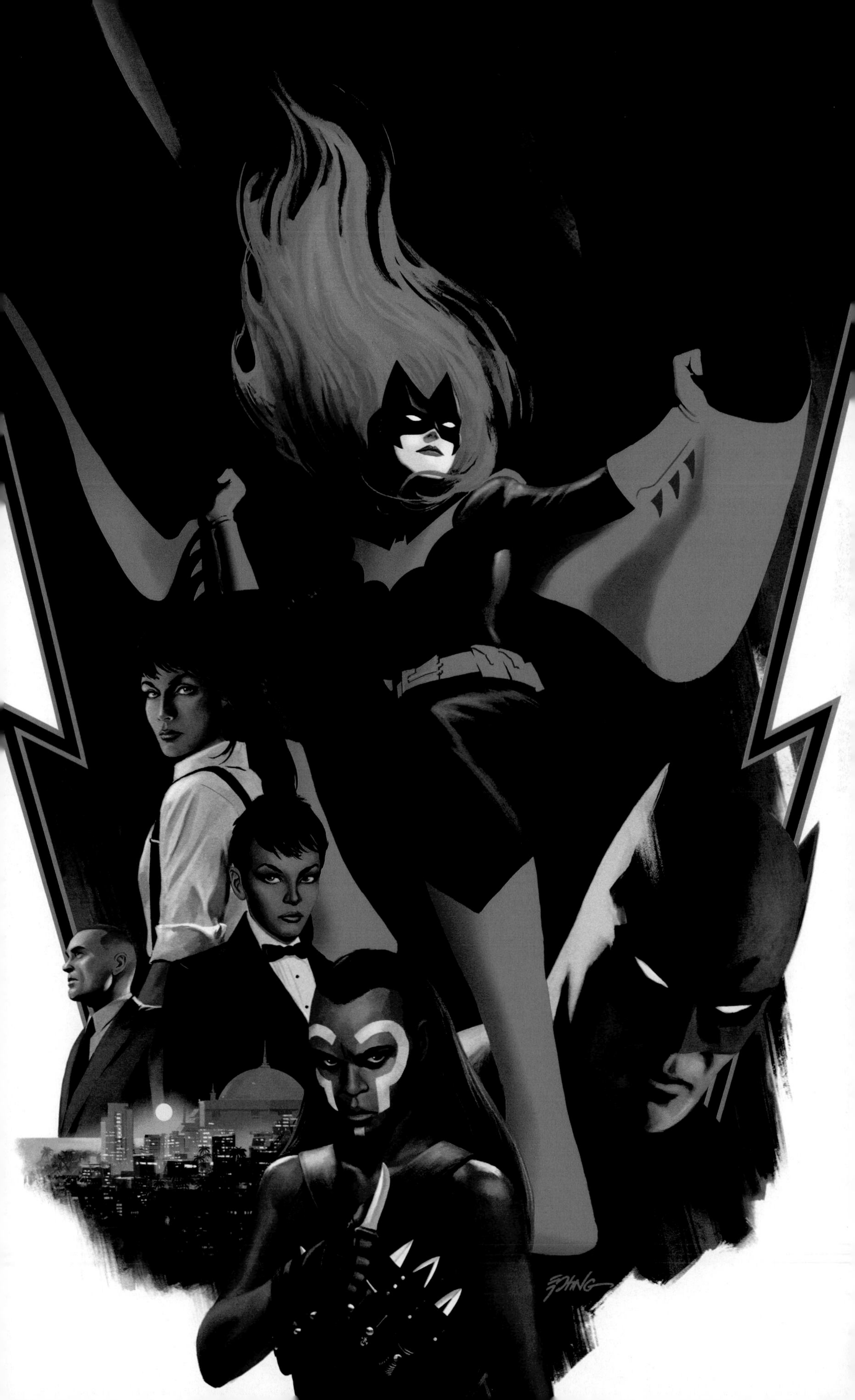

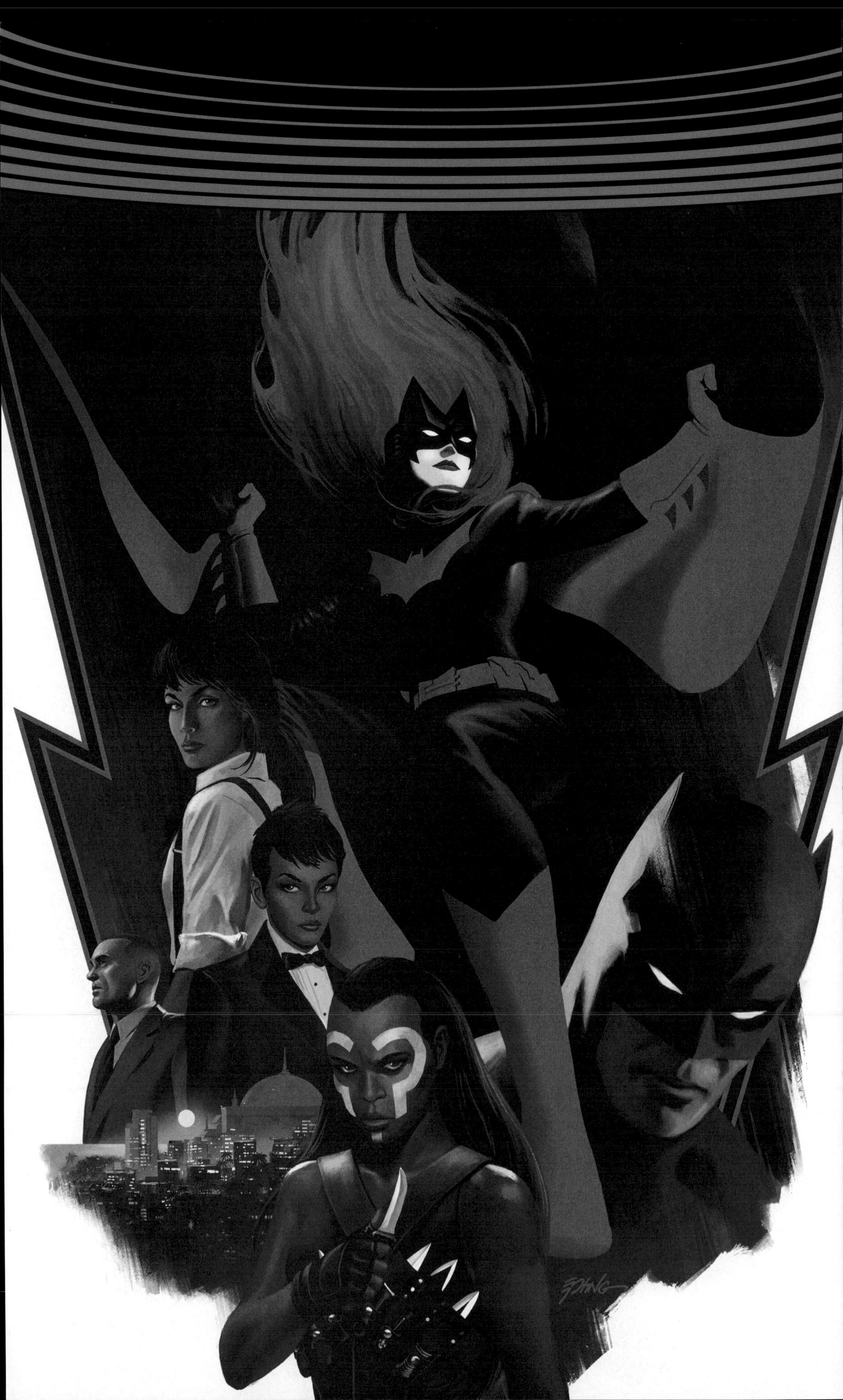

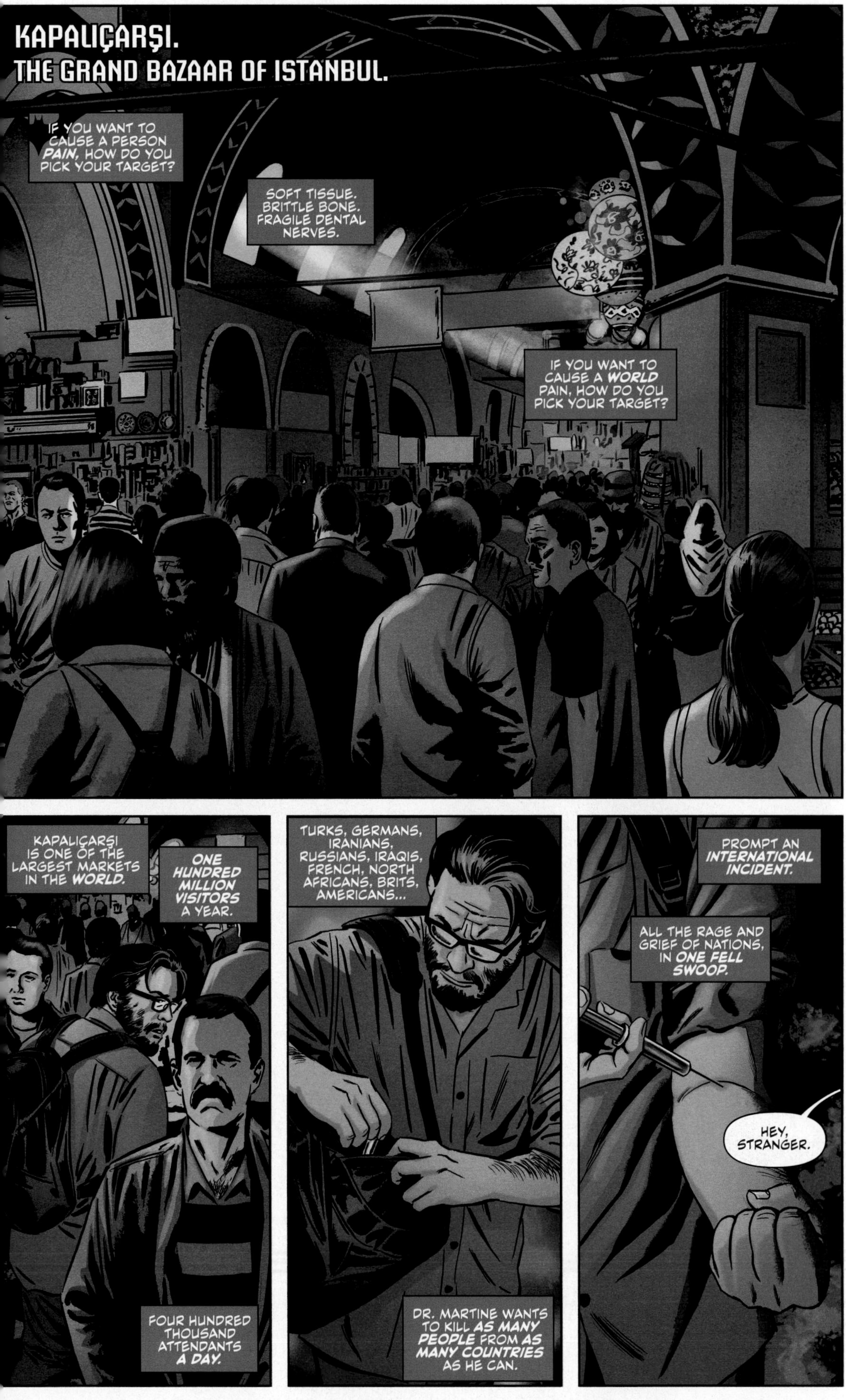
KAPALIÇARŞI.
THE GRAND BAZAAR OF ISTANBUL.
IF YOU WANT TO CAUSE A PERSON PAIN, HOW DO YOU PICK YOUR TARGET?
SOFT TISSUE. BRITTLE BONE. FRAGILE DENTAL NERVES.
IF YOU WANT TO CAUSE A WORLD PAIN, HOW DO YOU PICK YOUR TARGET?
KAPALIÇARŞI IS ONE OF THE LARGEST MARKETS IN THE WORLD.
ONE HUNDRED MILLION VISITORS A YEAR.
FOUR HUNDRED THOUSAND ATTENDANTS A DAY.
TURKS, GERMANS, IRANIANS, RUSSIANS, IRAQIS, FRENCH, NORTH AFRICANS, BRITS, AMERICANS...
DR. MARTINE WANTS TO KILL AS MANY PEOPLE FROM AS MANY COUNTRIES AS HE CAN.
PROMPT AN INTERNATIONAL INCIDENT.
ALL THE RAGE AND GRIEF OF NATIONS, IN ONE FELL SWOOP.
HEY, STRANGER.

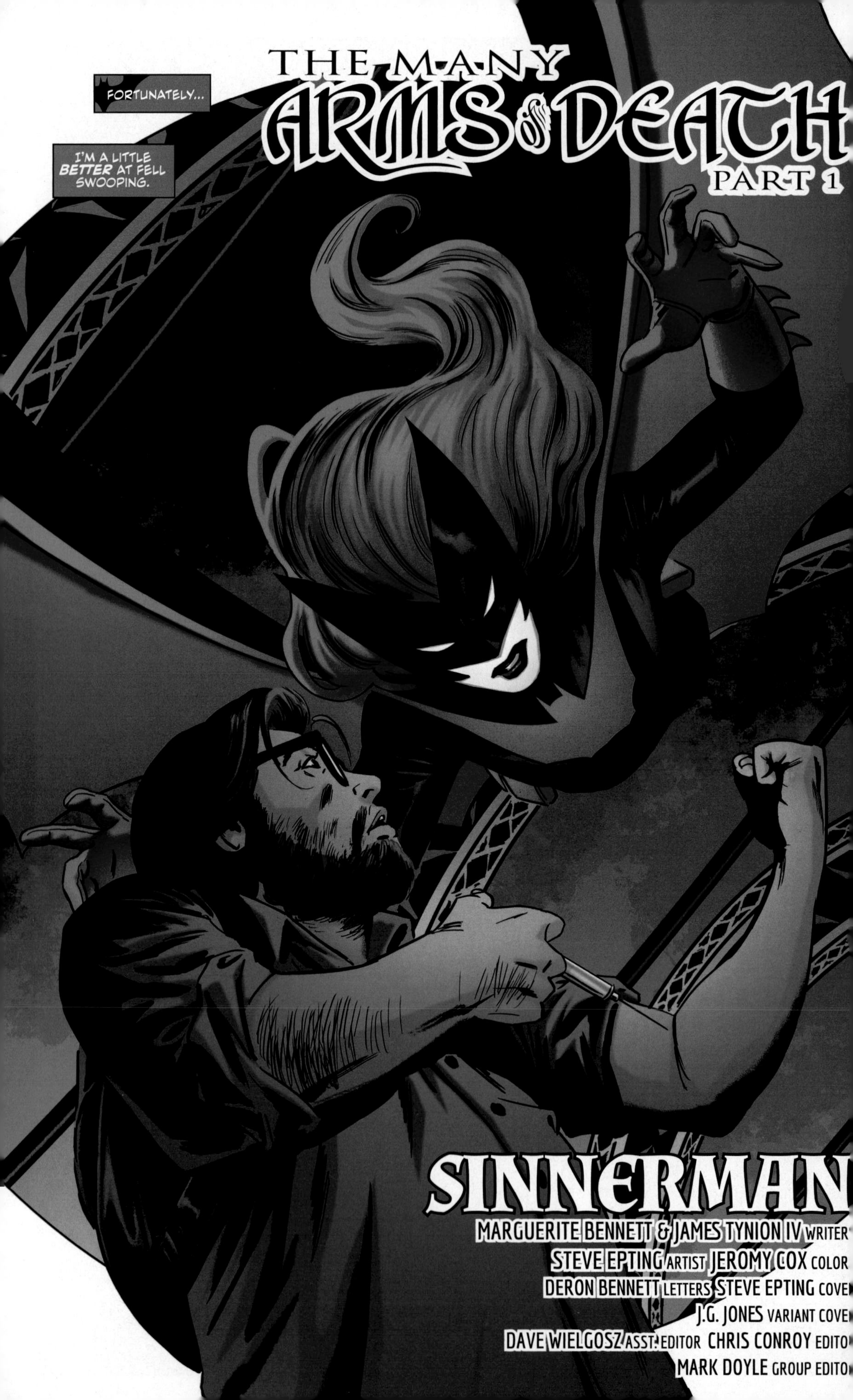
FORTUNATELY...
I'M A LITTLE BETTER AT FELL SWOOPING.
THE MANY ARMS of DEATH PART 1
SINNERMAN
MARGUERITE BENNETT & JAMES TYNION IV WRITER
STEVE EPTING ARTIST JEROMY COX COLOR
DERON BENNETT LETTERS STEVE EPTING COVE
J.G. JONES VARIANT COVE
DAVE WIELGOSZ ASST. EDITOR CHRIS CONROY EDITO
MARK DOYLE GROUP EDITO

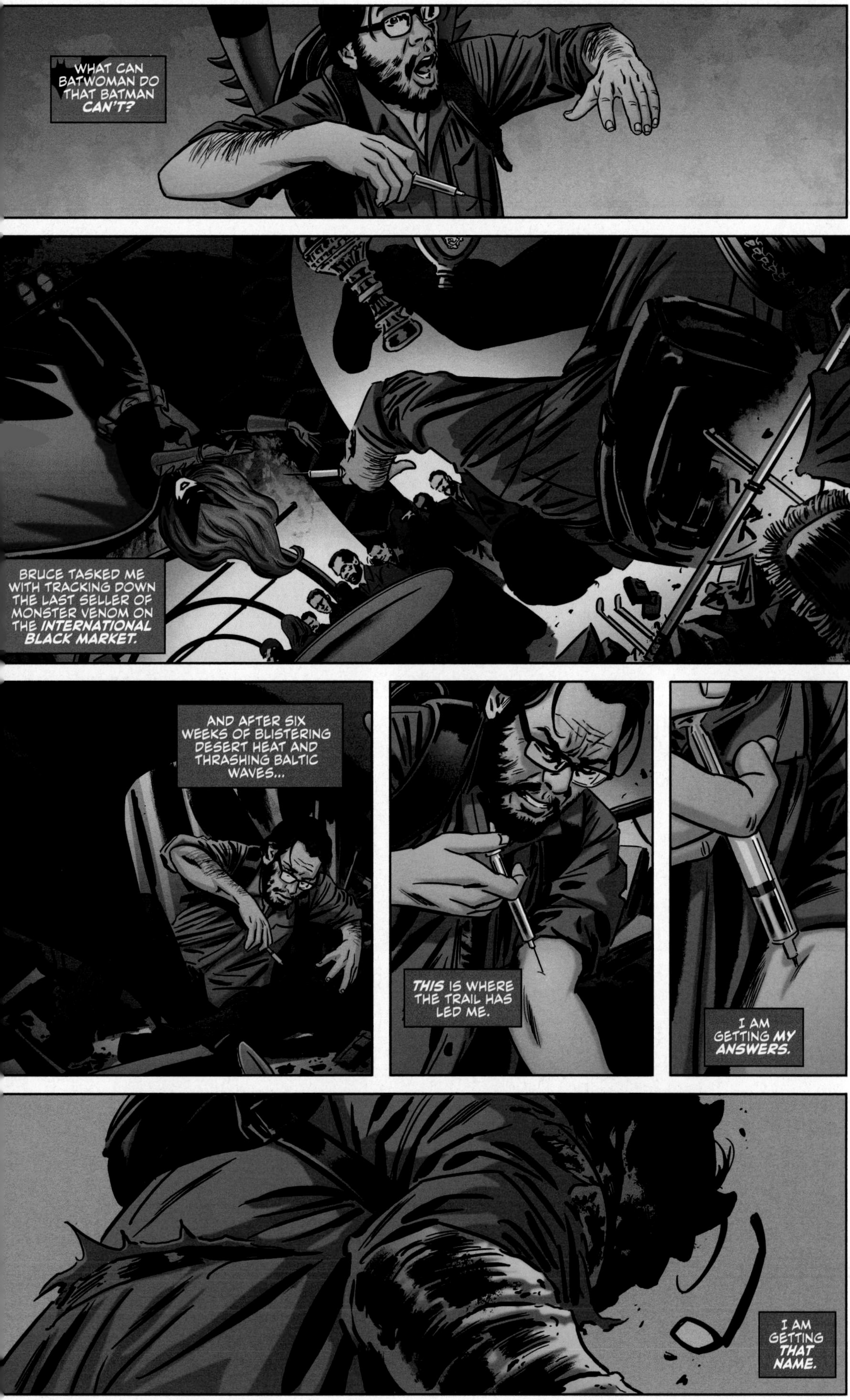
WHAT CAN BATWOMAN DO THAT BATMAN CAN'T?
BRUCE TASKED ME WITH TRACKING DOWN THE LAST SELLER OF MONSTER VENOM ON THE INTERNATIONAL BLACK MARKET.
AND AFTER SIX WEEKS OF BLISTERING DESERT HEAT AND THRASHING BALTIC WAVES...
THIS IS WHERE THE TRAIL HAS LED ME.
I AM GETTING MY ANSWERS.
I AM GETTING THAT NAME.

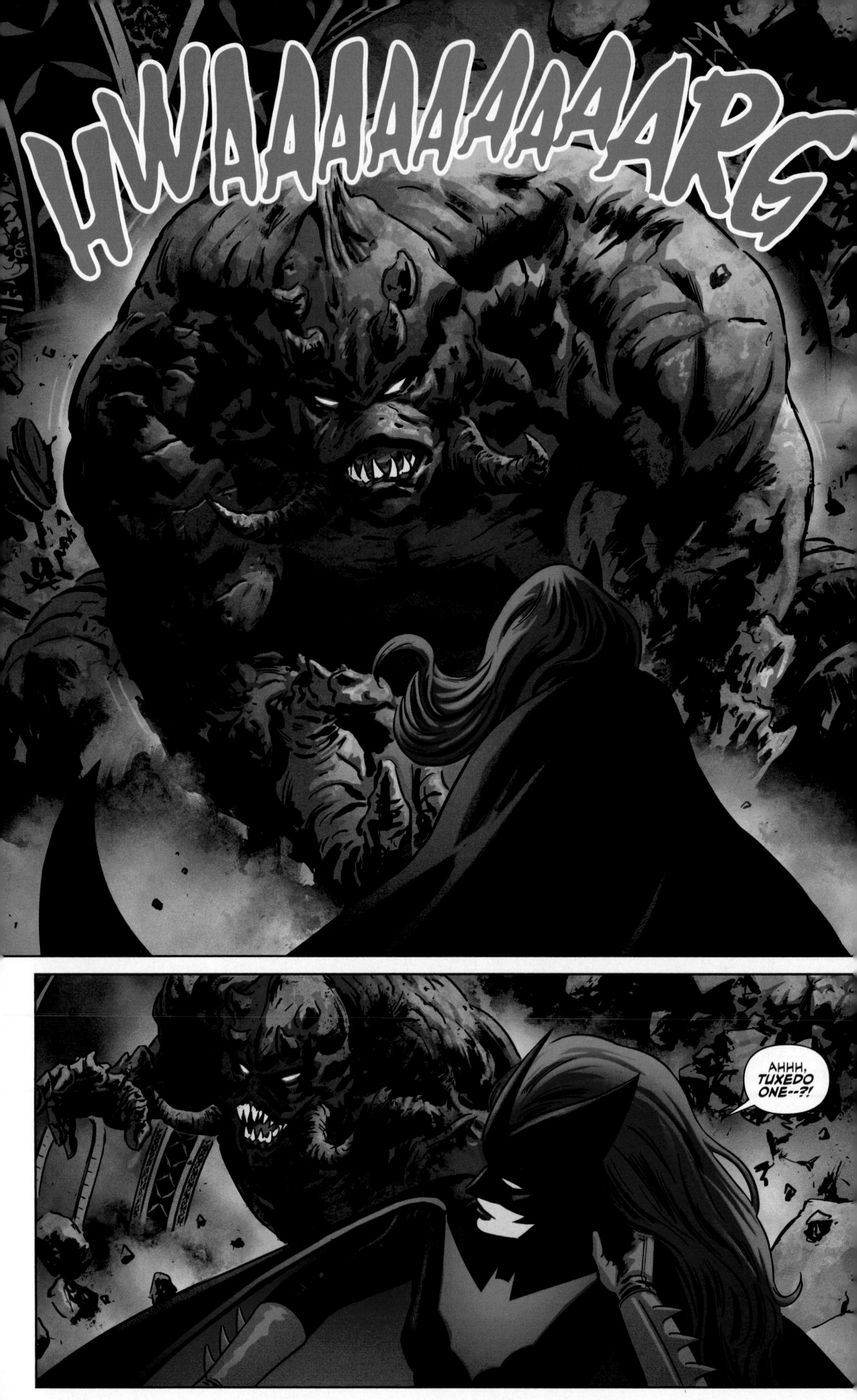
HWAAAAAAAAAARG
AHHH, TUXEDO ONE--?!

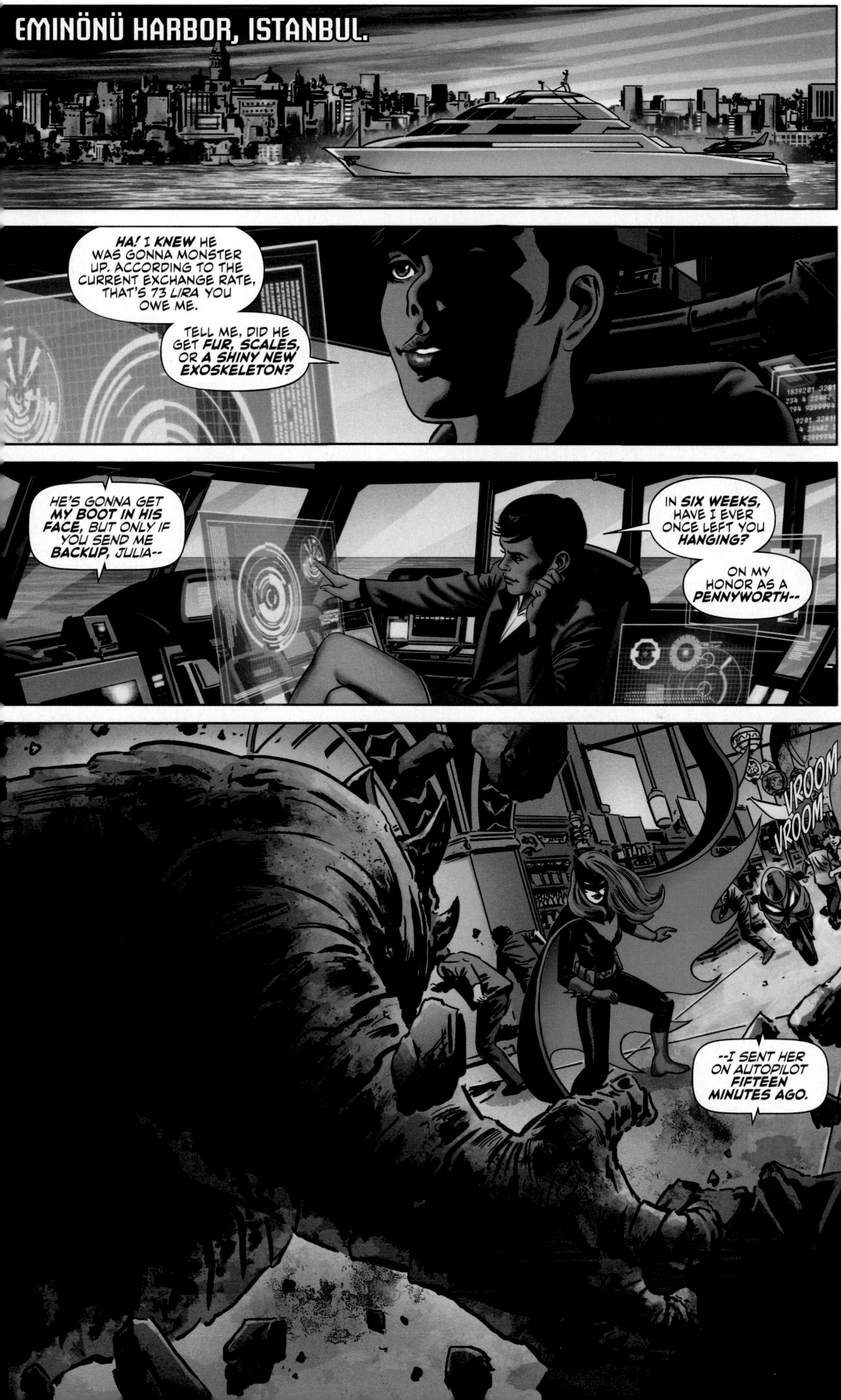
EMINÖNÜ HARBOR, ISTANBUL.
HA! I KNEW HE WAS GONNA MONSTER UP. ACCORDING TO THE CURRENT EXCHANGE RATE, THAT'S 73 LIRA YOU OWE ME.
TELL ME, DID HE GET FUR, SCALES, OR A SHINY NEW EXOSKELETON?
HE'S GONNA GET MY BOOT IN HIS FACE, BUT ONLY IF YOU SEND ME BACKUP, JULIA--
IN SIX WEEKS, HAVE I EVER ONCE LEFT YOU HANGING?
ON MY HONOR AS A PENNYWORTH--
VROOM
VROOM
--I SENT HER ON AUTOPILOT FIFTEEN MINUTES AGO.

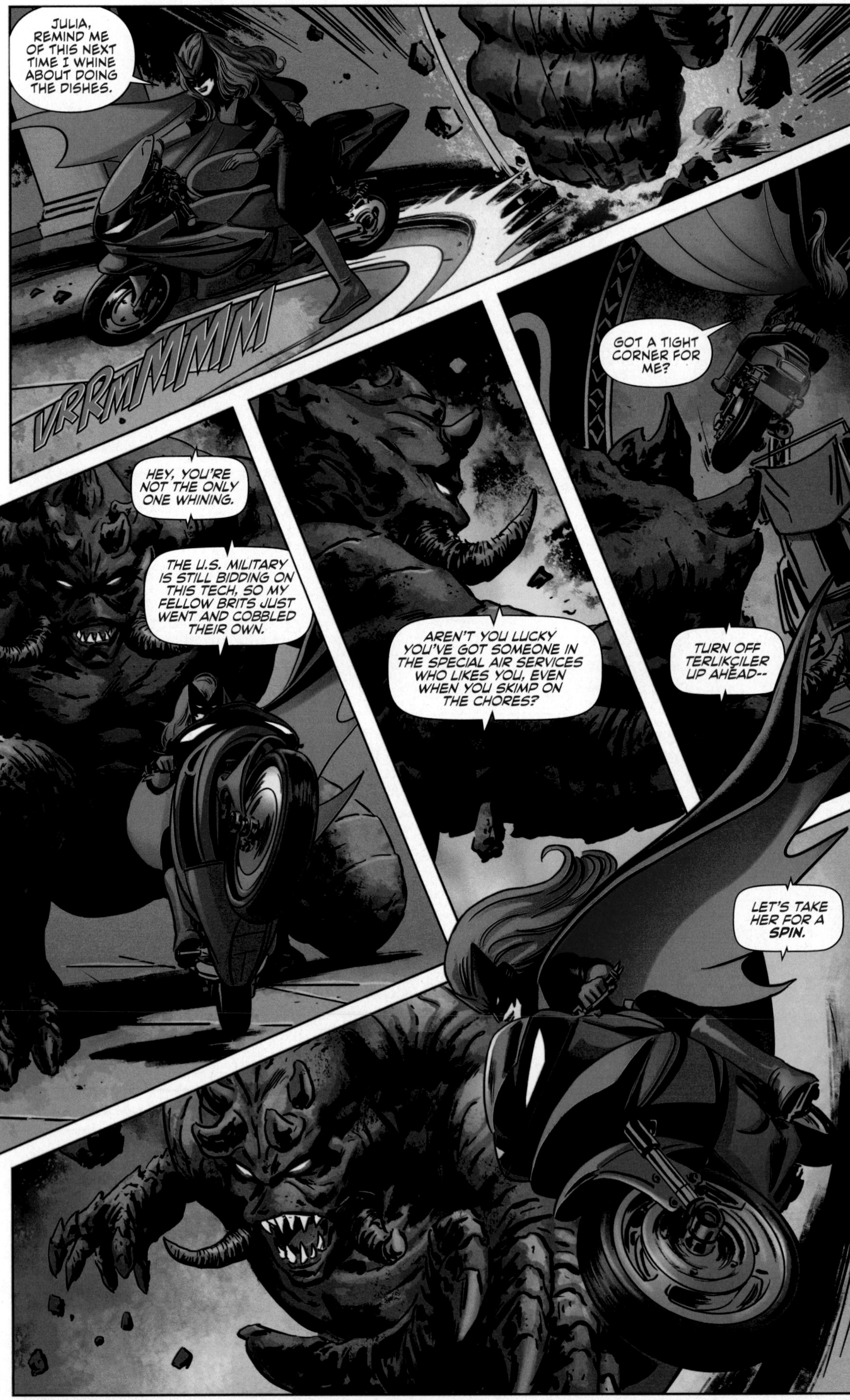

JULIA, REMIND ME OF THIS NEXT TIME I WHINE ABOUT DOING THE DISHES.
VRRMMMMM
GOT A TIGHT CORNER FOR ME?
HEY, YOU'RE NOT THE ONLY ONE WHINING.
THE U.S. MILITARY IS STILL BIDDING ON THIS TECH, SO MY FELLOW BRITS JUST WENT AND COBBLED THEIR OWN.
AREN'T YOU LUCKY YOU'VE GOT SOMEONE IN THE SPECIAL AIR SERVICES WHO LIKES YOU, EVEN WHEN YOU SKIMP ON THE CHORES?
TURN OFF TERLIKÇILER UP AHEAD--
LET'S TAKE HER FOR A SPIN.

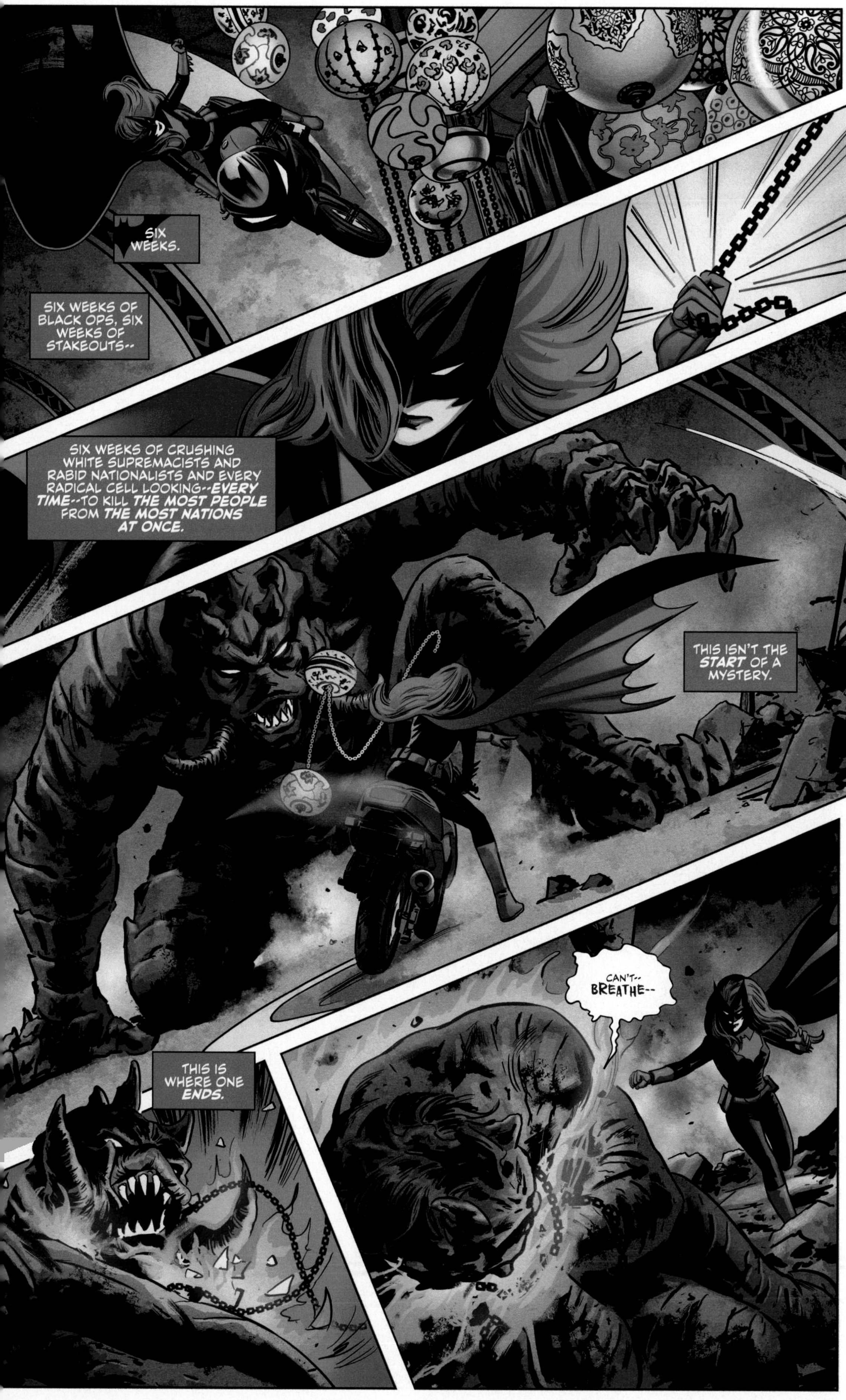
SIX WEEKS.
SIX WEEKS OF BLACK OPS, SIX WEEKS OF STAKEOUTS--
SIX WEEKS OF CRUSHING WHITE SUPREMACISTS AND RABID NATIONALISTS AND EVERY RADICAL CELL LOOKING--EVERY TIME--TO KILL THE MOST PEOPLE FROM THE MOST NATIONS AT ONCE.
THIS ISN'T THE START OF A MYSTERY.
THIS IS WHERE ONE ENDS.
CAN'T-- BREATHE--

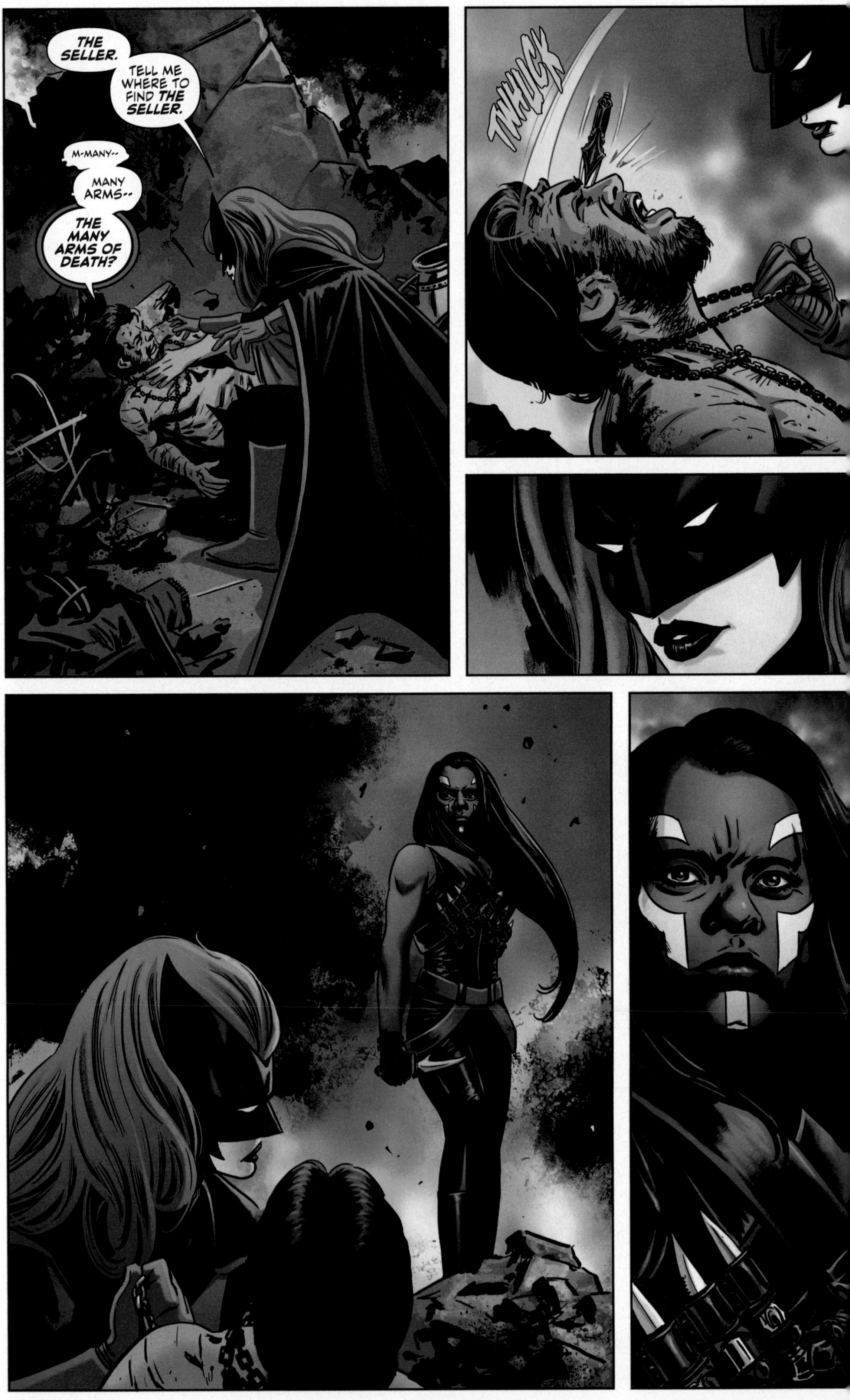
THE SELLER.
TELL ME WHERE TO FIND THE SELLER.
M-MANY--
MANY ARMS--
THE MANY ARMS OF DEATH?
THWACK

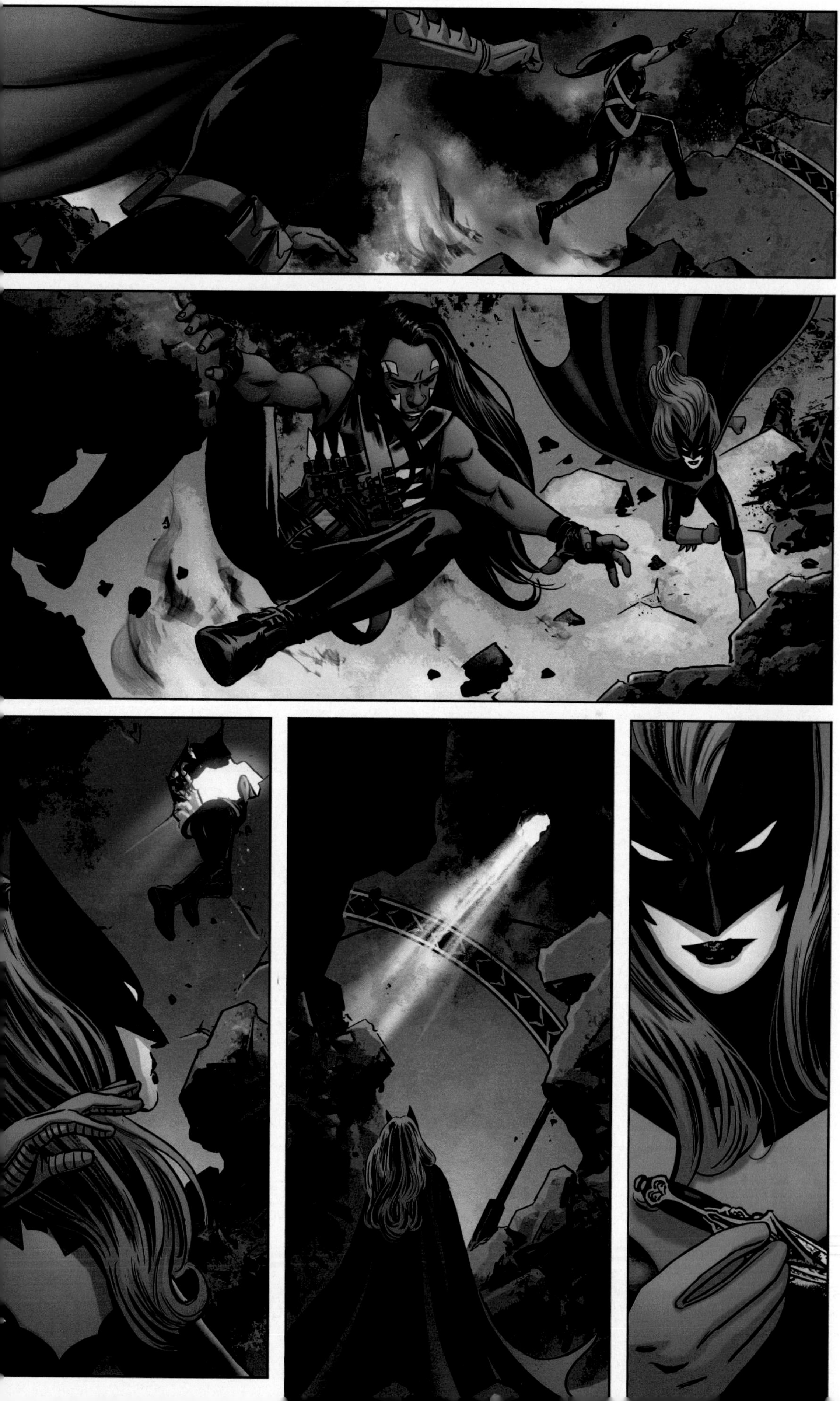

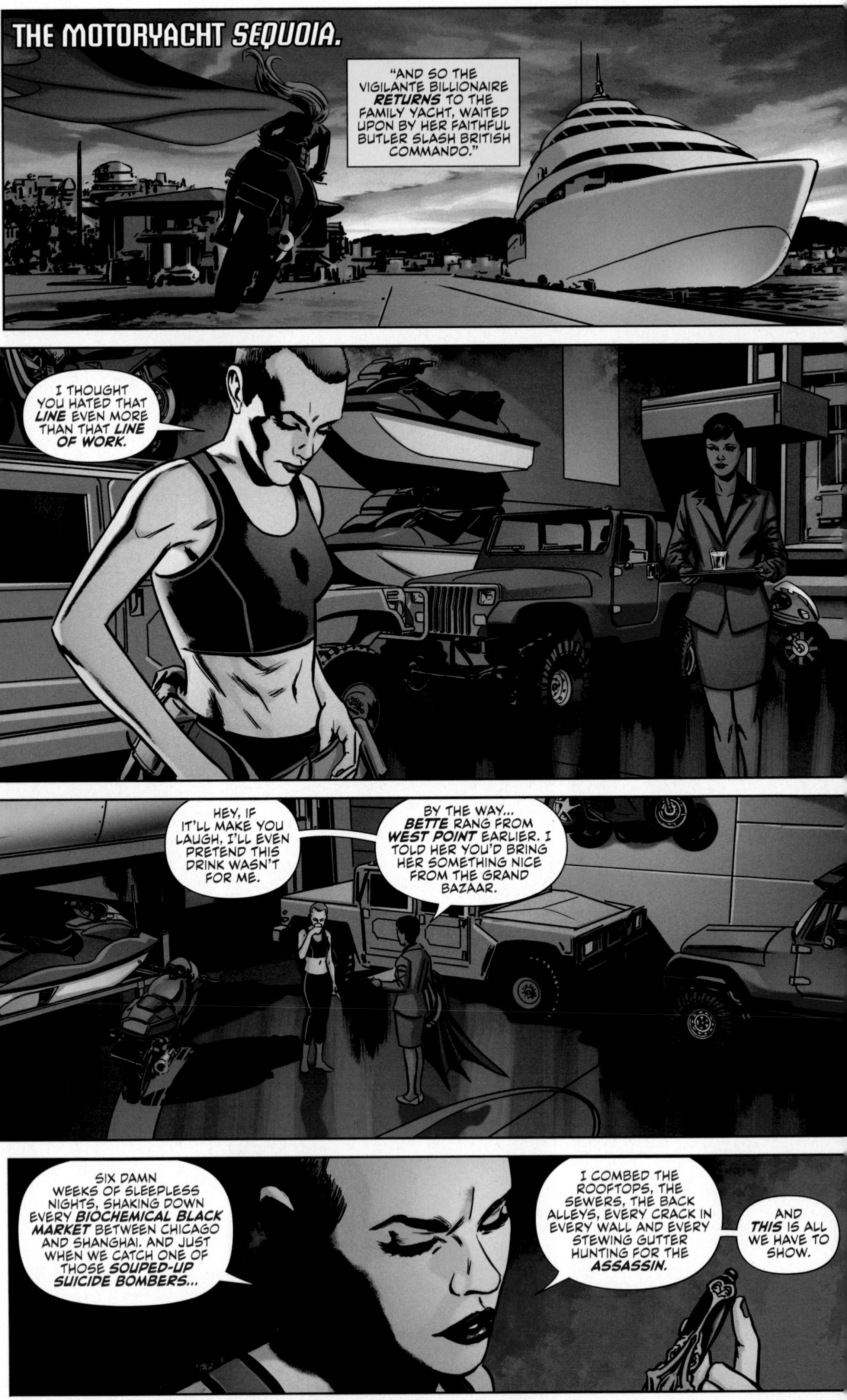
THE MOTORYACHT SEQUOIA.
"AND SO THE VIGILANTE BILLIONAIRE RETURNS TO THE FAMILY YACHT, WAITED UPON BY HER FAITHFUL BUTLER SLASH BRITISH COMMANDO."
I THOUGHT YOU HATED THAT LINE EVEN MORE THAN THAT LINE OF WORK.
HEY, IF IT'LL MAKE YOU LAUGH, I'LL EVEN PRETEND THIS DRINK WASN'T FOR ME.
BY THE WAY... BETTE RANG FROM WEST POINT EARLIER. I TOLD HER YOU'D BRING HER SOMETHING NICE FROM THE GRAND BAZAAR.
SIX DAMN WEEKS OF SLEEPLESS NIGHTS, SHAKING DOWN EVERY BIOCHEMICAL BLACK MARKET BETWEEN CHICAGO AND SHANGHAI. AND JUST WHEN WE CATCH ONE OF THOSE SOUPED-UP SUICIDE BOMBERS...
I COMBED THE ROOFTOPS, THE SEWERS, THE BACK ALLEYS, EVERY CRACK IN EVERY WALL AND EVERY STEWING GUTTER HUNTING FOR THE ASSASSIN.
AND THIS IS ALL WE HAVE TO SHOW.

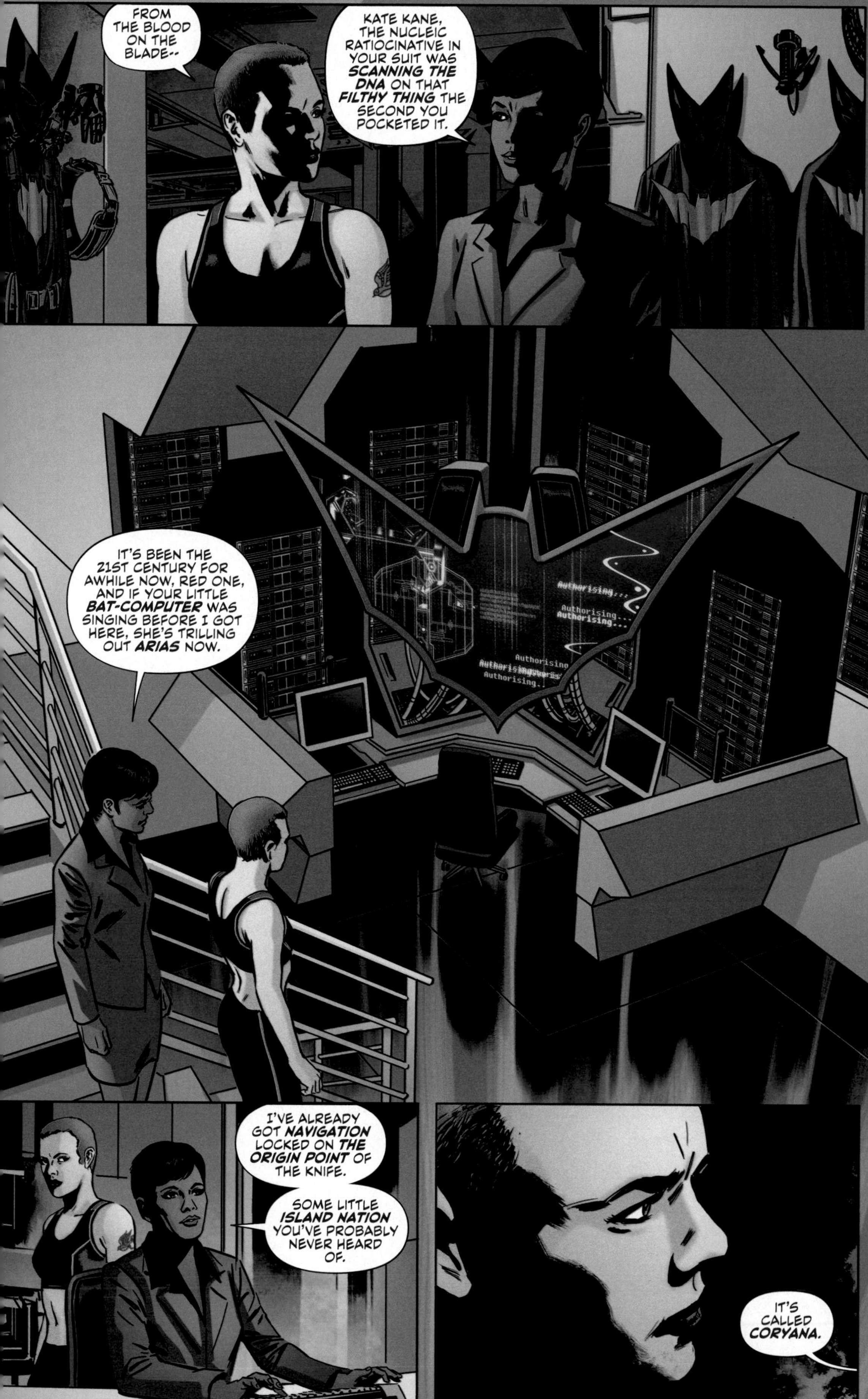
FROM THE BLOOD ON THE BLADE--
KATE KANE, THE NUCLEIC RATIOCINATIVE IN YOUR SUIT WAS SCANNING THE DNA ON THAT FILTHY THING THE SECOND YOU POCKETED IT.
IT'S BEEN THE 21ST CENTURY FOR AWHILE NOW, RED ONE, AND IF YOUR LITTLE BAT-COMPUTER WAS SINGING BEFORE I GOT HERE, SHE'S TRILLING OUT ARIAS NOW.
Authorising...
Authorising...
Authorising...
Authorising
Authorising..
I'VE ALREADY GOT NAVIGATION LOCKED ON THE ORIGIN POINT OF THE KNIFE.
SOME LITTLE ISLAND NATION YOU'VE PROBABLY NEVER HEARD OF.
IT'S CALLED CORYANA.

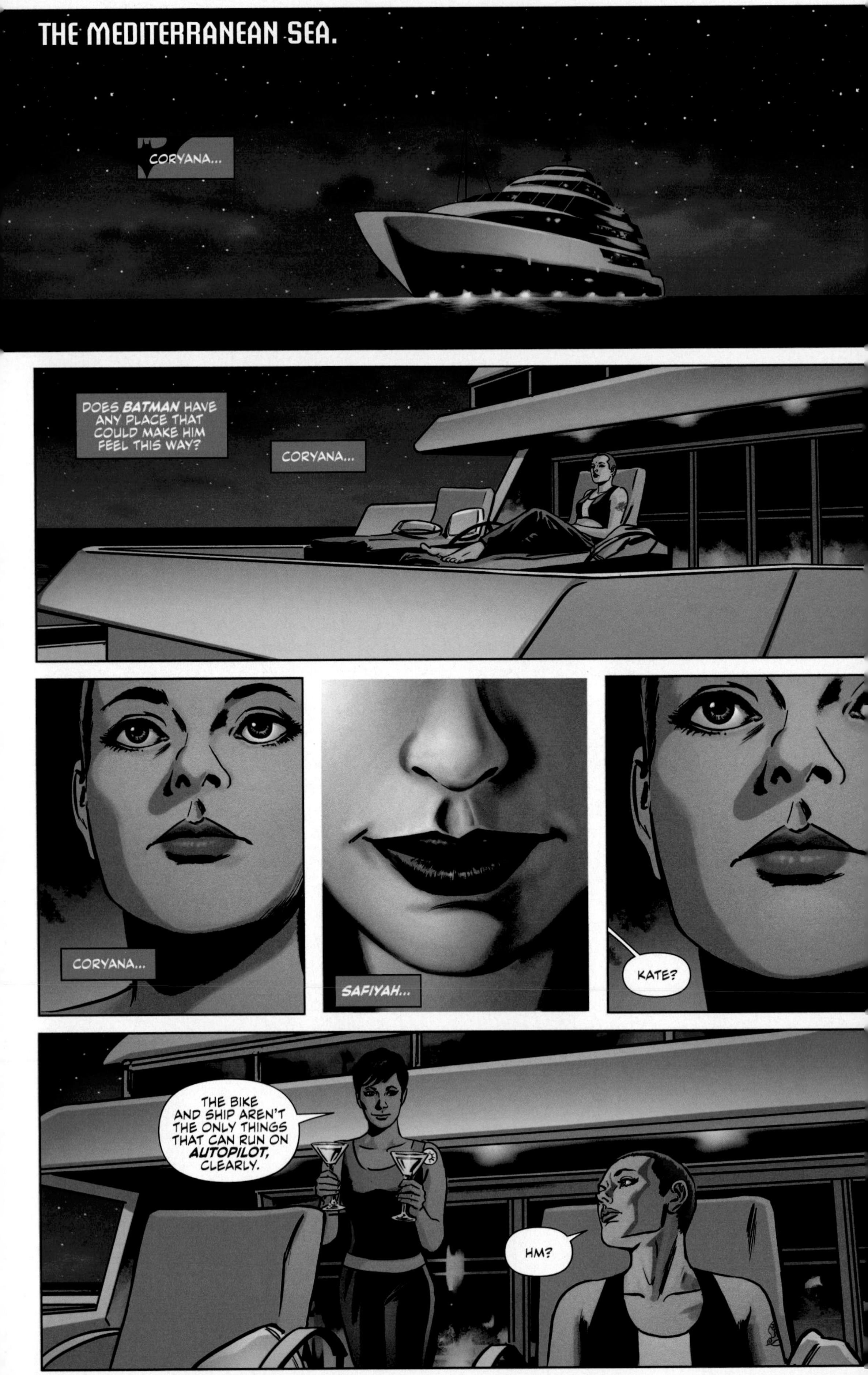
THE MEDITERRANEAN SEA.
CORYANA...
DOES BATMAN HAVE ANY PLACE THAT COULD MAKE HIM FEEL THIS WAY?
CORYANA...
CORYANA...
SAFIYAH...
KATE?
THE BIKE AND SHIP AREN'T THE ONLY THINGS THAT CAN RUN ON AUTOPILOT, CLEARLY.
HM?

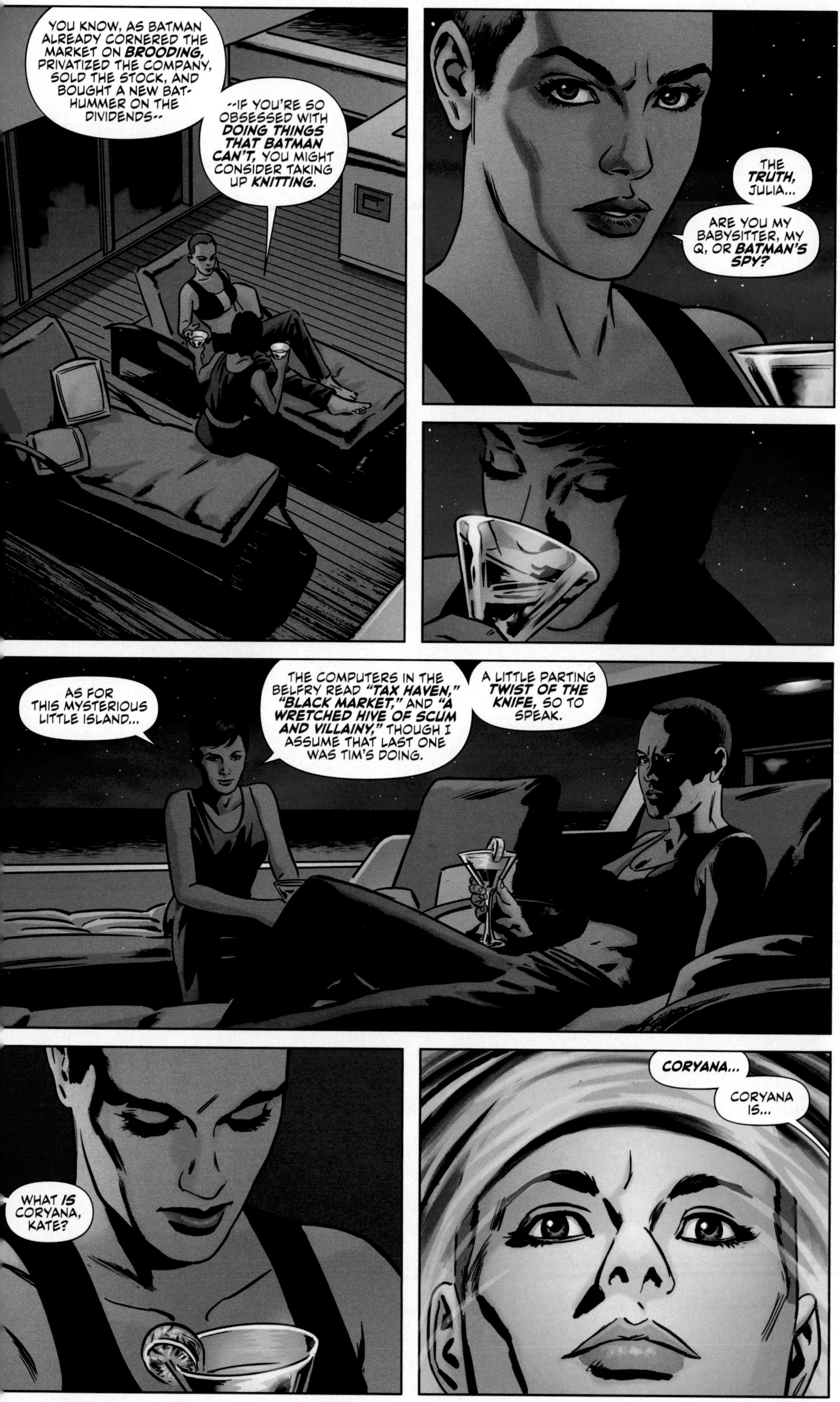
YOU KNOW, AS BATMAN ALREADY CORNERED THE MARKET ON BROODING, PRIVATIZED THE COMPANY, SOLD THE STOCK, AND BOUGHT A NEW BAT-HUMMER ON THE DIVIDENDS--
--IF YOU'RE SO OBSESSED WITH DOING THINGS THAT BATMAN CAN'T, YOU MIGHT CONSIDER TAKING UP KNITTING.
THE TRUTH, JULIA...
ARE YOU MY BABYSITTER, MY Q, OR BATMAN'S SPY?
AS FOR THIS MYSTERIOUS LITTLE ISLAND...
THE COMPUTERS IN THE BELFRY READ "TAX HAVEN," "BLACK MARKET," AND "A WRETCHED HIVE OF SCUM AND VILLAINY," THOUGH I ASSUME THAT LAST ONE WAS TIM'S DOING.
A LITTLE PARTING TWIST OF THE KNIFE, SO TO SPEAK.
WHAT IS CORYANA, KATE?
CORYANA...
CORYANA IS...

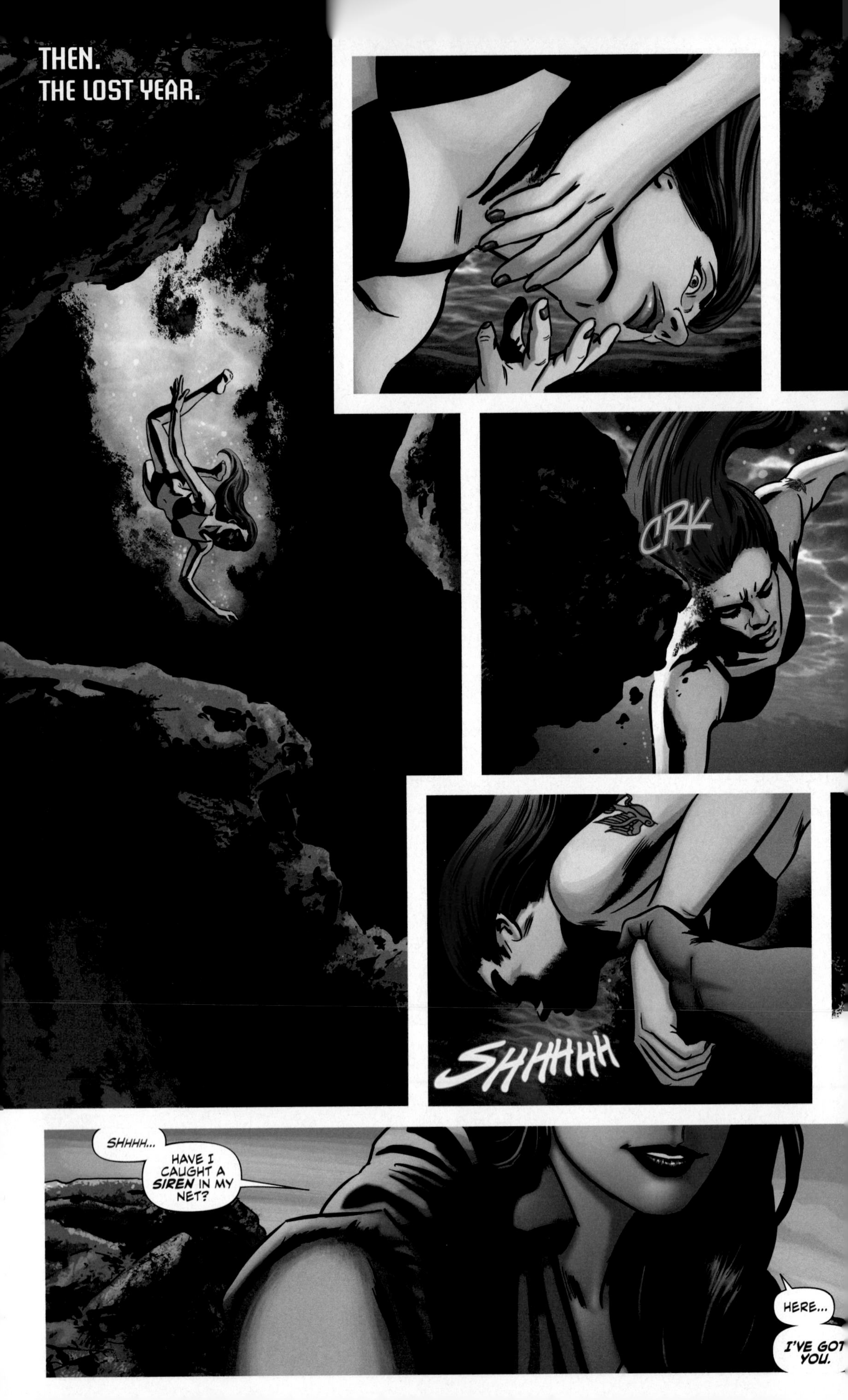
THEN.
THE LOST YEAR.
CRK
SHHHHH
SHHHH...
HAVE I CAUGHT A SIREN IN MY NET?
HERE...
I'VE GOT YOU.

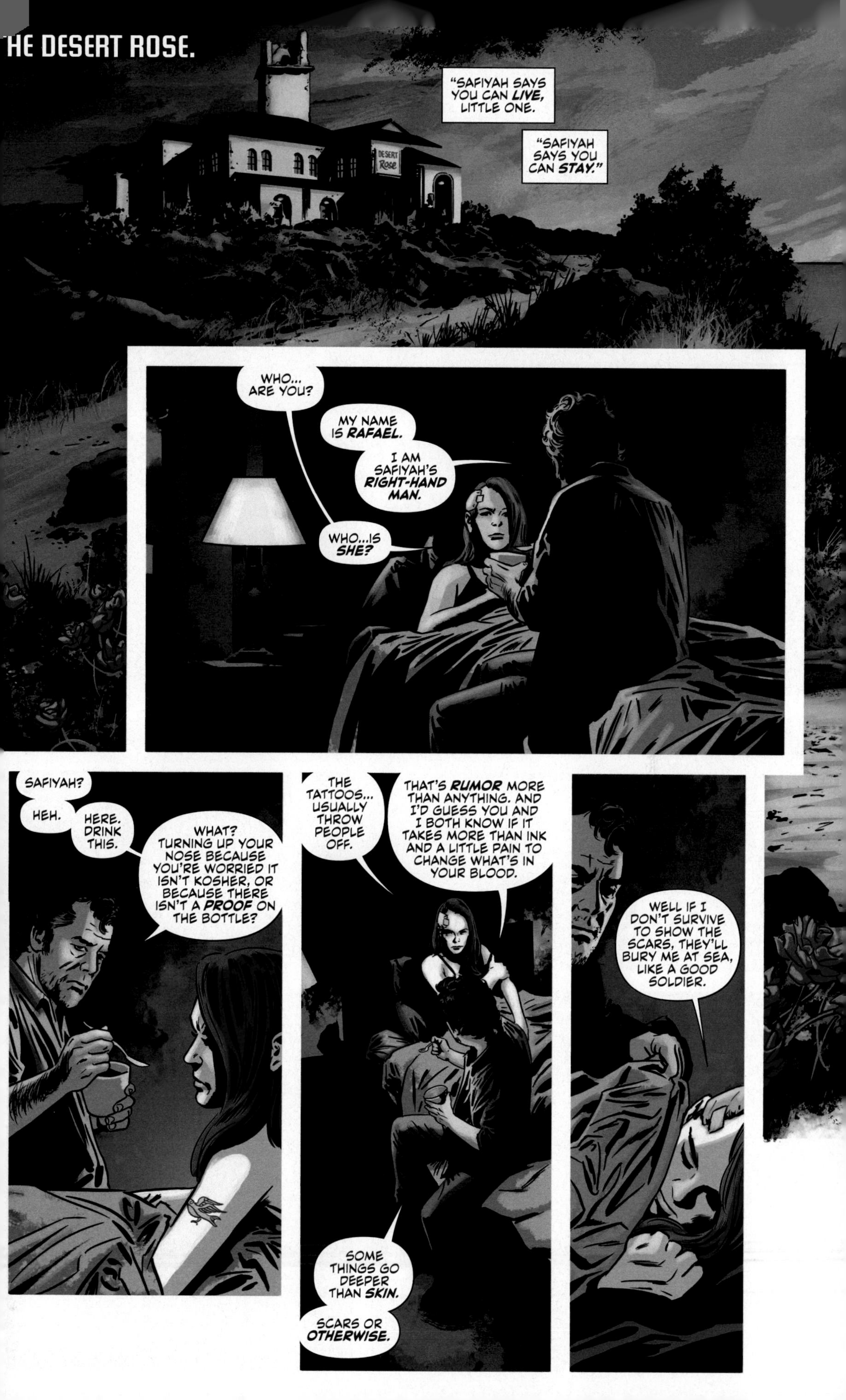
THE DESERT ROSE.
"SAFIYAH SAYS YOU CAN LIVE, LITTLE ONE.
"SAFIYAH SAYS YOU CAN STAY."
DESERT Rose
WHO... ARE YOU?
MY NAME IS RAFAEL.
I AM SAFIYAH'S RIGHT-HAND MAN.
WHO...IS SHE?
SAFIYAH?
HEH.
HERE. DRINK THIS.
WHAT? TURNING UP YOUR NOSE BECAUSE YOU'RE WORRIED IT ISN'T KOSHER, OR BECAUSE THERE ISN'T A PROOF ON THE BOTTLE?
THE TATTOOS... USUALLY THROW PEOPLE OFF.
THAT'S RUMOR MORE THAN ANYTHING. AND I'D GUESS YOU AND I BOTH KNOW IF IT TAKES MORE THAN INK AND A LITTLE PAIN TO CHANGE WHAT'S IN YOUR BLOOD.
SOME THINGS GO DEEPER THAN SKIN.
SCARS OR OTHERWISE.
WELL IF I DON'T SURVIVE TO SHOW THE SCARS, THEY'LL BURY ME AT SEA, LIKE A GOOD SOLDIER.

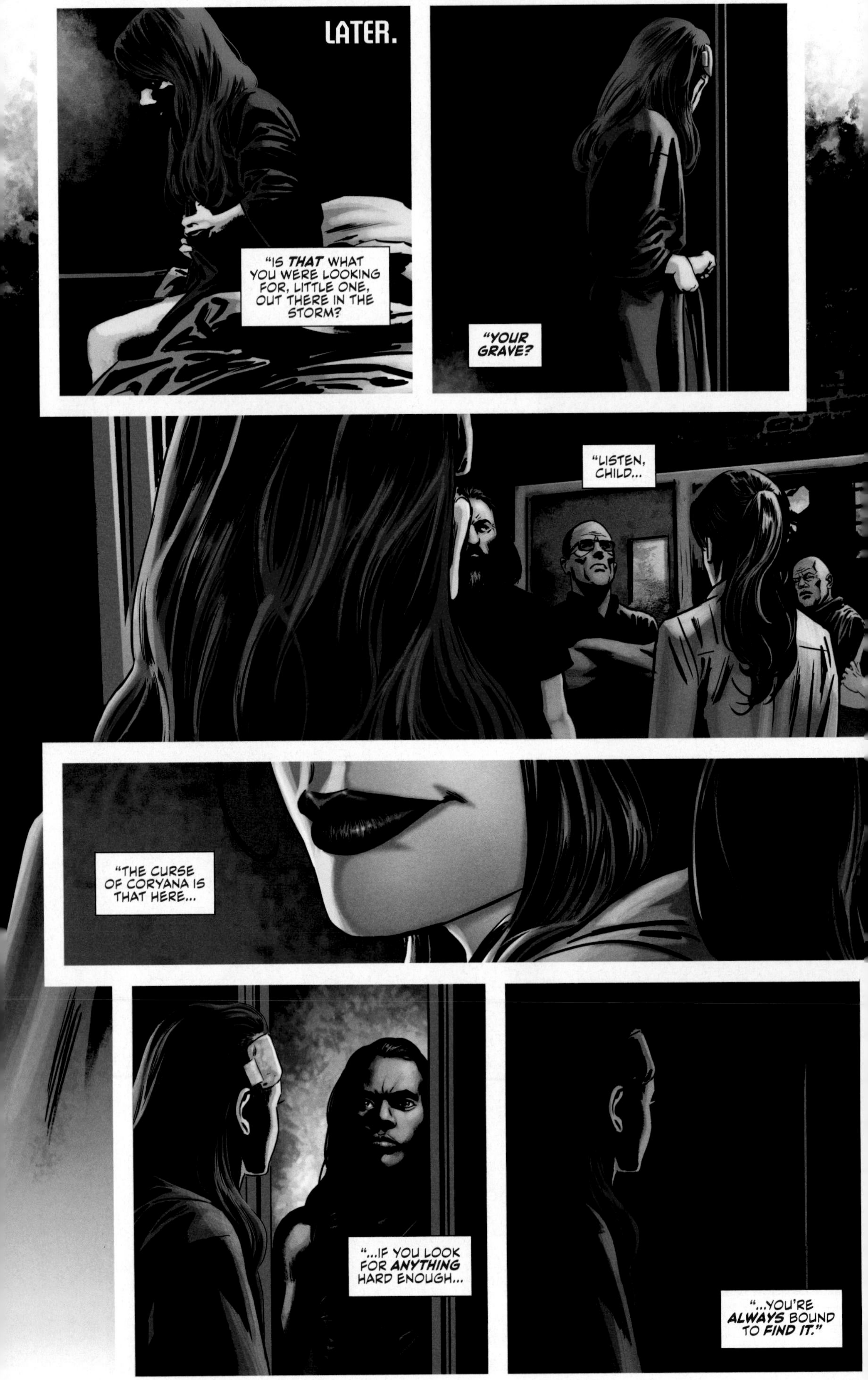
LATER.
"IS THAT WHAT YOU WERE LOOKING FOR, LITTLE ONE, OUT THERE IN THE STORM?
"YOUR GRAVE?
"LISTEN, CHILD...
"THE CURSE OF CORYANA IS THAT HERE...
"...IF YOU LOOK FOR ANYTHING HARD ENOUGH...
"...YOU'RE ALWAYS BOUND TO FIND IT."

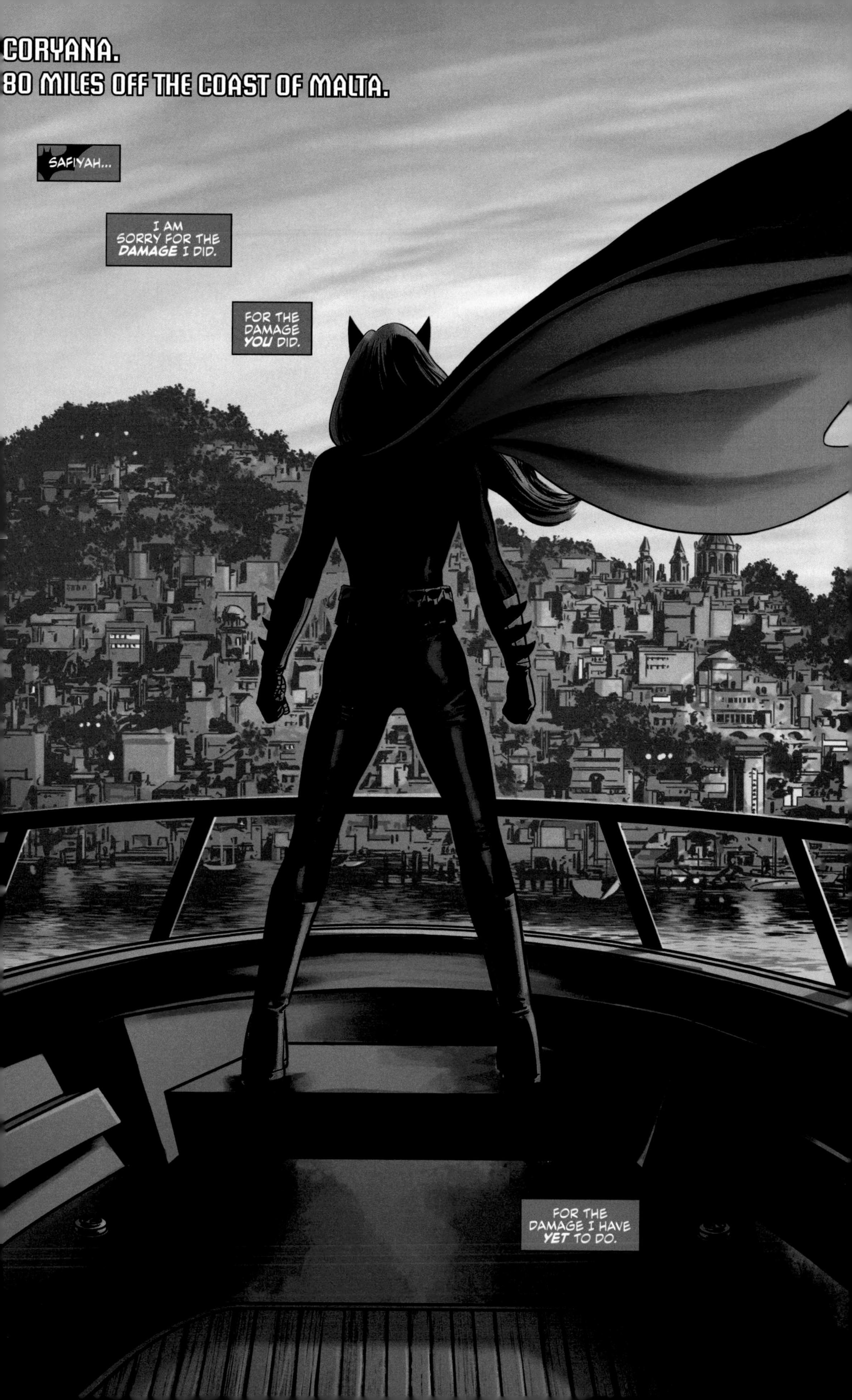
CORYANA.
80 MILES OFF THE COAST OF MALTA.
SAFIYAH...
I AM SORRY FOR THE DAMAGE I DID.
FOR THE DAMAGE YOU DID.
FOR THE DAMAGE I HAVE YET TO DO.

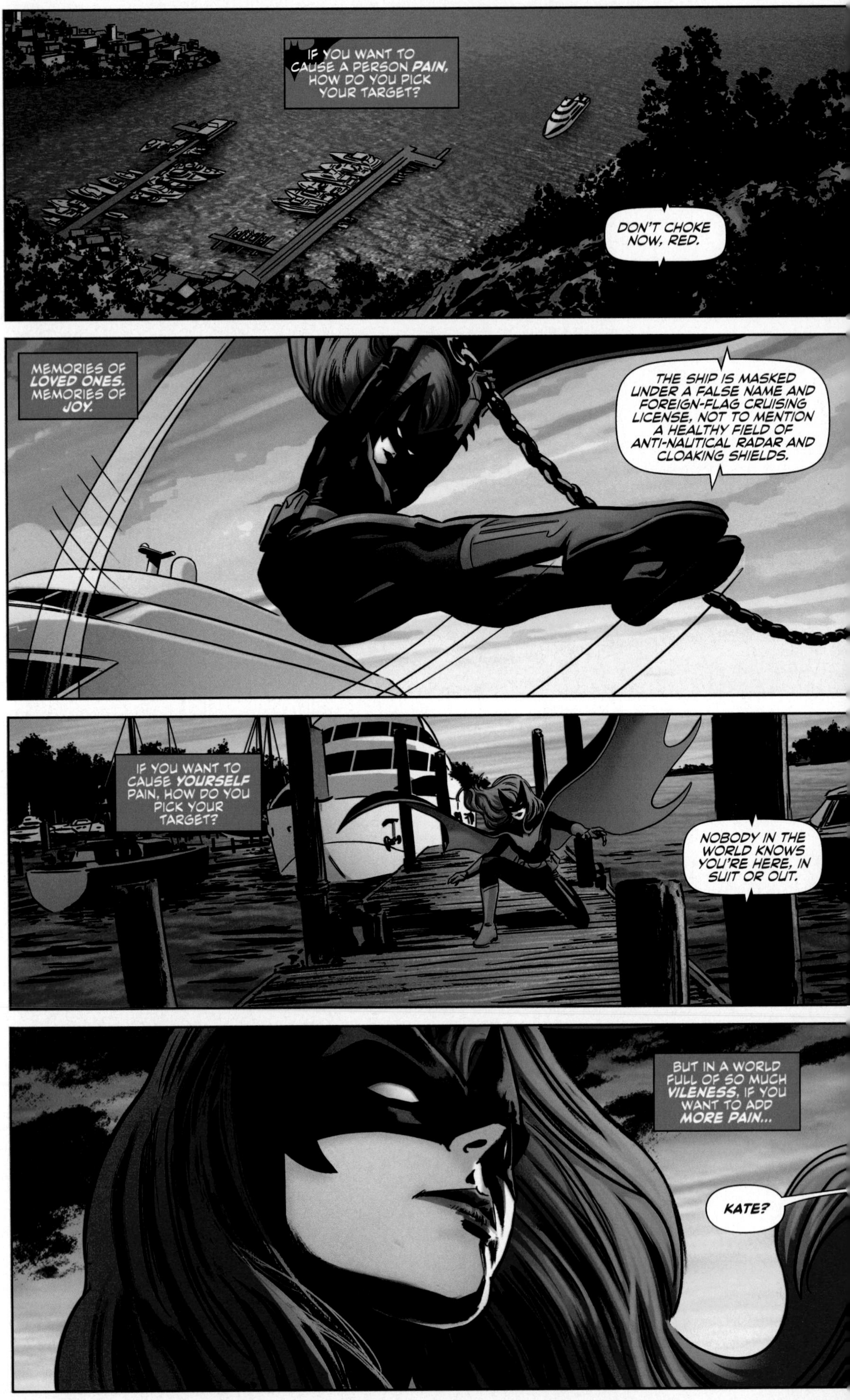
IF YOU WANT TO CAUSE A PERSON PAIN, HOW DO YOU PICK YOUR TARGET?
DON'T CHOKE NOW, RED.
MEMORIES OF LOVED ONES. MEMORIES OF JOY.
THE SHIP IS MASKED UNDER A FALSE NAME AND FOREIGN-FLAG CRUISING LICENSE, NOT TO MENTION A HEALTHY FIELD OF ANTI-NAUTICAL RADAR AND CLOAKING SHIELDS.
IF YOU WANT TO CAUSE YOURSELF PAIN, HOW DO YOU PICK YOUR TARGET?
NOBODY IN THE WORLD KNOWS YOU'RE HERE, IN SUIT OR OUT.
BUT IN A WORLD FULL OF SO MUCH VILENESS, IF YOU WANT TO ADD MORE PAIN...
KATE?

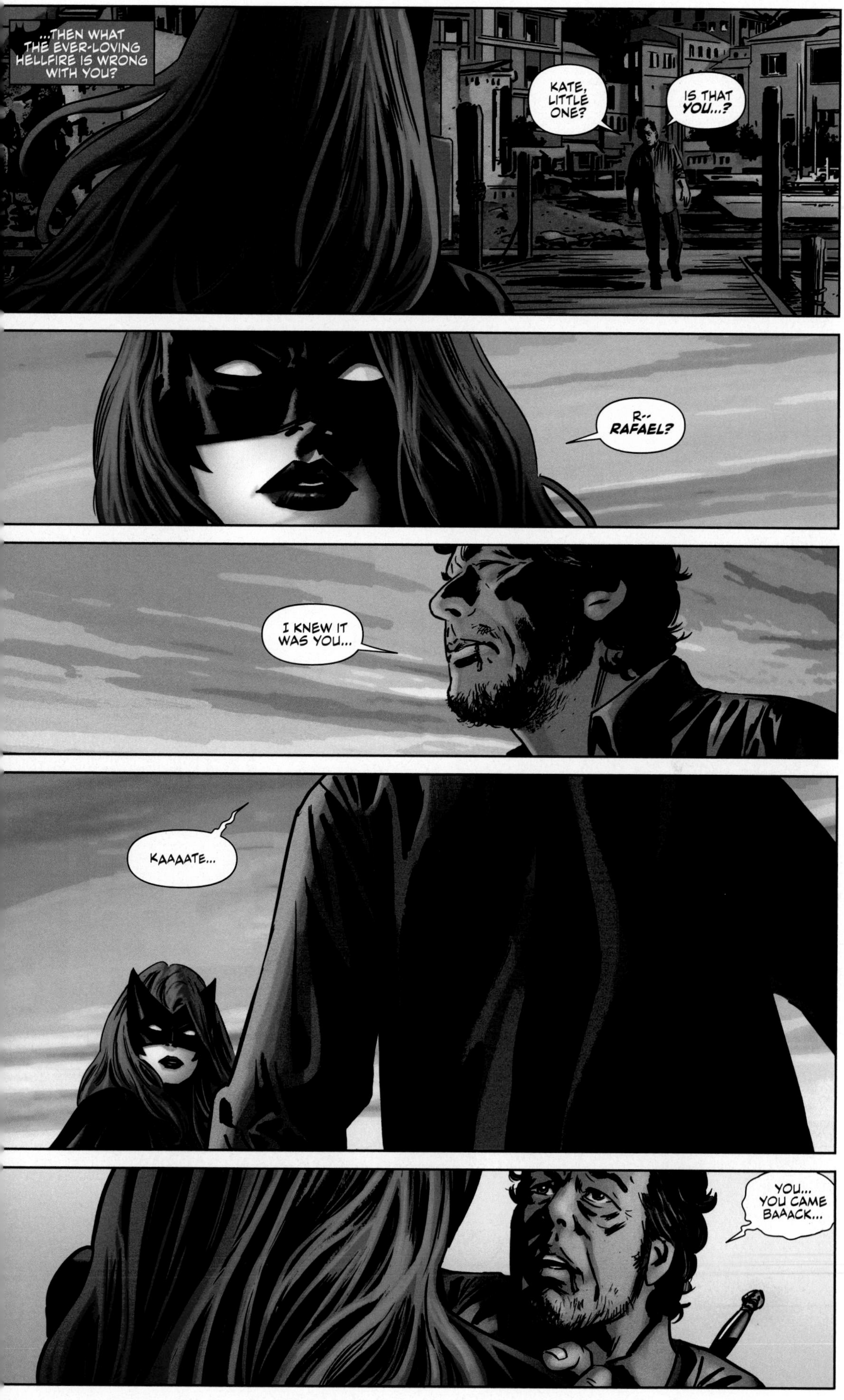
...THEN WHAT THE EVER-LOVING HELLFIRE IS WRONG WITH YOU?
KATE, LITTLE ONE?
IS THAT *YOU...?*
R-- *RAFAEL?*
I KNEW IT WAS YOU...
KAAAATE...
YOU... YOU CAME BAAACK...

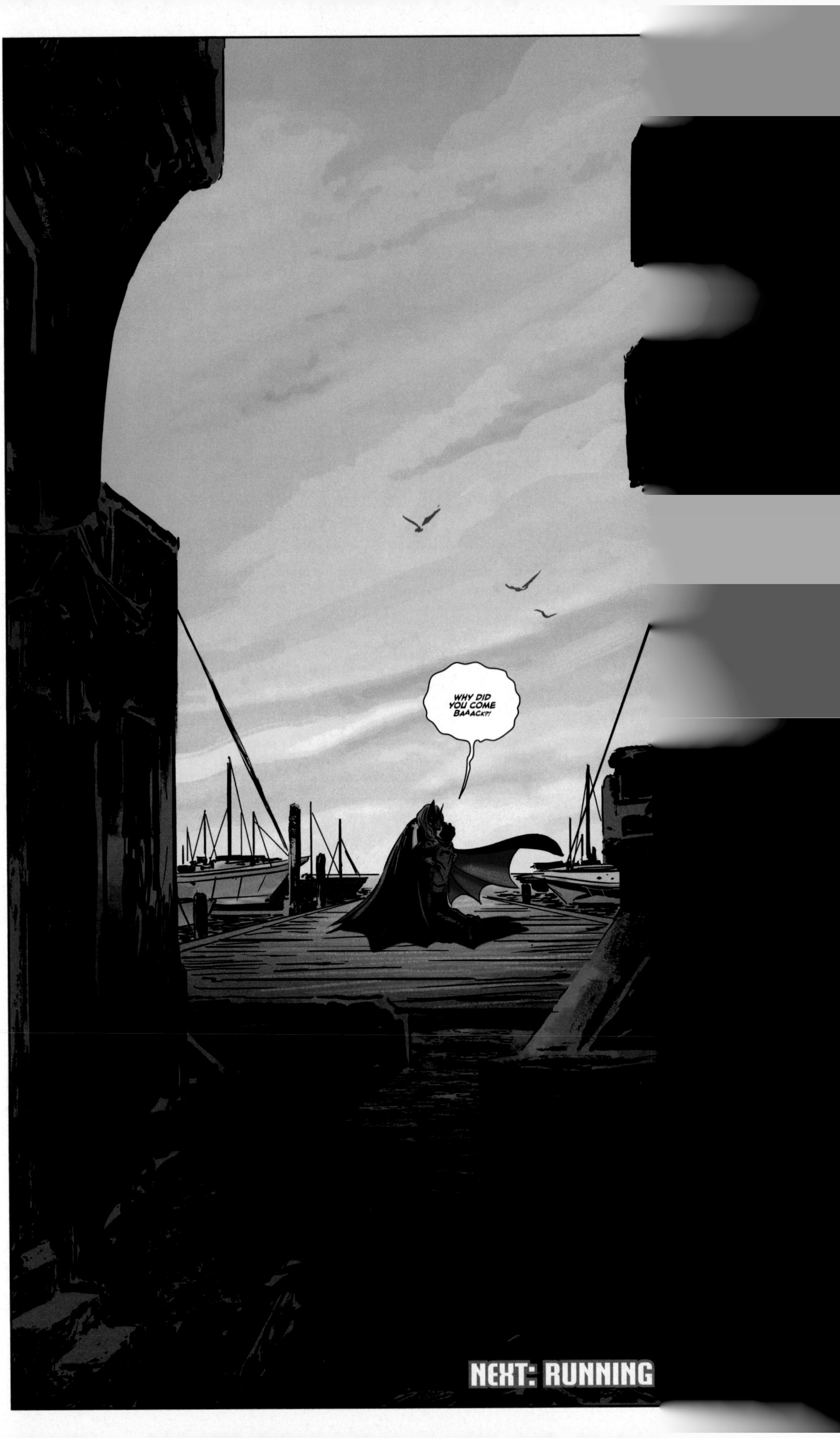
WHY DID YOU COME BAAACK?!
NEXT: RUNNING

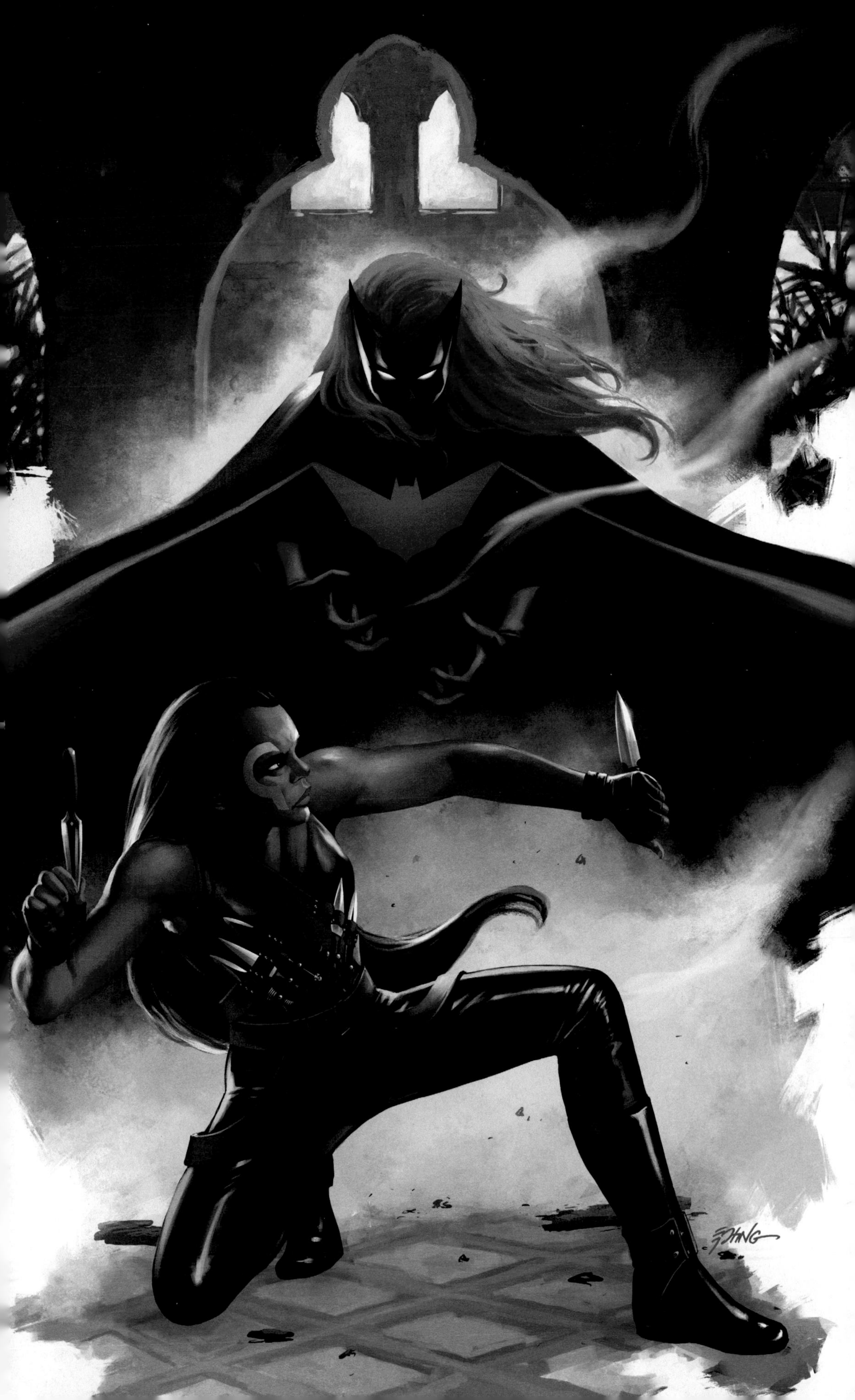

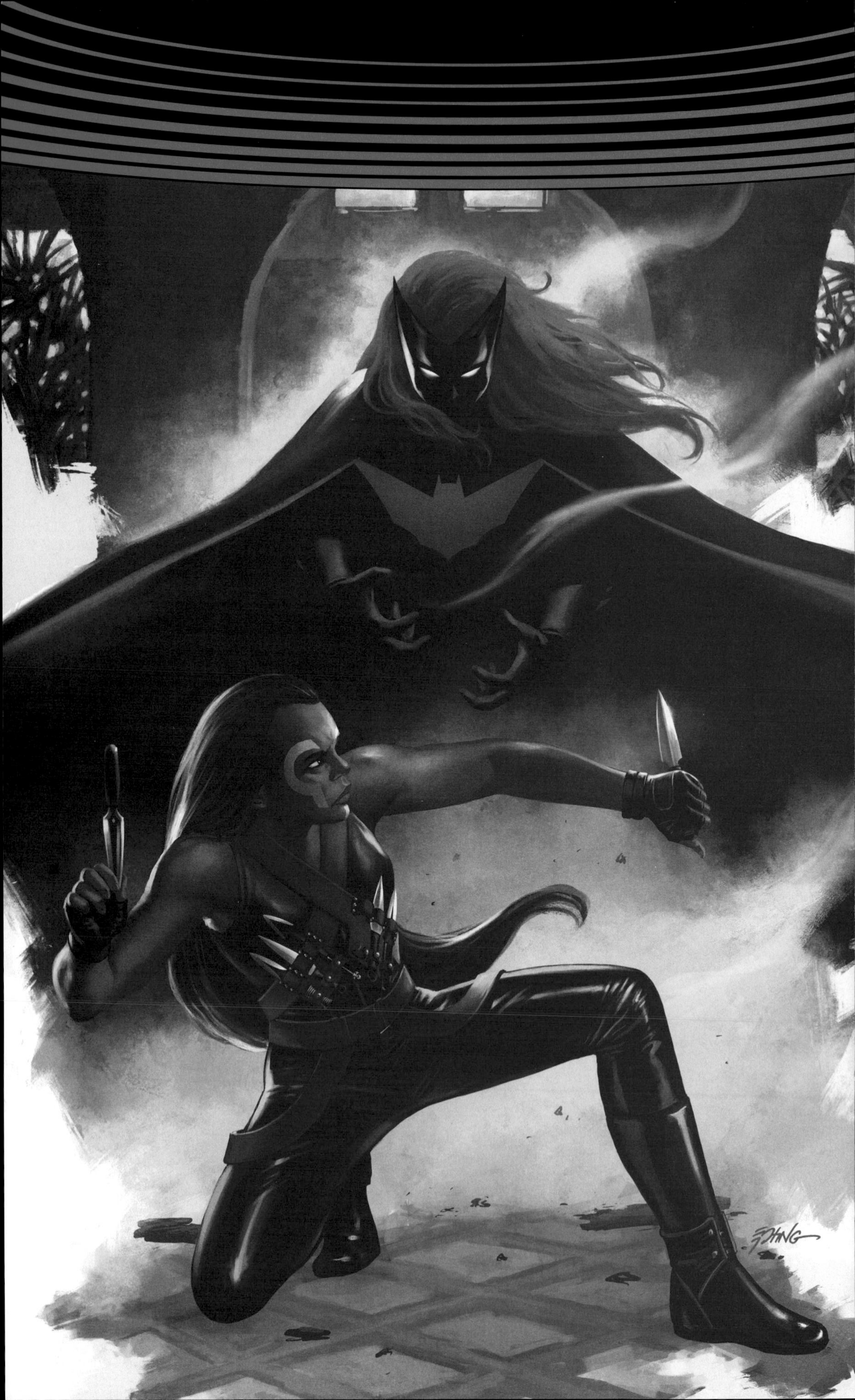

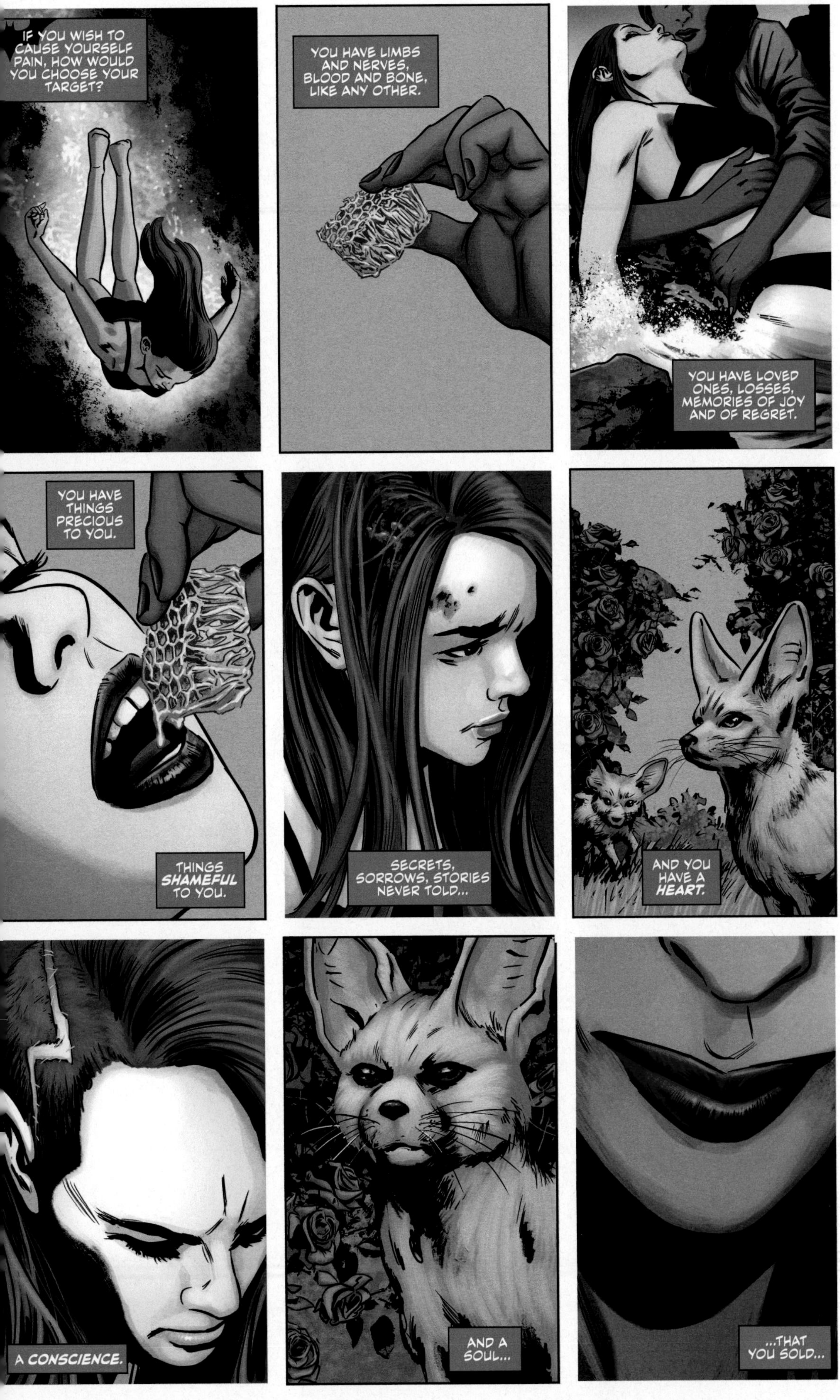
IF YOU WISH TO CAUSE YOURSELF PAIN, HOW WOULD YOU CHOOSE YOUR TARGET?
YOU HAVE LIMBS AND NERVES, BLOOD AND BONE, LIKE ANY OTHER.
YOU HAVE LOVED ONES, LOSSES, MEMORIES OF JOY AND OF REGRET.
YOU HAVE THINGS PRECIOUS TO YOU.
THINGS *SHAMEFUL* TO YOU.
SECRETS, SORROWS, STORIES NEVER TOLD...
AND YOU HAVE A *HEART.*
A *CONSCIENCE.*
AND A SOUL...
...THAT YOU SOLD...

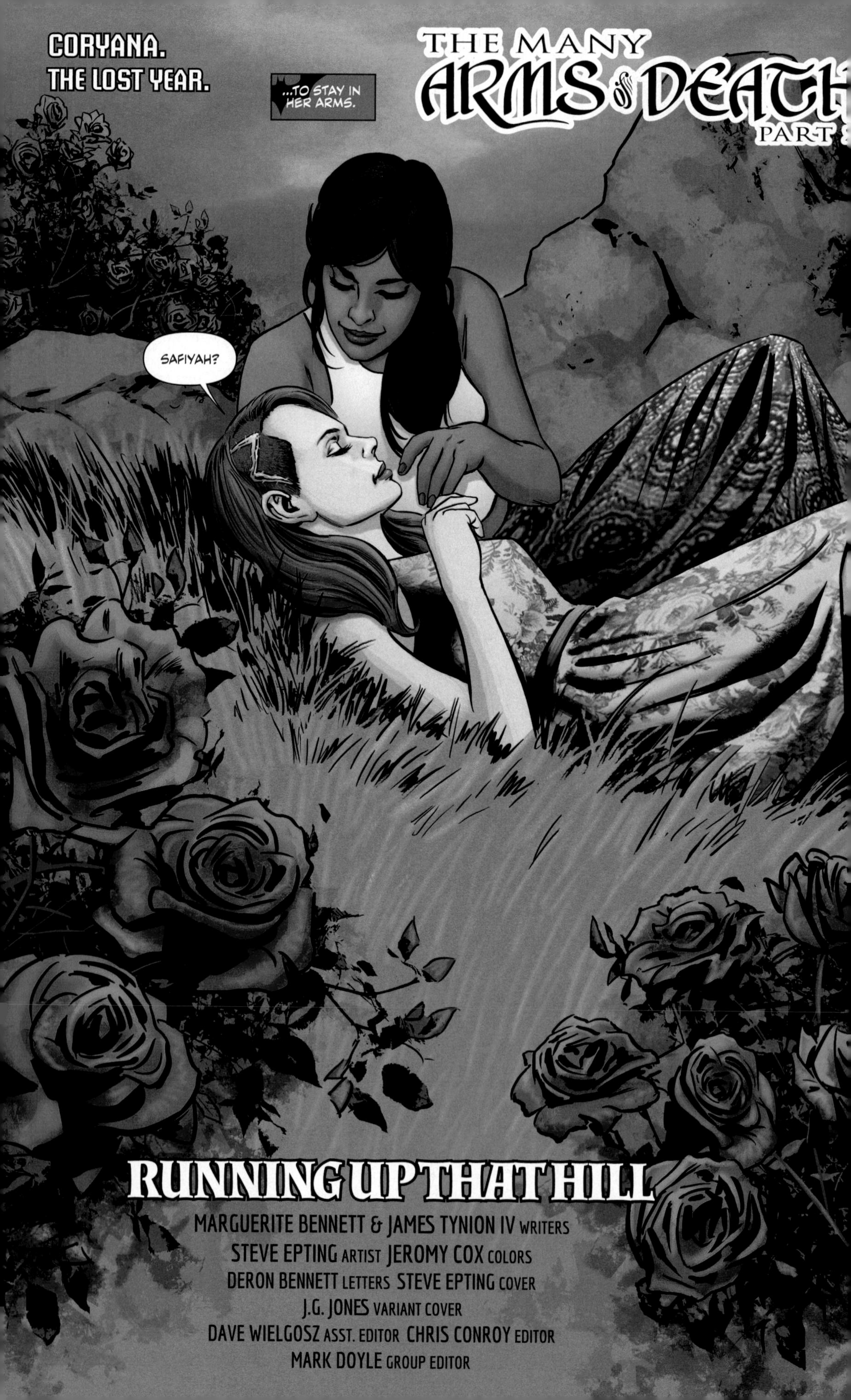

CORYANA.
THE LOST YEAR.
...TO STAY IN HER ARMS.
THE MANY ARMS of DEATH PART
SAFIYAH?
RUNNING UP THAT HILL
MARGUERITE BENNETT & JAMES TYNION IV WRITERS
STEVE EPTING ARTIST JEROMY COX COLORS
DERON BENNETT LETTERS STEVE EPTING COVER
J.G. JONES VARIANT COVER
DAVE WIELGOSZ ASST. EDITOR CHRIS CONROY EDITOR
MARK DOYLE GROUP EDITOR

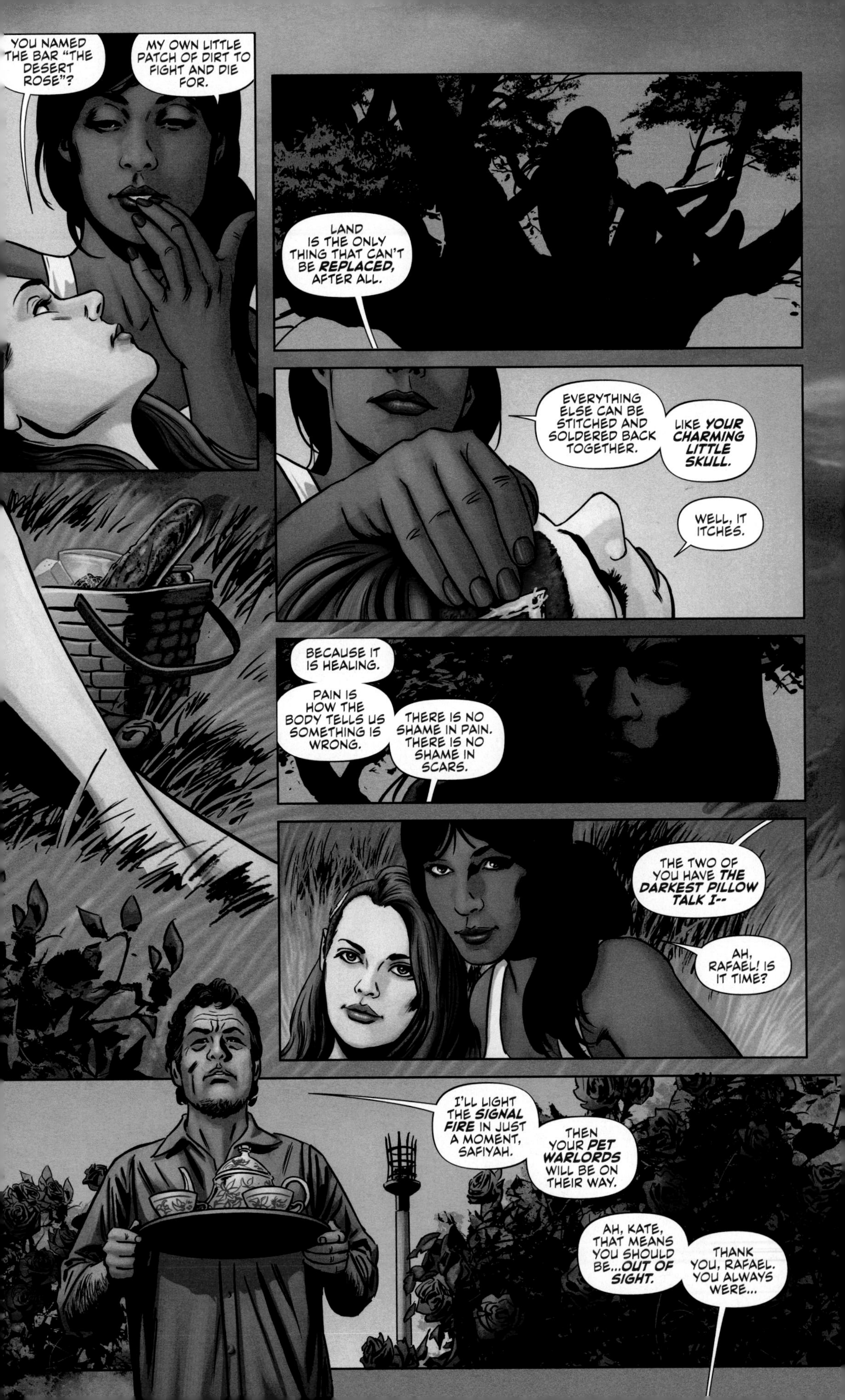
YOU NAMED THE BAR "THE DESERT ROSE"?
MY OWN LITTLE PATCH OF DIRT TO FIGHT AND DIE FOR.
LAND IS THE ONLY THING THAT CAN'T BE *REPLACED,* AFTER ALL.
EVERYTHING ELSE CAN BE STITCHED AND SOLDERED BACK TOGETHER.
LIKE ***YOUR CHARMING LITTLE SKULL.***
WELL, IT ITCHES.
BECAUSE IT IS HEALING.
PAIN IS HOW THE BODY TELLS US SOMETHING IS WRONG.
THERE IS NO SHAME IN PAIN. THERE IS NO SHAME IN SCARS.
THE TWO OF YOU HAVE ***THE DARKEST PILLOW TALK I--***
AH, RAFAEL! IS IT TIME?
I'LL LIGHT THE ***SIGNAL FIRE*** IN JUST A MOMENT, SAFIYAH.
THEN YOUR ***PET WARLORDS*** WILL BE ON THEIR WAY.
AH, KATE, THAT MEANS YOU SHOULD BE...***OUT OF SIGHT.***
THANK YOU, RAFAEL. YOU ALWAYS WERE...

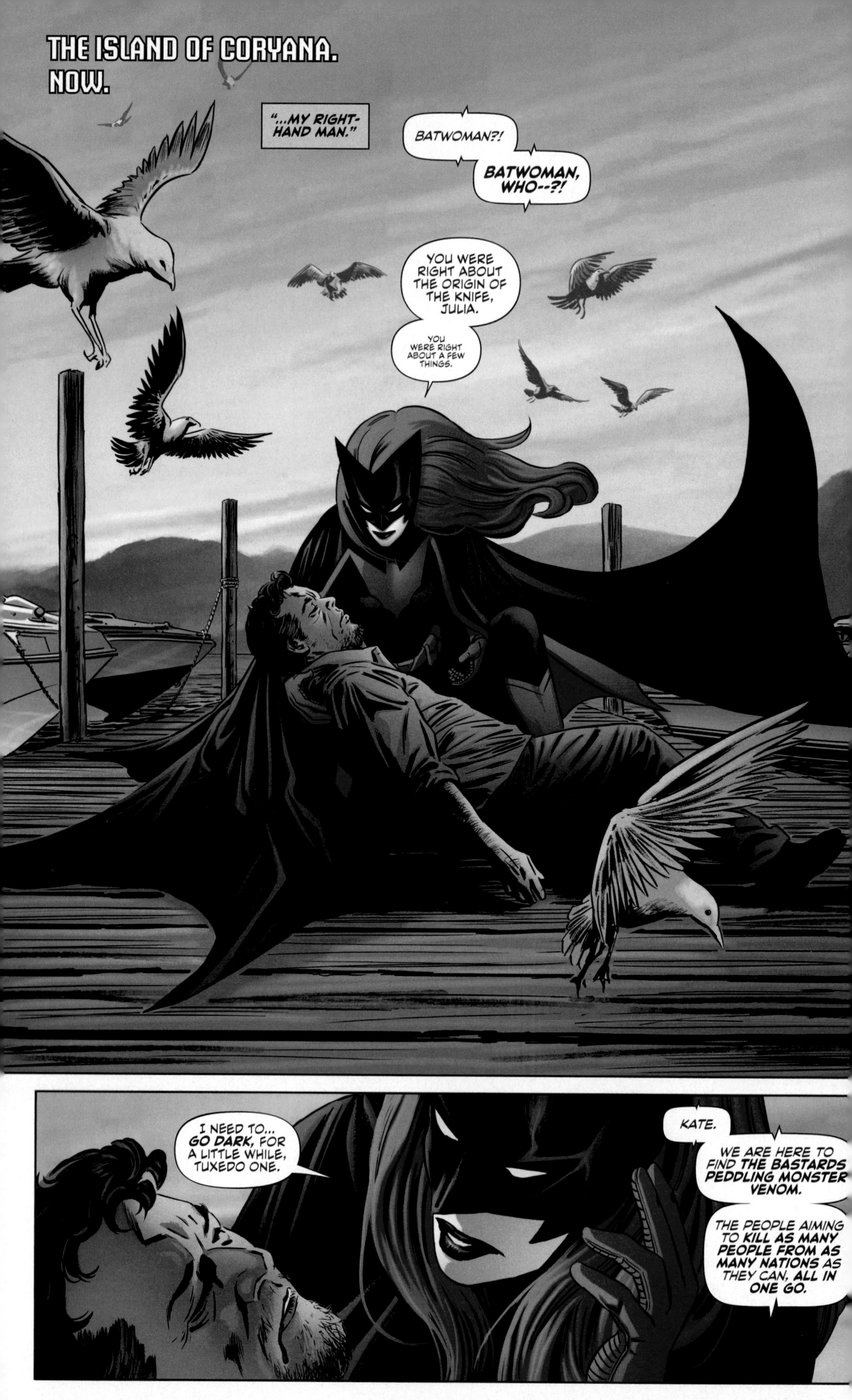
THE ISLAND OF CORYANA. NOW.
"...MY RIGHT-HAND MAN."
BATWOMAN?!
BATWOMAN, WHO--?!
YOU WERE RIGHT ABOUT THE ORIGIN OF THE KNIFE, JULIA.
YOU WERE RIGHT ABOUT A FEW THINGS.
I NEED TO... GO DARK, FOR A LITTLE WHILE, TUXEDO ONE.
KATE.
WE ARE HERE TO FIND THE BASTARDS PEDDLING MONSTER VENOM.
THE PEOPLE AIMING TO KILL AS MANY PEOPLE FROM AS MANY NATIONS AS THEY CAN, ALL IN ONE GO.

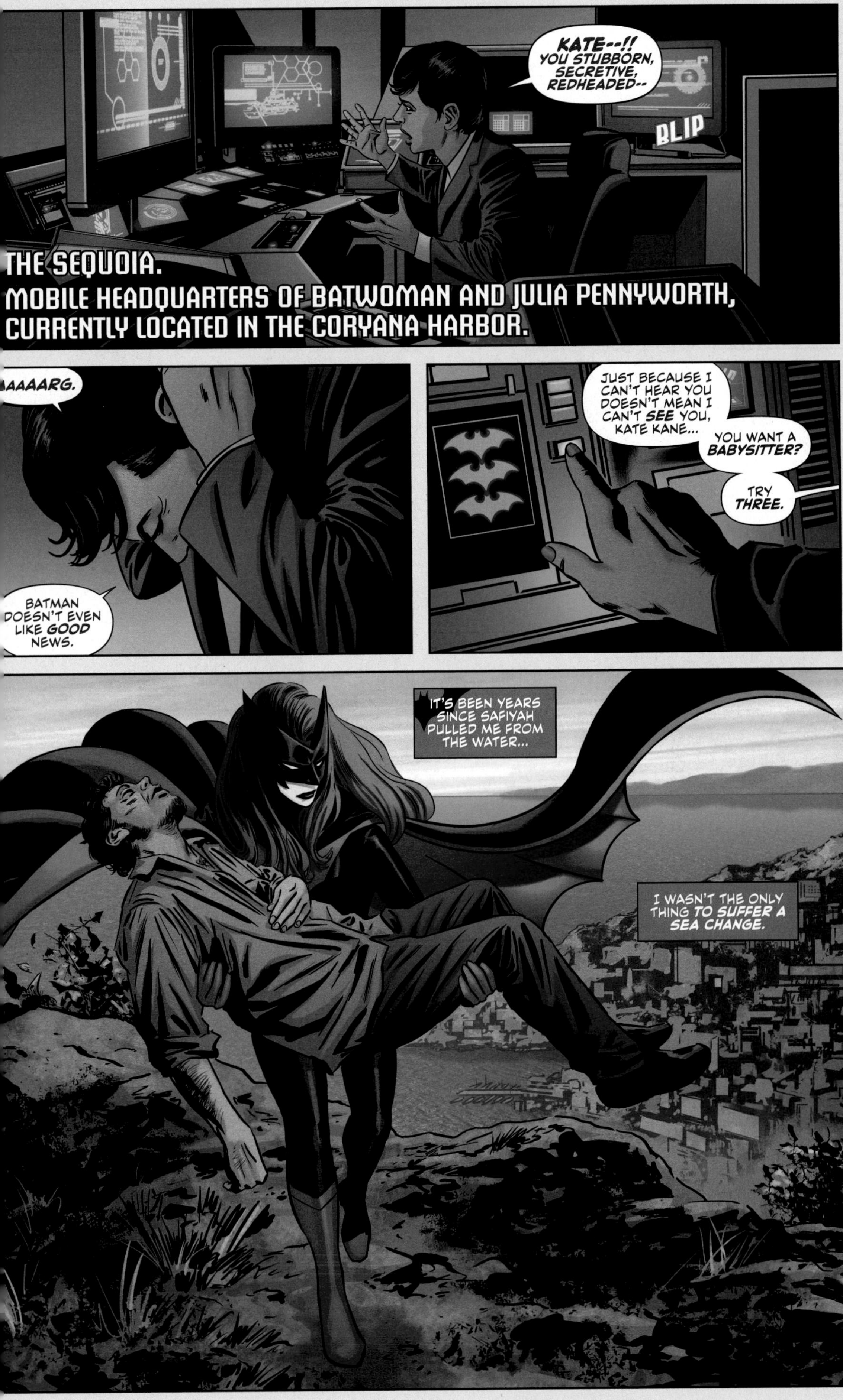
KATE--!! YOU STUBBORN, SECRETIVE, REDHEADED--
BLIP
THE SEQUOIA.
MOBILE HEADQUARTERS OF BATWOMAN AND JULIA PENNYWORTH, CURRENTLY LOCATED IN THE CORYANA HARBOR.
AAAAARG.
BATMAN DOESN'T EVEN LIKE GOOD NEWS.
JUST BECAUSE I CAN'T HEAR YOU DOESN'T MEAN I CAN'T SEE YOU, KATE KANE...
YOU WANT A BABYSITTER?
TRY THREE.
IT'S BEEN YEARS SINCE SAFIYAH PULLED ME FROM THE WATER...
I WASN'T THE ONLY THING TO SUFFER A SEA CHANGE.

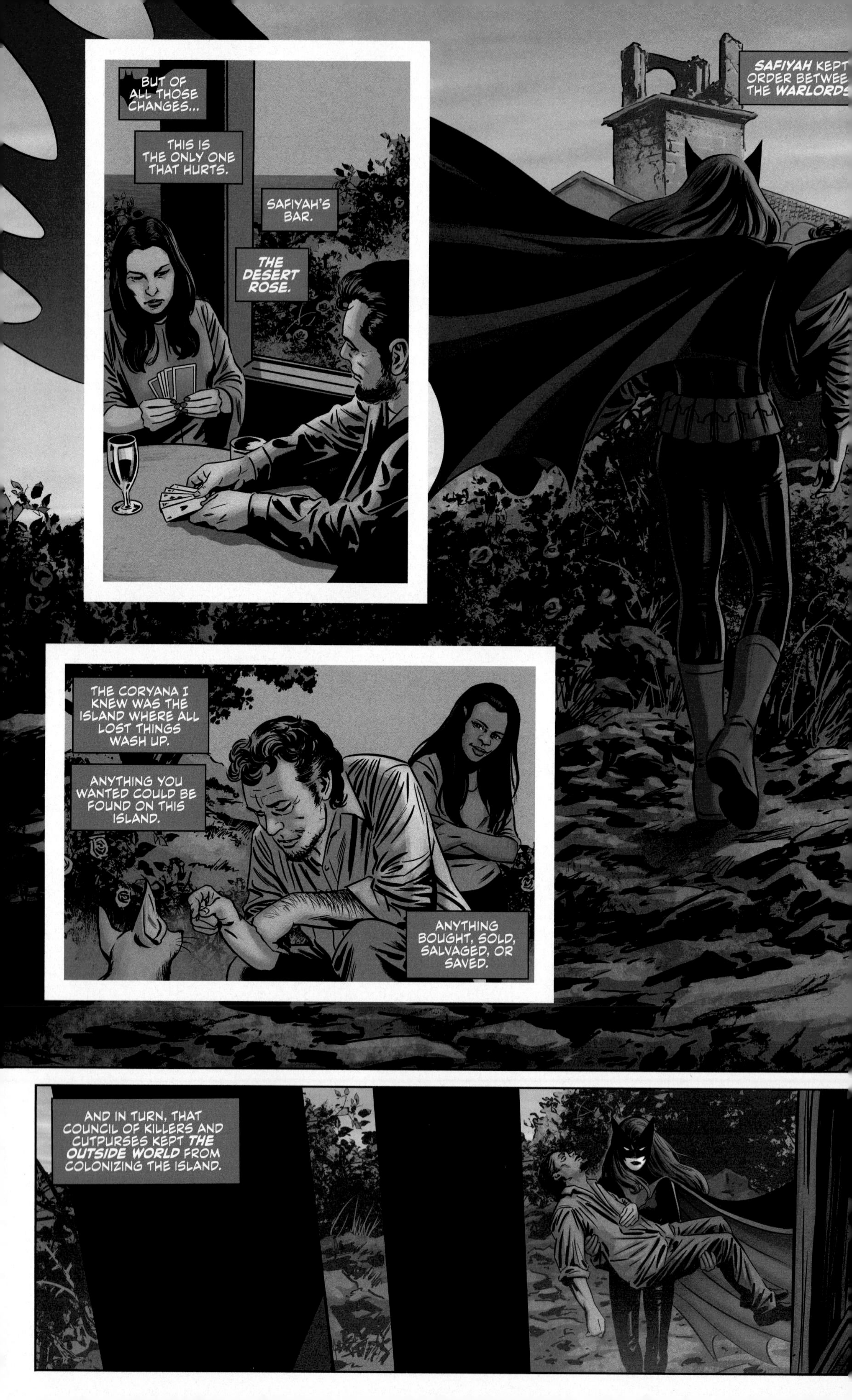
BUT OF ALL THOSE CHANGES...
THIS IS THE ONLY ONE THAT HURTS.
SAFIYAH'S BAR.
THE DESERT ROSE.
SAFIYAH KEPT ORDER BETWEE THE WARLORDS
THE CORYANA I KNEW WAS THE ISLAND WHERE ALL LOST THINGS WASH UP.
ANYTHING YOU WANTED COULD BE FOUND ON THIS ISLAND.
ANYTHING BOUGHT, SOLD, SALVAGED, OR SAVED.
AND IN TURN, THAT COUNCIL OF KILLERS AND CUTPURSES KEPT THE OUTSIDE WORLD FROM COLONIZING THE ISLAND.

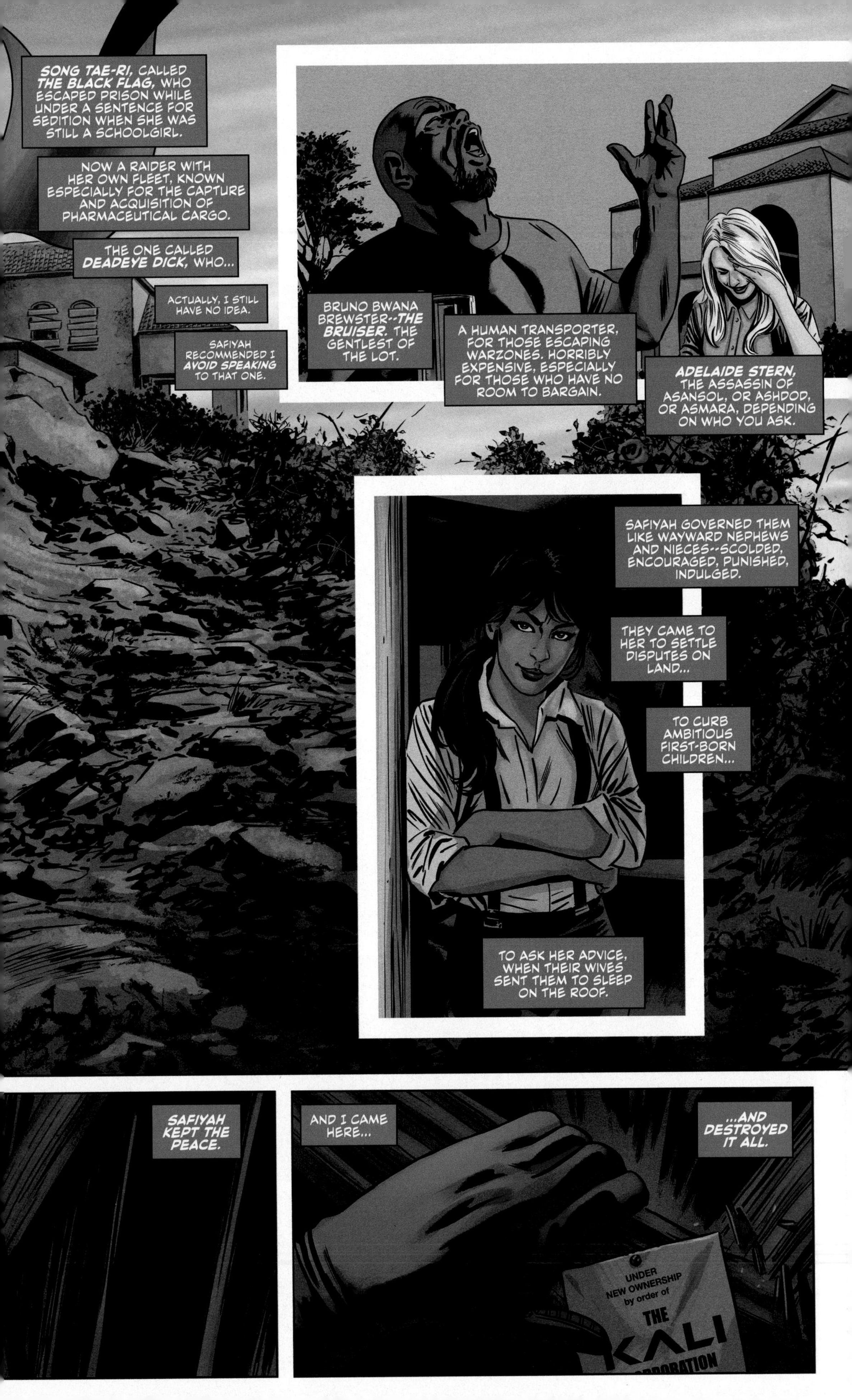
SONG TAE-RI, CALLED THE BLACK FLAG, WHO ESCAPED PRISON WHILE UNDER A SENTENCE FOR SEDITION WHEN SHE WAS STILL A SCHOOLGIRL.
NOW A RAIDER WITH HER OWN FLEET, KNOWN ESPECIALLY FOR THE CAPTURE AND ACQUISITION OF PHARMACEUTICAL CARGO.
THE ONE CALLED DEADEYE DICK, WHO...
ACTUALLY, I STILL HAVE NO IDEA.
SAFIYAH RECOMMENDED I AVOID SPEAKING TO THAT ONE.
BRUNO BWANA BREWSTER--THE BRUISER. THE GENTLEST OF THE LOT.
A HUMAN TRANSPORTER, FOR THOSE ESCAPING WARZONES. HORRIBLY EXPENSIVE, ESPECIALLY FOR THOSE WHO HAVE NO ROOM TO BARGAIN.
ADELAIDE STERN, THE ASSASSIN OF ASANSOL, OR ASHDOD, OR ASMARA, DEPENDING ON WHO YOU ASK.
SAFIYAH GOVERNED THEM LIKE WAYWARD NEPHEWS AND NIECES--SCOLDED, ENCOURAGED, PUNISHED, INDULGED.
THEY CAME TO HER TO SETTLE DISPUTES ON LAND...
TO CURB AMBITIOUS FIRST-BORN CHILDREN...
TO ASK HER ADVICE, WHEN THEIR WIVES SENT THEM TO SLEEP ON THE ROOF.
SAFIYAH KEPT THE PEACE.
AND I CAME HERE...
...AND DESTROYED IT ALL.
UNDER NEW OWNERSHIP by order of THE KALI

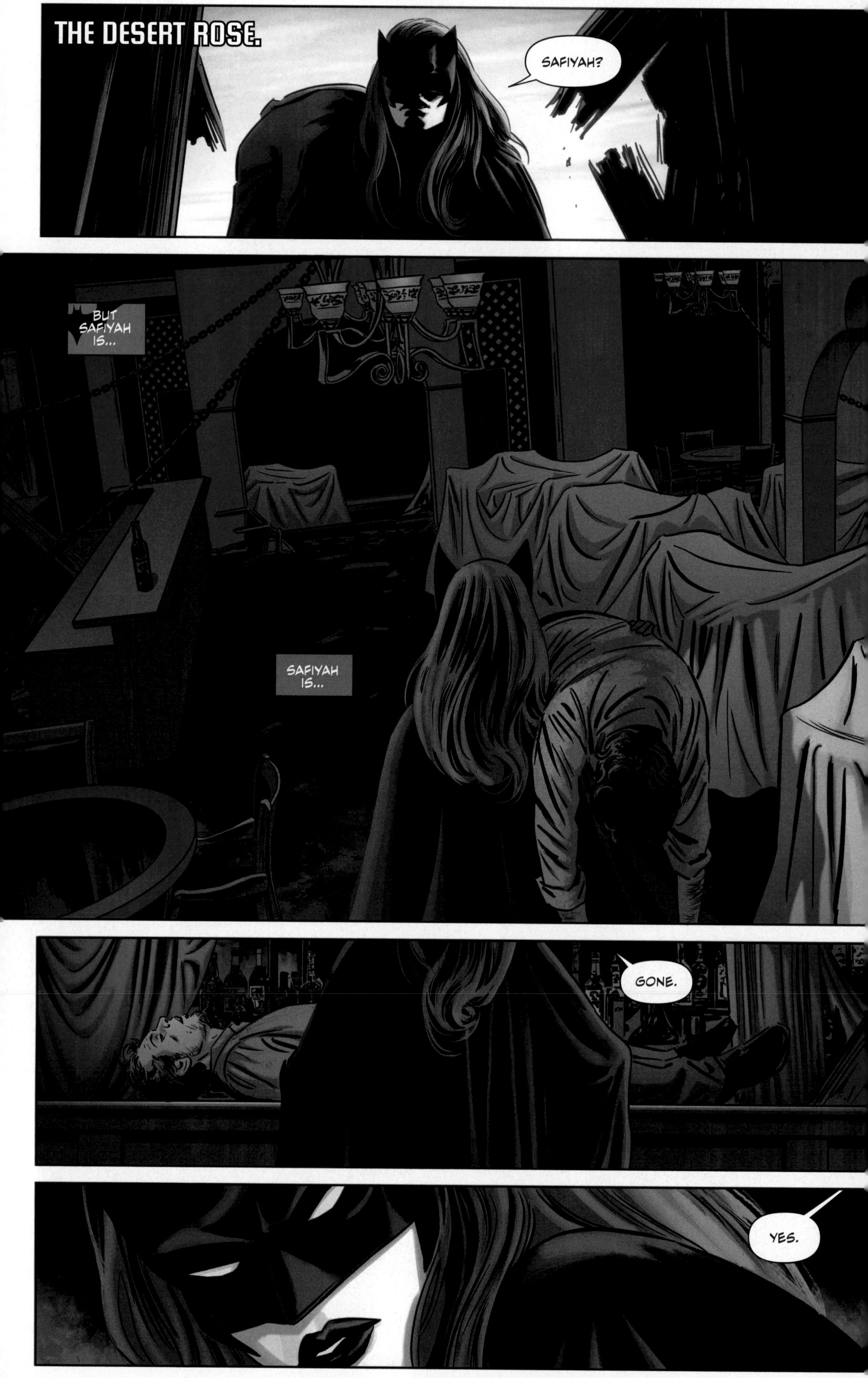
THE DESERT ROSE.
SAFIYAH?
BUT SAFIYAH IS...
SAFIYAH IS...
GONE.
YES.

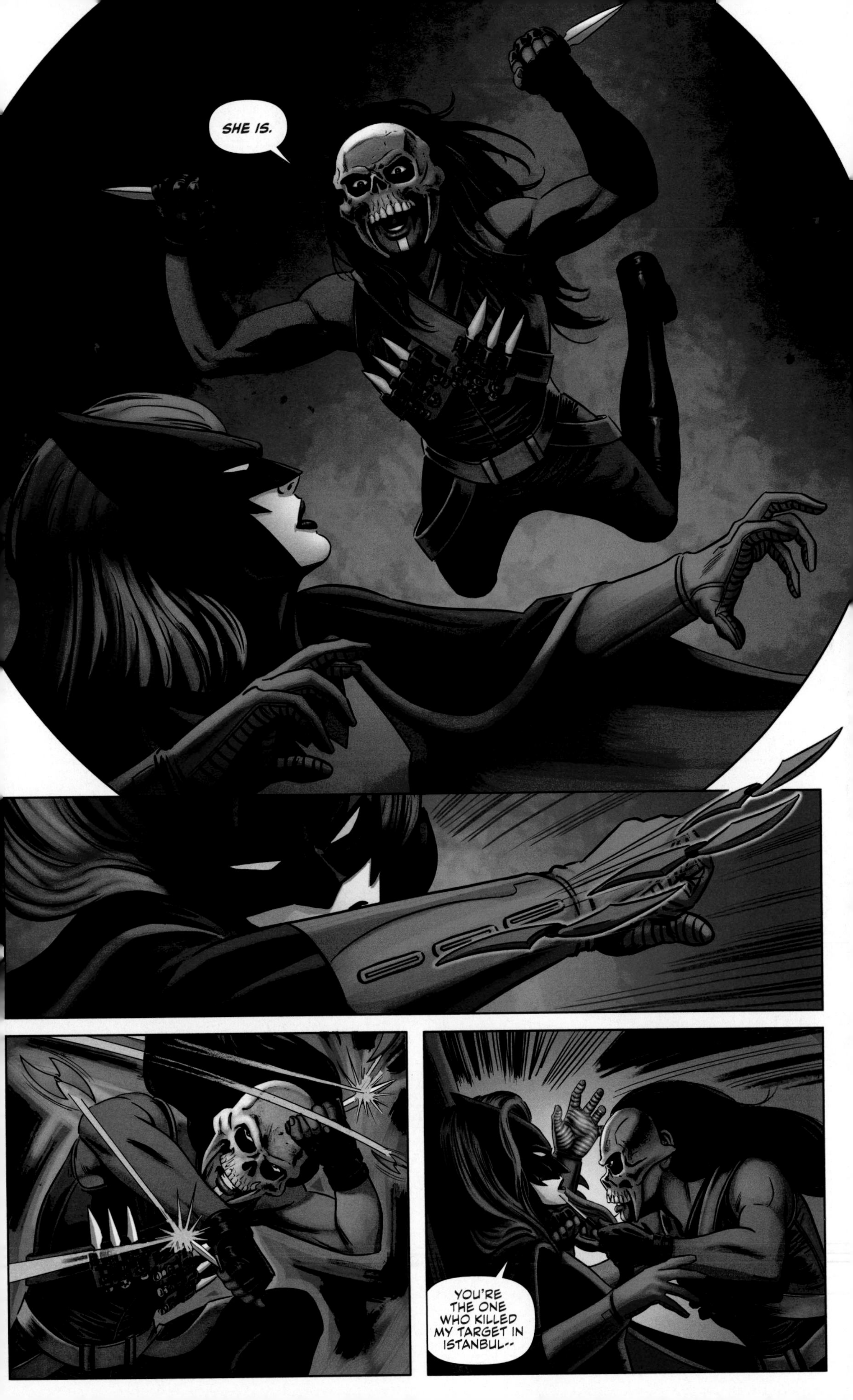
SHE IS.
YOU'RE THE ONE WHO KILLED MY TARGET IN ISTANBUL--

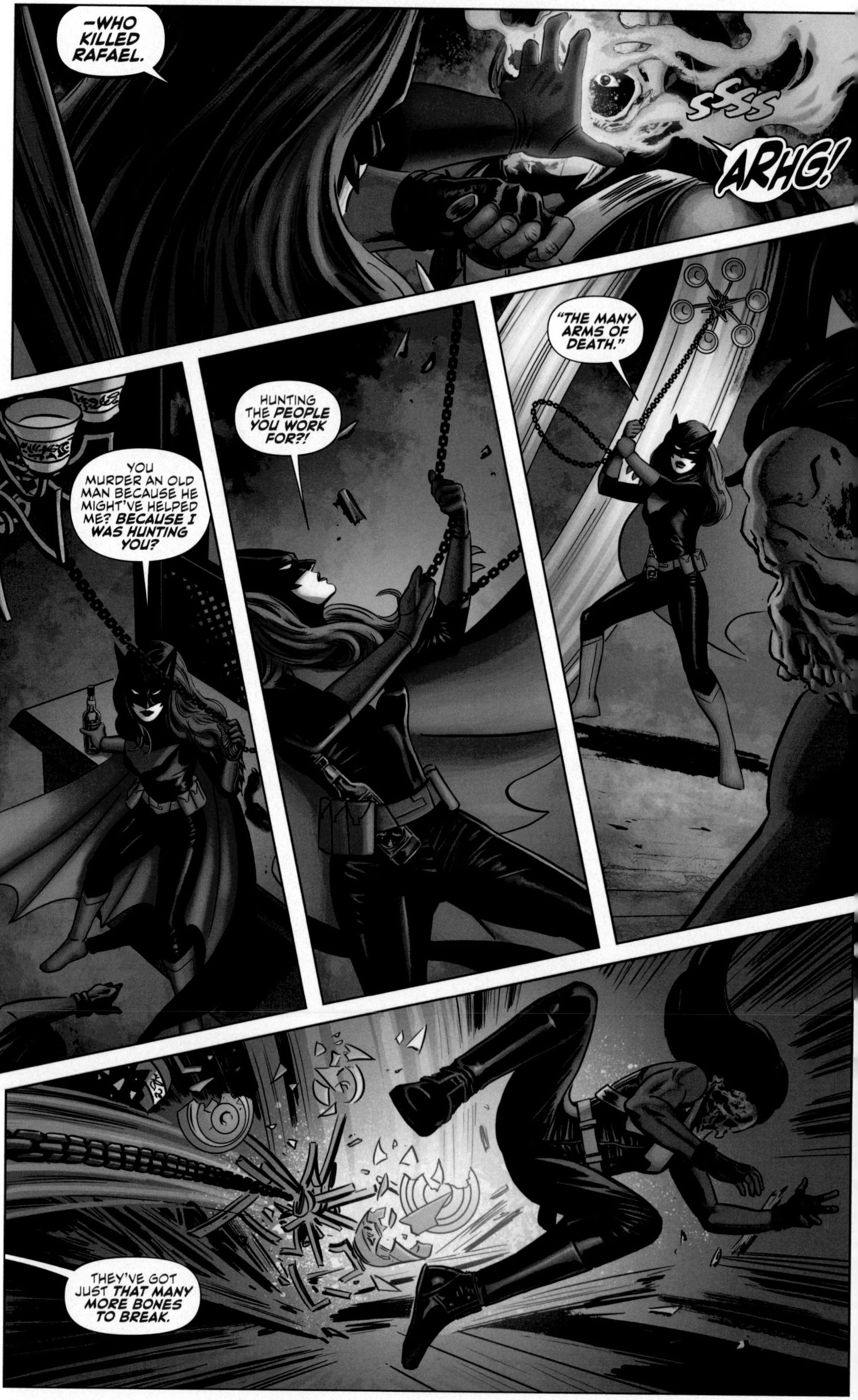
-WHO KILLED RAFAEL.
SSSS
ARHG!
YOU MURDER AN OLD MAN BECAUSE HE MIGHT'VE HELPED ME? BECAUSE I WAS HUNTING YOU?
HUNTING THE PEOPLE YOU WORK FOR?!
"THE MANY ARMS OF DEATH."
THEY'VE GOT JUST THAT MANY MORE BONES TO BREAK.

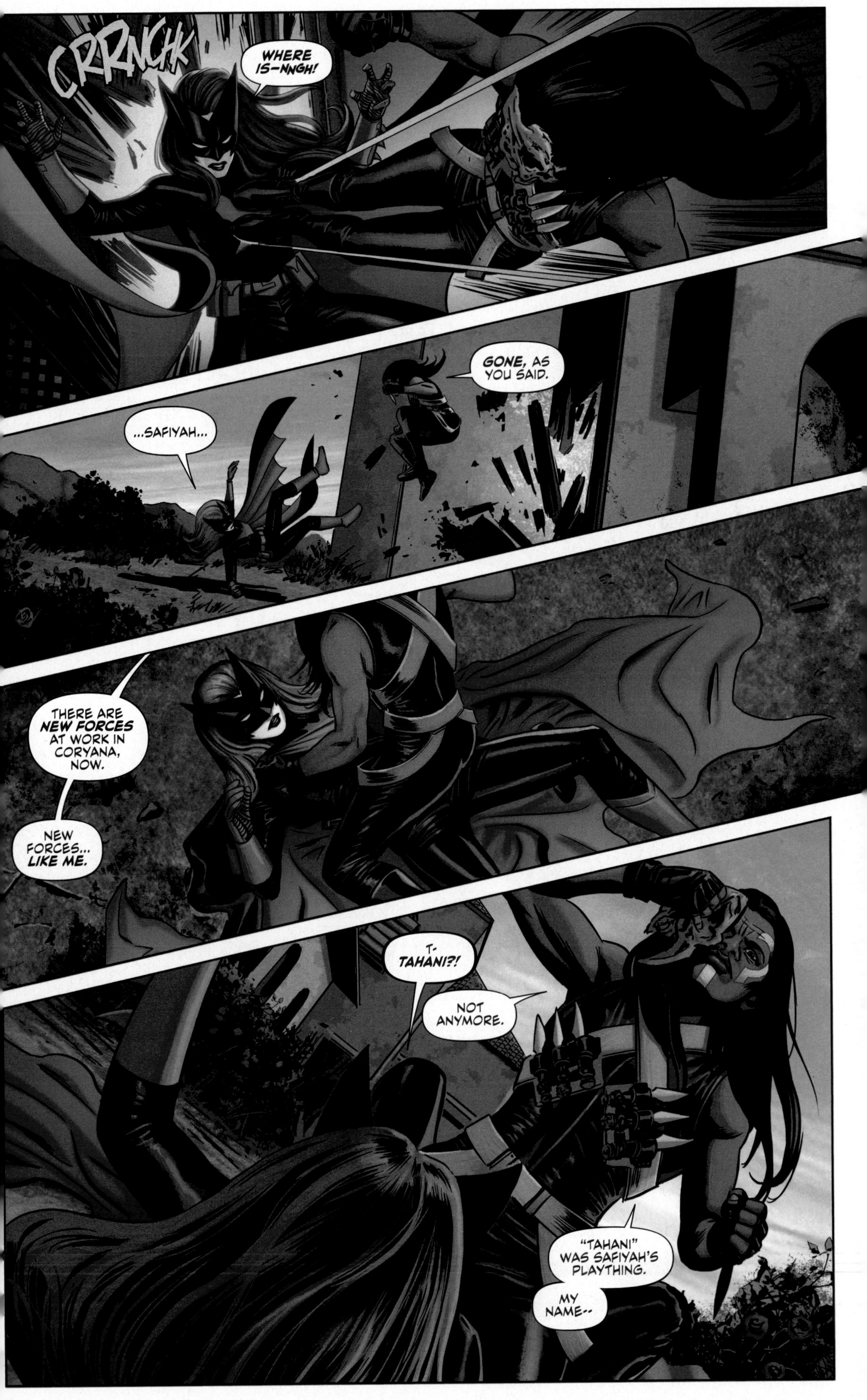
CRRNCHK
WHERE IS--NNGH!
GONE, AS YOU SAID.
...SAFIYAH...
THERE ARE NEW FORCES AT WORK IN CORYANA, NOW.
NEW FORCES... LIKE ME.
T-TAHANI?!
NOT ANYMORE.
"TAHANI" WAS SAFIYAH'S PLAYTHING.
MY NAME--

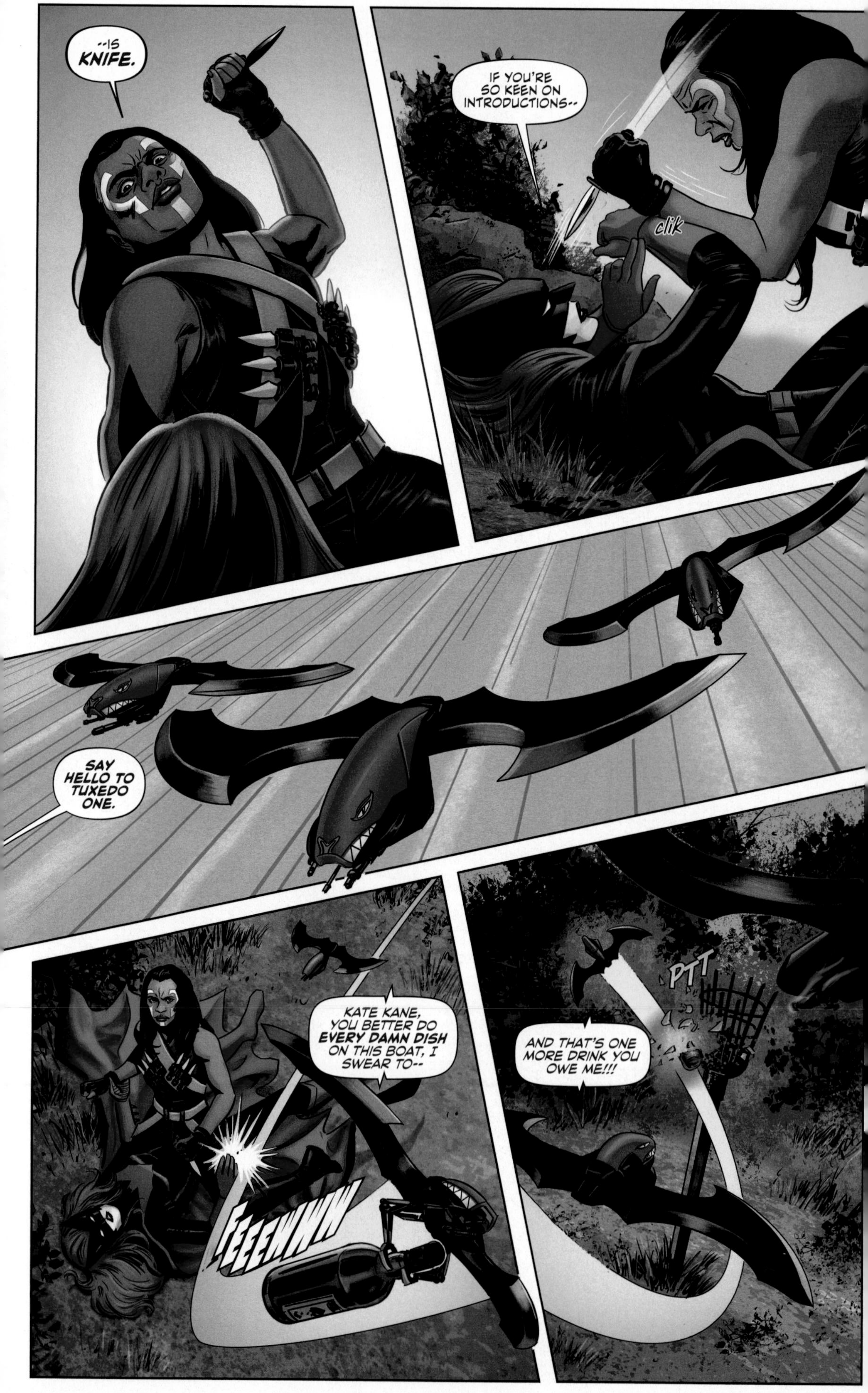
--IS KNIFE.
IF YOU'RE SO KEEN ON INTRODUCTIONS--
clik
SAY HELLO TO TUXEDO ONE.
KATE KANE, YOU BETTER DO EVERY DAMN DISH ON THIS BOAT, I SWEAR TO--
FEEEWWW
PTT
AND THAT'S ONE MORE DRINK YOU OWE ME!!!

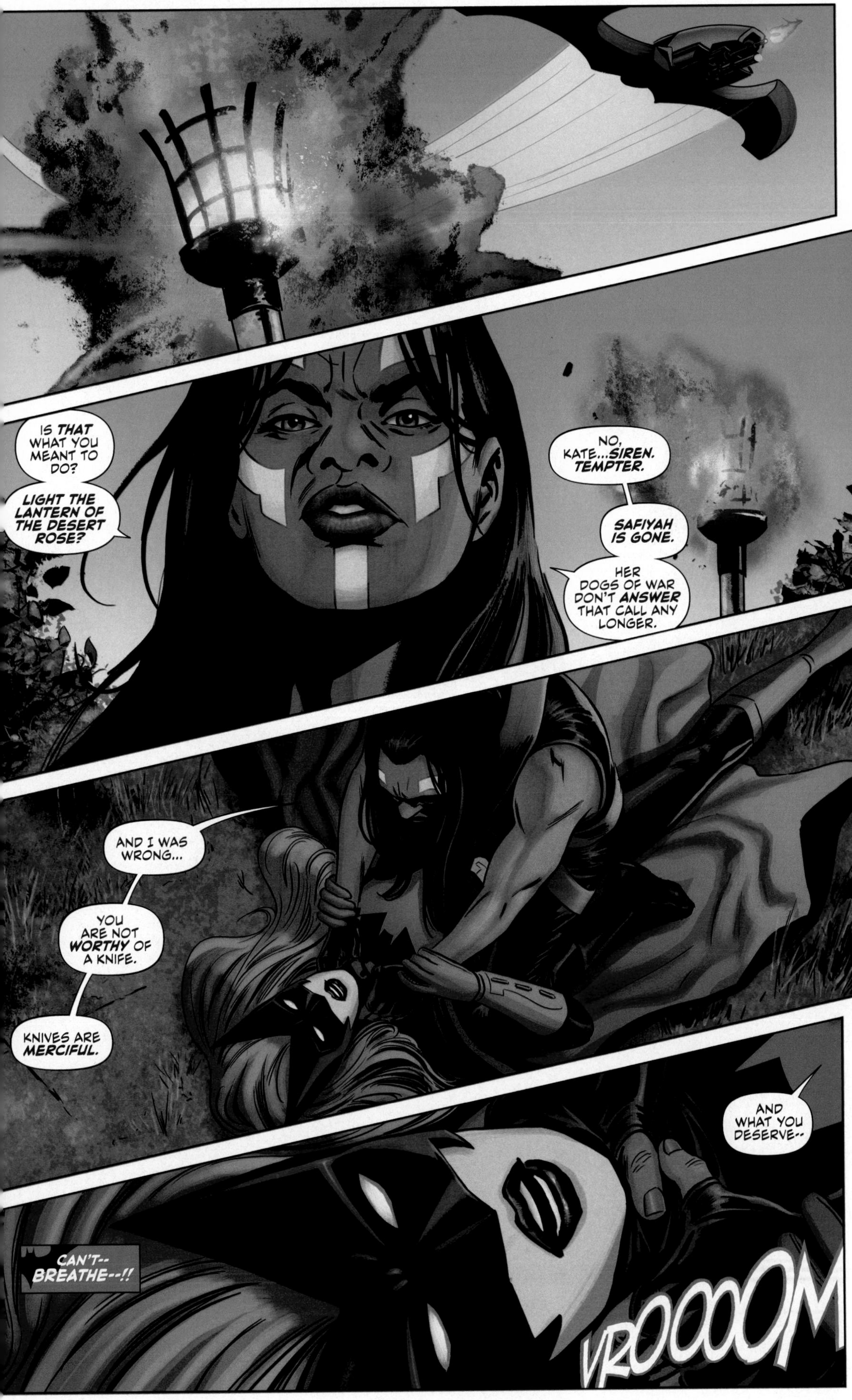
IS THAT WHAT YOU MEANT TO DO?
LIGHT THE LANTERN OF THE DESERT ROSE?
NO, KATE...SIREN. TEMPTER.
SAFIYAH IS GONE.
HER DOGS OF WAR DON'T ANSWER THAT CALL ANY LONGER.
AND I WAS WRONG...
YOU ARE NOT WORTHY OF A KNIFE.
KNIVES ARE MERCIFUL.
AND WHAT YOU DESERVE--
CAN'T-- BREATHE--!!
VROOOOM

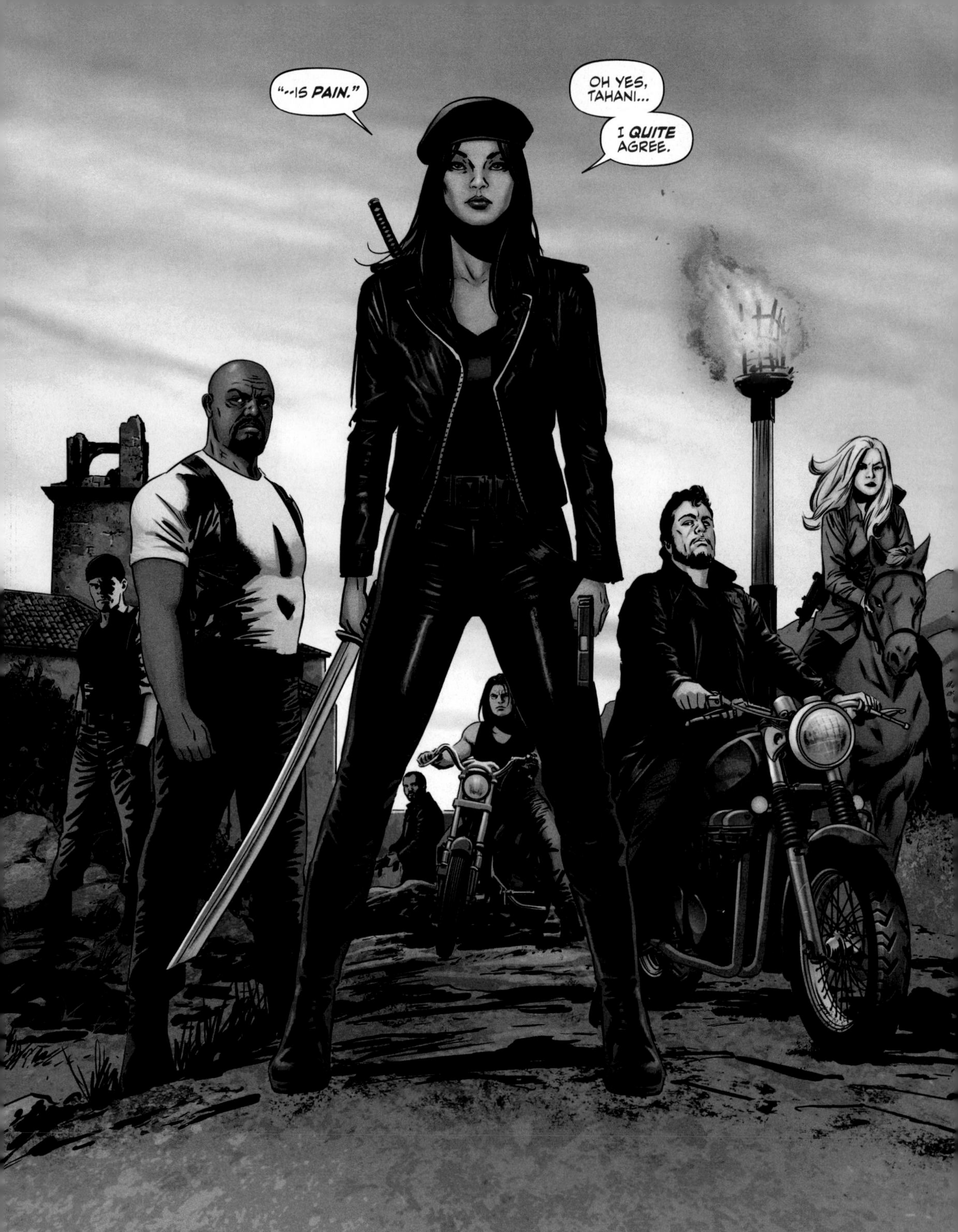
"--IS PAIN."
OH YES, TAHANI...
I QUITE AGREE.
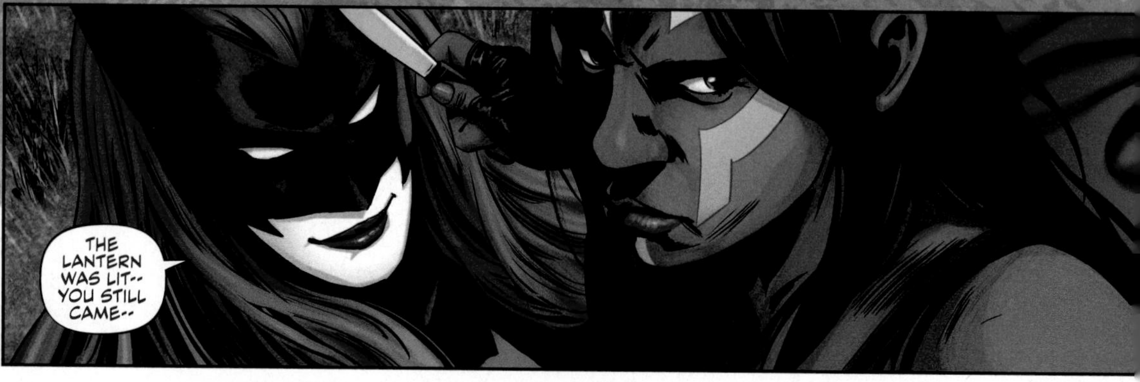
THE LANTERN WAS LIT-- YOU STILL CAME--

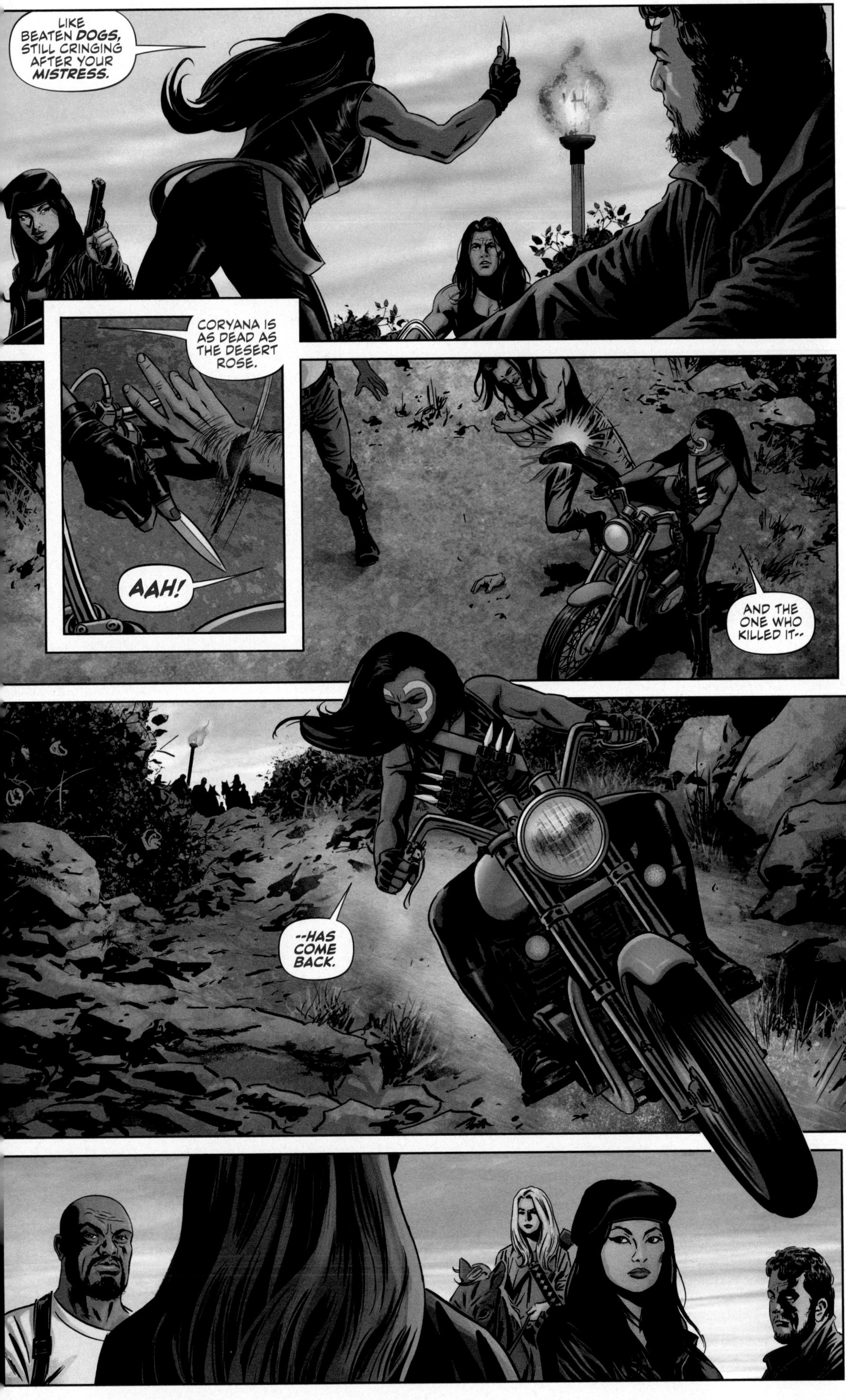
LIKE BEATEN DOGS, STILL CRINGING AFTER YOUR MISTRESS.
CORYANA IS AS DEAD AS THE DESERT ROSE.
AAH!
AND THE ONE WHO KILLED IT--
--HAS COME BACK.

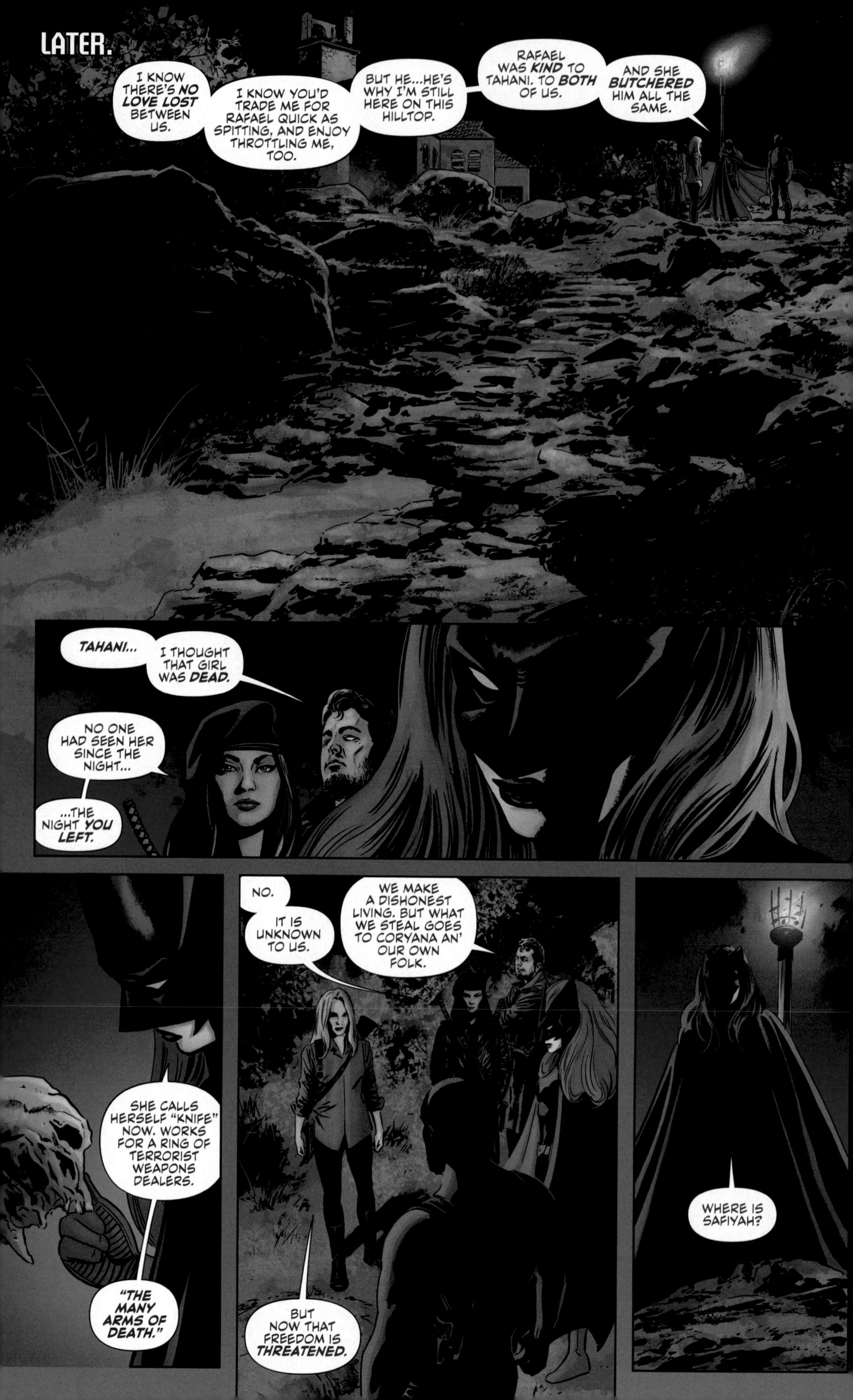
LATER.
I KNOW THERE'S NO LOVE LOST BETWEEN US.
I KNOW YOU'D TRADE ME FOR RAFAEL QUICK AS SPITTING, AND ENJOY THROTTLING ME, TOO.
BUT HE...HE'S WHY I'M STILL HERE ON THIS HILLTOP.
RAFAEL WAS KIND TO TAHANI. TO BOTH OF US.
AND SHE BUTCHERED HIM ALL THE SAME.
TAHANI...
I THOUGHT THAT GIRL WAS DEAD.
NO ONE HAD SEEN HER SINCE THE NIGHT...
...THE NIGHT YOU LEFT.
SHE CALLS HERSELF "KNIFE" NOW. WORKS FOR A RING OF TERRORIST WEAPONS DEALERS.
"THE MANY ARMS OF DEATH."
NO.
IT IS UNKNOWN TO US.
WE MAKE A DISHONEST LIVING. BUT WHAT WE STEAL GOES TO CORYANA AN' OUR OWN FOLK.
BUT NOW THAT FREEDOM IS THREATENED.
WHERE IS SAFIYAH?

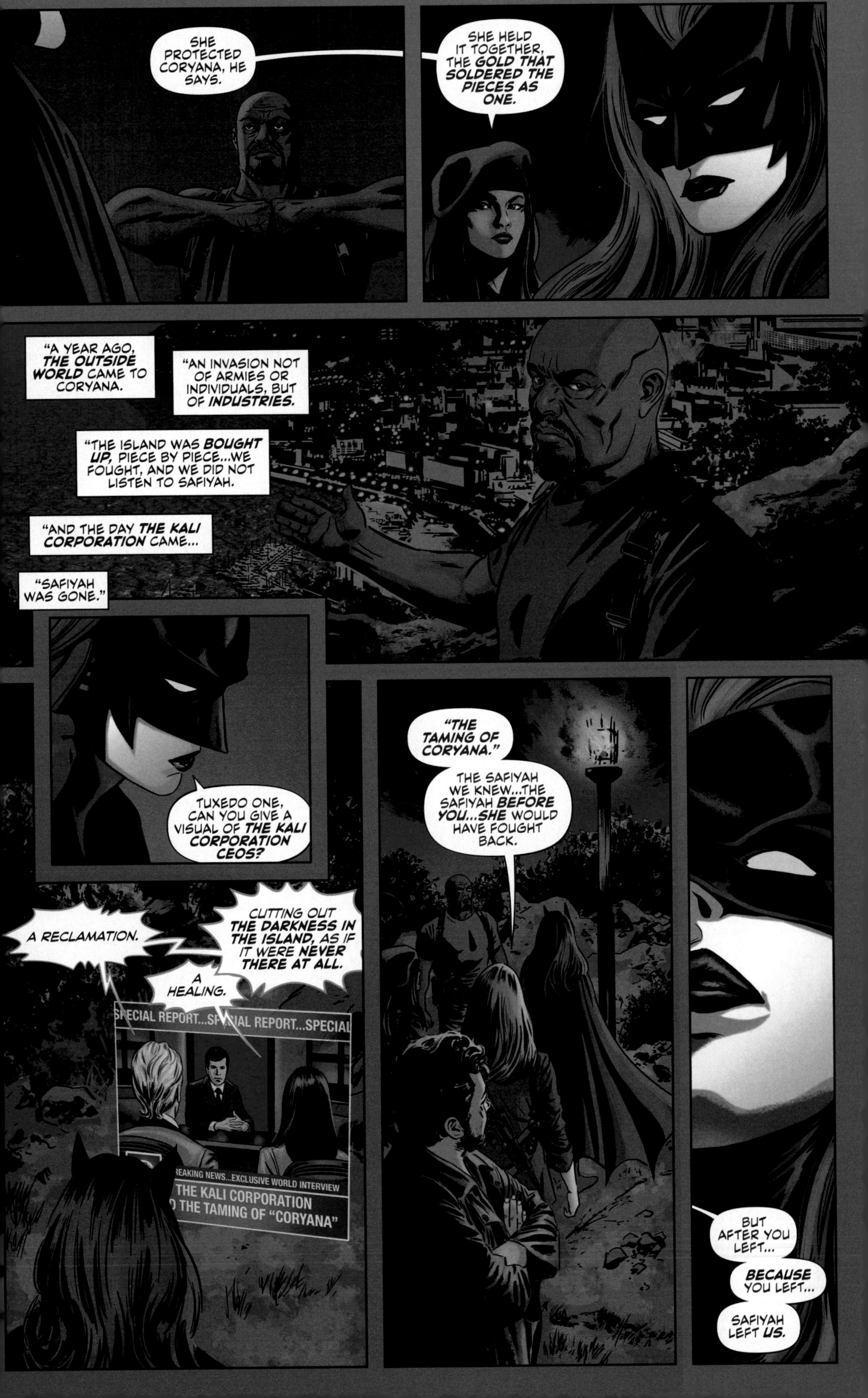
SHE PROTECTED CORYANA, HE SAYS.
SHE HELD IT TOGETHER, THE GOLD THAT SOLDERED THE PIECES AS ONE.
"A YEAR AGO, THE OUTSIDE WORLD CAME TO CORYANA.
"AN INVASION NOT OF ARMIES OR INDIVIDUALS, BUT OF INDUSTRIES.
"THE ISLAND WAS BOUGHT UP, PIECE BY PIECE...WE FOUGHT, AND WE DID NOT LISTEN TO SAFIYAH.
"AND THE DAY THE KALI CORPORATION CAME...
"SAFIYAH WAS GONE."
TUXEDO ONE, CAN YOU GIVE A VISUAL OF THE KALI CORPORATION CEOS?
A RECLAMATION.
A HEALING.
CUTTING OUT THE DARKNESS IN THE ISLAND, AS IF IT WERE NEVER THERE AT ALL.
SPECIAL REPORT...SPECIAL REPORT...SPECIAL
REAKING NEWS...EXCLUSIVE WORLD INTERVIEW
THE KALI CORPORATION
THE TAMING OF "CORYANA"
"THE TAMING OF CORYANA."
THE SAFIYAH WE KNEW...THE SAFIYAH BEFORE YOU...SHE WOULD HAVE FOUGHT BACK.
BUT AFTER YOU LEFT...
BECAUSE YOU LEFT...
SAFIYAH LEFT US.

"AND THE OUTSIDE WORLD SLITHERED IN."

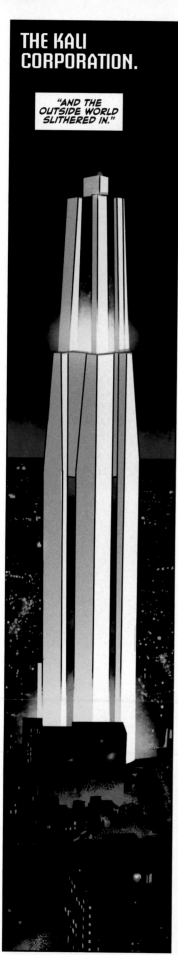

WE HAVE RECEIVED ANOTHER REQUEST FOR PROPERTY ON THE NORTHERN SHORE.

THAT PROPERTY IS NOT YET ACQUIRED.

SEND THE FIST TO THE NORTH, AND TELL THE BIDDERS IT WILL BE READY IN TEN DAYS.

A REPORTER FROM THAT LONDON PAPER SEEKS AN INTERVIEW. THEIR PUBLICITY *WOULD* ASSIST SALES...

ONLY IF WE HAVE GUARANTEED TRANSLATION AND DISTRIBUTION.

WE MUST NOT GIVE ANY ONE TONGUE OR NATION THE ADVANTAGE.

AND THE, AH...

...THE SUDANESE GENTLEMAN HAS INQUIRED IF WE SELL...IF YOU SELL...

...NERVE AGENTS.

AND HOW DID YOU ANSWER HIM?

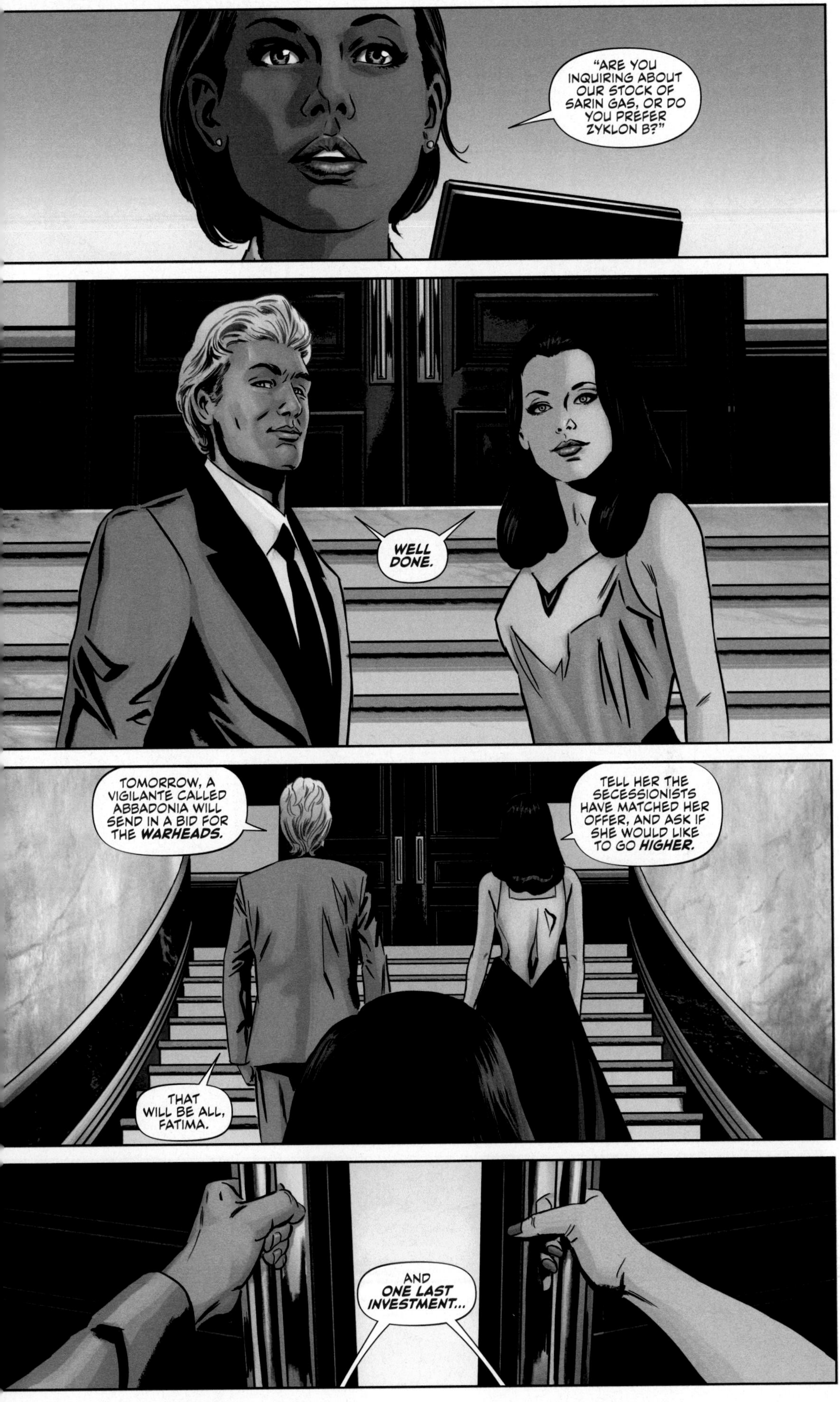
"ARE YOU INQUIRING ABOUT OUR STOCK OF SARIN GAS, OR DO YOU PREFER ZYKLON B?"
WELL DONE.
TOMORROW, A VIGILANTE CALLED ABBADONIA WILL SEND IN A BID FOR THE WARHEADS.
TELL HER THE SECESSIONISTS HAVE MATCHED HER OFFER, AND ASK IF SHE WOULD LIKE TO GO HIGHER.
THAT WILL BE ALL, FATIMA.
AND ONE LAST INVESTMENT...

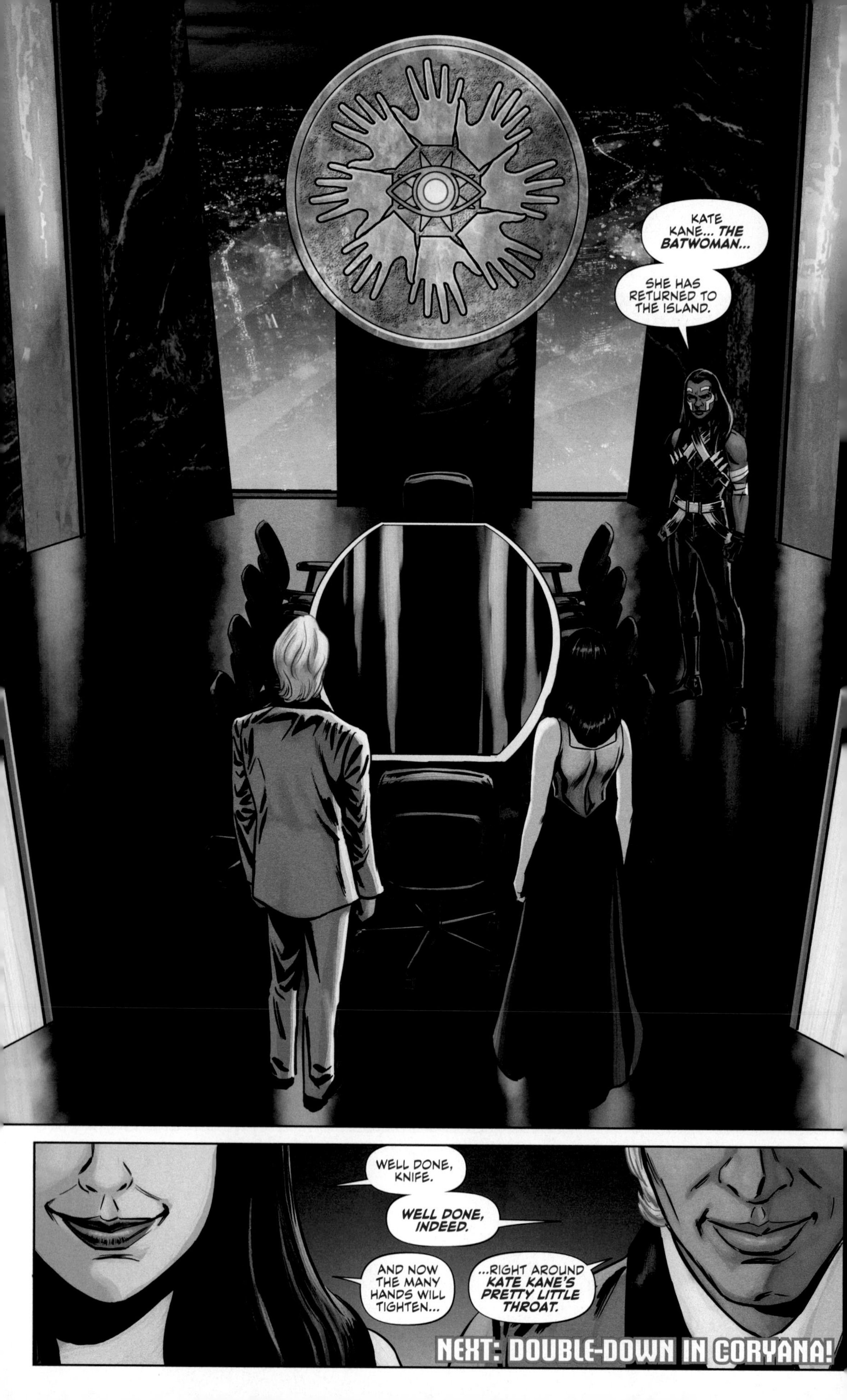
KATE KANE... THE BATWOMAN...
SHE HAS RETURNED TO THE ISLAND.
WELL DONE, KNIFE.
WELL DONE, INDEED.
AND NOW THE MANY HANDS WILL TIGHTEN...
...RIGHT AROUND KATE KANE'S PRETTY LITTLE THROAT.
NEXT: DOUBLE-DOWN IN CORYANA!

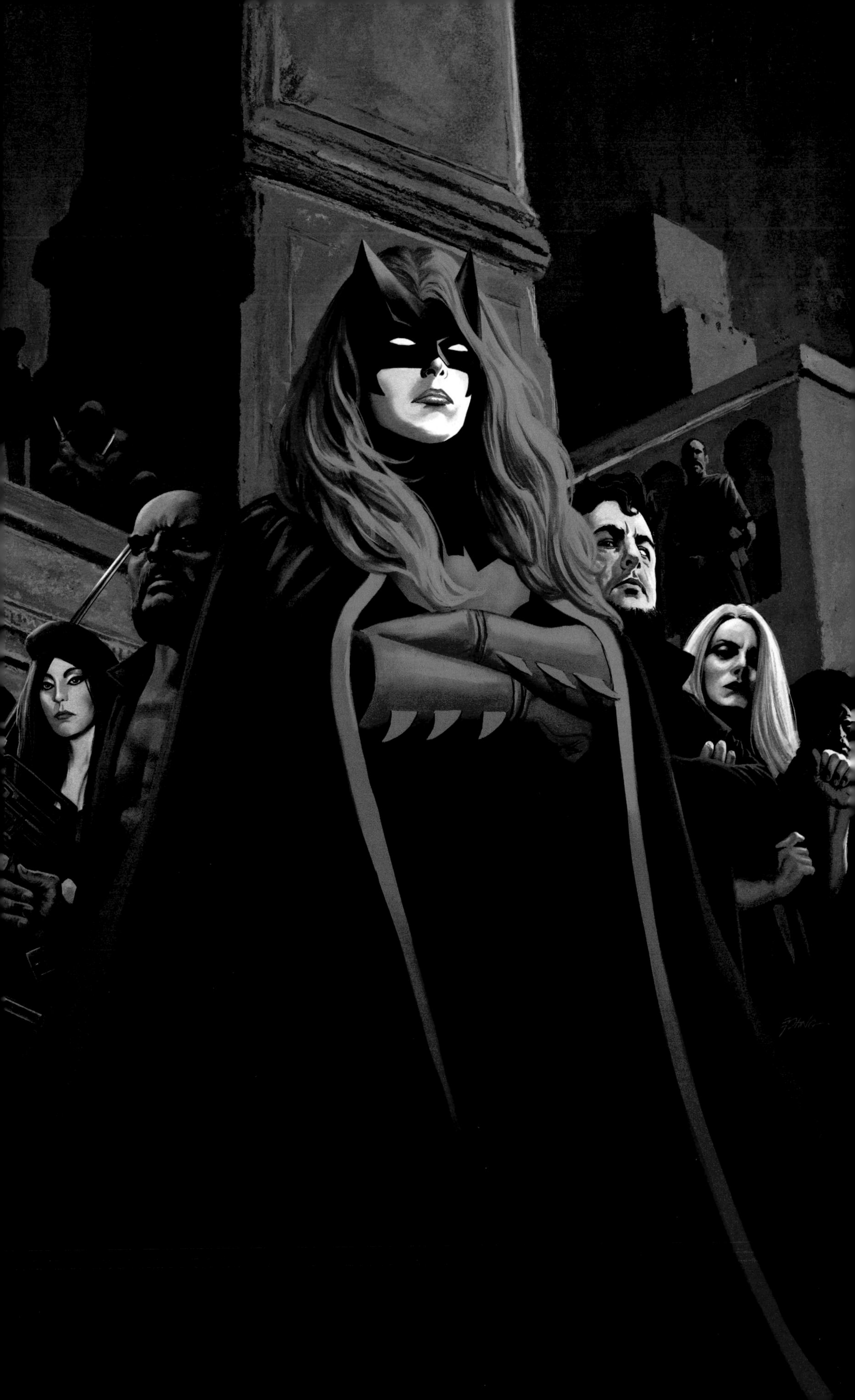

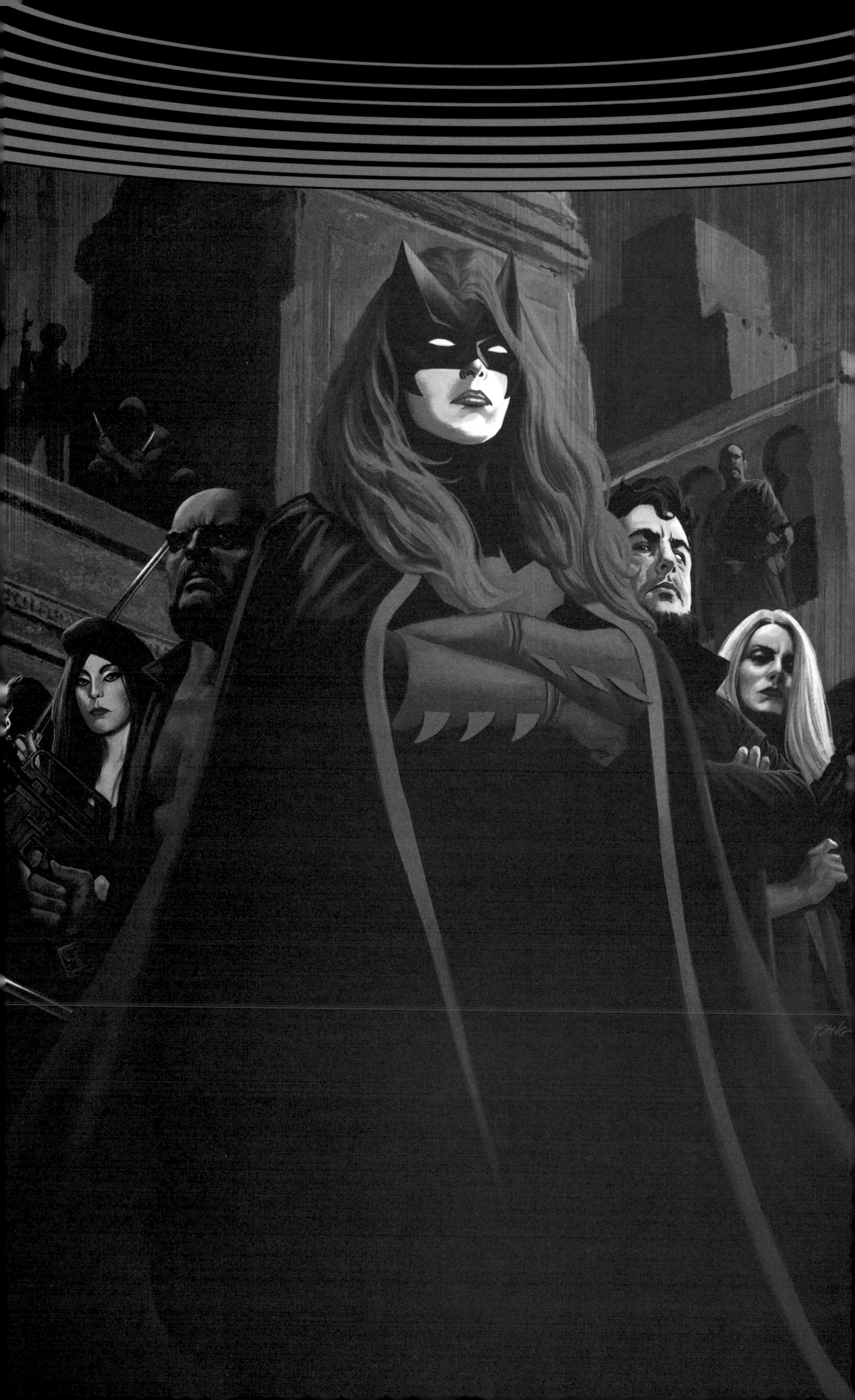

"WHAT ARE YOU DOING HERE, VERMIN?

"I TOLD YOU, IF I EVER FOUND YOU BEGGING HERE AGAIN--

"--I'D MAKE YOU **BEG** THAT YOUR DOG MOTHER NEVER SQUATTED DOWN TO WHELP YOU.

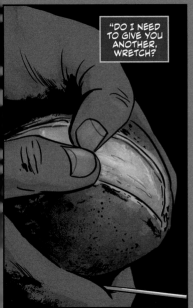

"DO I NEED TO GIVE YOU ANOTHER, WRETCH?

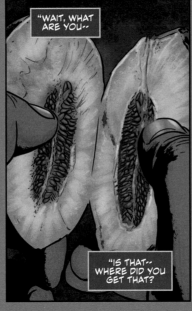

"WAIT, WHAT ARE YOU--

"IS THAT-- WHERE DID YOU GET THAT?

"DON'T.

"PLEASE.

"STOP.

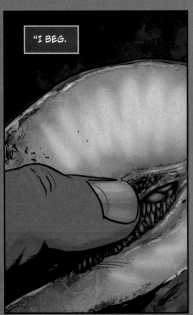

"I BEG.

"BEG.

"BEG.

"BEG.

"NOOOO."

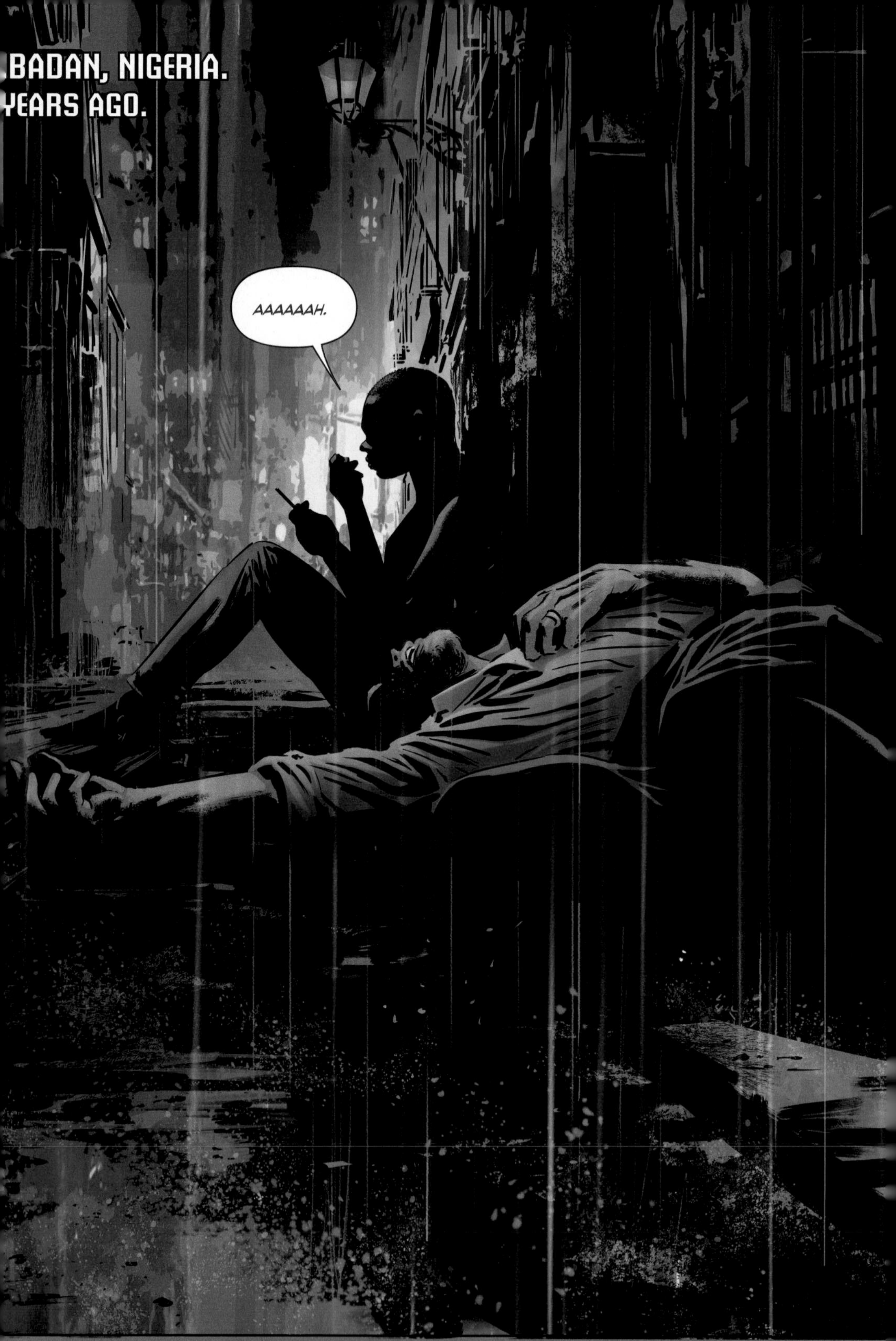
BADAN, NIGERIA.
YEARS AGO.
AAAAAAH.

THE MANY ARMS OF DEATH PART 3

IF I HAD A HEART

MARGUERITE BENNETT & JAMES TYNION IV WRIT
STEVE EPTING ARTIST JEROMY COX COLORS
DERON BENNETT LETTERS STEVE EPTING COVER
J.G. JONES VARIANT COVER
DAVE WIELGOSZ ASST. EDITOR CHRIS CONROY EDITO
MARK DOYLE GROUP EDITOR

HOW TERRIBLY AWKWARD.

I SEEM TO HAVE ARRIVED AN HOUR LATE AND THIRTY KILLING BLOWS SHORT.

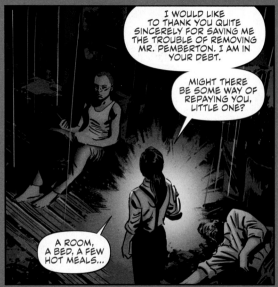

I WOULD LIKE TO THANK YOU QUITE SINCERELY FOR SAVING ME THE TROUBLE OF REMOVING MR. PEMBERTON. I AM IN YOUR DEBT.

MIGHT THERE BE SOME WAY OF REPAYING YOU, LITTLE ONE?

A ROOM, A BED, A FEW HOT MEALS...

PERHAPS EVEN... ...AN **APPRENTICESHIP?**

AND MY NAME IS SAFIYAH.

TAHANI.

I THINK YOU WILL FIND MY HOME OF CORYANA A FASCINATING PLACE, TAHANI...

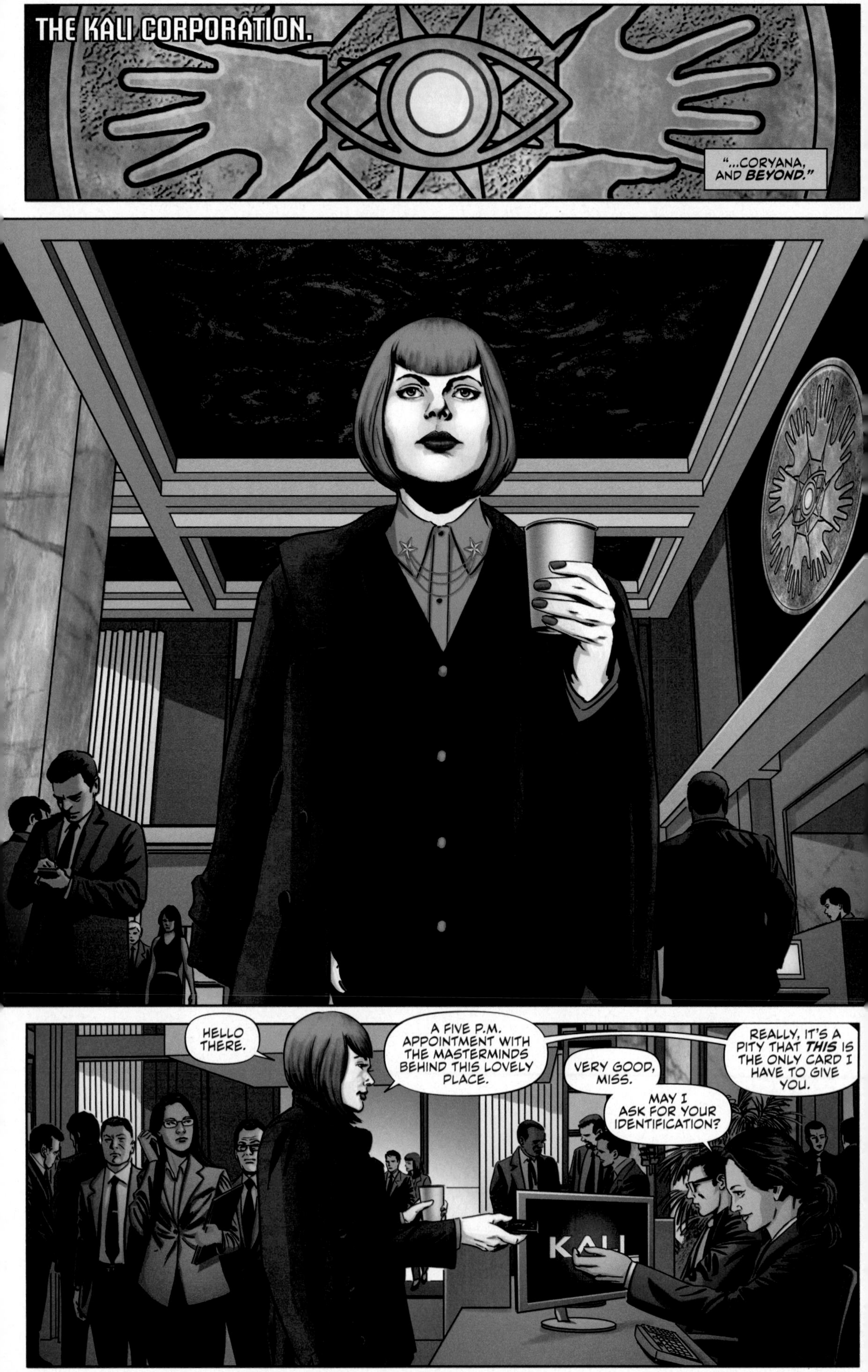
THE KALI CORPORATION.
"...CORYANA, AND BEYOND."
HELLO THERE.
A FIVE P.M. APPOINTMENT WITH THE MASTERMINDS BEHIND THIS LOVELY PLACE.
VERY GOOD, MISS.
MAY I ASK FOR YOUR IDENTIFICATION?
REALLY, IT'S A PITY THAT THIS IS THE ONLY CARD I HAVE TO GIVE YOU.
KALI

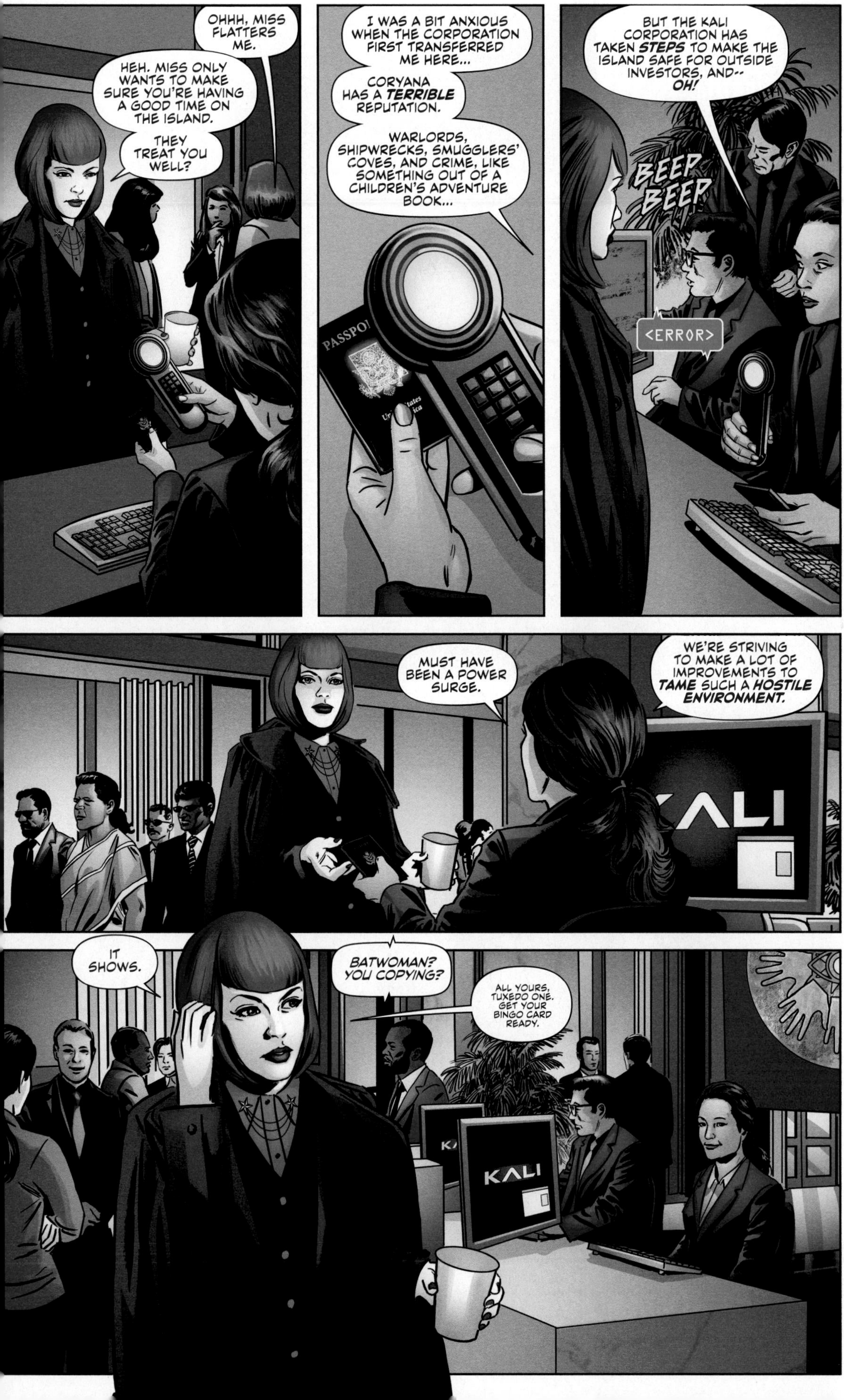
OHHH, MISS FLATTERS ME.
HEH. MISS ONLY WANTS TO MAKE SURE YOU'RE HAVING A GOOD TIME ON THE ISLAND.
THEY TREAT YOU WELL?
I WAS A BIT ANXIOUS WHEN THE CORPORATION FIRST TRANSFERRED ME HERE...
CORYANA HAS A TERRIBLE REPUTATION.
WARLORDS, SHIPWRECKS, SMUGGLERS' COVES, AND CRIME, LIKE SOMETHING OUT OF A CHILDREN'S ADVENTURE BOOK...
PASSPORT
BUT THE KALI CORPORATION HAS TAKEN STEPS TO MAKE THE ISLAND SAFE FOR OUTSIDE INVESTORS, AND-- OH!
BEEP BEEP
<ERROR>
MUST HAVE BEEN A POWER SURGE.
WE'RE STRIVING TO MAKE A LOT OF IMPROVEMENTS TO TAME SUCH A HOSTILE ENVIRONMENT.
KALI
IT SHOWS.
BATWOMAN? YOU COPYING?
ALL YOURS, TUXEDO ONE. GET YOUR BINGO CARD READY.
KALI

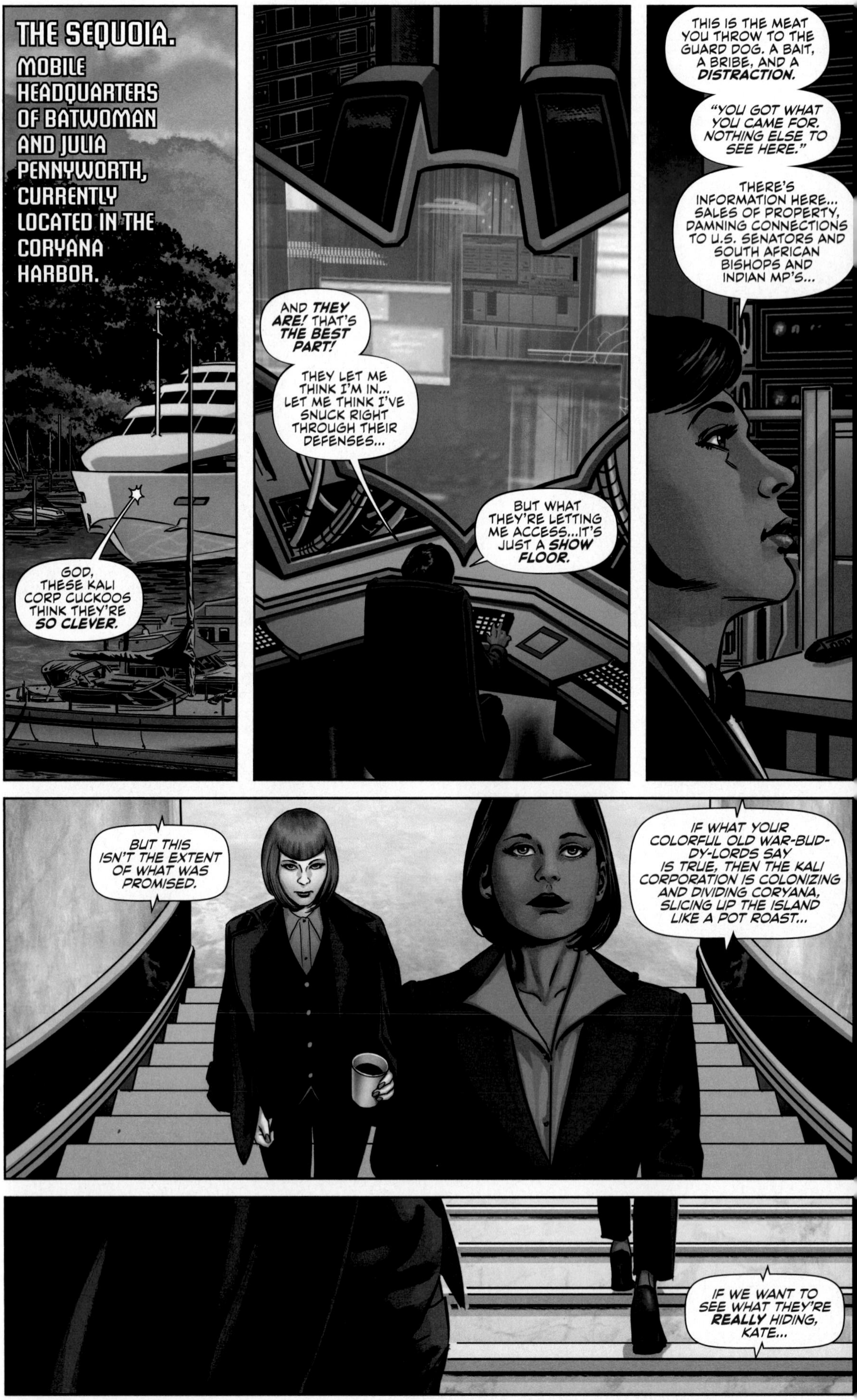
THE SEQUOIA.
MOBILE HEADQUARTERS OF BATWOMAN AND JULIA PENNYWORTH, CURRENTLY LOCATED IN THE CORYANA HARBOR.
GOD, THESE KALI CORP CUCKOOS THINK THEY'RE SO CLEVER.
AND THEY ARE! THAT'S THE BEST PART!
THEY LET ME THINK I'M IN... LET ME THINK I'VE SNUCK RIGHT THROUGH THEIR DEFENSES...
BUT WHAT THEY'RE LETTING ME ACCESS...IT'S JUST A SHOW FLOOR.
THIS IS THE MEAT YOU THROW TO THE GUARD DOG. A BAIT, A BRIBE, AND A DISTRACTION.
"YOU GOT WHAT YOU CAME FOR. NOTHING ELSE TO SEE HERE."
THERE'S INFORMATION HERE... SALES OF PROPERTY, DAMNING CONNECTIONS TO U.S. SENATORS AND SOUTH AFRICAN BISHOPS AND INDIAN MP'S...
BUT THIS ISN'T THE EXTENT OF WHAT WAS PROMISED.
IF WHAT YOUR COLORFUL OLD WAR-BUDDY-LORDS SAY IS TRUE, THEN THE KALI CORPORATION IS COLONIZING AND DIVIDING CORYANA, SLICING UP THE ISLAND LIKE A POT ROAST...
IF WE WANT TO SEE WHAT THEY'RE REALLY HIDING, KATE...

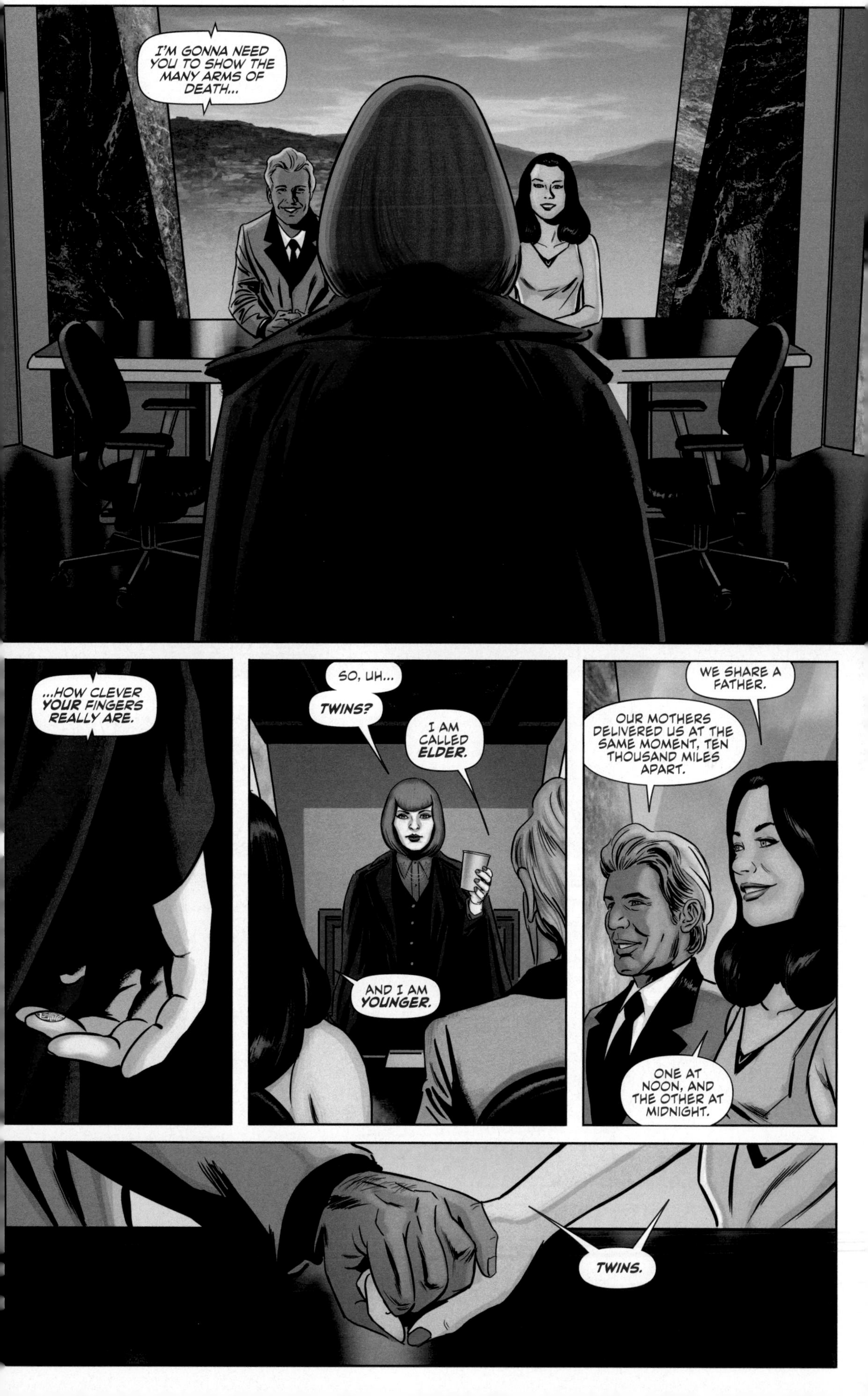
I'M GONNA NEED YOU TO SHOW THE MANY ARMS OF DEATH...
...HOW CLEVER YOUR FINGERS REALLY ARE.
SO, UH...
TWINS?
I AM CALLED ELDER.
AND I AM YOUNGER.
WE SHARE A FATHER.
OUR MOTHERS DELIVERED US AT THE SAME MOMENT, TEN THOUSAND MILES APART.
ONE AT NOON, AND THE OTHER AT MIDNIGHT.
TWINS.

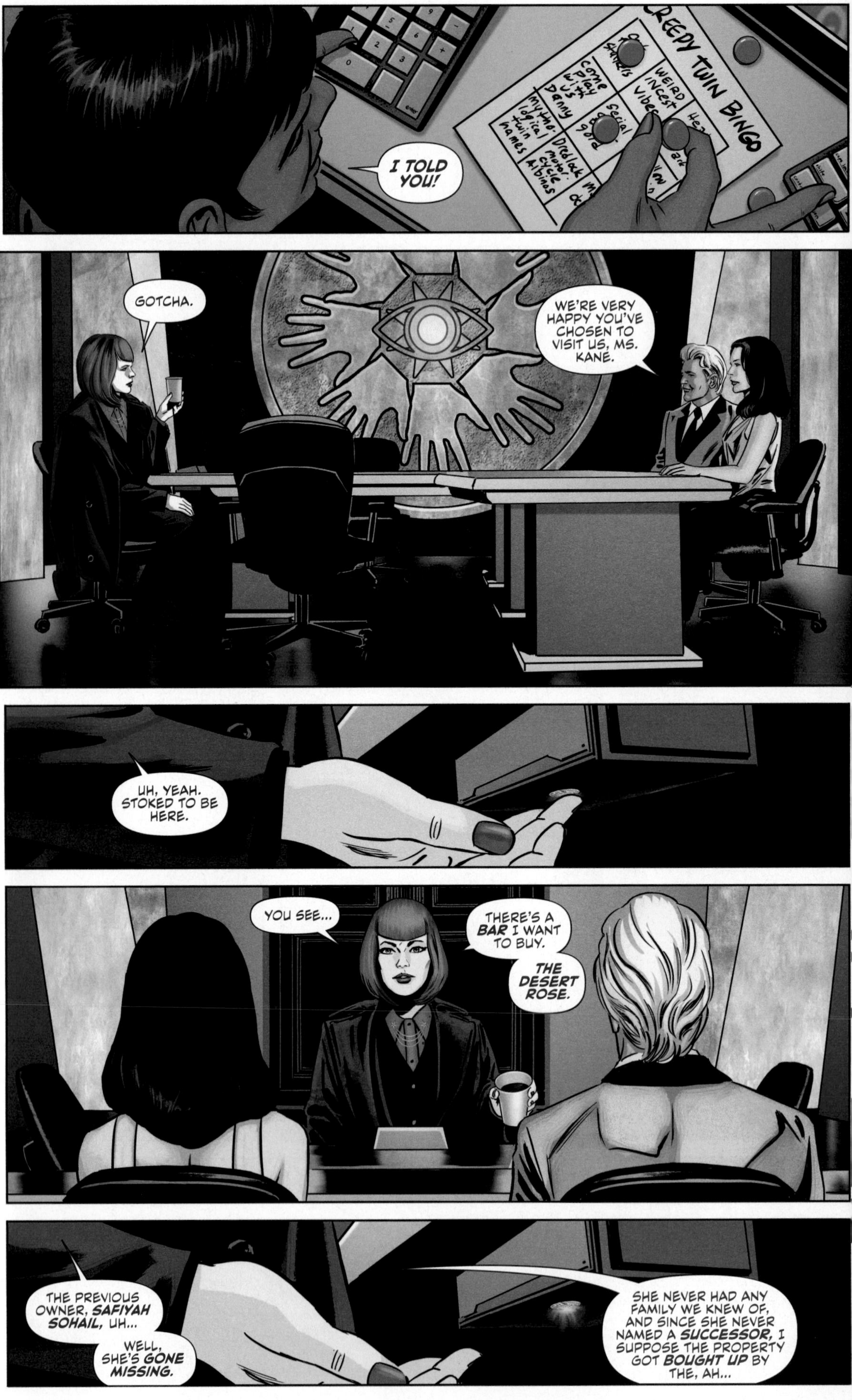
CREEPY TWIN BINGO
WEIRD incest vibes
come play with us Danny
mytho-logical twin names
Dredlak motor cycle Albinos
I TOLD YOU!
GOTCHA.
WE'RE VERY HAPPY YOU'VE CHOSEN TO VISIT US, MS. KANE.
UH, YEAH. STOKED TO BE HERE.
YOU SEE...
THERE'S A BAR I WANT TO BUY.
THE DESERT ROSE.
THE PREVIOUS OWNER, SAFIYAH SOHAIL, UH...
WELL, SHE'S GONE MISSING.
SHE NEVER HAD ANY FAMILY WE KNEW OF, AND SINCE SHE NEVER NAMED A SUCCESSOR, I SUPPOSE THE PROPERTY GOT BOUGHT UP BY THE, AH...

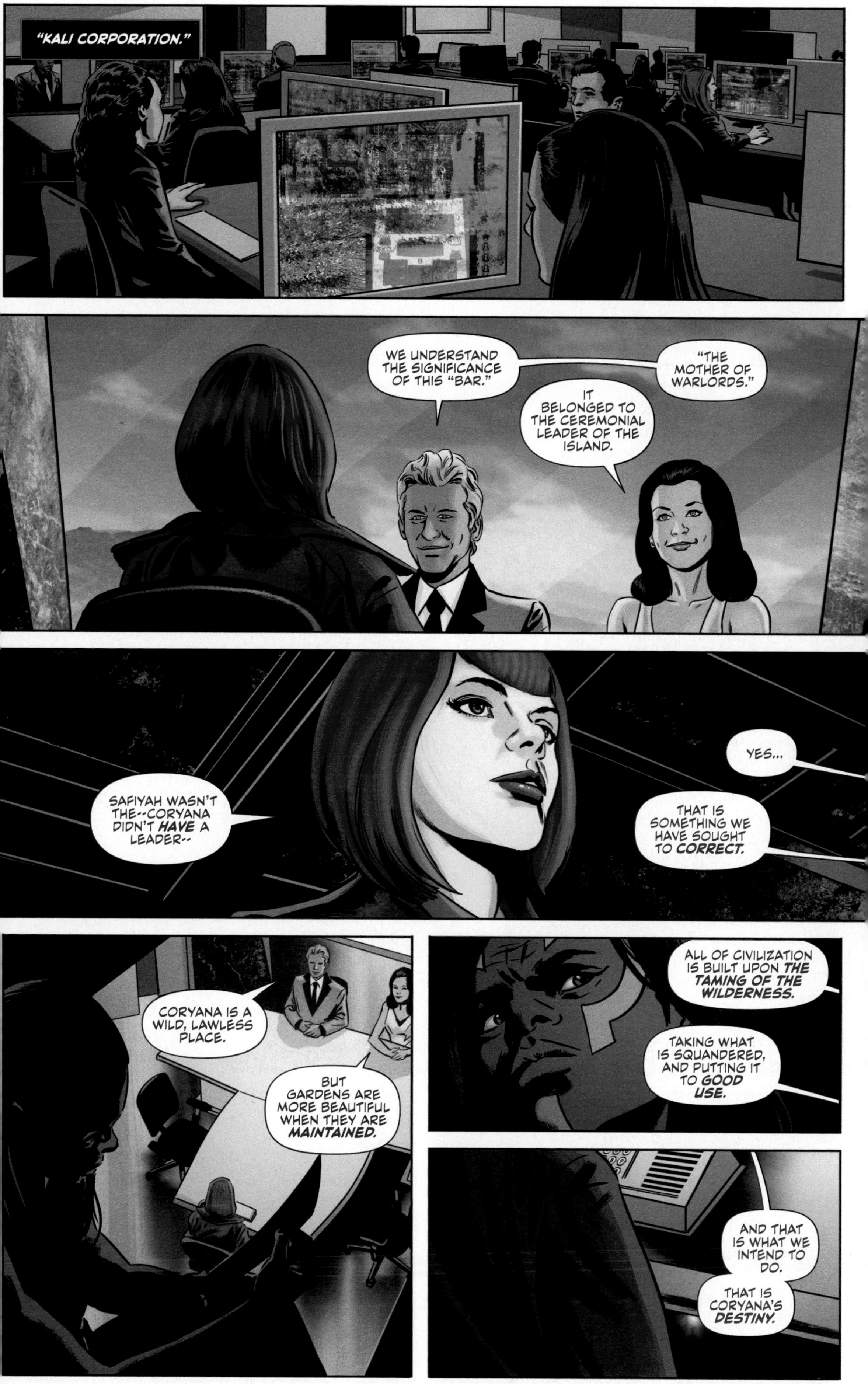
"KALI CORPORATION."
WE UNDERSTAND THE SIGNIFICANCE OF THIS "BAR."
"THE MOTHER OF WARLORDS."
IT BELONGED TO THE CEREMONIAL LEADER OF THE ISLAND.
SAFIYAH WASN'T THE--CORYANA DIDN'T *HAVE* A LEADER--
YES...
THAT IS SOMETHING WE HAVE SOUGHT TO *CORRECT.*
CORYANA IS A WILD, LAWLESS PLACE.
BUT GARDENS ARE MORE BEAUTIFUL WHEN THEY ARE *MAINTAINED.*
ALL OF CIVILIZATION IS BUILT UPON *THE TAMING OF THE WILDERNESS.*
TAKING WHAT IS SQUANDERED, AND PUTTING IT TO *GOOD USE.*
AND THAT IS WHAT WE INTEND TO DO.
THAT IS CORYANA'S *DESTINY.*

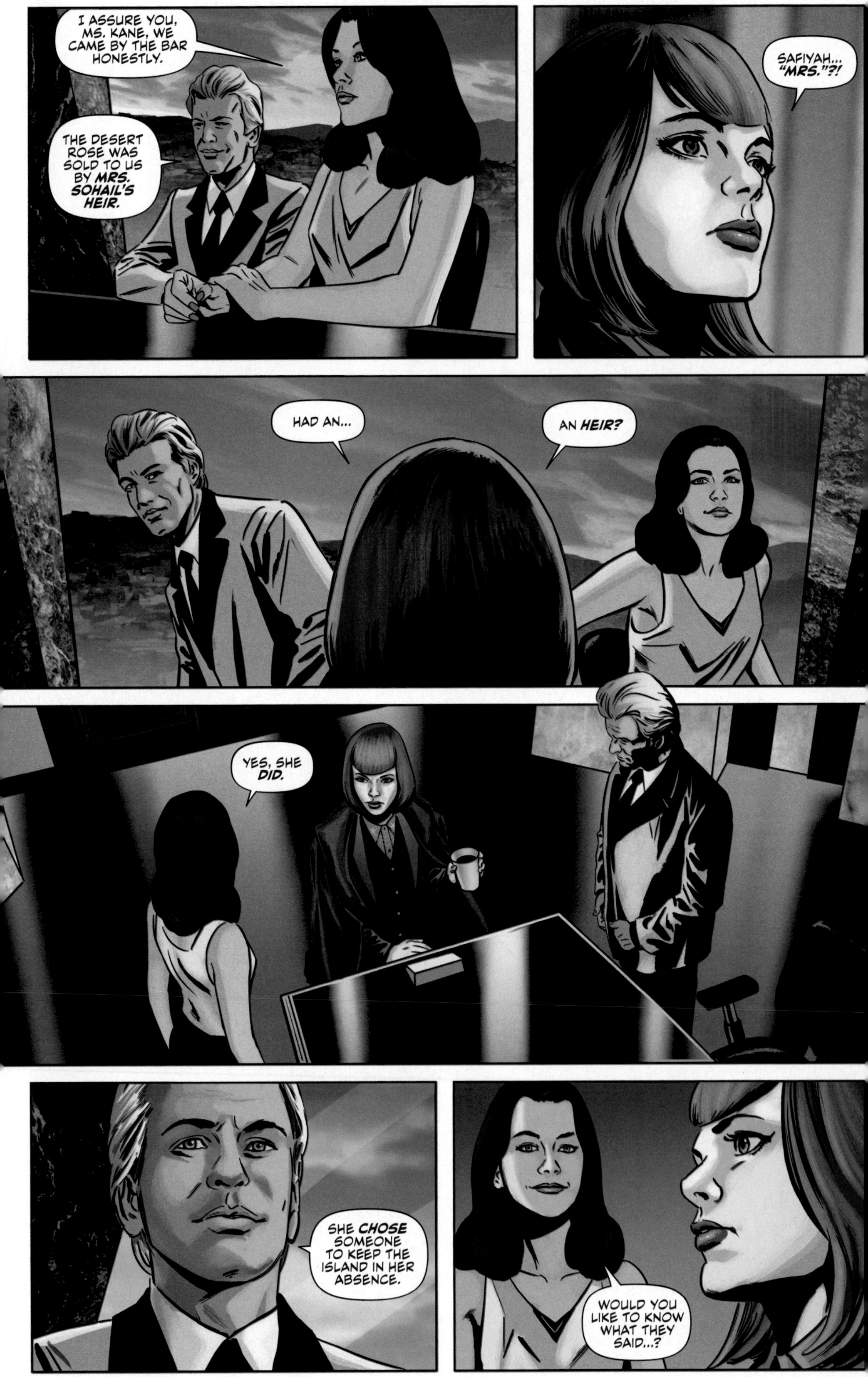
I ASSURE YOU, MS. KANE, WE CAME BY THE BAR HONESTLY.
THE DESERT ROSE WAS SOLD TO US BY **MRS. SOHAIL'S HEIR.**
SAFIYAH... **"MRS."?!**
HAD AN...
AN **HEIR?**
YES, SHE **DID.**
SHE **CHOSE** SOMEONE TO KEEP THE ISLAND IN HER ABSENCE.
WOULD YOU LIKE TO KNOW WHAT THEY SAID...?

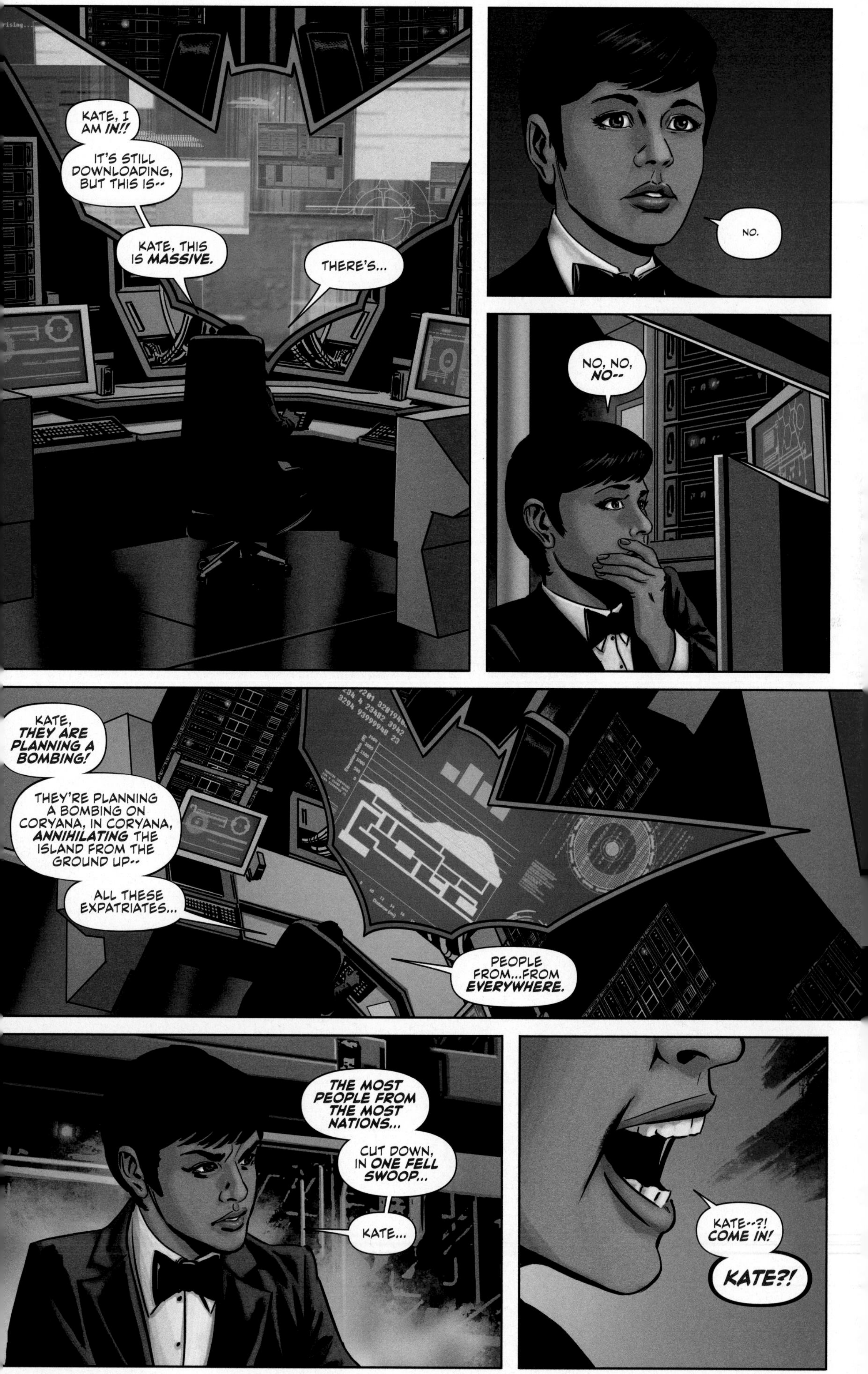
KATE, I AM IN!!
IT'S STILL DOWNLOADING, BUT THIS IS--
KATE, THIS IS MASSIVE.
THERE'S...
NO.
NO, NO, NO--
KATE, THEY ARE PLANNING A BOMBING!
THEY'RE PLANNING A BOMBING ON CORYANA, IN CORYANA, ANNIHILATING THE ISLAND FROM THE GROUND UP--
ALL THESE EXPATRIATES...
PEOPLE FROM...FROM EVERYWHERE.
THE MOST PEOPLE FROM THE MOST NATIONS...
CUT DOWN, IN ONE FELL SWOOP...
KATE...
KATE--?! COME IN!
KATE?!

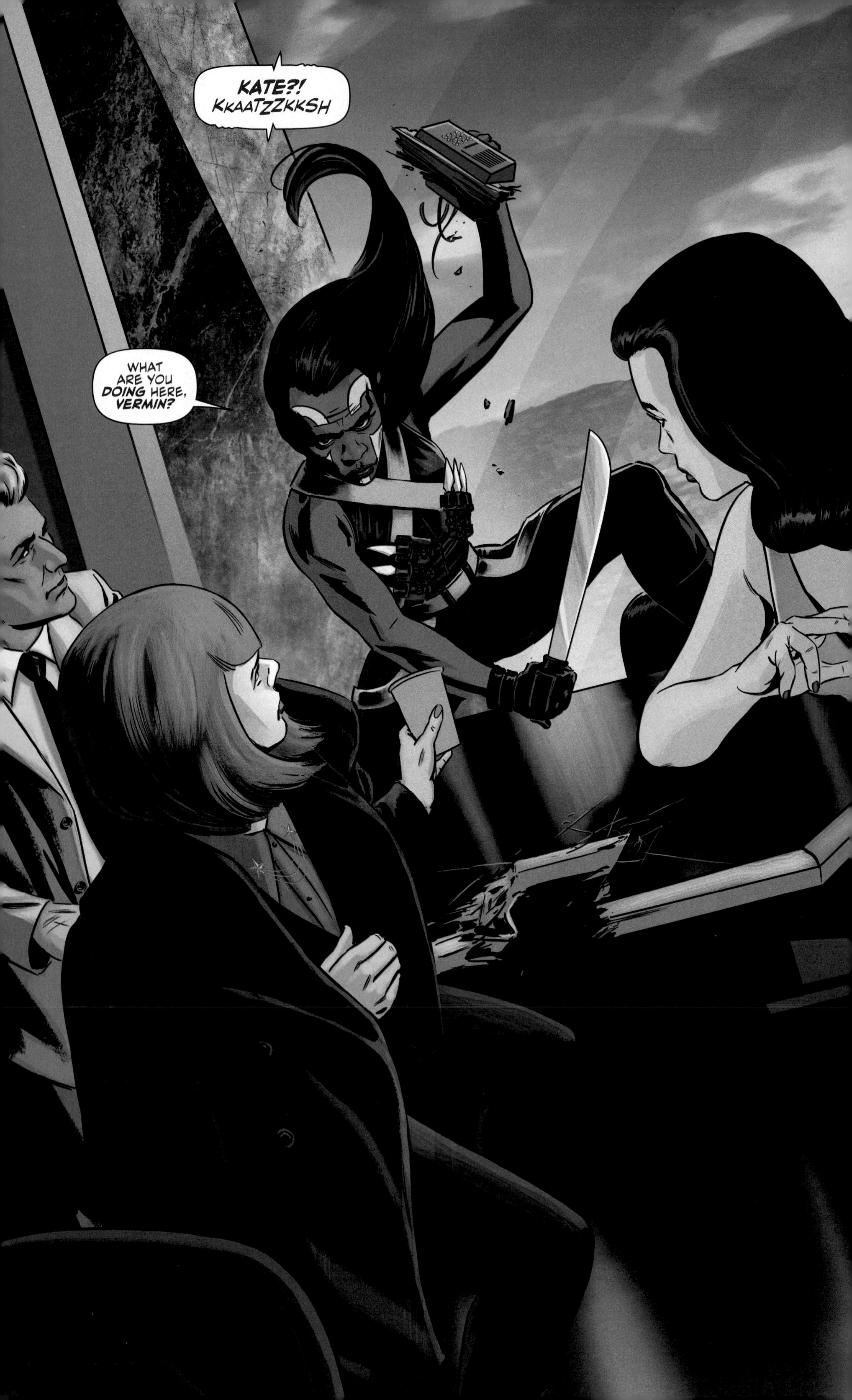
KATE?! KKAATZZKKSH
WHAT ARE YOU DOING HERE, VERMIN?

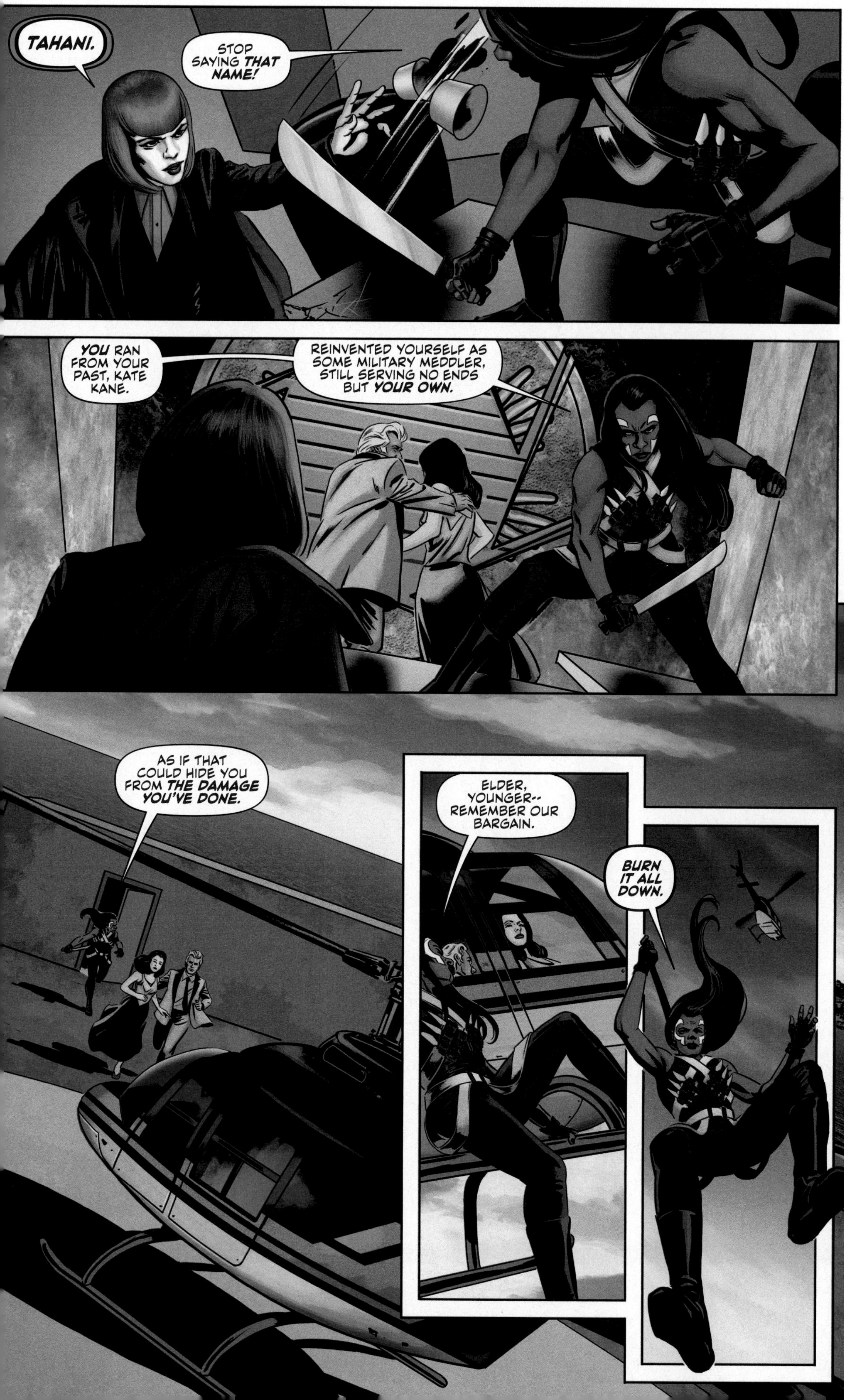
TAHANI.
STOP SAYING THAT NAME!
YOU RAN FROM YOUR PAST, KATE KANE.
REINVENTED YOURSELF AS SOME MILITARY MEDDLER, STILL SERVING NO ENDS BUT YOUR OWN.
AS IF THAT COULD HIDE YOU FROM THE DAMAGE YOU'VE DONE.
ELDER, YOUNGER-- REMEMBER OUR BARGAIN.
BURN IT ALL DOWN.

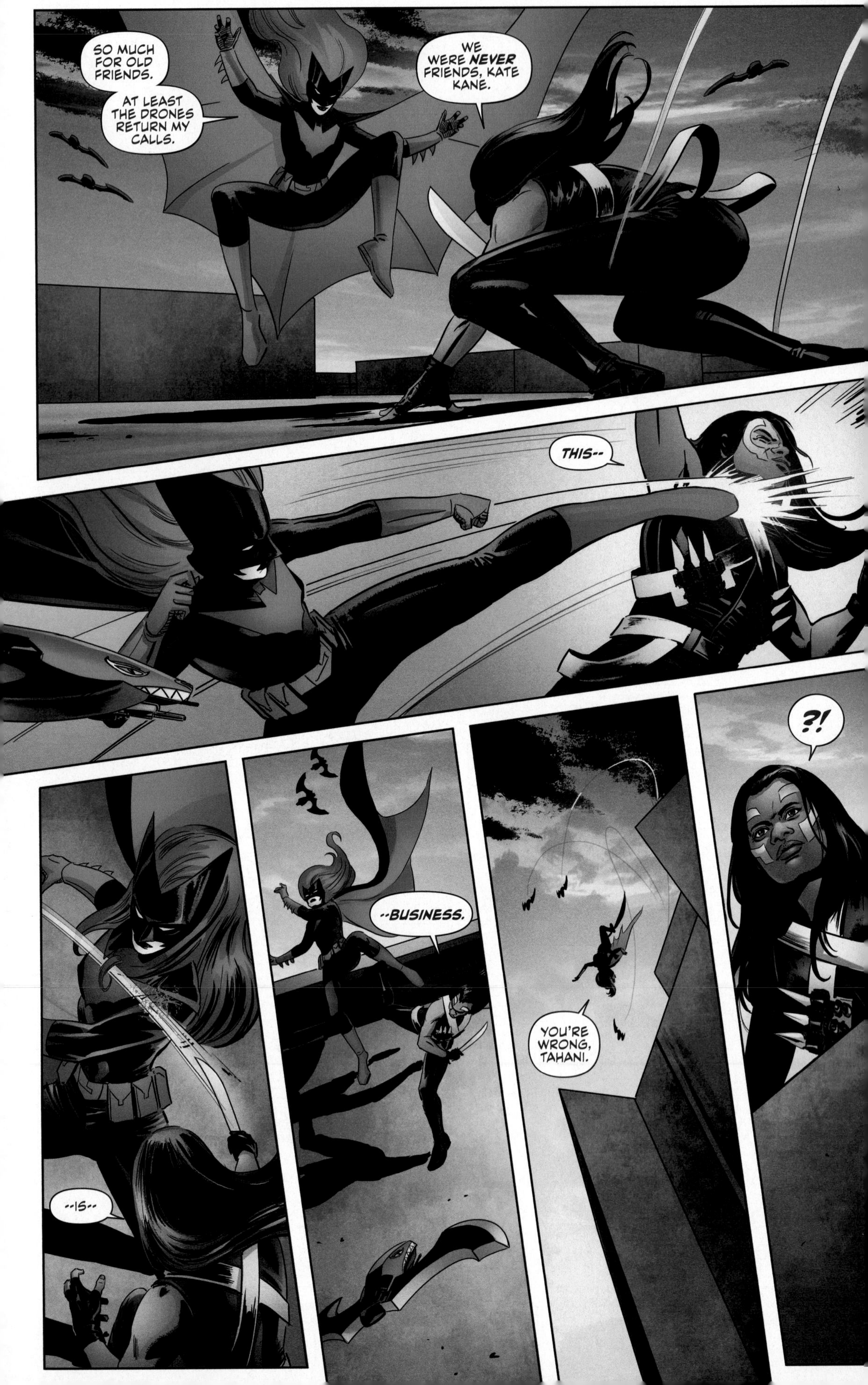

SO MUCH FOR OLD FRIENDS.
AT LEAST THE DRONES RETURN MY CALLS.
WE WERE NEVER FRIENDS, KATE KANE.
THIS--
--IS--
--BUSINESS.
YOU'RE WRONG, TAHANI.
?!

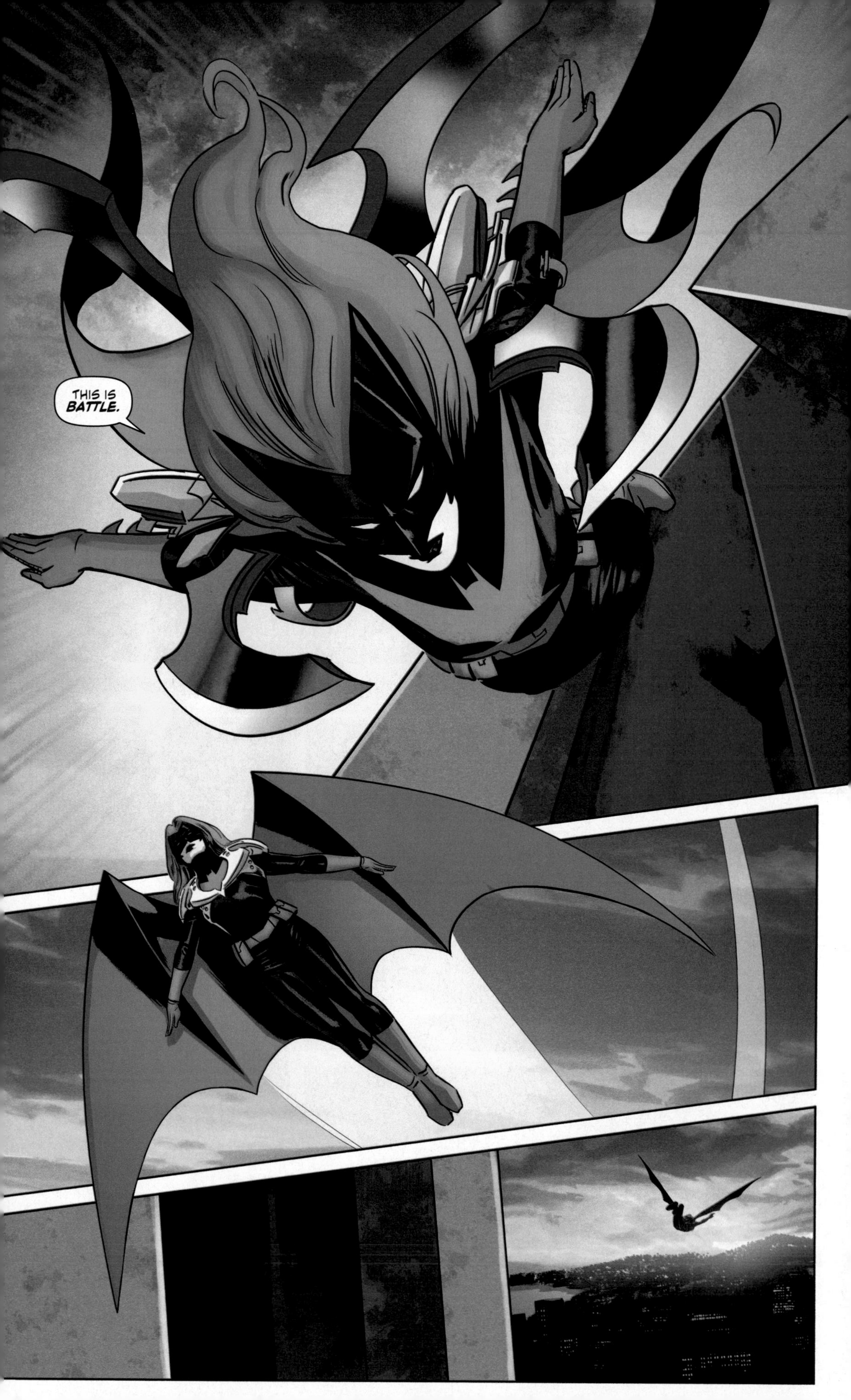
THIS IS BATTLE.

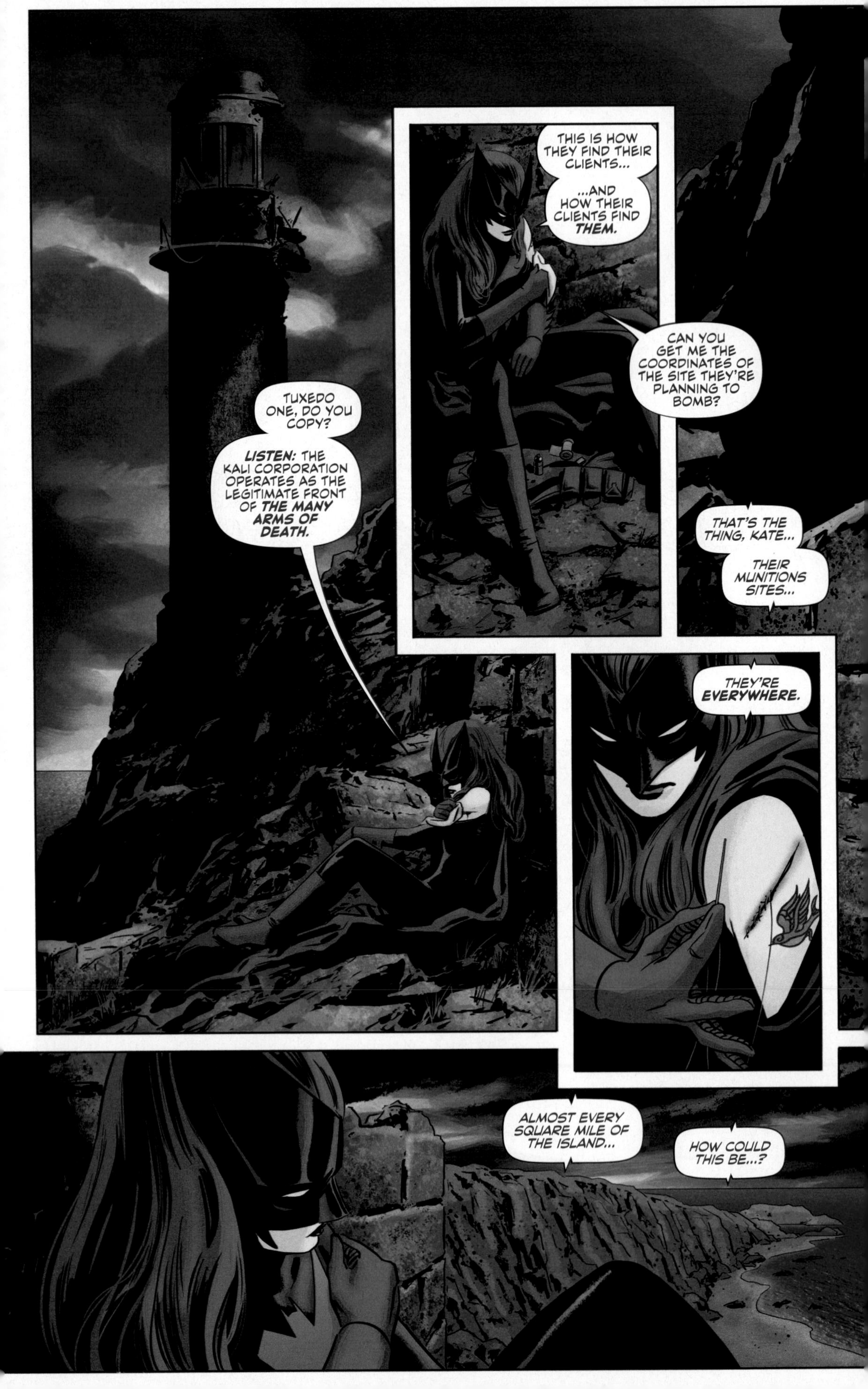
TUXEDO ONE, DO YOU COPY?
LISTEN: THE KALI CORPORATION OPERATES AS THE LEGITIMATE FRONT OF THE MANY ARMS OF DEATH.
THIS IS HOW THEY FIND THEIR CLIENTS...
...AND HOW THEIR CLIENTS FIND THEM.
CAN YOU GET ME THE COORDINATES OF THE SITE THEY'RE PLANNING TO BOMB?
THAT'S THE THING, KATE...
THEIR MUNITIONS SITES...
THEY'RE EVERYWHERE.
ALMOST EVERY SQUARE MILE OF THE ISLAND...
HOW COULD THIS BE...?

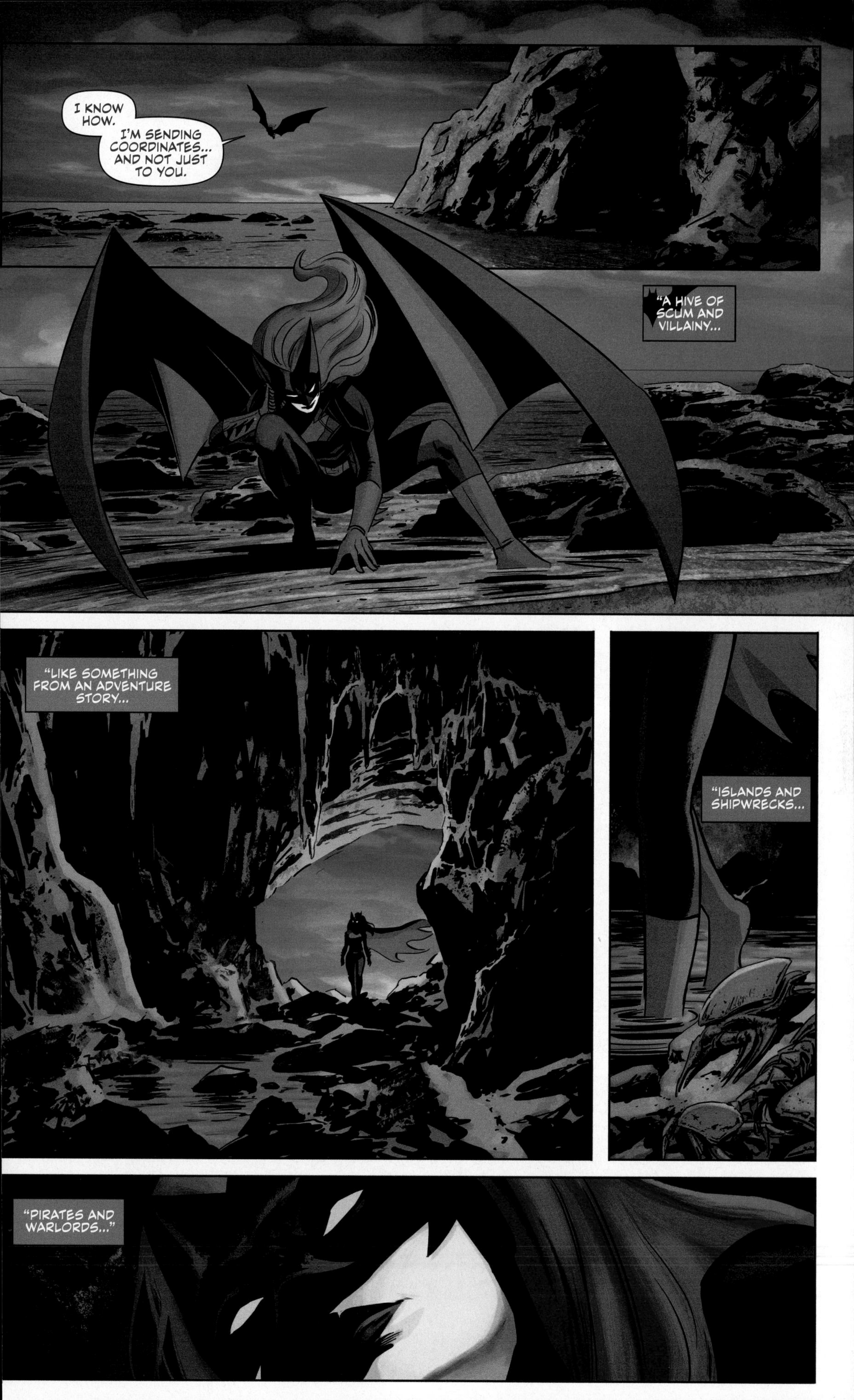
I KNOW HOW.
I'M SENDING COORDINATES... AND NOT JUST TO YOU.
"A HIVE OF SCUM AND VILLAINY...
"LIKE SOMETHING FROM AN ADVENTURE STORY...
"ISLANDS AND SHIPWRECKS...
"PIRATES AND WARLORDS..."

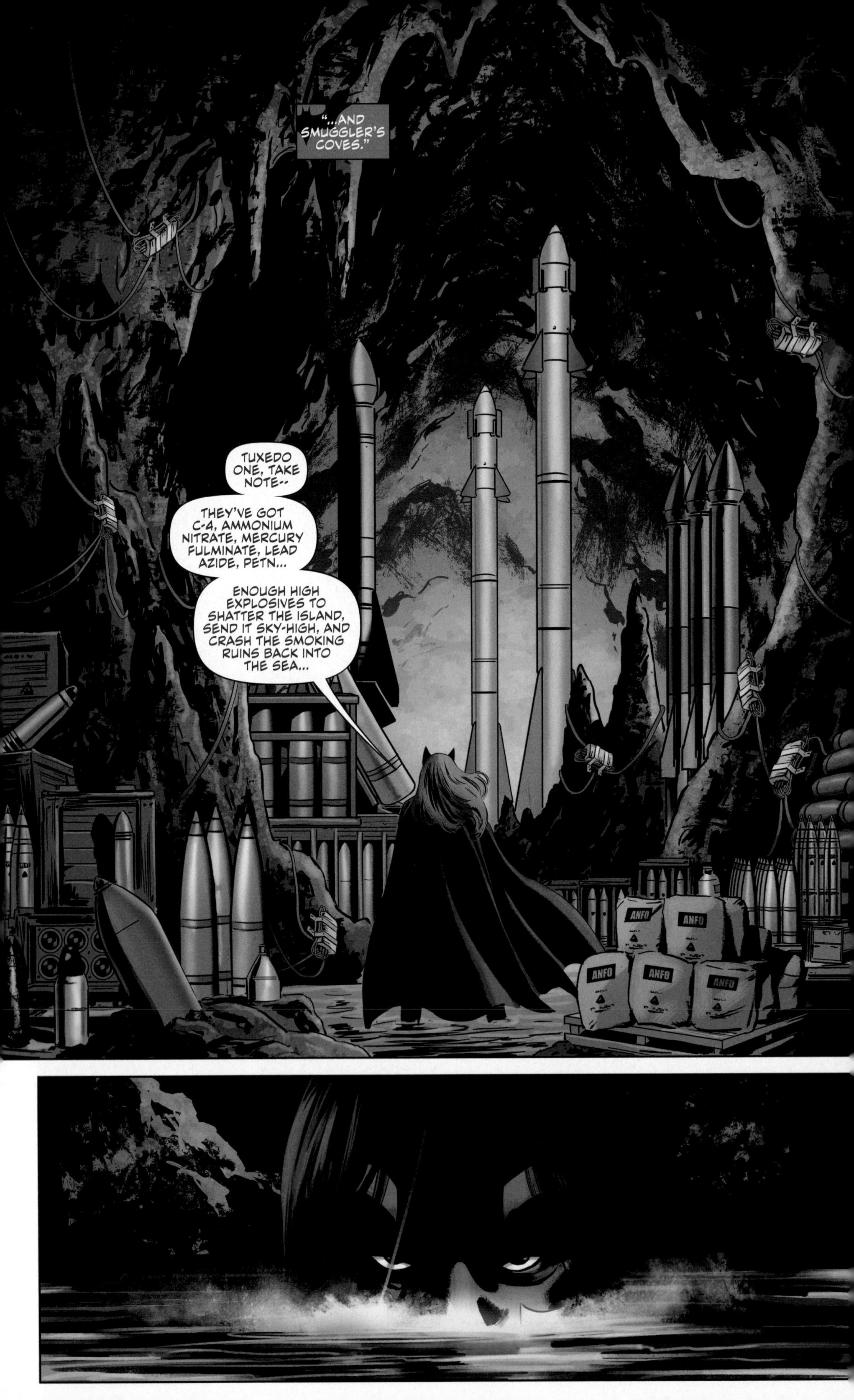
"...AND SMUGGLER'S COVES."
TUXEDO ONE, TAKE NOTE--
THEY'VE GOT C-4, AMMONIUM NITRATE, MERCURY FULMINATE, LEAD AZIDE, PETN...
ENOUGH HIGH EXPLOSIVES TO SHATTER THE ISLAND, SEND IT SKY-HIGH, AND CRASH THE SMOKING RUINS BACK INTO THE SEA...
ANFO
ANFO
ANFO
ANFO
ANFO

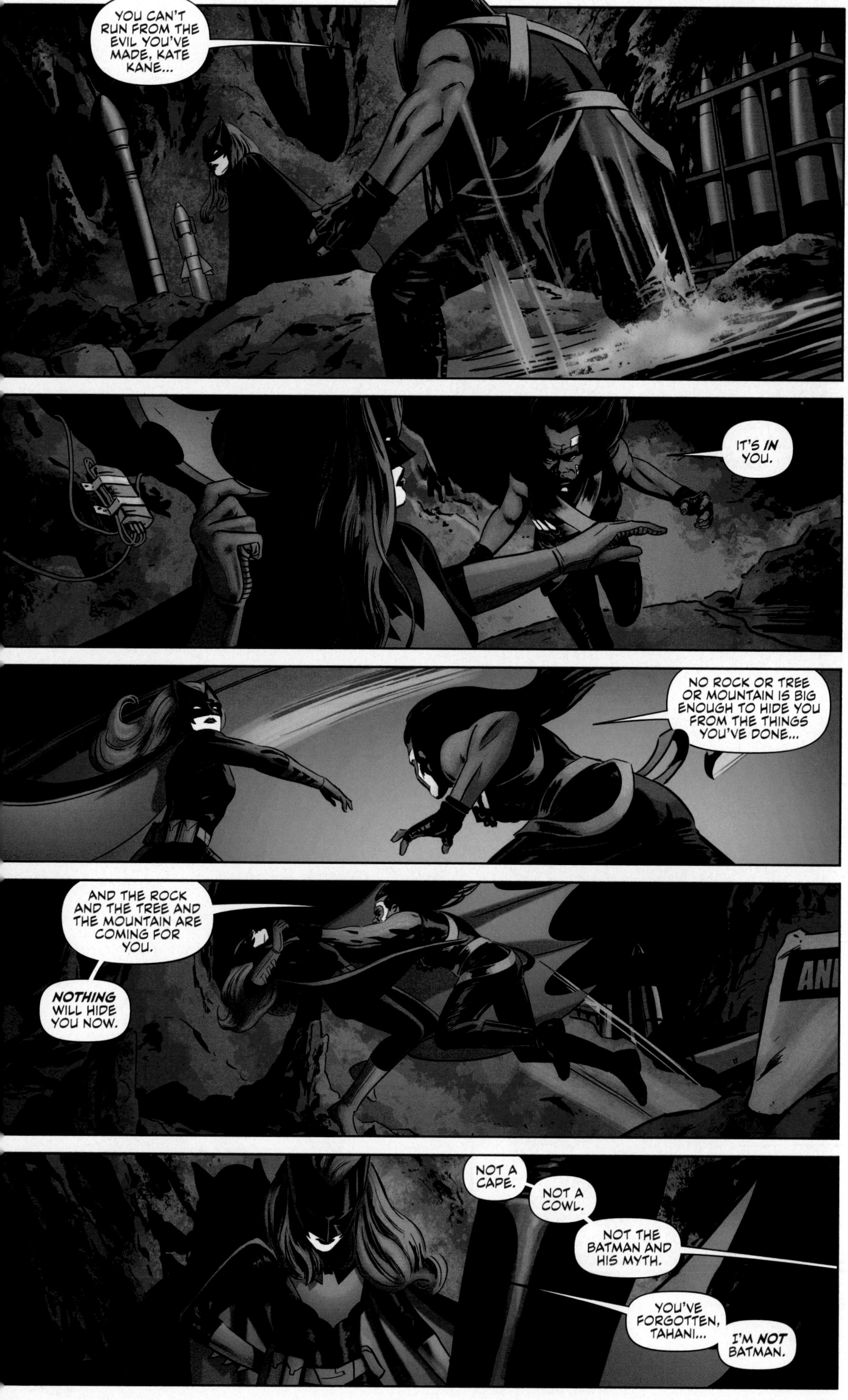
YOU CAN'T RUN FROM THE EVIL YOU'VE MADE, KATE KANE...
IT'S *IN* YOU.
NO ROCK OR TREE OR MOUNTAIN IS BIG ENOUGH TO HIDE YOU FROM THE THINGS YOU'VE DONE...
AND THE ROCK AND THE TREE AND THE MOUNTAIN ARE COMING FOR YOU.
NOTHING WILL HIDE YOU NOW.
NOT A CAPE.
NOT A COWL.
NOT THE BATMAN AND HIS MYTH.
YOU'VE FORGOTTEN, TAHANI...
I'M *NOT* BATMAN.

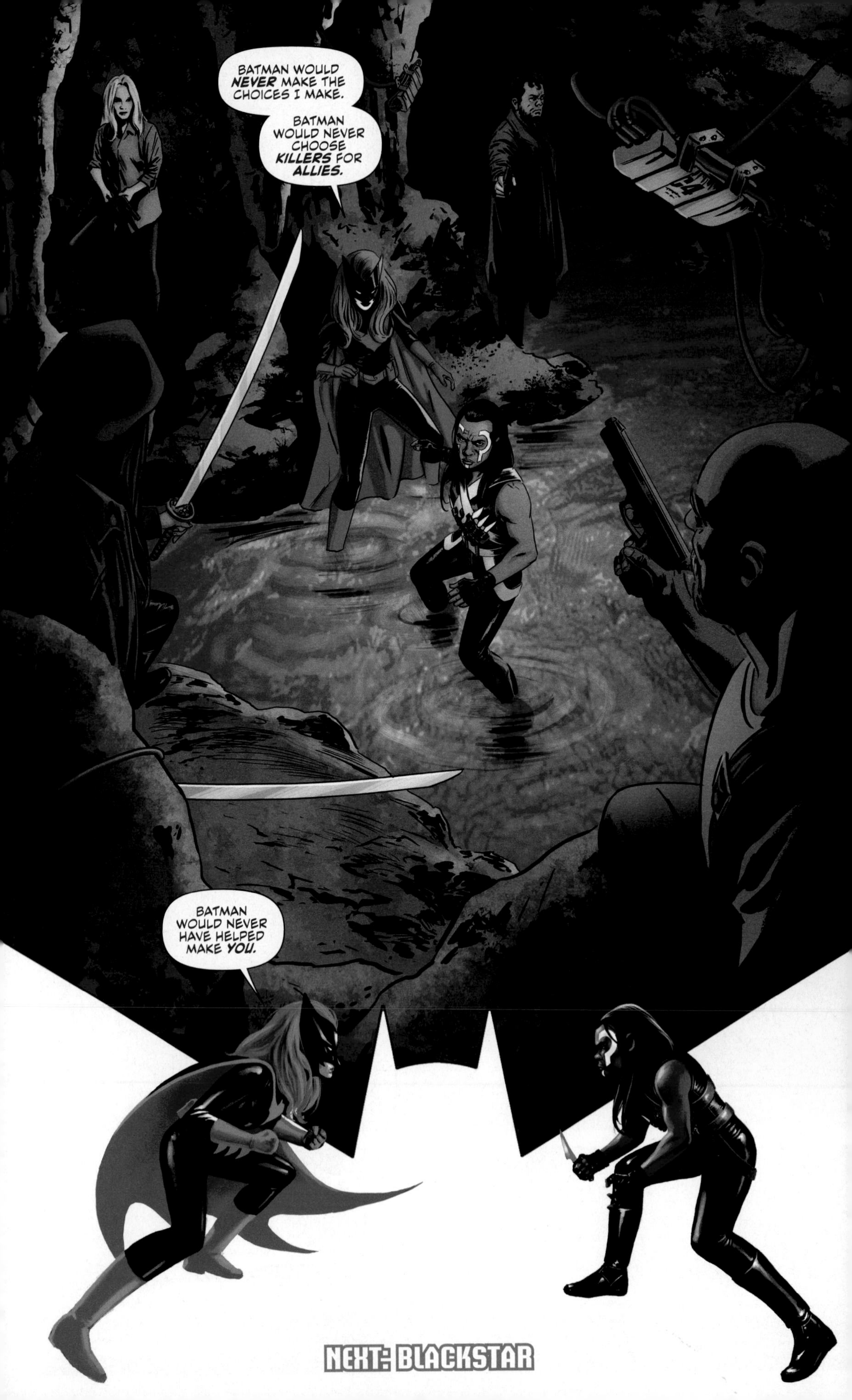
BATMAN WOULD NEVER MAKE THE CHOICES I MAKE.
BATMAN WOULD NEVER CHOOSE KILLERS FOR ALLIES.
BATMAN WOULD NEVER HAVE HELPED MAKE YOU.
NEXT: BLACKSTAR

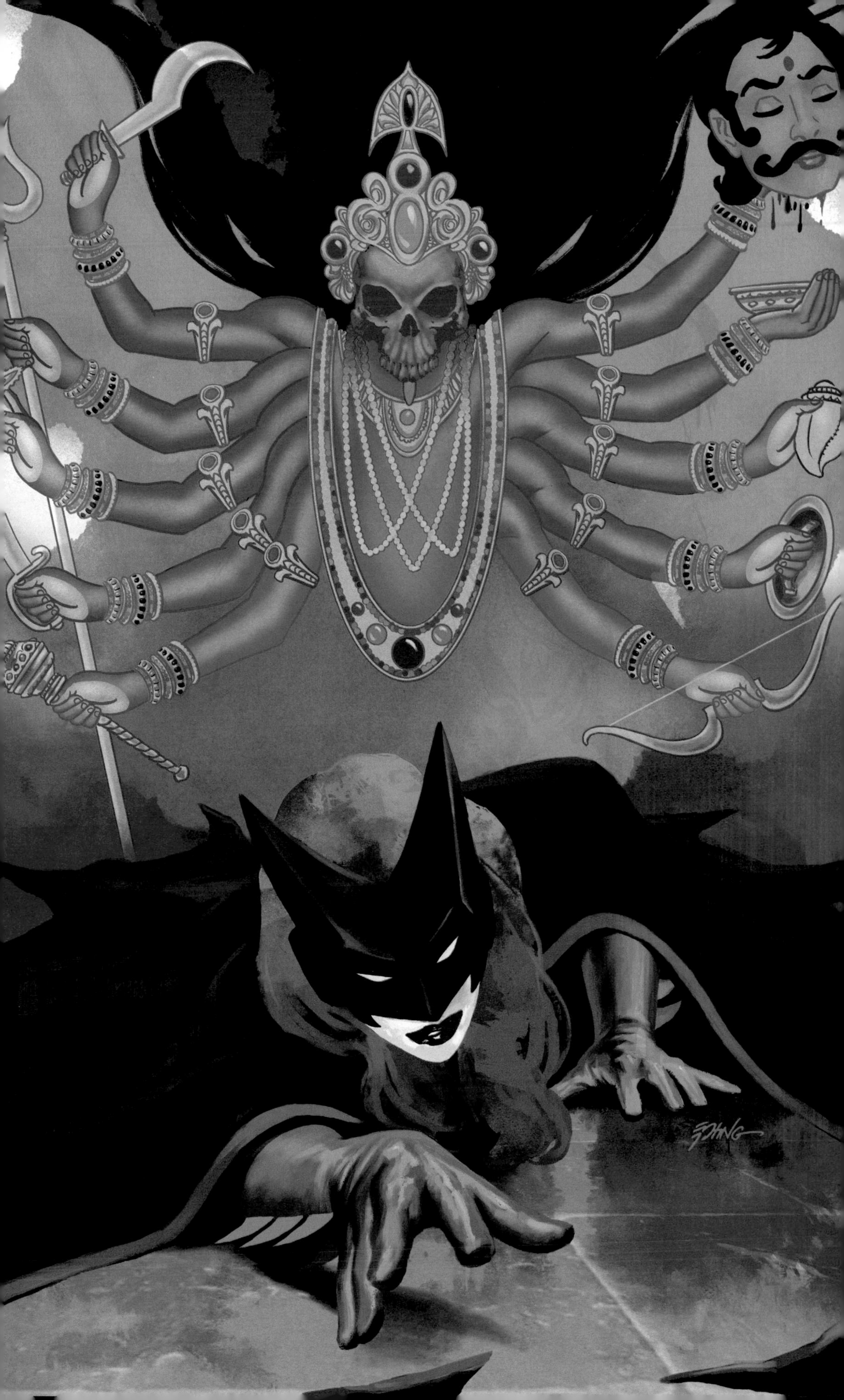

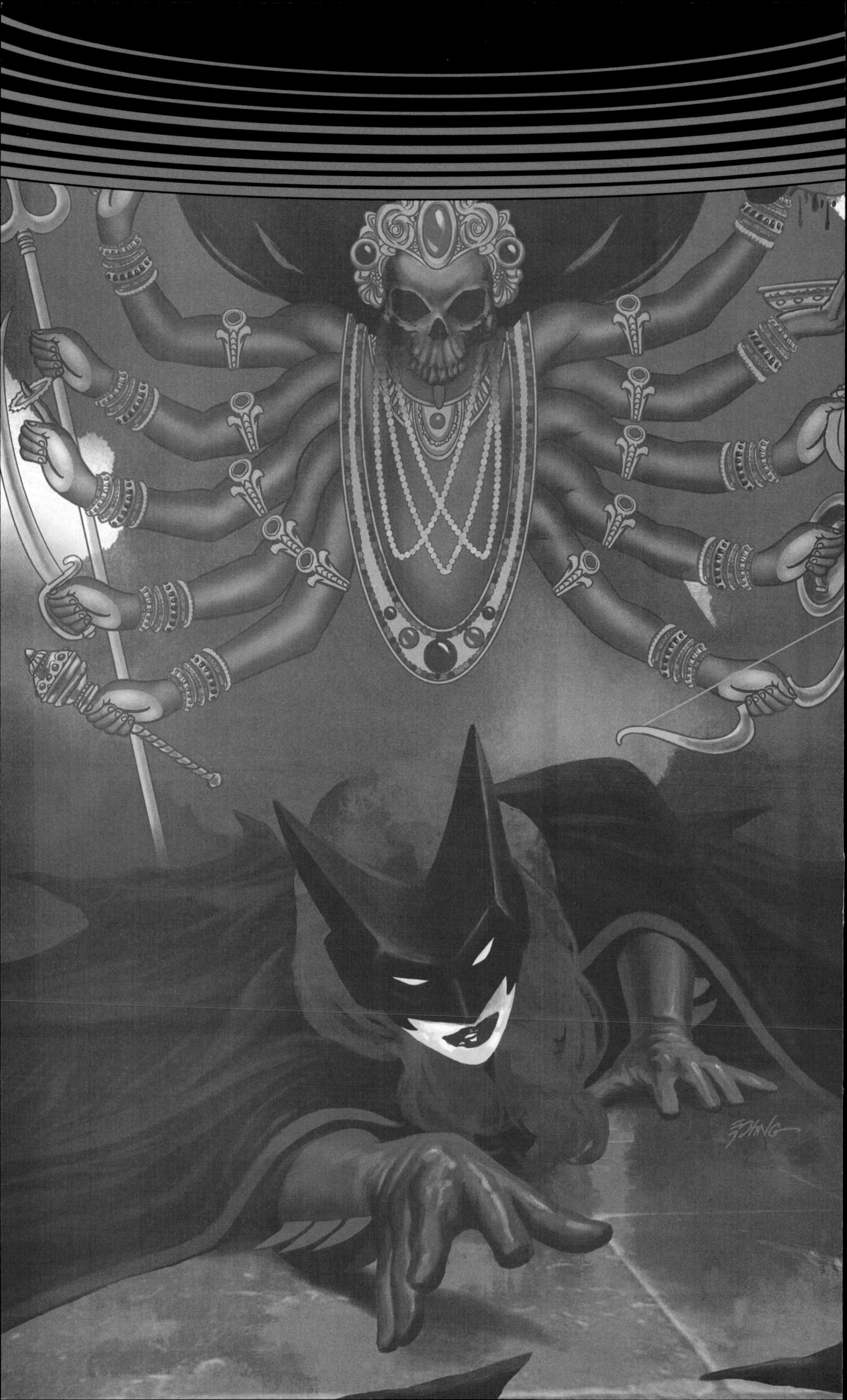

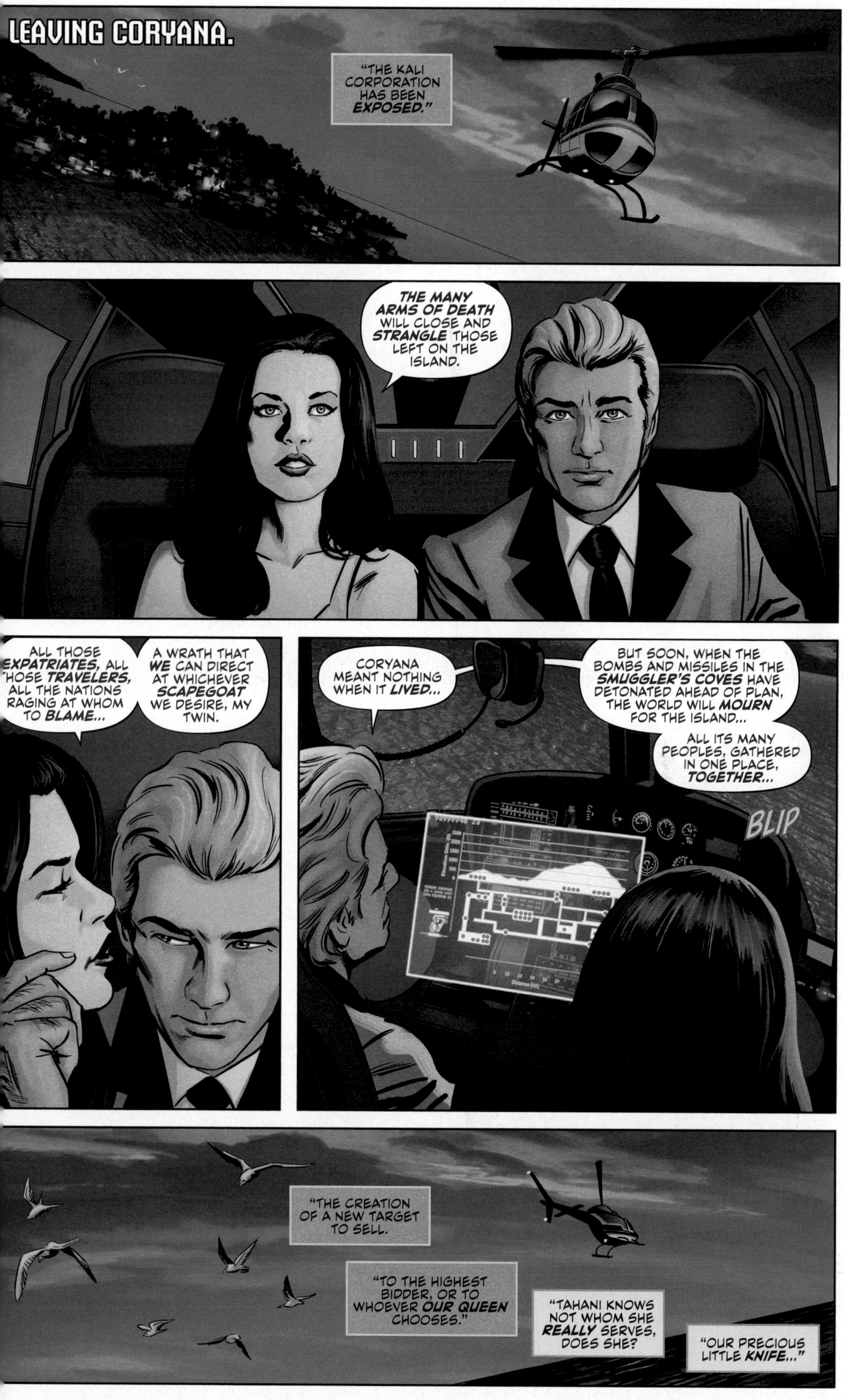
LEAVING CORYANA.
"THE KALI CORPORATION HAS BEEN EXPOSED."
THE MANY ARMS OF DEATH WILL CLOSE AND STRANGLE THOSE LEFT ON THE ISLAND.
ALL THOSE EXPATRIATES, ALL THOSE TRAVELERS, ALL THE NATIONS RAGING AT WHOM TO BLAME...
A WRATH THAT WE CAN DIRECT AT WHICHEVER SCAPEGOAT WE DESIRE, MY TWIN.
CORYANA MEANT NOTHING WHEN IT LIVED...
BUT SOON, WHEN THE BOMBS AND MISSILES IN THE SMUGGLER'S COVES HAVE DETONATED AHEAD OF PLAN, THE WORLD WILL MOURN FOR THE ISLAND...
ALL ITS MANY PEOPLES, GATHERED IN ONE PLACE, TOGETHER...
BLIP
"THE CREATION OF A NEW TARGET TO SELL.
"TO THE HIGHEST BIDDER, OR TO WHOEVER OUR QUEEN CHOOSES."
"TAHANI KNOWS NOT WHOM SHE REALLY SERVES, DOES SHE?
"OUR PRECIOUS LITTLE KNIFE..."

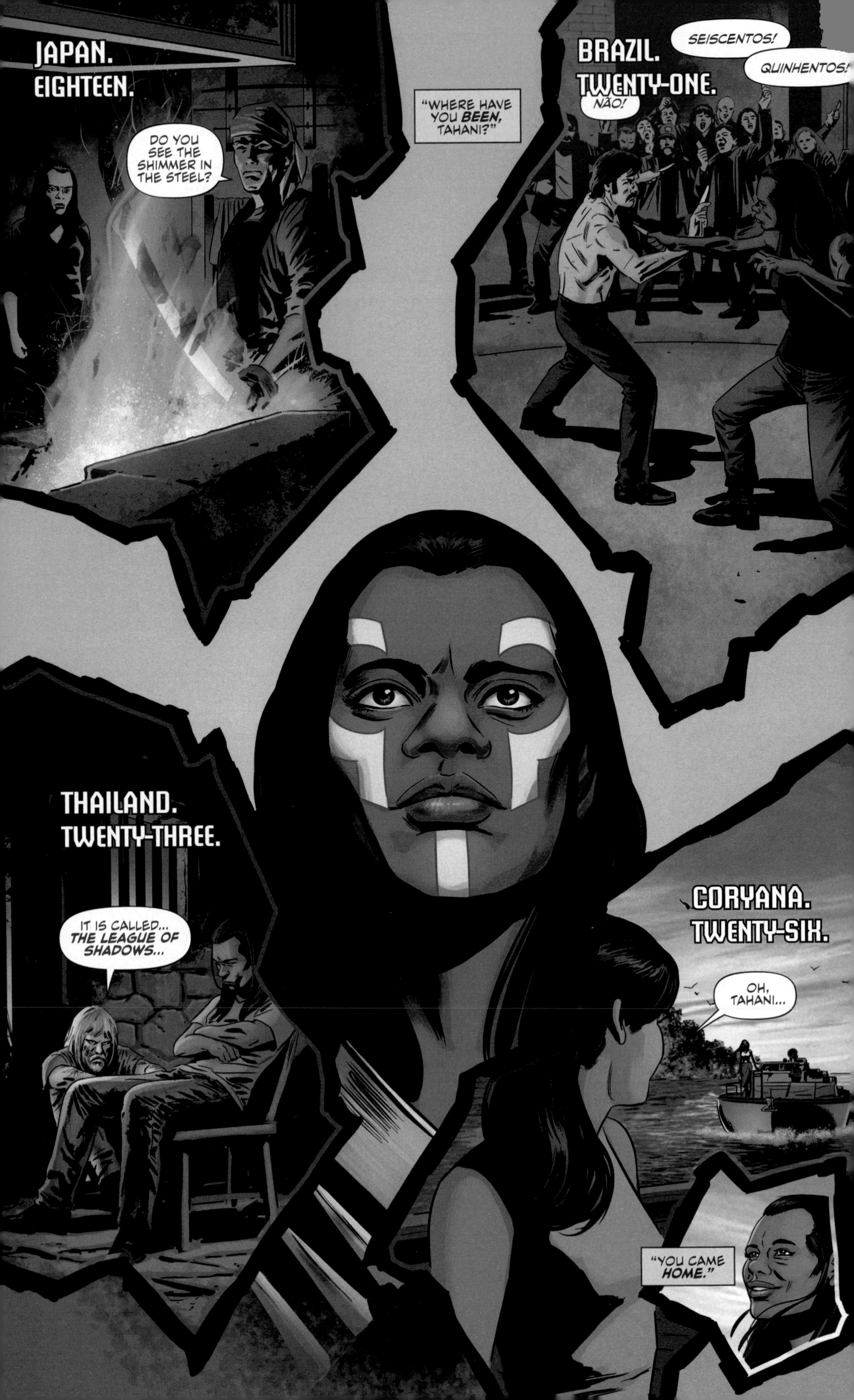
JAPAN.
EIGHTEEN.
DO YOU SEE THE SHIMMER IN THE STEEL?
"WHERE HAVE YOU BEEN, TAHANI?"
BRAZIL.
TWENTY-ONE.
SEISCENTOS!
QUINHENTOS!
NÃO!
THAILAND.
TWENTY-THREE.
IT IS CALLED... THE LEAGUE OF SHADOWS...
CORYANA.
TWENTY-SIX.
OH, TAHANI...
"YOU CAME HOME."

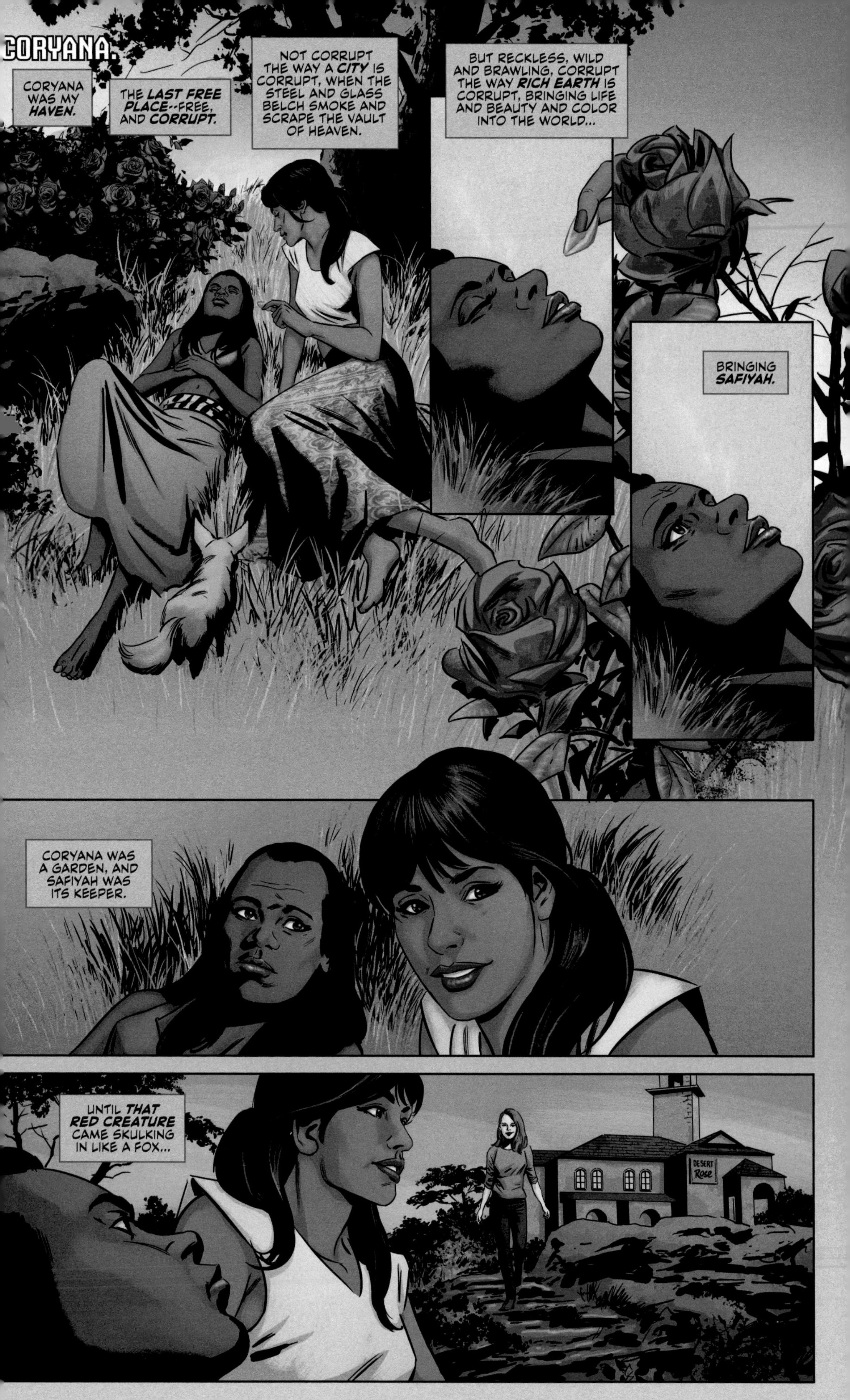
CORYANA.
CORYANA WAS MY HAVEN.
THE LAST FREE PLACE--FREE, AND CORRUPT.
NOT CORRUPT THE WAY A CITY IS CORRUPT, WHEN THE STEEL AND GLASS BELCH SMOKE AND SCRAPE THE VAULT OF HEAVEN.
BUT RECKLESS, WILD AND BRAWLING, CORRUPT THE WAY RICH EARTH IS CORRUPT, BRINGING LIFE AND BEAUTY AND COLOR INTO THE WORLD...
BRINGING SAFIYAH.
CORYANA WAS A GARDEN, AND SAFIYAH WAS ITS KEEPER.
UNTIL THAT RED CREATURE CAME SKULKING IN LIKE A FOX...
DESERT Rose

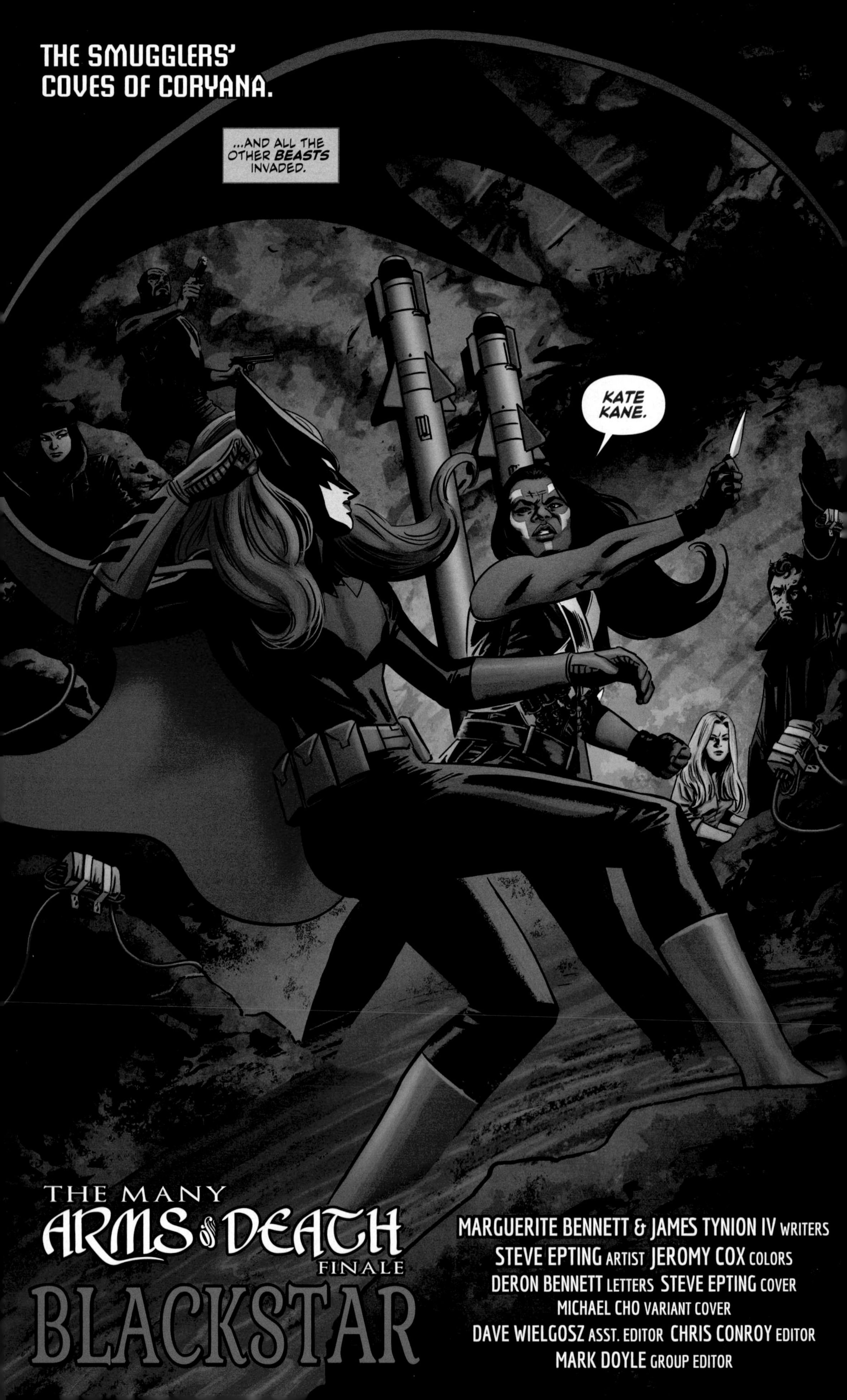
THE SMUGGLERS' COVES OF CORYANA.
...AND ALL THE OTHER BEASTS INVADED.
KATE KANE.
THE MANY ARMS of DEATH FINALE
BLACKSTAR
MARGUERITE BENNETT & JAMES TYNION IV WRITERS
STEVE EPTING ARTIST JEROMY COX COLORS
DERON BENNETT LETTERS STEVE EPTING COVER
MICHAEL CHO VARIANT COVER
DAVE WIELGOSZ ASST. EDITOR CHRIS CONROY EDITOR
MARK DOYLE GROUP EDITOR

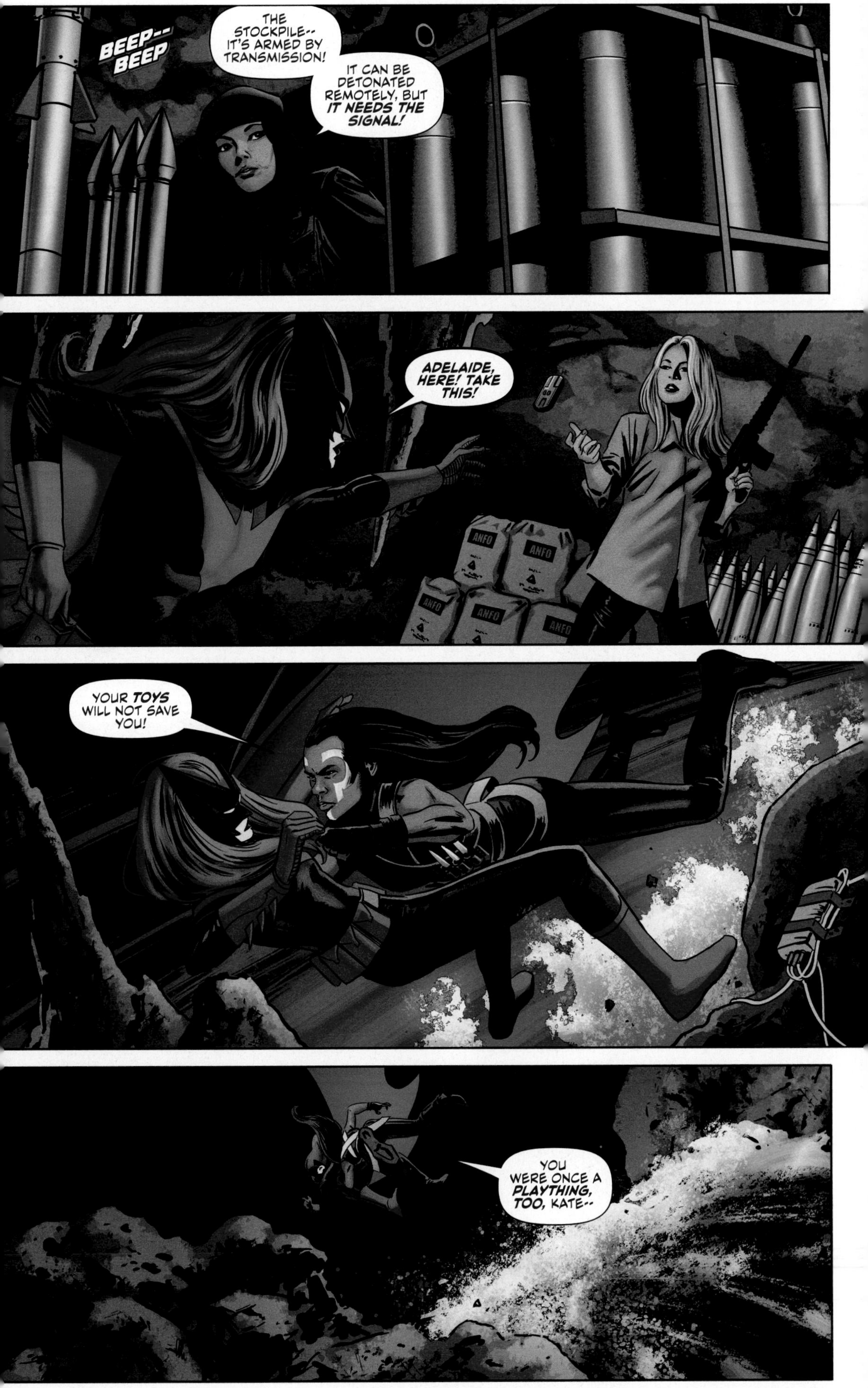
BEEP-- BEEP
THE STOCKPILE-- IT'S ARMED BY TRANSMISSION!
IT CAN BE DETONATED REMOTELY, BUT *IT NEEDS THE SIGNAL!*
ADELAIDE, HERE! TAKE THIS!
ANFO
YOUR *TOYS* WILL NOT SAVE YOU!
YOU WERE ONCE A *PLAYTHING, TOO,* KATE--

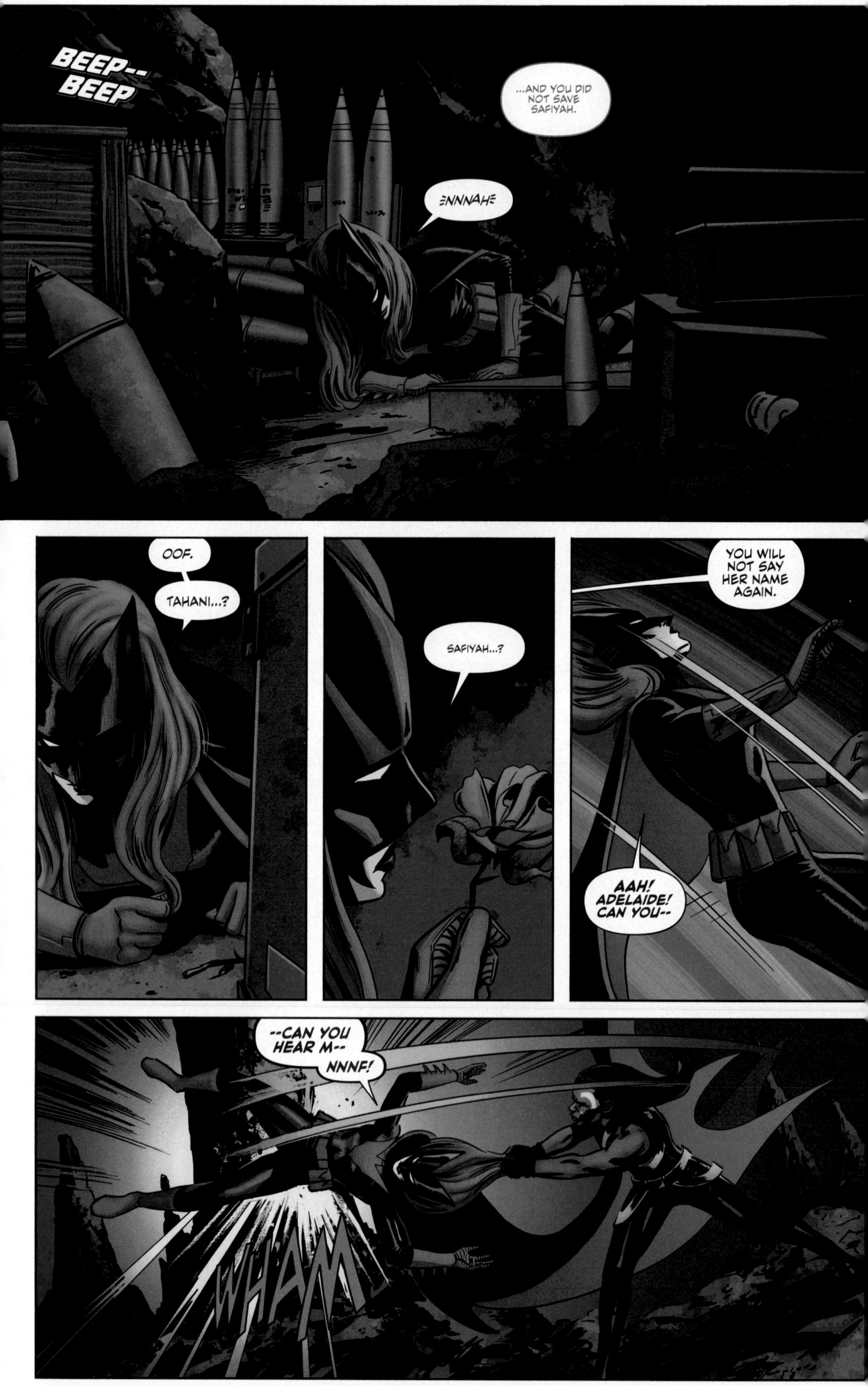
BEEP--
BEEP
...AND YOU DID NOT SAVE SAFIYAH.
ENNNAH
OOF.
TAHANI...?
SAFIYAH...?
YOU WILL NOT SAY HER NAME AGAIN.
AAH! ADELAIDE! CAN YOU--
--CAN YOU HEAR M--
NNNF!
WHAM

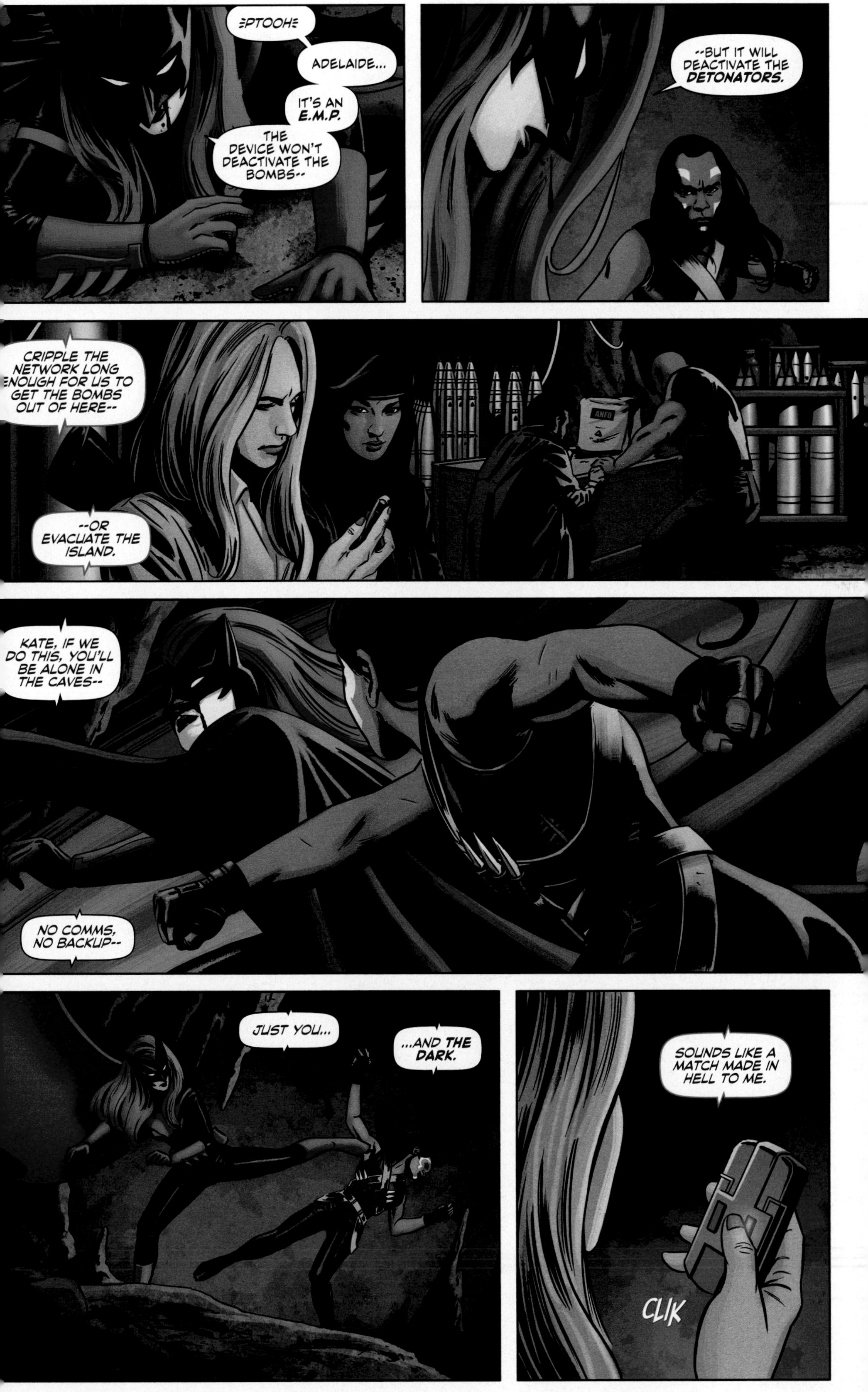

=PTOOH=
ADELAIDE...
IT'S AN E.M.P.
THE DEVICE WON'T DEACTIVATE THE BOMBS--
--BUT IT WILL DEACTIVATE THE DETONATORS.
CRIPPLE THE NETWORK LONG ENOUGH FOR US TO GET THE BOMBS OUT OF HERE--
ANFO
--OR EVACUATE THE ISLAND.
KATE, IF WE DO THIS, YOU'LL BE ALONE IN THE CAVES--
NO COMMS, NO BACKUP--
JUST YOU...
...AND THE DARK.
SOUNDS LIKE A MATCH MADE IN HELL TO ME.
CLIK

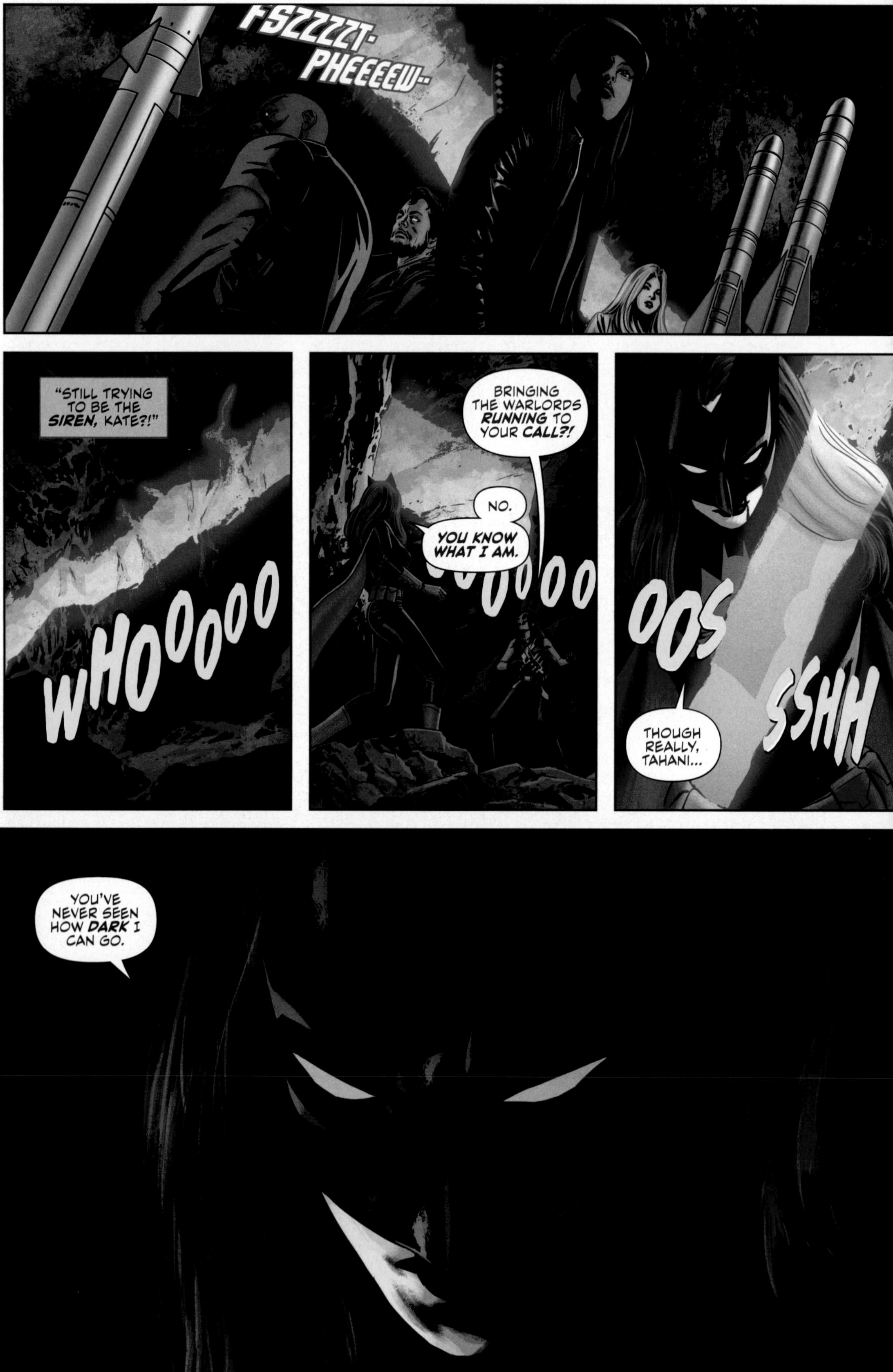
FSZZZZT-
PHEEEEW--
"STILL TRYING TO BE THE SIREN, KATE?!"
WHOOOOO
BRINGING THE WARLORDS RUNNING TO YOUR CALL?!
NO.
YOU KNOW WHAT I AM.
OOOOOO
OOS
THOUGH REALLY, TAHANI...
SSHH
YOU'VE NEVER SEEN HOW DARK I CAN GO.

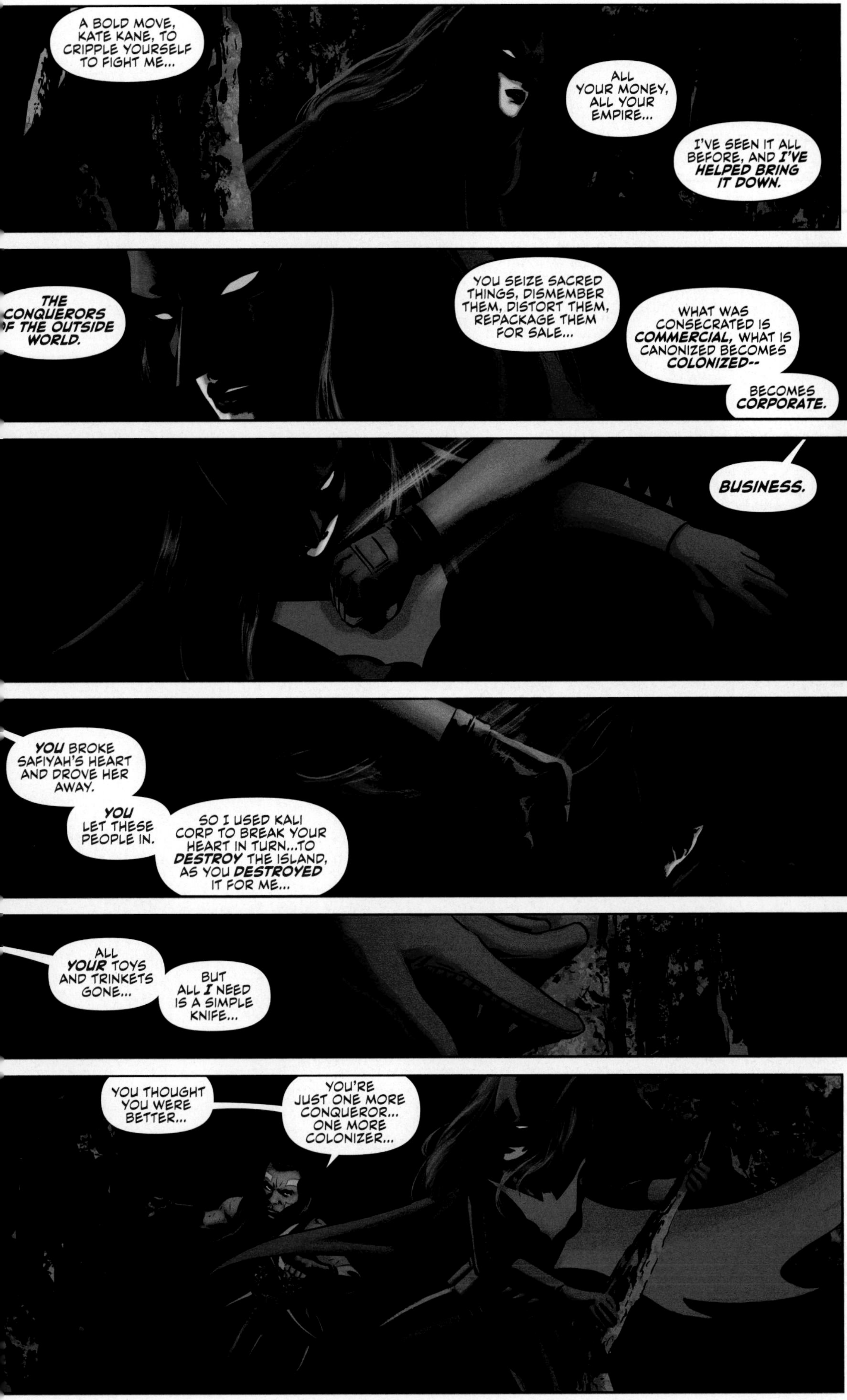
A BOLD MOVE, KATE KANE, TO CRIPPLE YOURSELF TO FIGHT ME...
ALL YOUR MONEY, ALL YOUR EMPIRE...
I'VE SEEN IT ALL BEFORE, AND I'VE HELPED BRING IT DOWN.
THE CONQUERORS OF THE OUTSIDE WORLD.
YOU SEIZE SACRED THINGS, DISMEMBER THEM, DISTORT THEM, REPACKAGE THEM FOR SALE...
WHAT WAS CONSECRATED IS COMMERCIAL, WHAT IS CANONIZED BECOMES COLONIZED--
BECOMES CORPORATE.
BUSINESS.
YOU BROKE SAFIYAH'S HEART AND DROVE HER AWAY.
YOU LET THESE PEOPLE IN.
SO I USED KALI CORP TO BREAK YOUR HEART IN TURN...TO DESTROY THE ISLAND, AS YOU DESTROYED IT FOR ME...
ALL YOUR TOYS AND TRINKETS GONE...
BUT ALL I NEED IS A SIMPLE KNIFE...
YOU THOUGHT YOU WERE BETTER...
YOU'RE JUST ONE MORE CONQUEROR... ONE MORE COLONIZER...

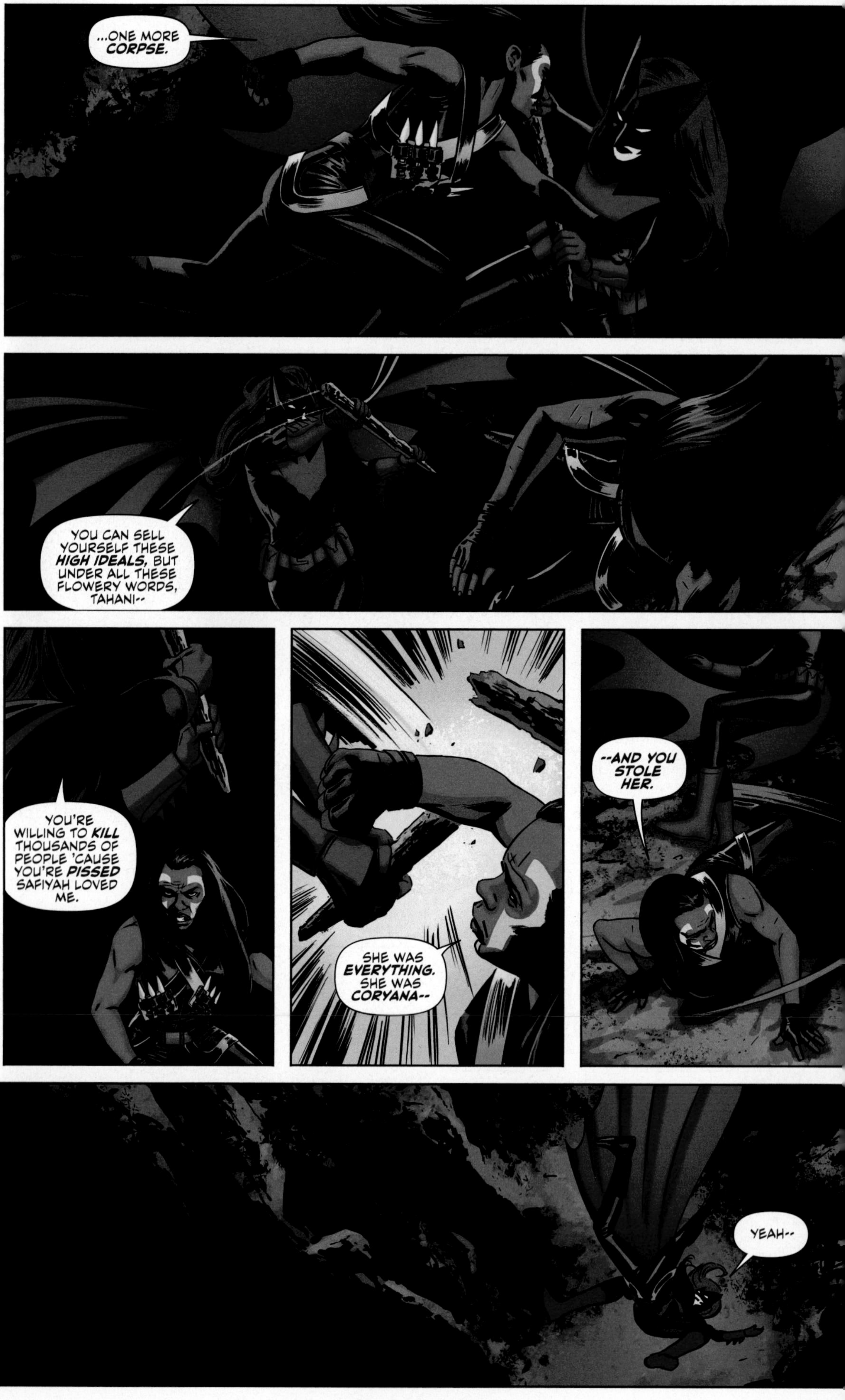
...ONE MORE CORPSE.
YOU CAN SELL YOURSELF THESE HIGH IDEALS, BUT UNDER ALL THESE FLOWERY WORDS, TAHANI--
YOU'RE WILLING TO KILL THOUSANDS OF PEOPLE 'CAUSE YOU'RE PISSED SAFIYAH LOVED ME.
SHE WAS EVERYTHING. SHE WAS CORYANA--
--AND YOU STOLE HER.
YEAH--

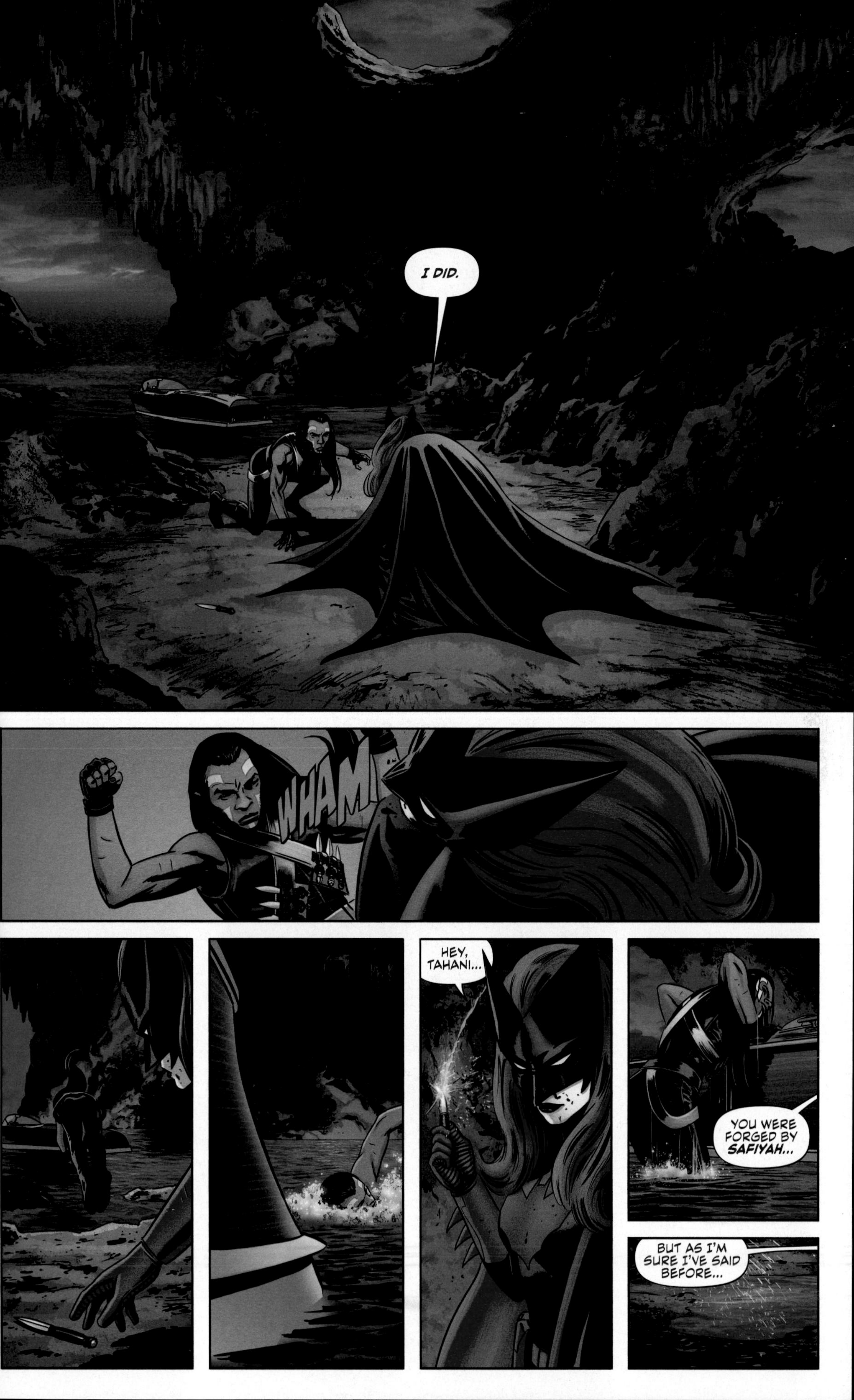
I DID.
WHAM!
HEY, TAHANI...
YOU WERE FORGED BY SAFIYAH...
BUT AS I'M SURE I'VE SAID BEFORE...

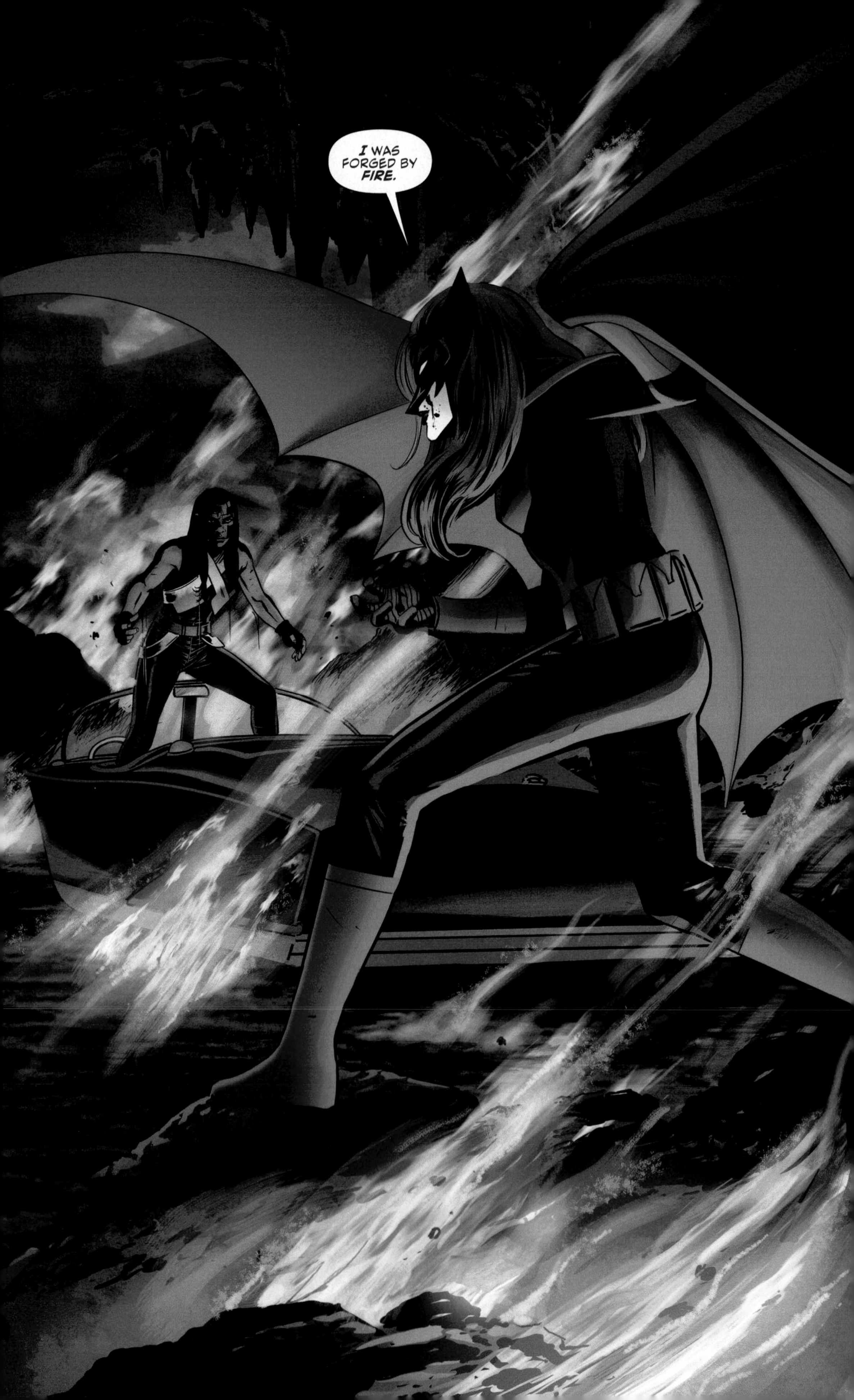
I WAS FORGED BY FIRE.

THE MANY ARMS OF DEATH ARE STILL OUT THERE.

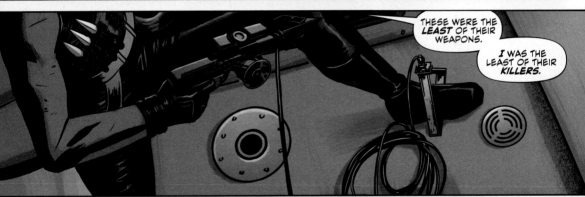

THESE WERE THE *LEAST* OF THEIR WEAPONS.

I WAS THE LEAST OF THEIR *KILLERS.*

KEEP CORYANA.

WATCH IT *ROT* IN FRONT OF YOUR EYES.

I'LL RETURN TO SERVE THE MANY ARMS.

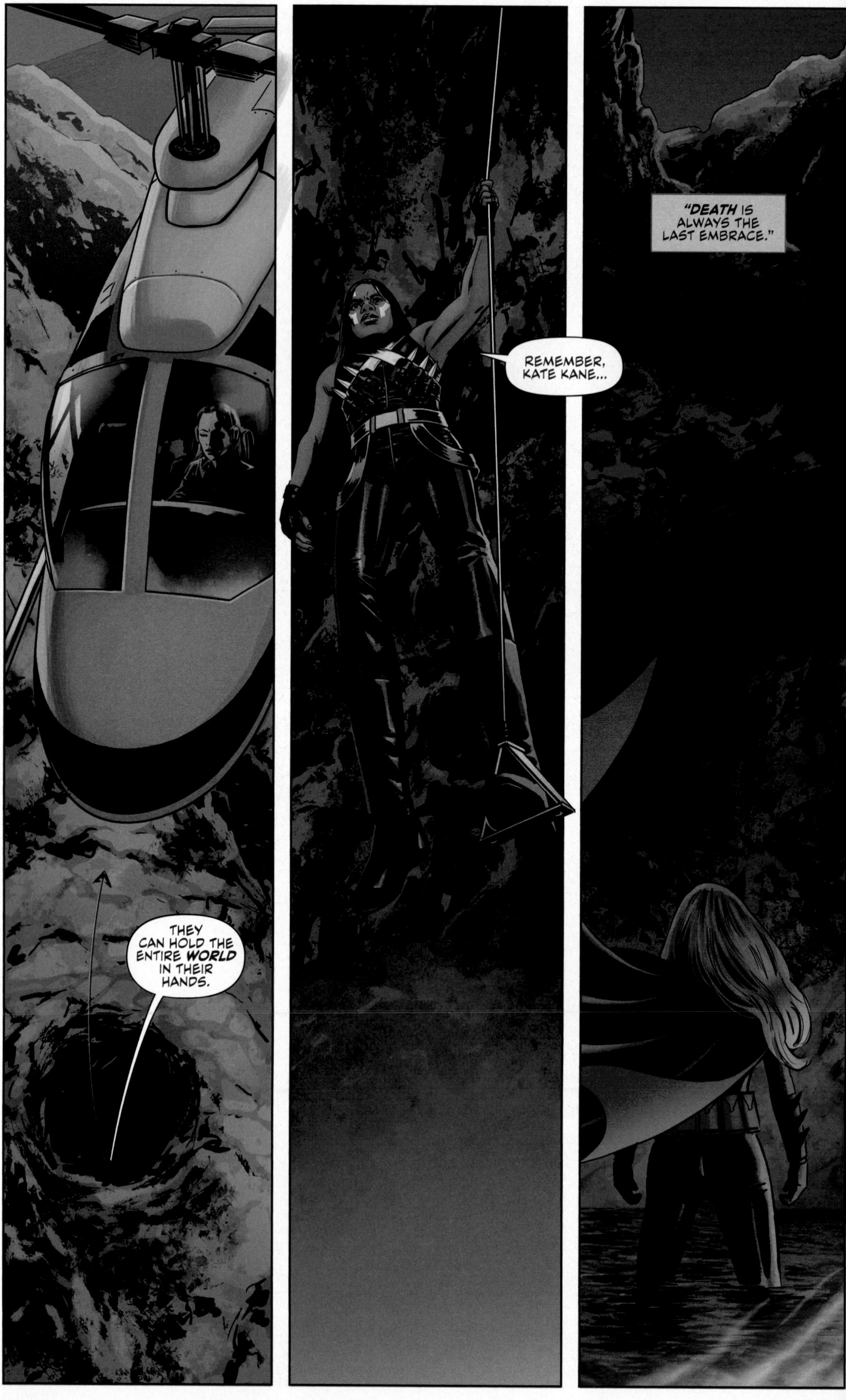
THEY CAN HOLD THE ENTIRE WORLD IN THEIR HANDS.
REMEMBER, KATE KANE...
"DEATH IS ALWAYS THE LAST EMBRACE."

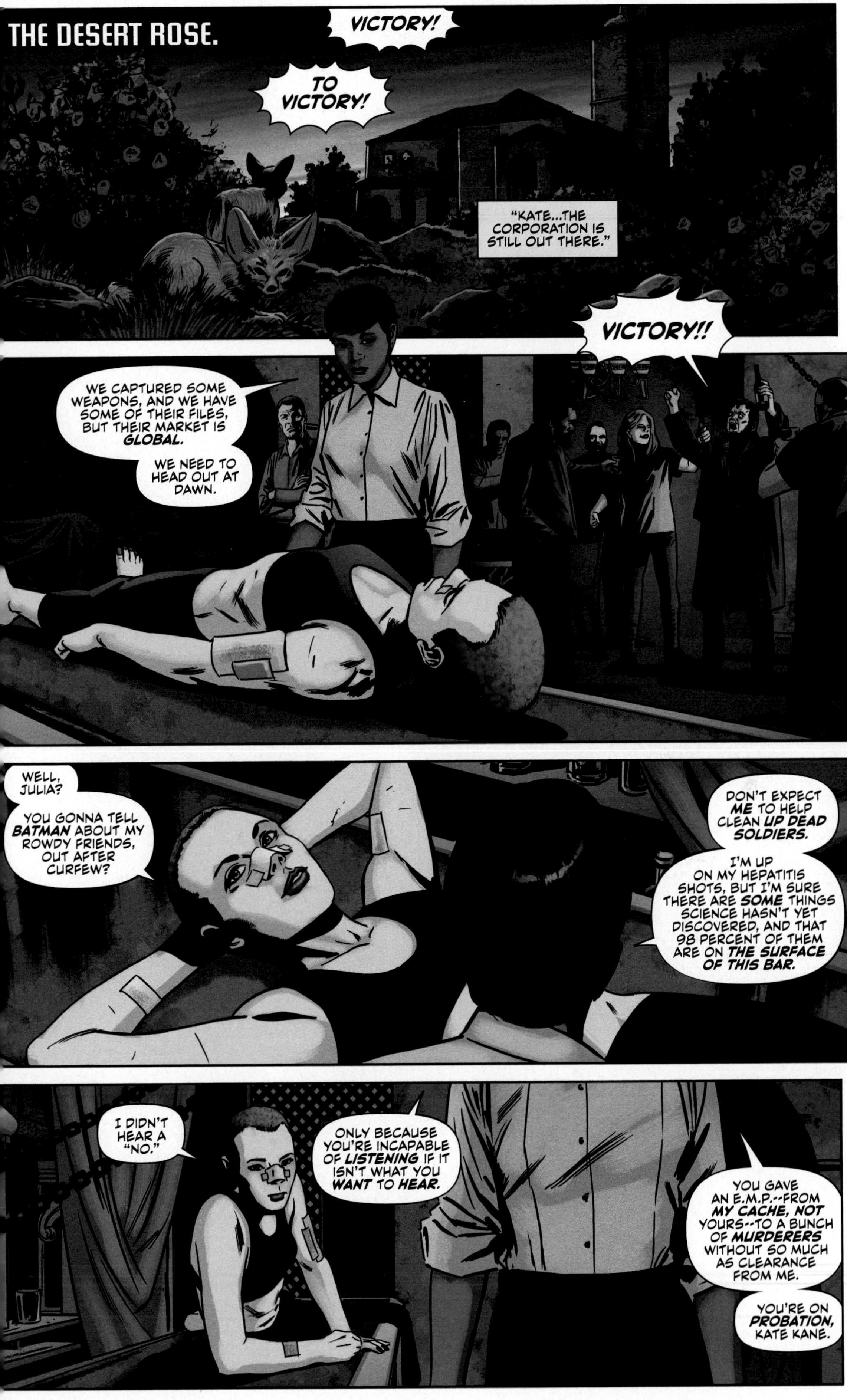
THE DESERT ROSE.
VICTORY!
TO VICTORY!
"KATE...THE CORPORATION IS STILL OUT THERE."
VICTORY!!
WE CAPTURED SOME WEAPONS, AND WE HAVE SOME OF THEIR FILES, BUT THEIR MARKET IS GLOBAL.
WE NEED TO HEAD OUT AT DAWN.
WELL, JULIA?
YOU GONNA TELL BATMAN ABOUT MY ROWDY FRIENDS, OUT AFTER CURFEW?
DON'T EXPECT ME TO HELP CLEAN UP DEAD SOLDIERS.
I'M UP ON MY HEPATITIS SHOTS, BUT I'M SURE THERE ARE SOME THINGS SCIENCE HASN'T YET DISCOVERED, AND THAT 98 PERCENT OF THEM ARE ON THE SURFACE OF THIS BAR.
I DIDN'T HEAR A "NO."
ONLY BECAUSE YOU'RE INCAPABLE OF LISTENING IF IT ISN'T WHAT YOU WANT TO HEAR.
YOU GAVE AN E.M.P.--FROM MY CACHE, NOT YOURS--TO A BUNCH OF MURDERERS WITHOUT SO MUCH AS CLEARANCE FROM ME.
YOU'RE ON PROBATION, KATE KANE.

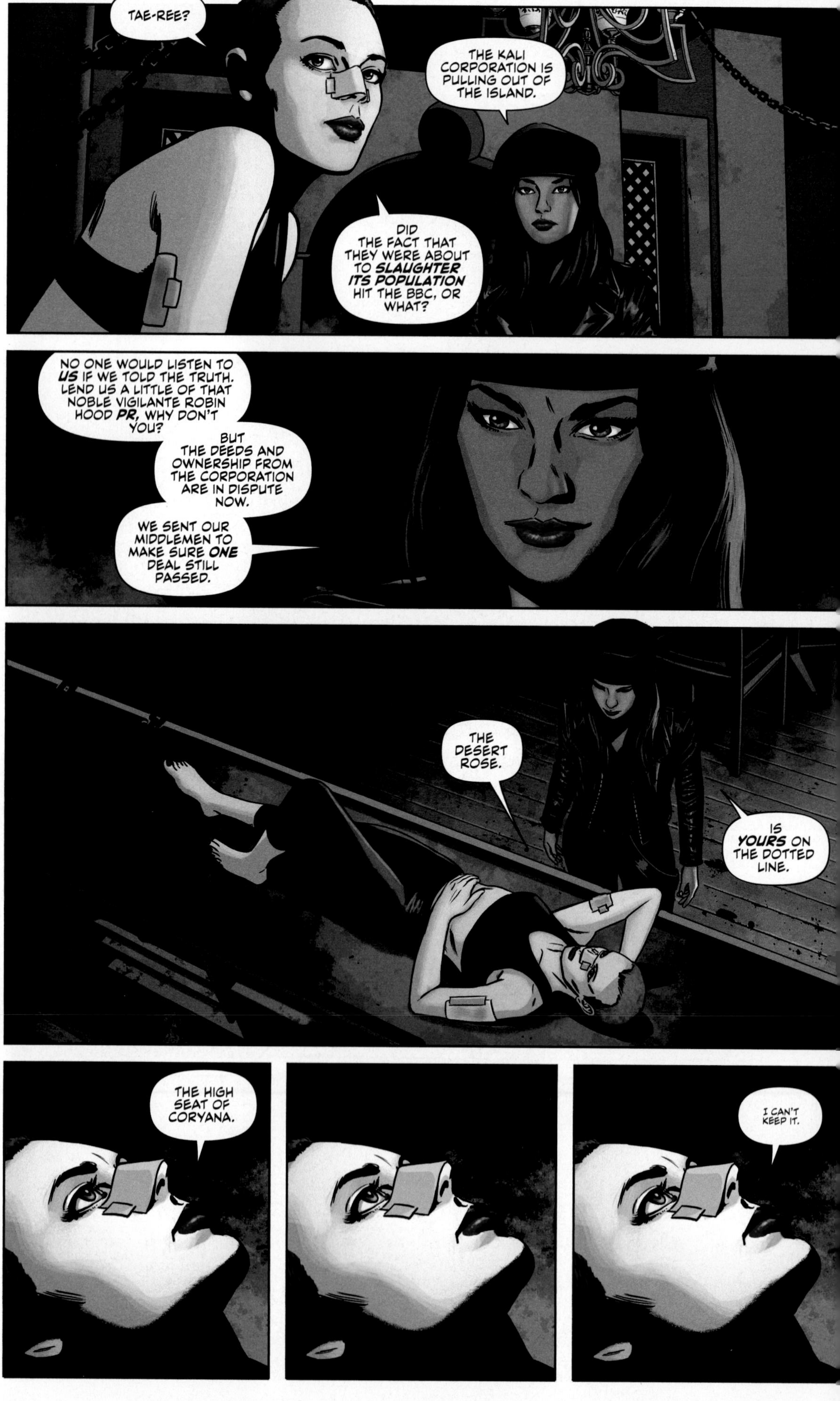
TAE-REE?
THE KALI CORPORATION IS PULLING OUT OF THE ISLAND.
DID THE FACT THAT THEY WERE ABOUT TO SLAUGHTER ITS POPULATION HIT THE BBC, OR WHAT?
NO ONE WOULD LISTEN TO US IF WE TOLD THE TRUTH. LEND US A LITTLE OF THAT NOBLE VIGILANTE ROBIN HOOD PR, WHY DON'T YOU?
BUT THE DEEDS AND OWNERSHIP FROM THE CORPORATION ARE IN DISPUTE NOW.
WE SENT OUR MIDDLEMEN TO MAKE SURE ONE DEAL STILL PASSED.
THE DESERT ROSE.
IS YOURS ON THE DOTTED LINE.
THE HIGH SEAT OF CORYANA.
I CAN'T KEEP IT.

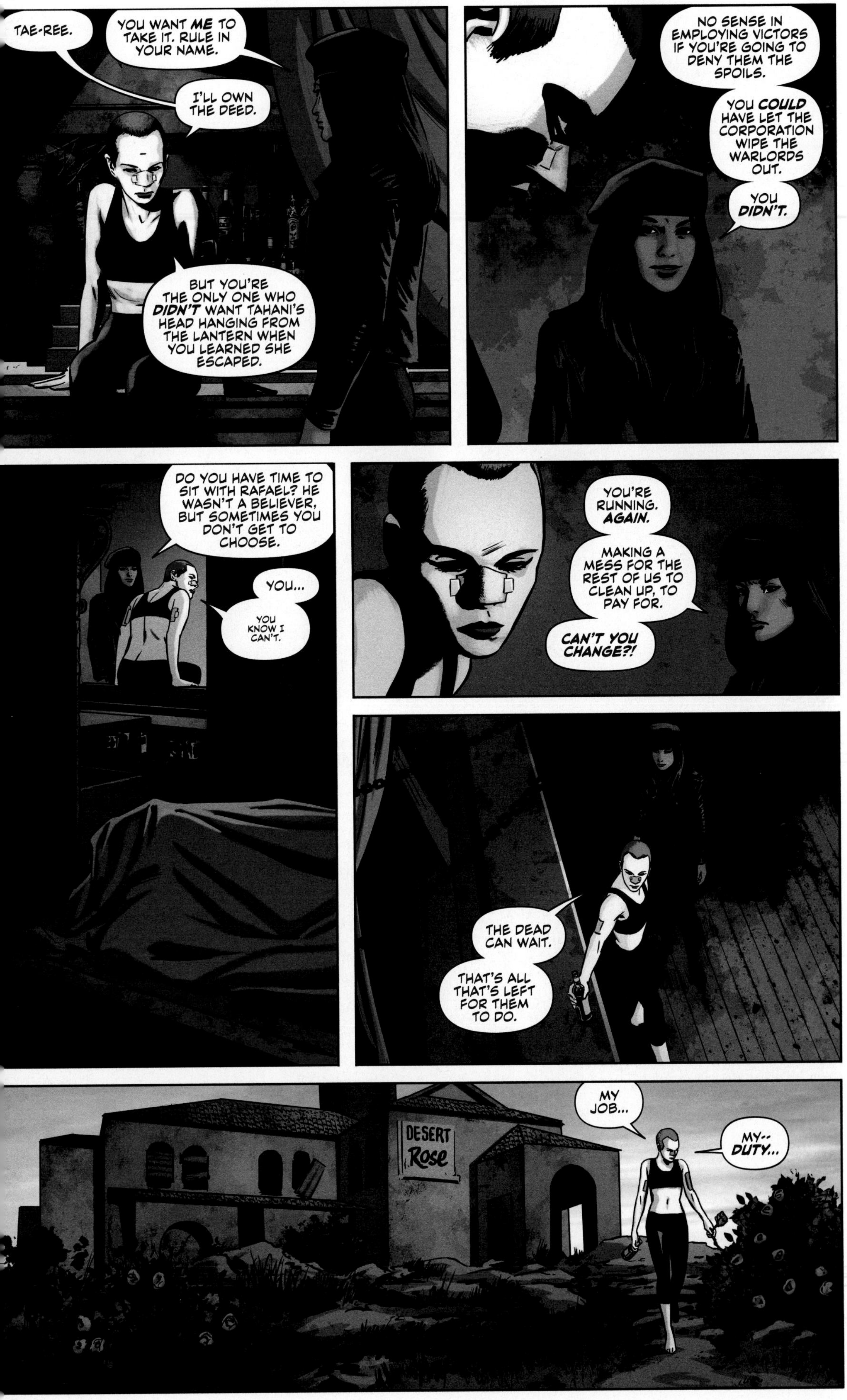
TAE-REE.
YOU WANT ME TO TAKE IT. RULE IN YOUR NAME.
I'LL OWN THE DEED.
BUT YOU'RE THE ONLY ONE WHO DIDN'T WANT TAHANI'S HEAD HANGING FROM THE LANTERN WHEN YOU LEARNED SHE ESCAPED.
NO SENSE IN EMPLOYING VICTORS IF YOU'RE GOING TO DENY THEM THE SPOILS.
YOU COULD HAVE LET THE CORPORATION WIPE THE WARLORDS OUT.
YOU DIDN'T.
DO YOU HAVE TIME TO SIT WITH RAFAEL? HE WASN'T A BELIEVER, BUT SOMETIMES YOU DON'T GET TO CHOOSE.
YOU...
YOU KNOW I CAN'T.
YOU'RE RUNNING. AGAIN.
MAKING A MESS FOR THE REST OF US TO CLEAN UP, TO PAY FOR.
CAN'T YOU CHANGE?!
THE DEAD CAN WAIT.
THAT'S ALL THAT'S LEFT FOR THEM TO DO.
DESERT Rose
MY JOB...
MY.. DUTY...

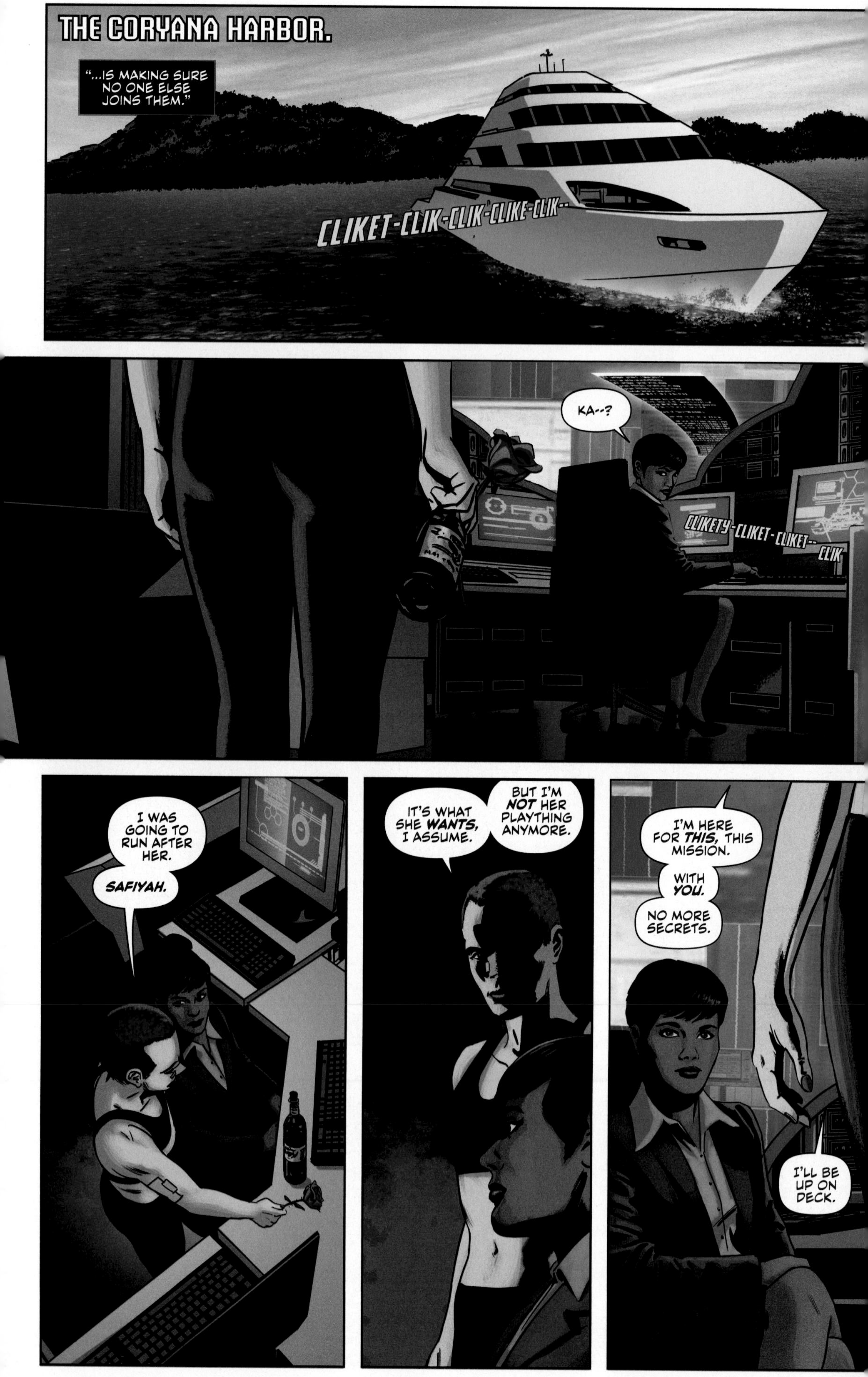

THE CORYANA HARBOR.
"...IS MAKING SURE NO ONE ELSE JOINS THEM."
CLIKET-CLIK-CLIK-CLIKE-CLIK--
KA--?
CLIKETY-CLIKET-CLIKET--CLIK
I WAS GOING TO RUN AFTER HER.
SAFIYAH.
IT'S WHAT SHE WANTS, I ASSUME.
BUT I'M NOT HER PLAYTHING ANYMORE.
I'M HERE FOR THIS, THIS MISSION.
WITH YOU.
NO MORE SECRETS.
I'LL BE UP ON DECK.

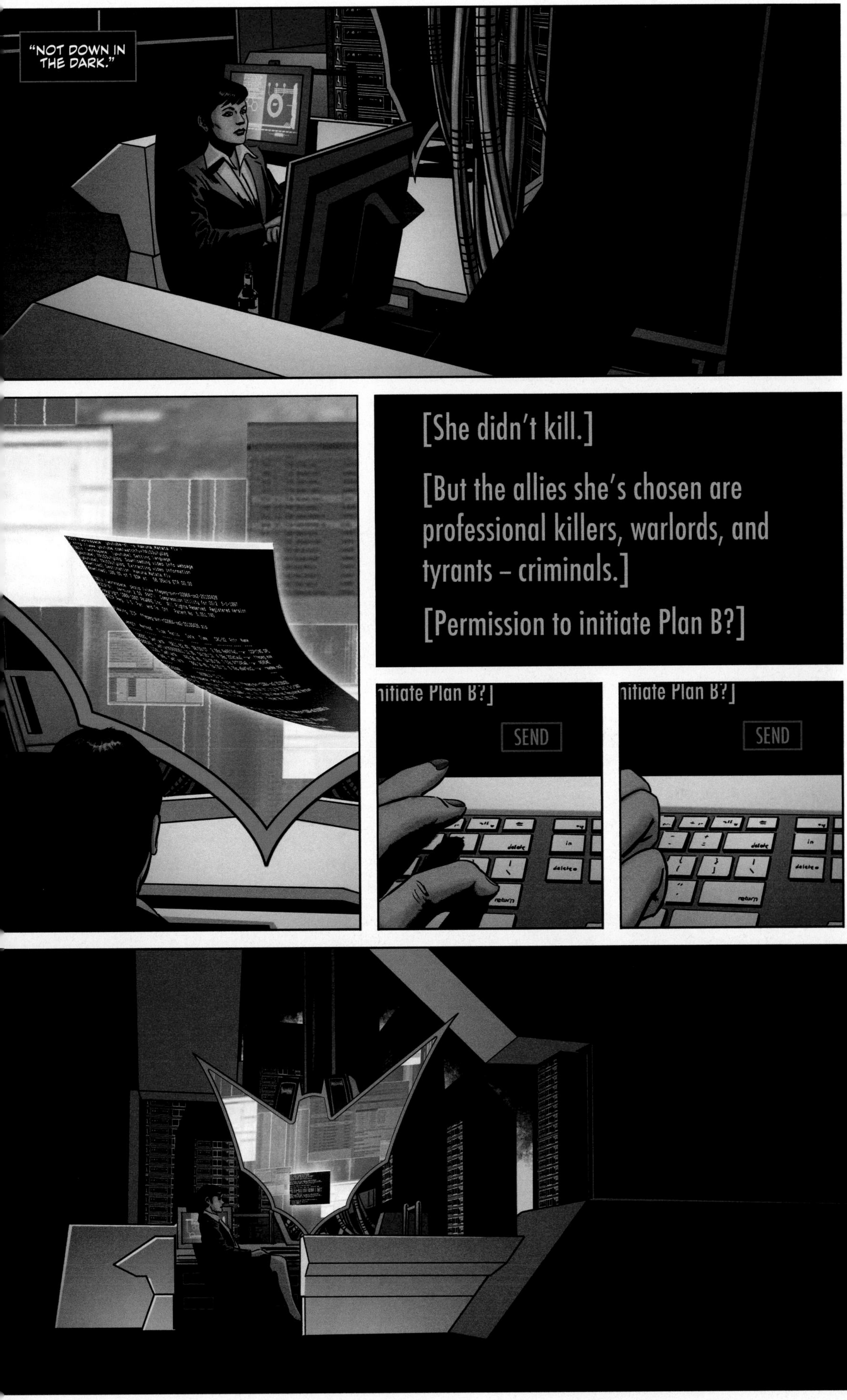
"NOT DOWN IN THE DARK."
[She didn't kill.]
[But the allies she's chosen are professional killers, warlords, and tyrants – criminals.]
[Permission to initiate Plan B?]
nitiate Plan B?]
SEND
nitiate Plan B?]
SEND

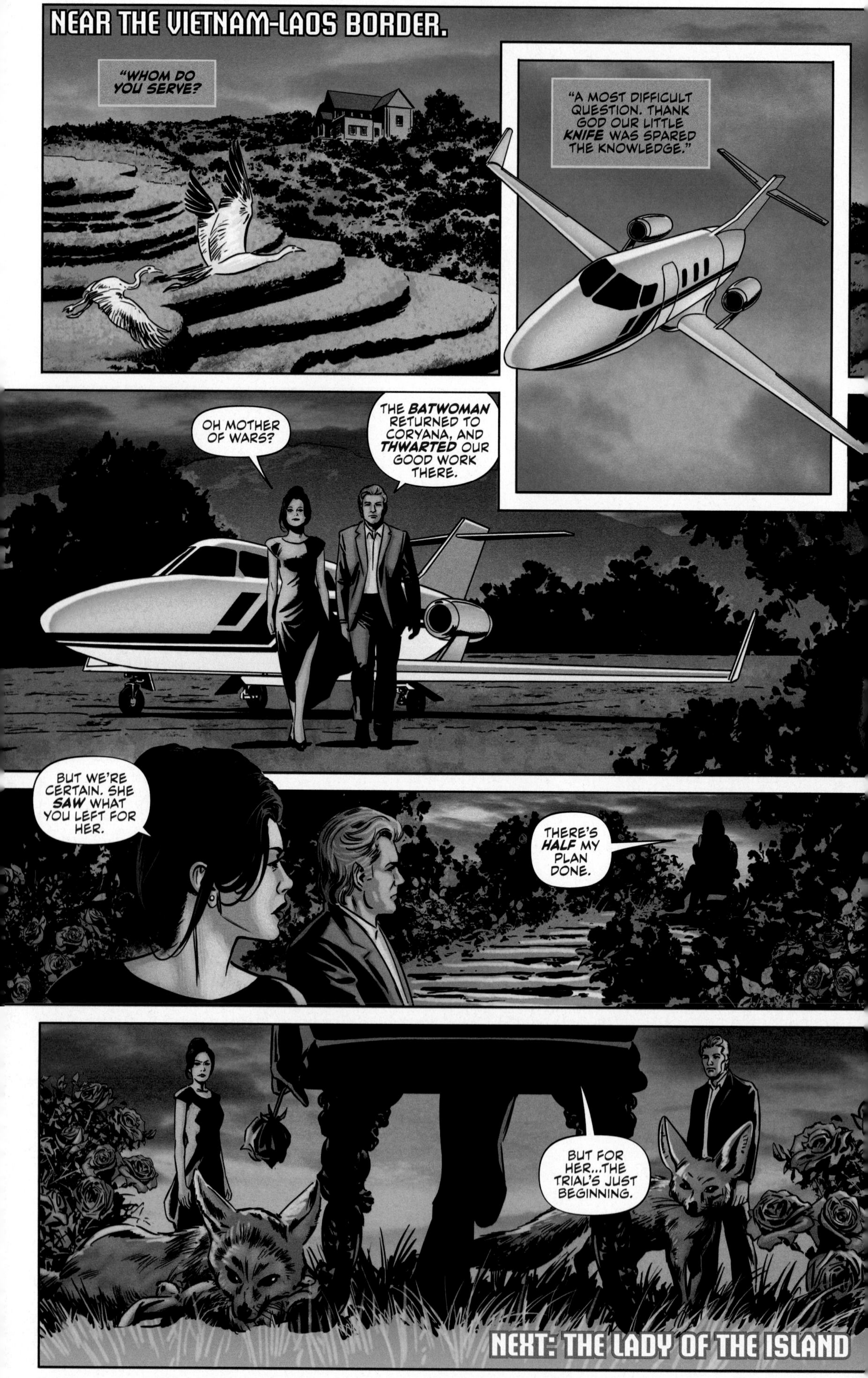
NEAR THE VIETNAM-LAOS BORDER.
"WHOM DO YOU SERVE?
"A MOST DIFFICULT QUESTION. THANK GOD OUR LITTLE KNIFE WAS SPARED THE KNOWLEDGE."
OH MOTHER OF WARS?
THE BATWOMAN RETURNED TO CORYANA, AND THWARTED OUR GOOD WORK THERE.
BUT WE'RE CERTAIN. SHE SAW WHAT YOU LEFT FOR HER.
THERE'S HALF MY PLAN DONE.
BUT FOR HER...THE TRIAL'S JUST BEGINNING.
NEXT: THE LADY OF THE ISLAND

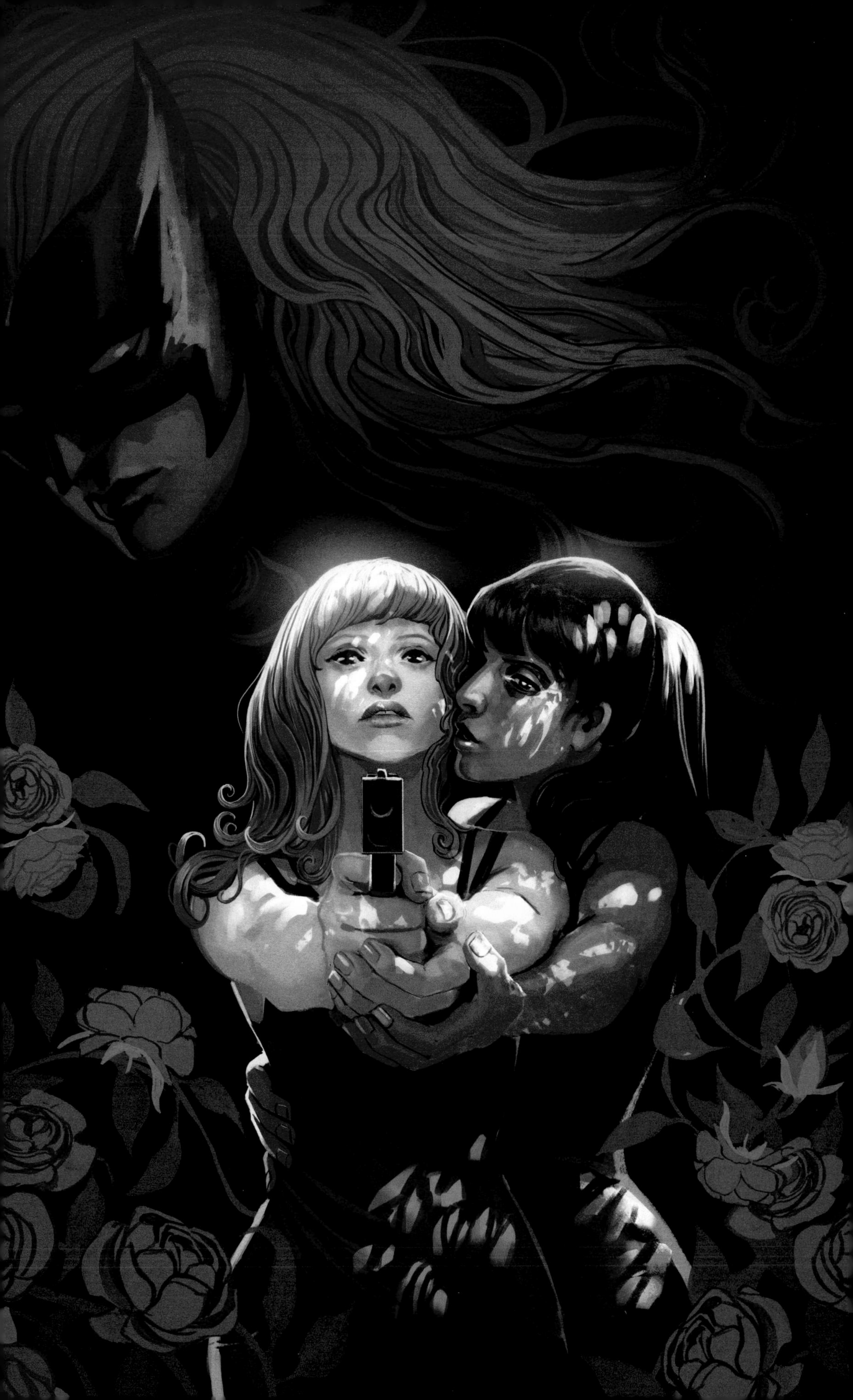

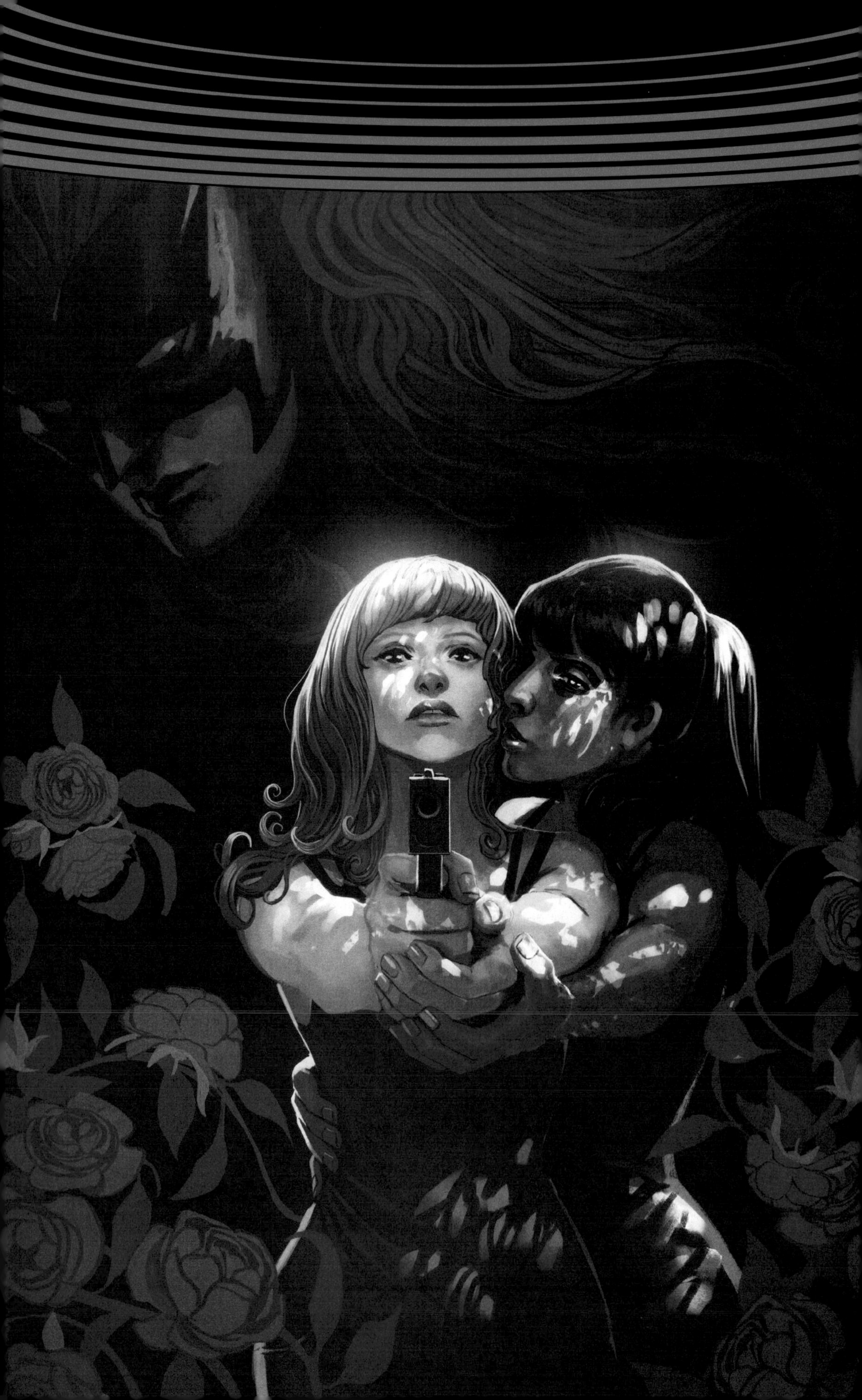

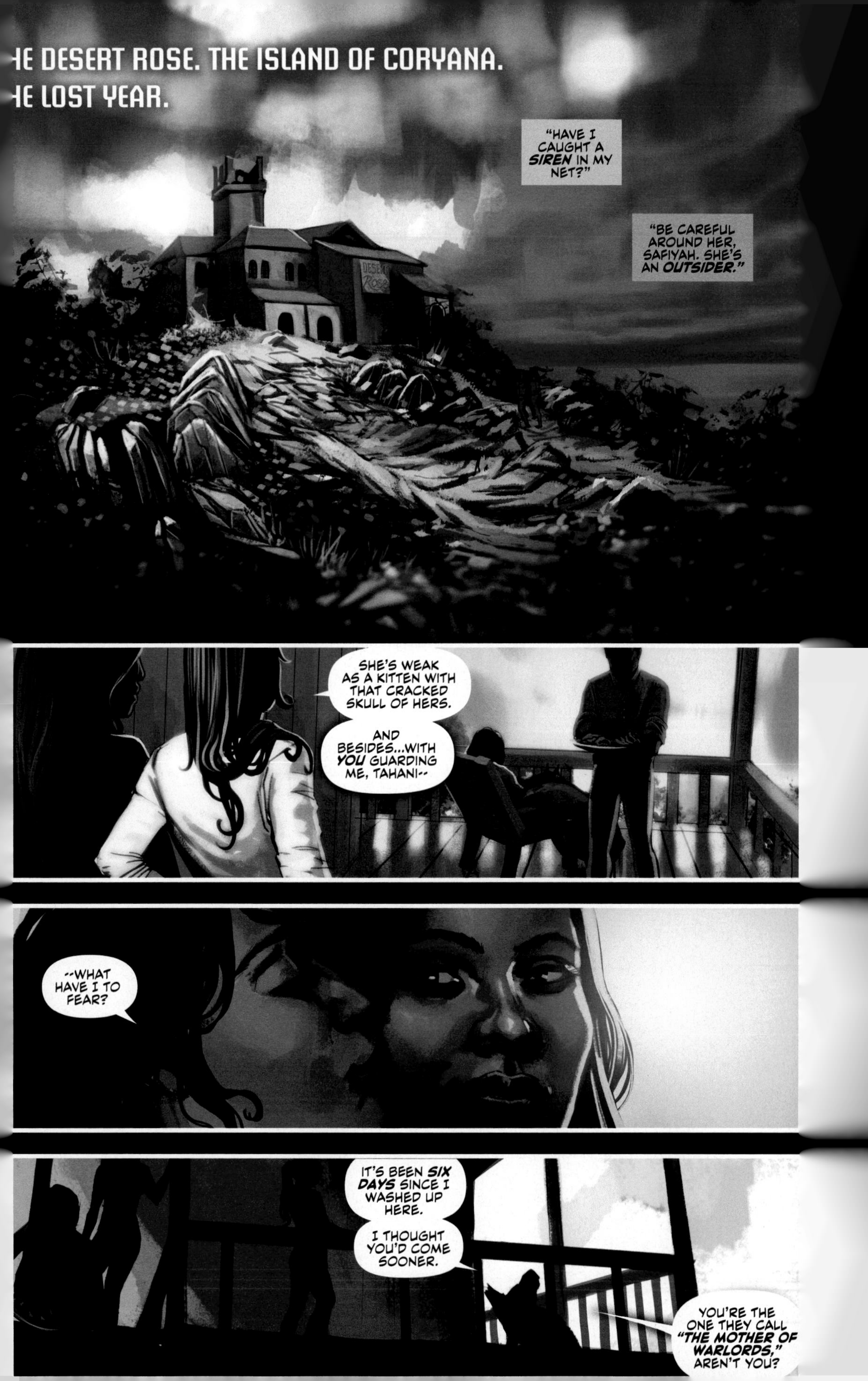
HE DESERT ROSE. THE ISLAND OF CORYANA.
HE LOST YEAR.
"HAVE I CAUGHT A SIREN IN MY NET?"
"BE CAREFUL AROUND HER, SAFIYAH. SHE'S AN OUTSIDER."
DESERT ROSE
SHE'S WEAK AS A KITTEN WITH THAT CRACKED SKULL OF HERS.
AND BESIDES...WITH YOU GUARDING ME, TAHANI--
--WHAT HAVE I TO FEAR?
IT'S BEEN SIX DAYS SINCE I WASHED UP HERE.
I THOUGHT YOU'D COME SOONER.
YOU'RE THE ONE THEY CALL "THE MOTHER OF WARLORDS," AREN'T YOU?

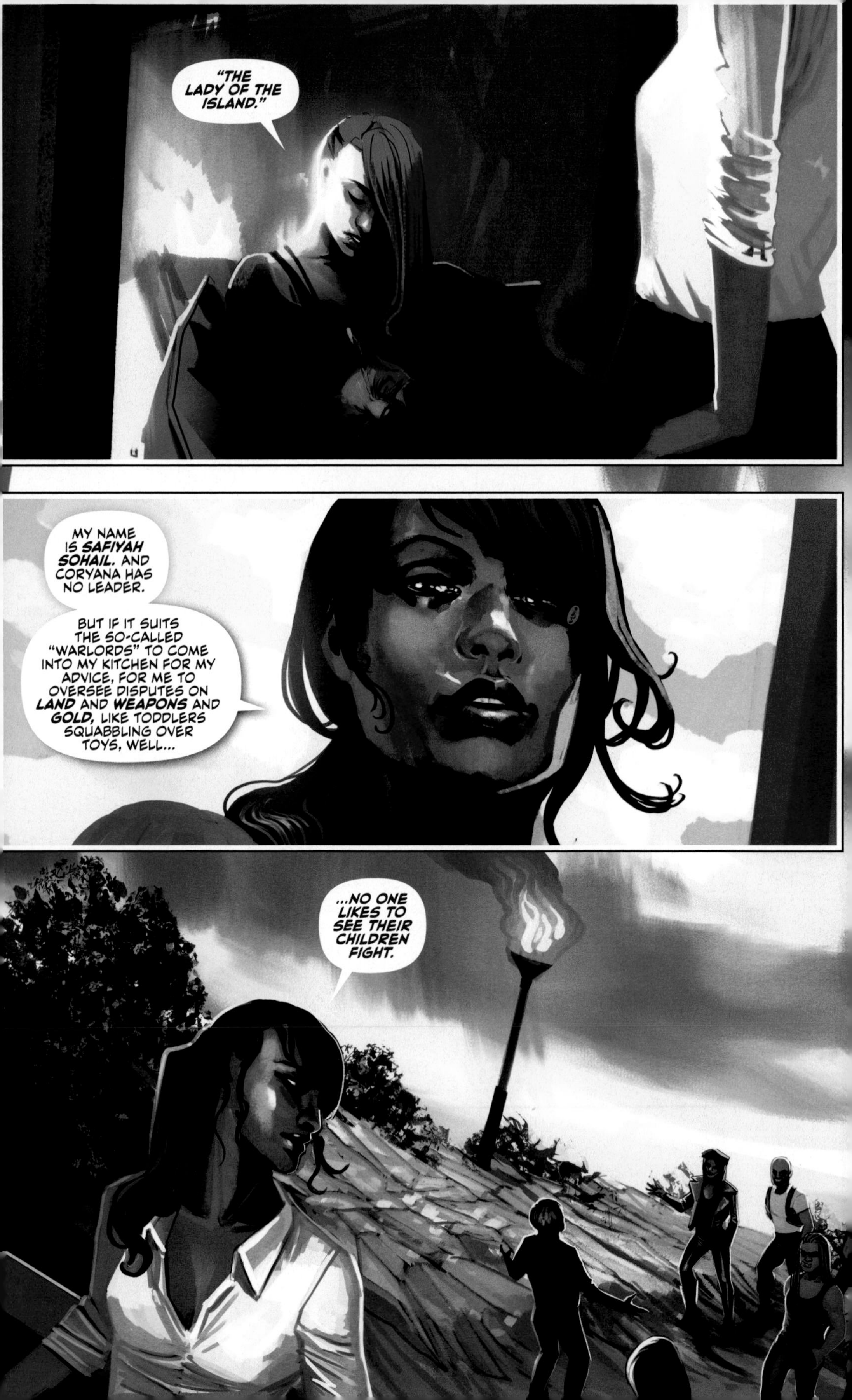
"THE LADY OF THE ISLAND."
MY NAME IS SAFIYAH SOHAIL. AND CORYANA HAS NO LEADER.
BUT IF IT SUITS THE SO-CALLED "WARLORDS" TO COME INTO MY KITCHEN FOR MY ADVICE, FOR ME TO OVERSEE DISPUTES ON LAND AND WEAPONS AND GOLD, LIKE TODDLERS SQUABBLING OVER TOYS, WELL...
...NO ONE LIKES TO SEE THEIR CHILDREN FIGHT.

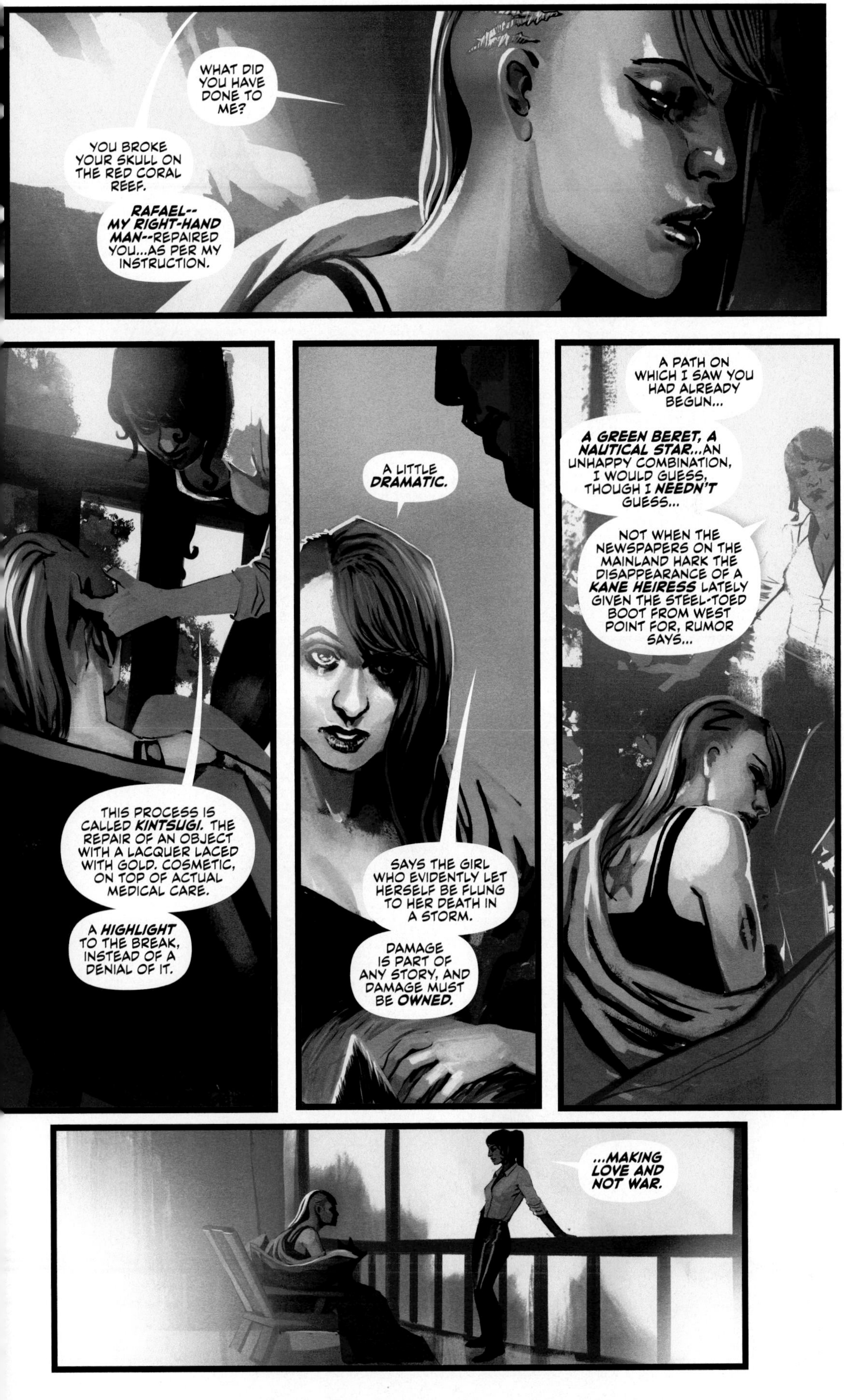
WHAT DID YOU HAVE DONE TO ME?
YOU BROKE YOUR SKULL ON THE RED CORAL REEF.
RAFAEL-- MY RIGHT-HAND MAN--REPAIRED YOU...AS PER MY INSTRUCTION.
THIS PROCESS IS CALLED KINTSUGI. THE REPAIR OF AN OBJECT WITH A LACQUER LACED WITH GOLD. COSMETIC, ON TOP OF ACTUAL MEDICAL CARE.
A HIGHLIGHT TO THE BREAK, INSTEAD OF A DENIAL OF IT.
A LITTLE DRAMATIC.
SAYS THE GIRL WHO EVIDENTLY LET HERSELF BE FLUNG TO HER DEATH IN A STORM.
DAMAGE IS PART OF ANY STORY, AND DAMAGE MUST BE OWNED.
A PATH ON WHICH I SAW YOU HAD ALREADY BEGUN...
A GREEN BERET, A NAUTICAL STAR...AN UNHAPPY COMBINATION, I WOULD GUESS, THOUGH I NEEDN'T GUESS...
NOT WHEN THE NEWSPAPERS ON THE MAINLAND HARK THE DISAPPEARANCE OF A KANE HEIRESS LATELY GIVEN THE STEEL-TOED BOOT FROM WEST POINT FOR, RUMOR SAYS...
...MAKING LOVE AND NOT WAR.

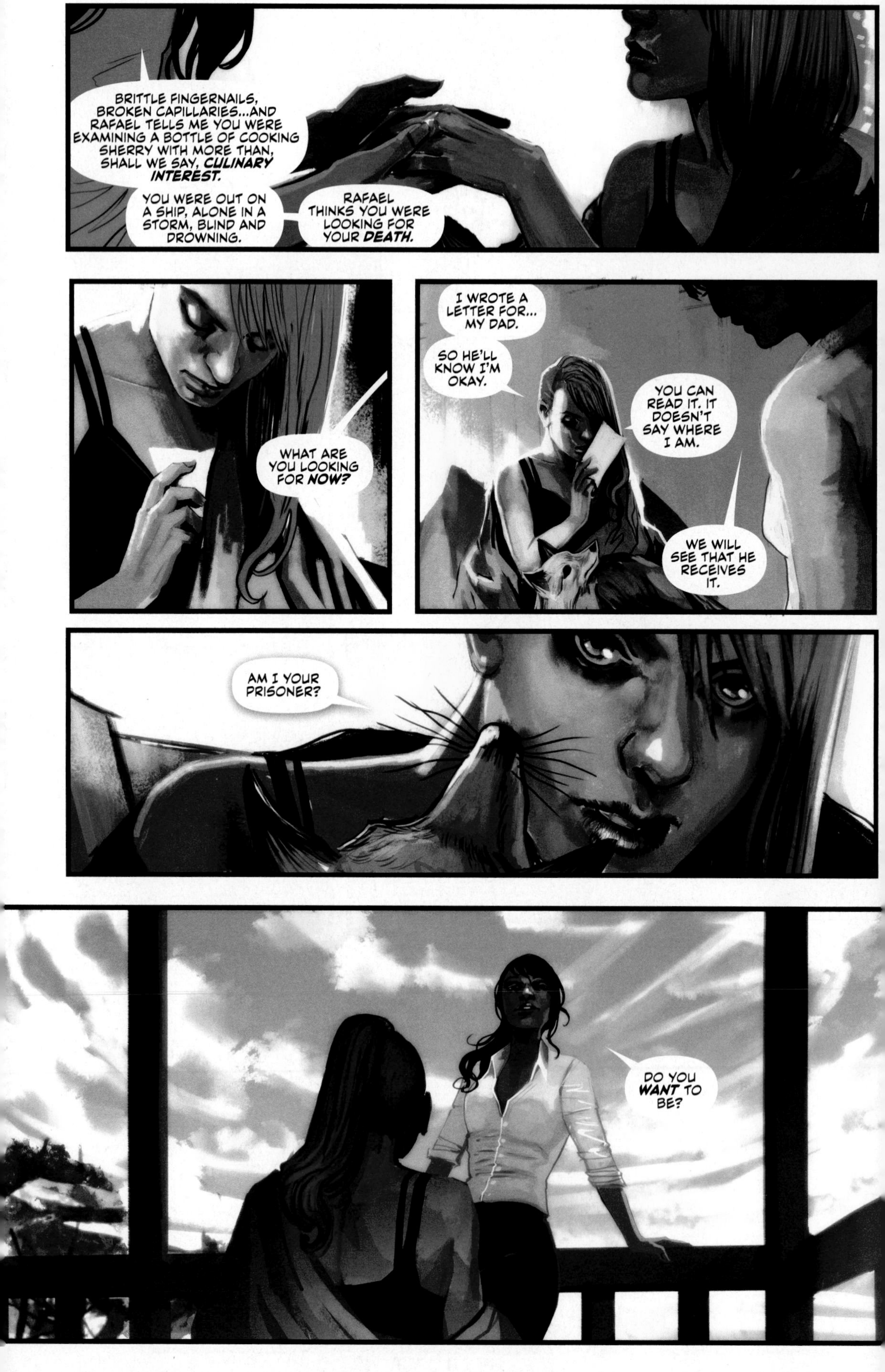
BRITTLE FINGERNAILS, BROKEN CAPILLARIES...AND RAFAEL TELLS ME YOU WERE EXAMINING A BOTTLE OF COOKING SHERRY WITH MORE THAN, SHALL WE SAY, CULINARY INTEREST.
YOU WERE OUT ON A SHIP, ALONE IN A STORM, BLIND AND DROWNING.
RAFAEL THINKS YOU WERE LOOKING FOR YOUR DEATH.
WHAT ARE YOU LOOKING FOR NOW?
I WROTE A LETTER FOR... MY DAD.
SO HE'LL KNOW I'M OKAY.
YOU CAN READ IT. IT DOESN'T SAY WHERE I AM.
WE WILL SEE THAT HE RECEIVES IT.
AM I YOUR PRISONER?
DO YOU WANT TO BE?

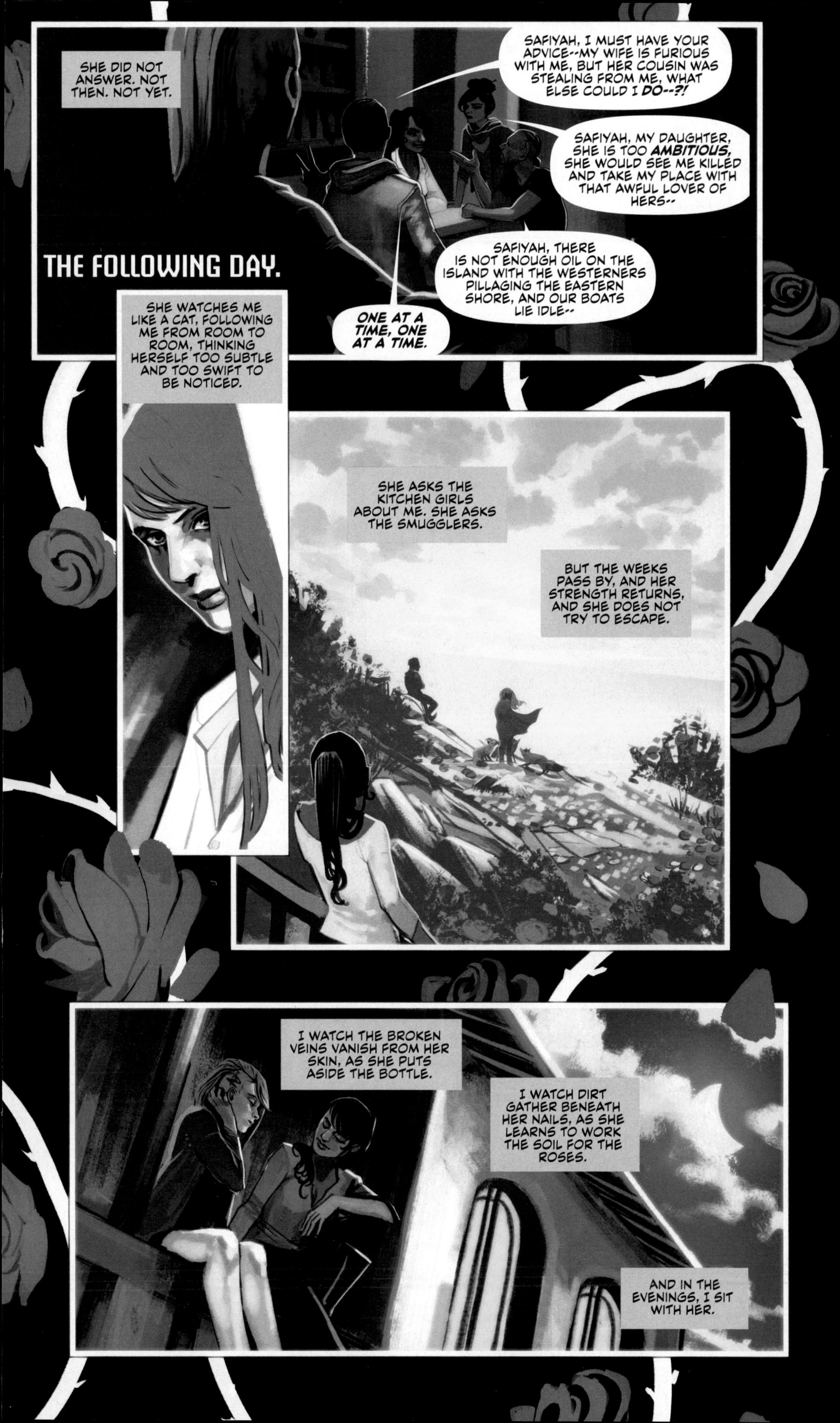
SHE DID NOT ANSWER. NOT THEN. NOT YET.
THE FOLLOWING DAY.
SAFIYAH, I MUST HAVE YOUR ADVICE--MY WIFE IS FURIOUS WITH ME, BUT HER COUSIN WAS STEALING FROM ME, WHAT ELSE COULD I DO--?!
SAFIYAH, MY DAUGHTER, SHE IS TOO AMBITIOUS, SHE WOULD SEE ME KILLED AND TAKE MY PLACE WITH THAT AWFUL LOVER OF HERS--
SAFIYAH, THERE IS NOT ENOUGH OIL ON THE ISLAND WITH THE WESTERNERS PILLAGING THE EASTERN SHORE, AND OUR BOATS LIE IDLE--
ONE AT A TIME, ONE AT A TIME.
SHE WATCHES ME LIKE A CAT, FOLLOWING ME FROM ROOM TO ROOM, THINKING HERSELF TOO SUBTLE AND TOO SWIFT TO BE NOTICED.
SHE ASKS THE KITCHEN GIRLS ABOUT ME. SHE ASKS THE SMUGGLERS.
BUT THE WEEKS PASS BY, AND HER STRENGTH RETURNS, AND SHE DOES NOT TRY TO ESCAPE.
I WATCH THE BROKEN VEINS VANISH FROM HER SKIN, AS SHE PUTS ASIDE THE BOTTLE.
I WATCH DIRT GATHER BENEATH HER NAILS, AS SHE LEARNS TO WORK THE SOIL FOR THE ROSES.
AND IN THE EVENINGS, I SIT WITH HER.

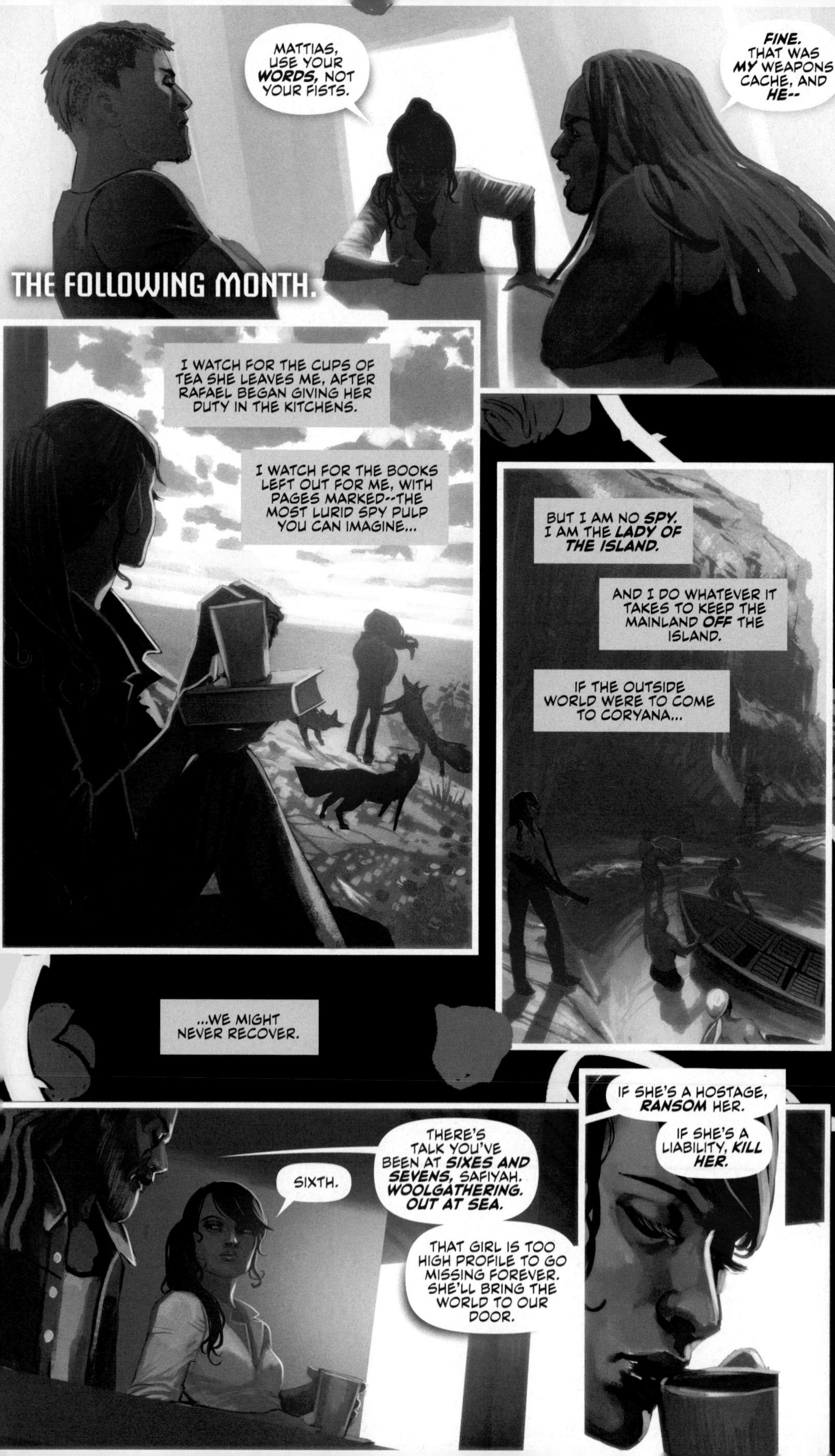
MATTIAS, USE YOUR WORDS, NOT YOUR FISTS.
FINE. THAT WAS MY WEAPONS CACHE, AND HE--
THE FOLLOWING MONTH.
I WATCH FOR THE CUPS OF TEA SHE LEAVES ME, AFTER RAFAEL BEGAN GIVING HER DUTY IN THE KITCHENS.
I WATCH FOR THE BOOKS LEFT OUT FOR ME, WITH PAGES MARKED--THE MOST LURID SPY PULP YOU CAN IMAGINE...
BUT I AM NO SPY. I AM THE LADY OF THE ISLAND.
AND I DO WHATEVER IT TAKES TO KEEP THE MAINLAND OFF THE ISLAND.
IF THE OUTSIDE WORLD WERE TO COME TO CORYANA...
...WE MIGHT NEVER RECOVER.
THERE'S TALK YOU'VE BEEN AT SIXES AND SEVENS, SAFIYAH. WOOLGATHERING. OUT AT SEA.
SIXTH.
THAT GIRL IS TOO HIGH PROFILE TO GO MISSING FOREVER. SHE'LL BRING THE WORLD TO OUR DOOR.
IF SHE'S A HOSTAGE, RANSOM HER.
IF SHE'S A LIABILITY, KILL HER.

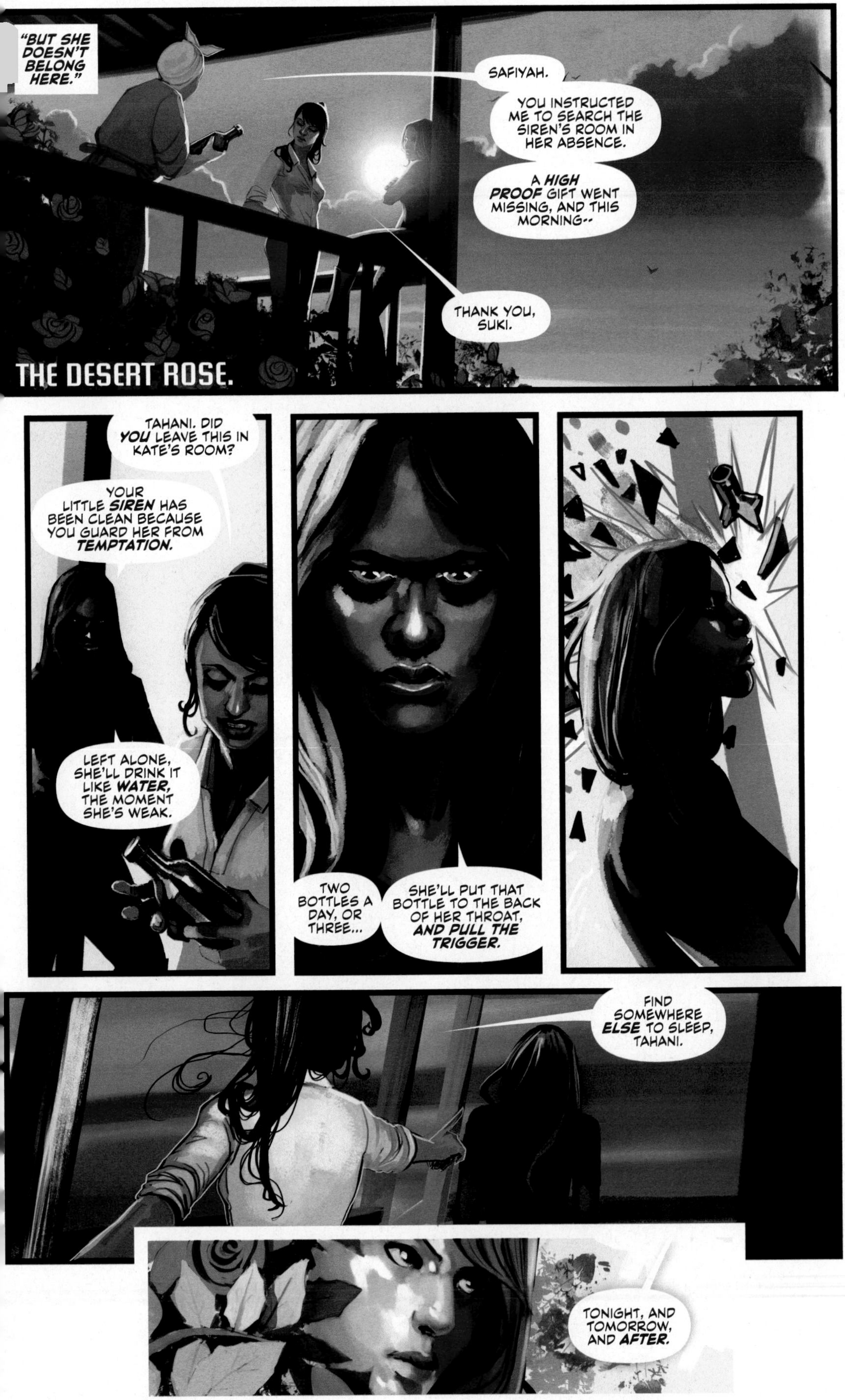

"BUT SHE DOESN'T BELONG HERE."
SAFIYAH.
YOU INSTRUCTED ME TO SEARCH THE SIREN'S ROOM IN HER ABSENCE.
A HIGH PROOF GIFT WENT MISSING, AND THIS MORNING--
THANK YOU, SUKI.
THE DESERT ROSE.
TAHANI. DID YOU LEAVE THIS IN KATE'S ROOM?
YOUR LITTLE SIREN HAS BEEN CLEAN BECAUSE YOU GUARD HER FROM TEMPTATION.
LEFT ALONE, SHE'LL DRINK IT LIKE WATER, THE MOMENT SHE'S WEAK.
TWO BOTTLES A DAY, OR THREE...
SHE'LL PUT THAT BOTTLE TO THE BACK OF HER THROAT, AND PULL THE TRIGGER.
FIND SOMEWHERE ELSE TO SLEEP, TAHANI.
TONIGHT, AND TOMORROW, AND AFTER.

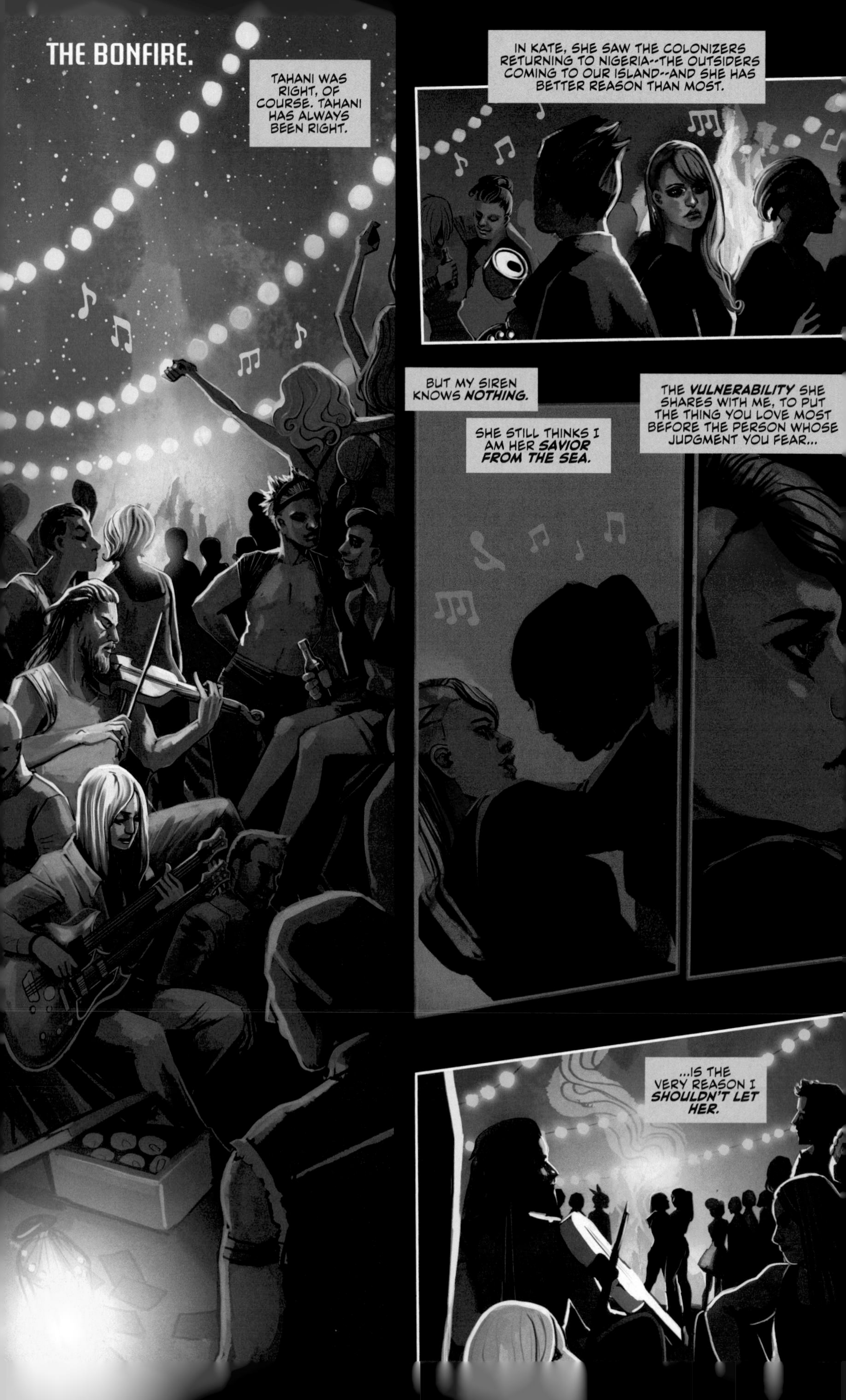
THE BONFIRE.
TAHANI WAS RIGHT, OF COURSE. TAHANI HAS ALWAYS BEEN RIGHT.
IN KATE, SHE SAW THE COLONIZERS RETURNING TO NIGERIA--THE OUTSIDERS COMING TO OUR ISLAND--AND SHE HAS BETTER REASON THAN MOST.
BUT MY SIREN KNOWS NOTHING.
SHE STILL THINKS I AM HER SAVIOR FROM THE SEA.
THE VULNERABILITY SHE SHARES WITH ME, TO PUT THE THING YOU LOVE MOST BEFORE THE PERSON WHOSE JUDGMENT YOU FEAR...
...IS THE VERY REASON I SHOULDN'T LET HER.

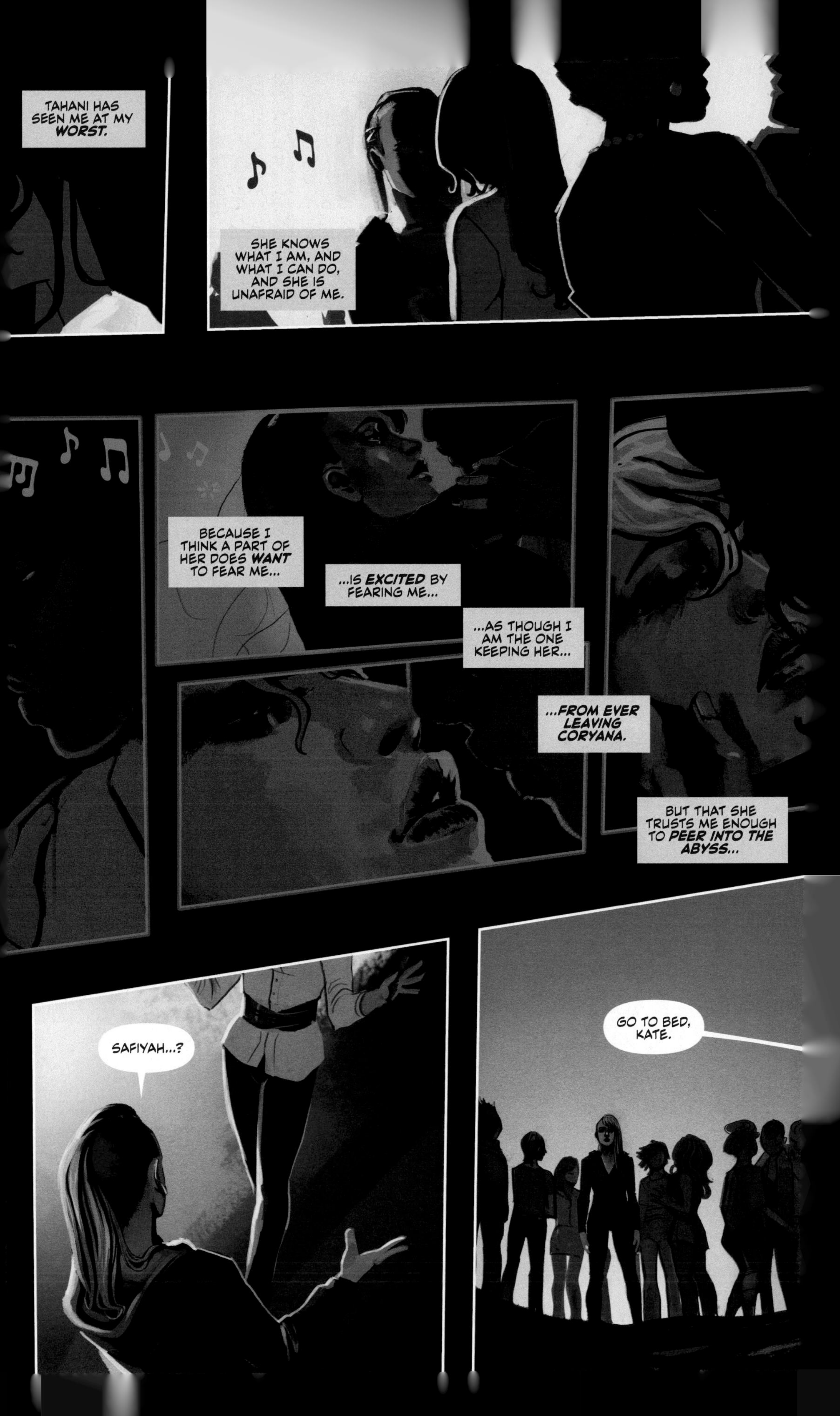

TAHANI HAS SEEN ME AT MY WORST.
SHE KNOWS WHAT I AM, AND WHAT I CAN DO, AND SHE IS UNAFRAID OF ME.
BECAUSE I THINK A PART OF HER DOES WANT TO FEAR ME...
...IS EXCITED BY FEARING ME...
...AS THOUGH I AM THE ONE KEEPING HER...
...FROM EVER LEAVING CORYANA.
BUT THAT SHE TRUSTS ME ENOUGH TO PEER INTO THE ABYSS...
SAFIYAH...?
GO TO BED, KATE.

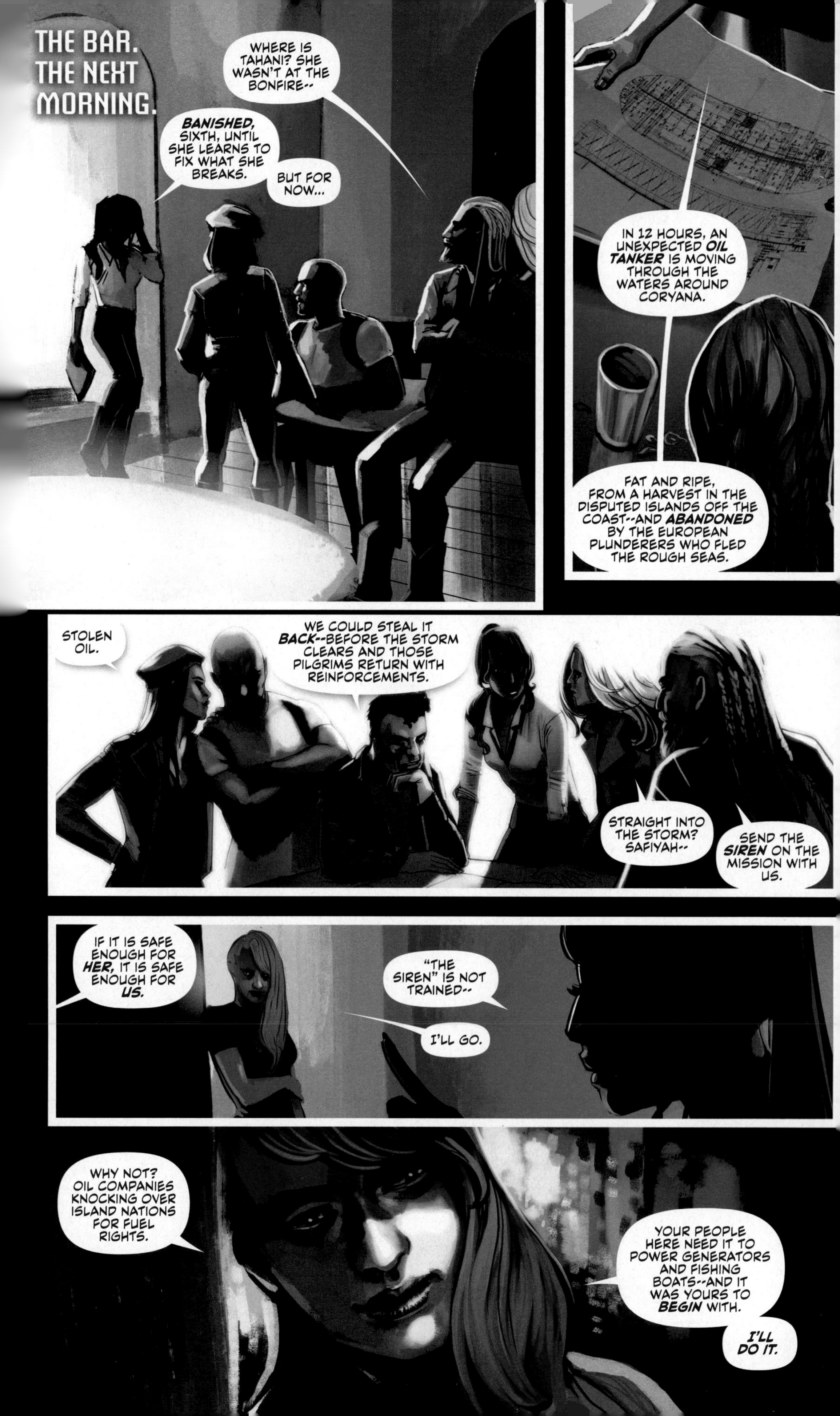
THE BAR. THE NEXT MORNING.
WHERE IS TAHANI? SHE WASN'T AT THE BONFIRE--
BANISHED, SIXTH, UNTIL SHE LEARNS TO FIX WHAT SHE BREAKS.
BUT FOR NOW...
IN 12 HOURS, AN UNEXPECTED OIL TANKER IS MOVING THROUGH THE WATERS AROUND CORYANA.
FAT AND RIPE, FROM A HARVEST IN THE DISPUTED ISLANDS OFF THE COAST--AND ABANDONED BY THE EUROPEAN PLUNDERERS WHO FLED THE ROUGH SEAS.
STOLEN OIL.
WE COULD STEAL IT BACK--BEFORE THE STORM CLEARS AND THOSE PILGRIMS RETURN WITH REINFORCEMENTS.
STRAIGHT INTO THE STORM? SAFIYAH--
SEND THE SIREN ON THE MISSION WITH US.
IF IT IS SAFE ENOUGH FOR HER, IT IS SAFE ENOUGH FOR US.
"THE SIREN" IS NOT TRAINED--
I'LL GO.
WHY NOT? OIL COMPANIES KNOCKING OVER ISLAND NATIONS FOR FUEL RIGHTS.
YOUR PEOPLE HERE NEED IT TO POWER GENERATORS AND FISHING BOATS--AND IT WAS YOURS TO BEGIN WITH.
I'LL DO IT.

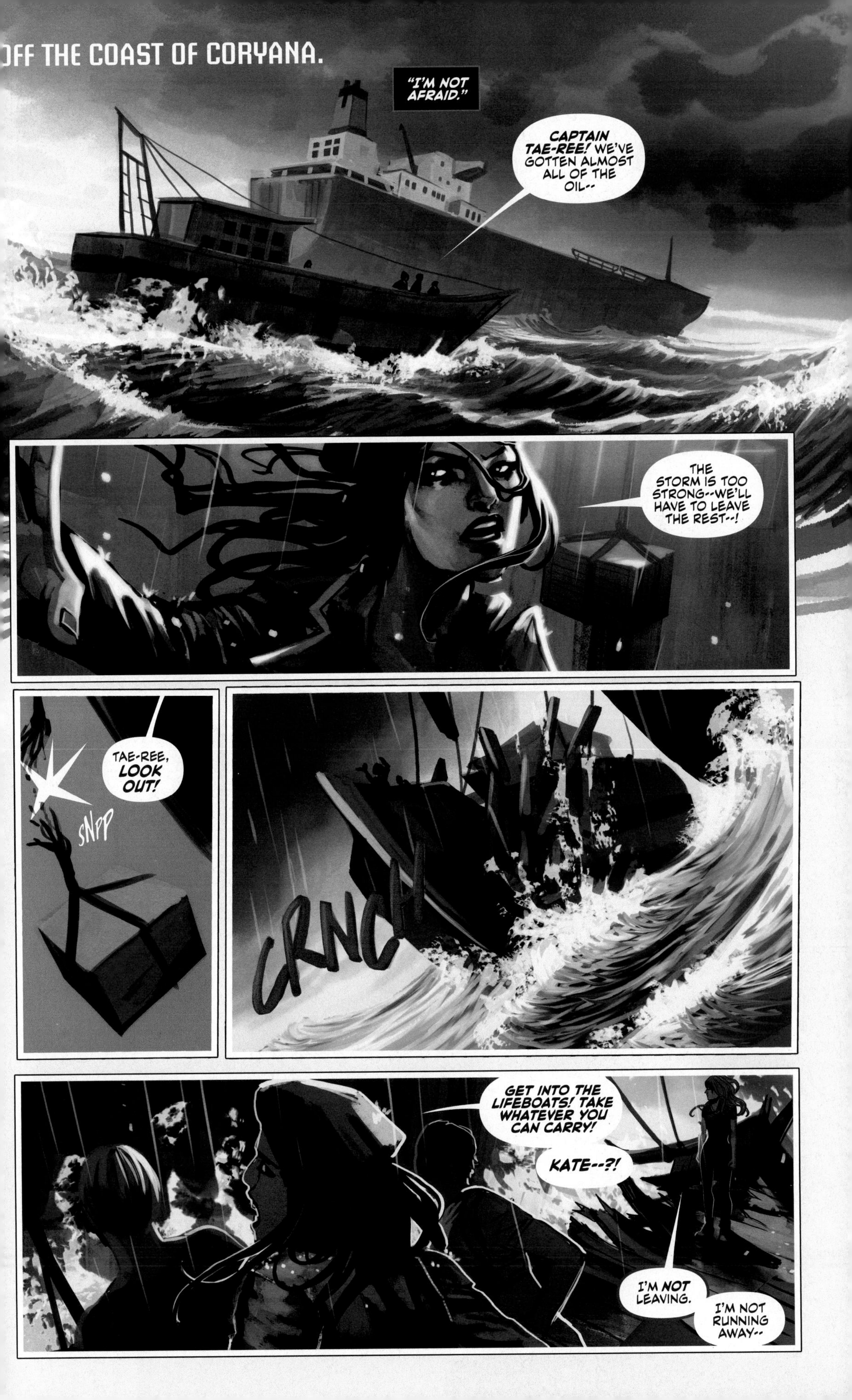
OFF THE COAST OF CORYANA.
"I'M NOT AFRAID."
CAPTAIN TAE-REE! WE'VE GOTTEN ALMOST ALL OF THE OIL--
THE STORM IS TOO STRONG--WE'LL HAVE TO LEAVE THE REST--!
TAE-REE, LOOK OUT!
SNPP
CRNCH
GET INTO THE LIFEBOATS! TAKE WHATEVER YOU CAN CARRY!
KATE--?!
I'M NOT LEAVING.
I'M NOT RUNNING AWAY--

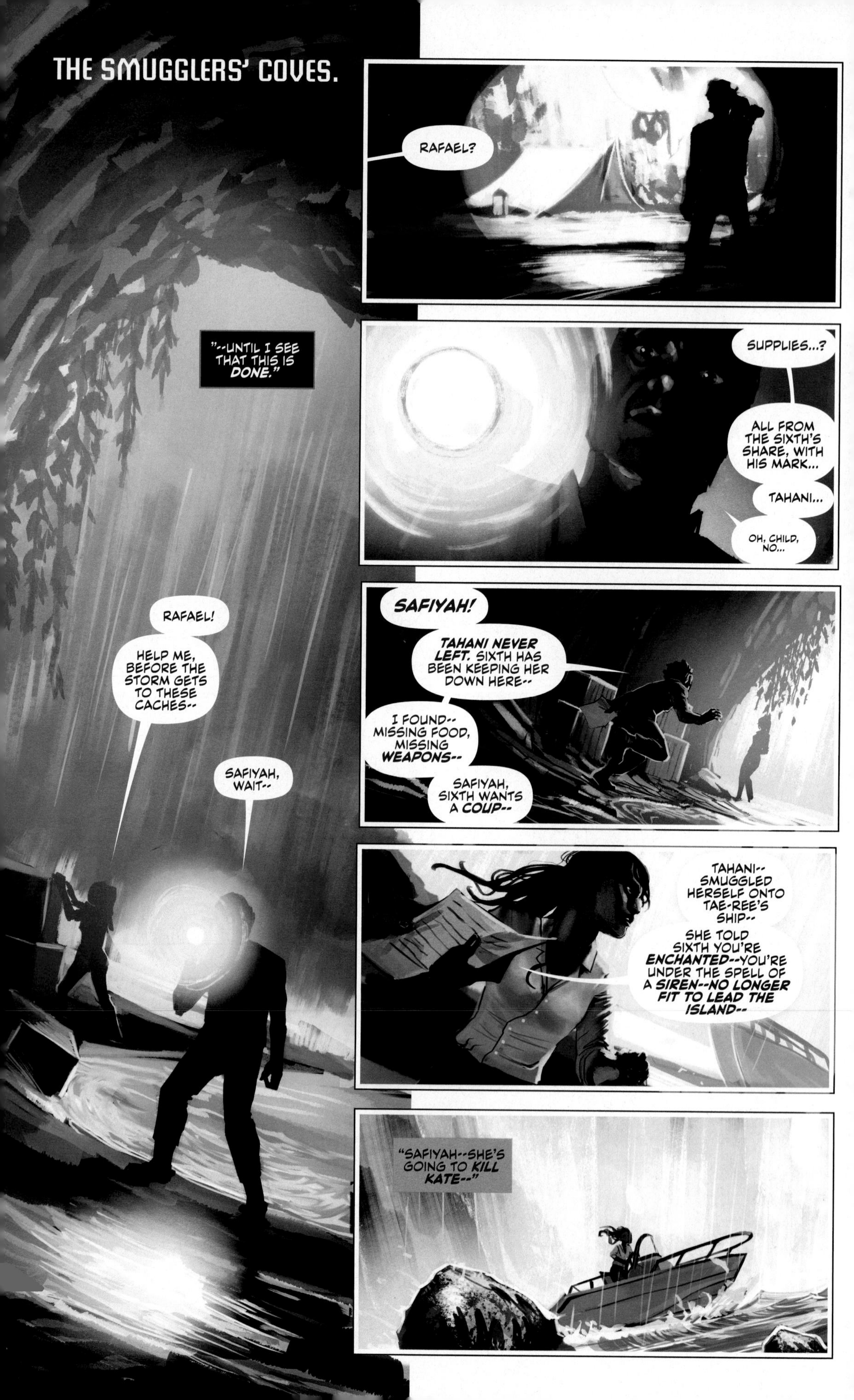
THE SMUGGLERS' COVES.
RAFAEL?
"--UNTIL I SEE THAT THIS IS DONE."
SUPPLIES...?
ALL FROM THE SIXTH'S SHARE, WITH HIS MARK...
TAHANI...
OH, CHILD, NO...
RAFAEL!
HELP ME, BEFORE THE STORM GETS TO THESE CACHES--
SAFIYAH, WAIT--
SAFIYAH!
TAHANI NEVER LEFT. SIXTH HAS BEEN KEEPING HER DOWN HERE--
I FOUND-- MISSING FOOD, MISSING WEAPONS--
SAFIYAH, SIXTH WANTS A COUP--
TAHANI-- SMUGGLED HERSELF ONTO TAE-REE'S SHIP--
SHE TOLD SIXTH YOU'RE ENCHANTED--YOU'RE UNDER THE SPELL OF A SIREN--NO LONGER FIT TO LEAD THE ISLAND--
"SAFIYAH--SHE'S GOING TO KILL KATE--"

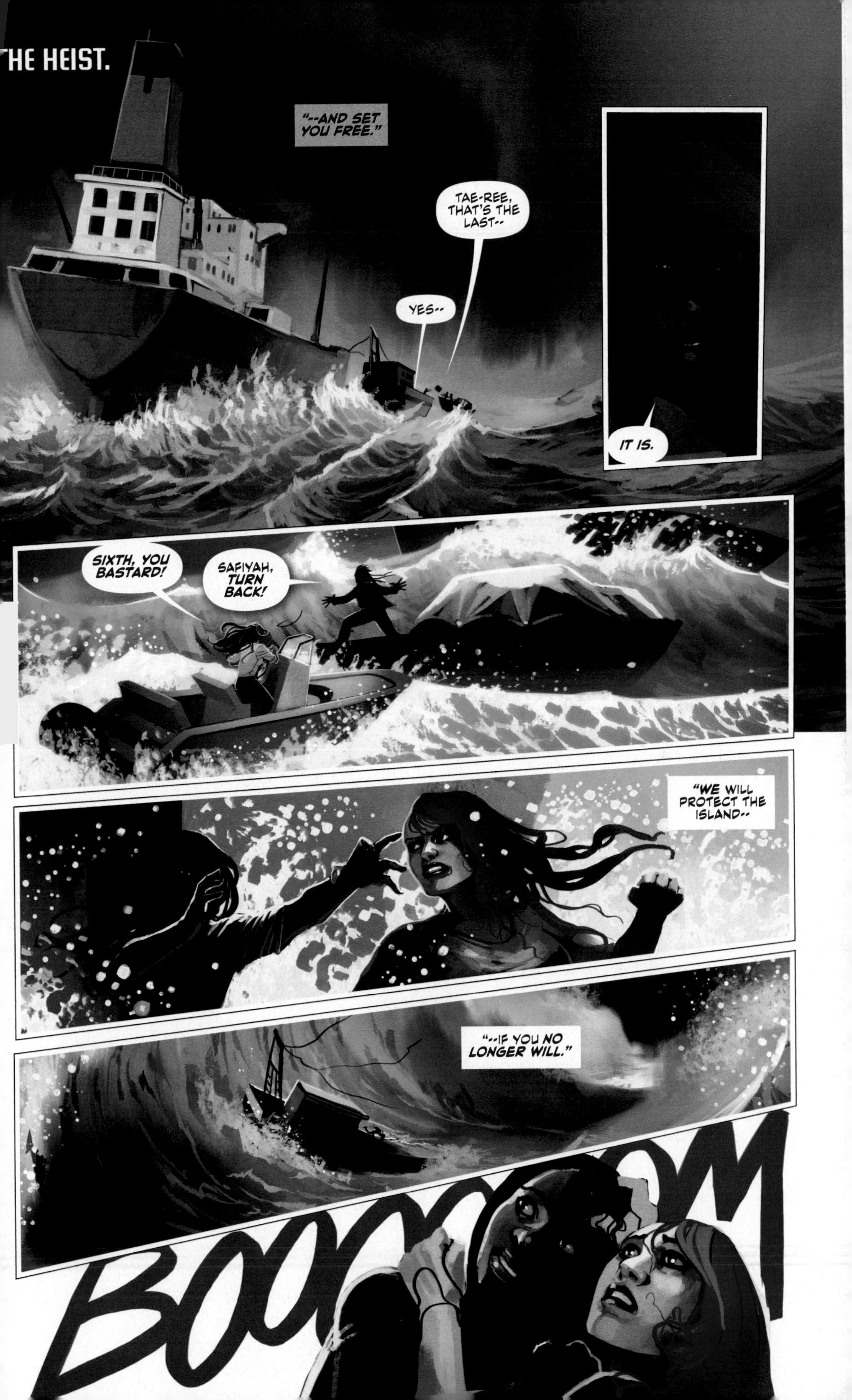
THE HEIST.
"--AND SET YOU FREE."
TAE-REE, THAT'S THE LAST--
YES--
IT IS.
SIXTH, YOU BASTARD!
SAFIYAH, TURN BACK!
"WE WILL PROTECT THE ISLAND--
"--IF YOU NO LONGER WILL."
BOOOOOM

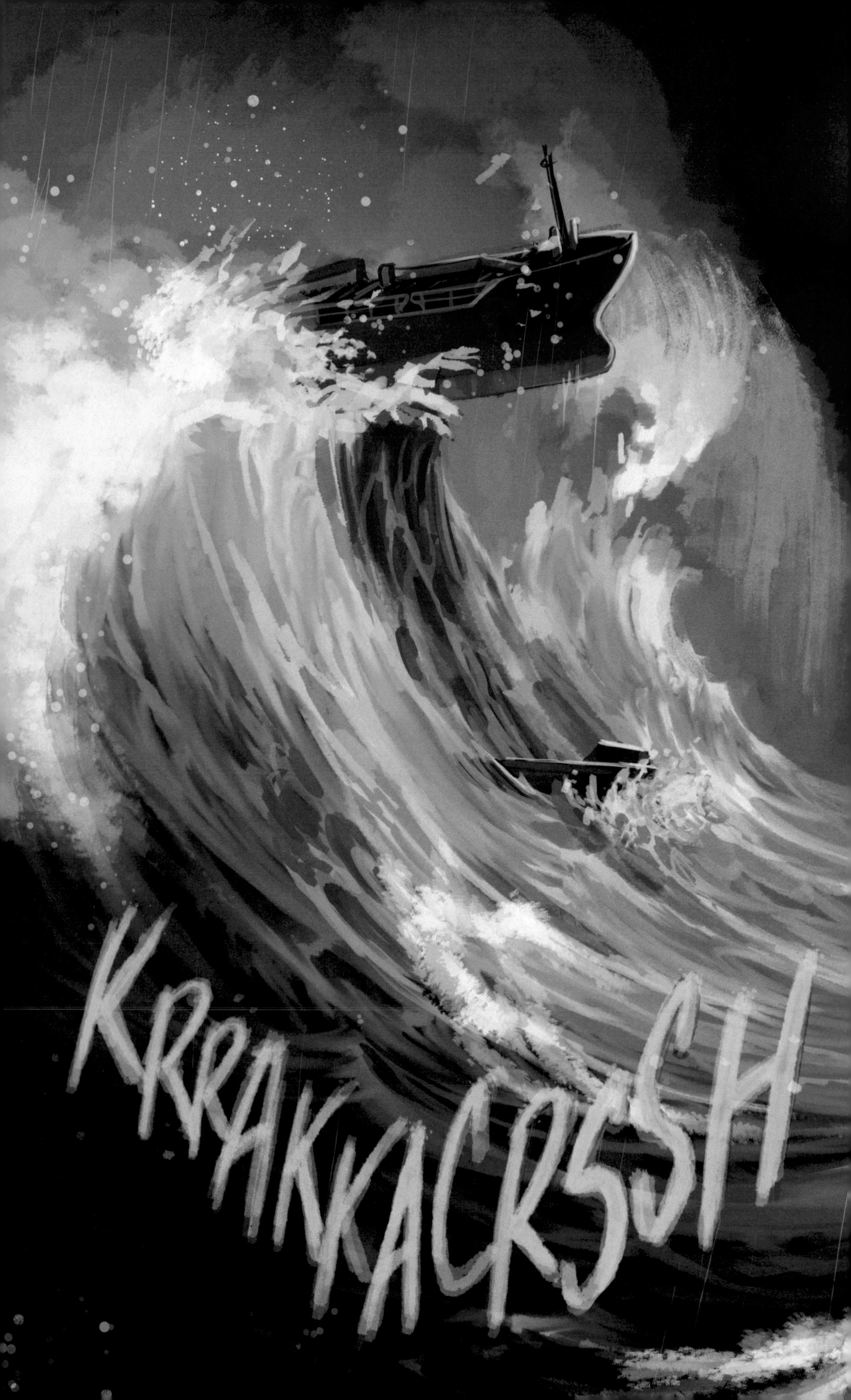
KRRAKKACRSSH

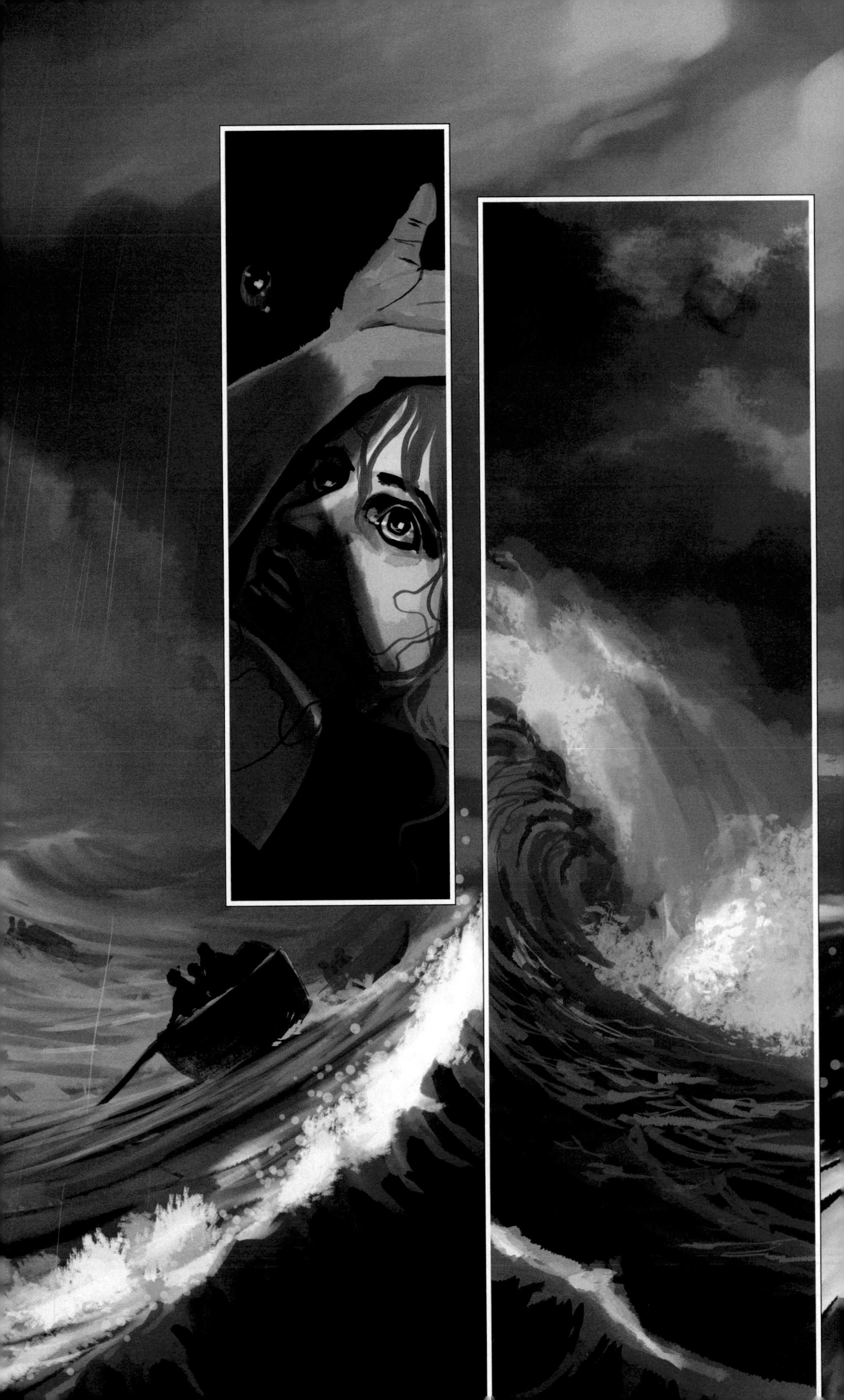

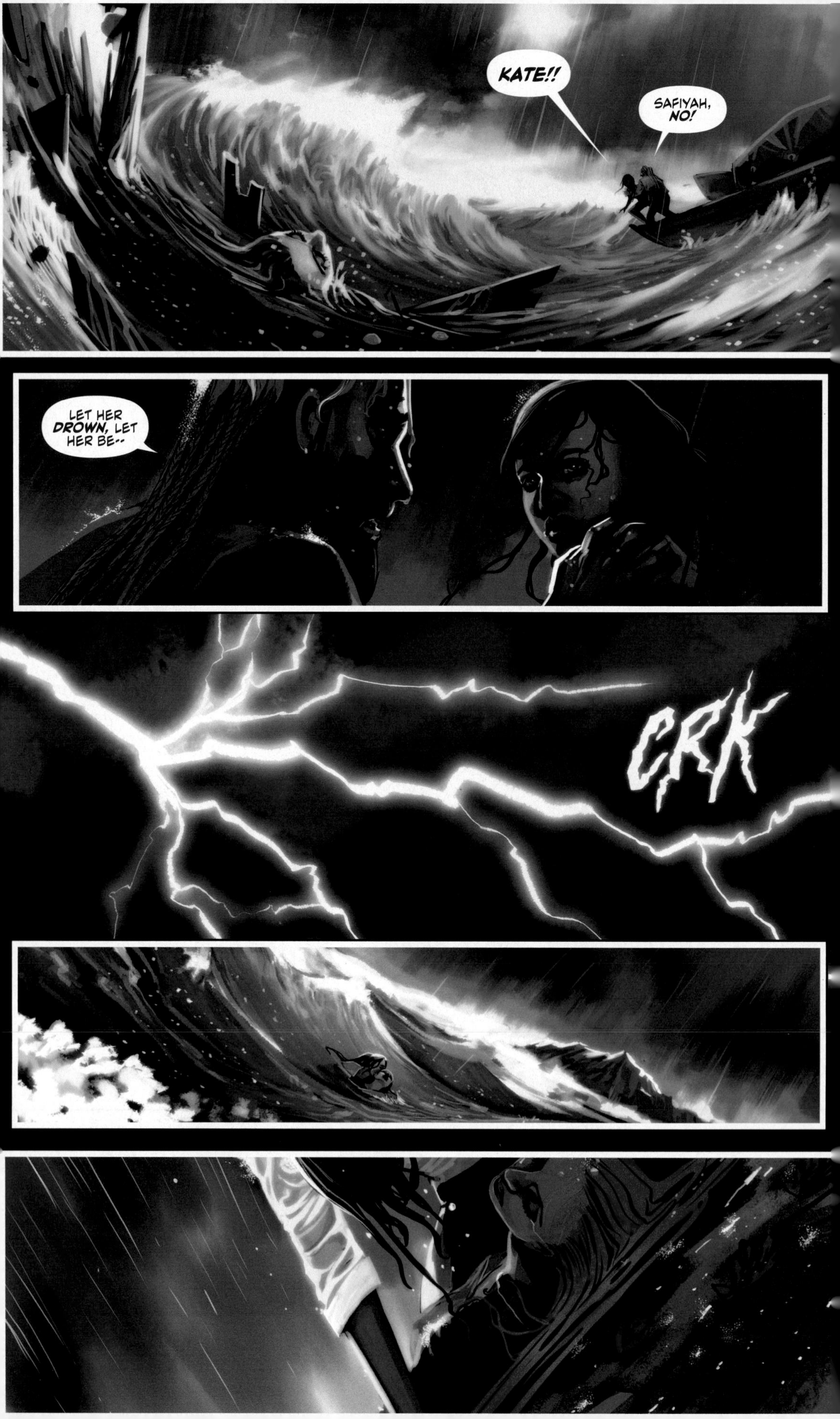

KATE!!
SAFIYAH, NO!
LET HER DROWN, LET HER BE--
CRK

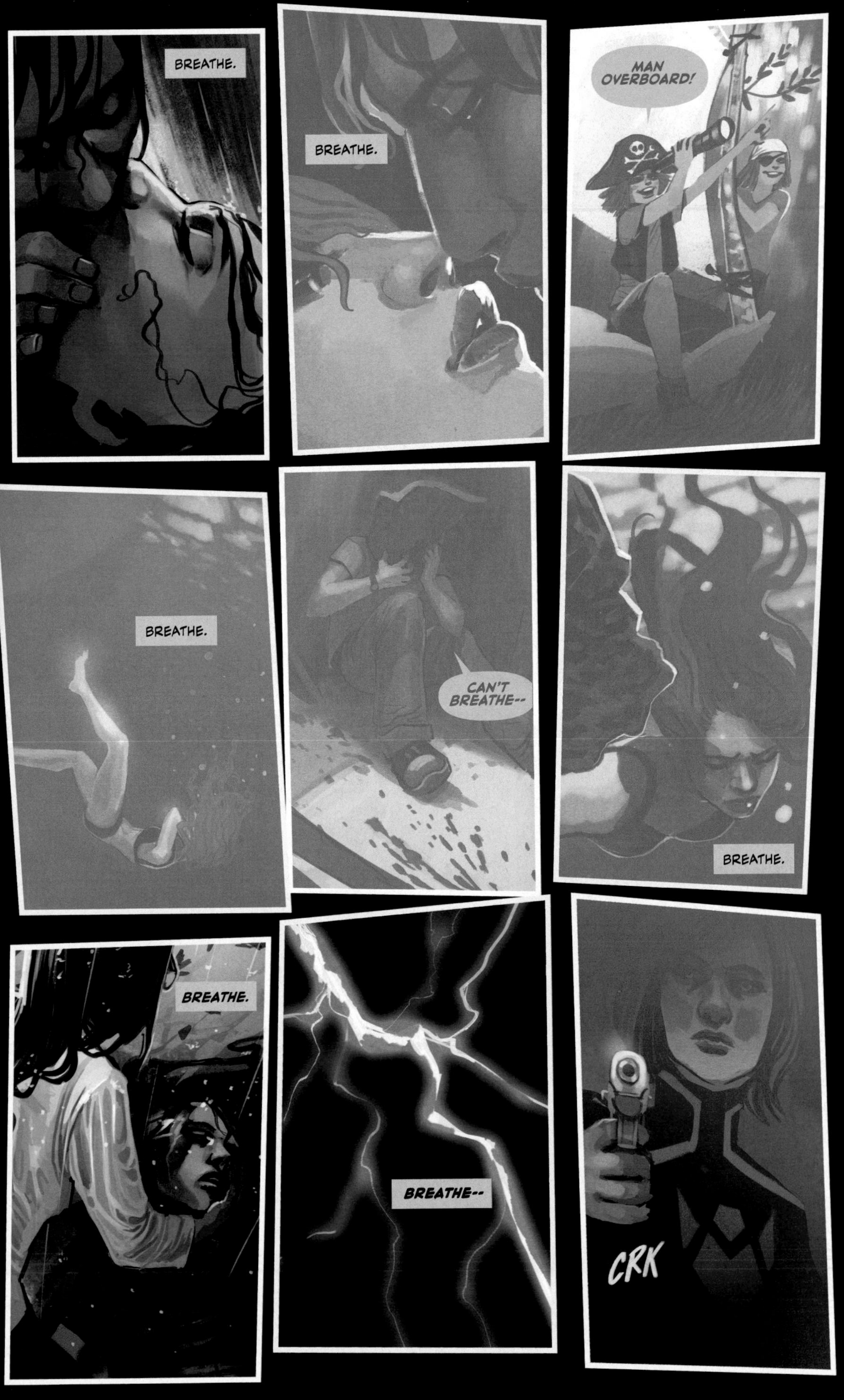
BREATHE.
BREATHE.
MAN OVERBOARD!
BREATHE.
CAN'T BREATHE--
BREATHE.
BREATHE.
BREATHE--
CRK

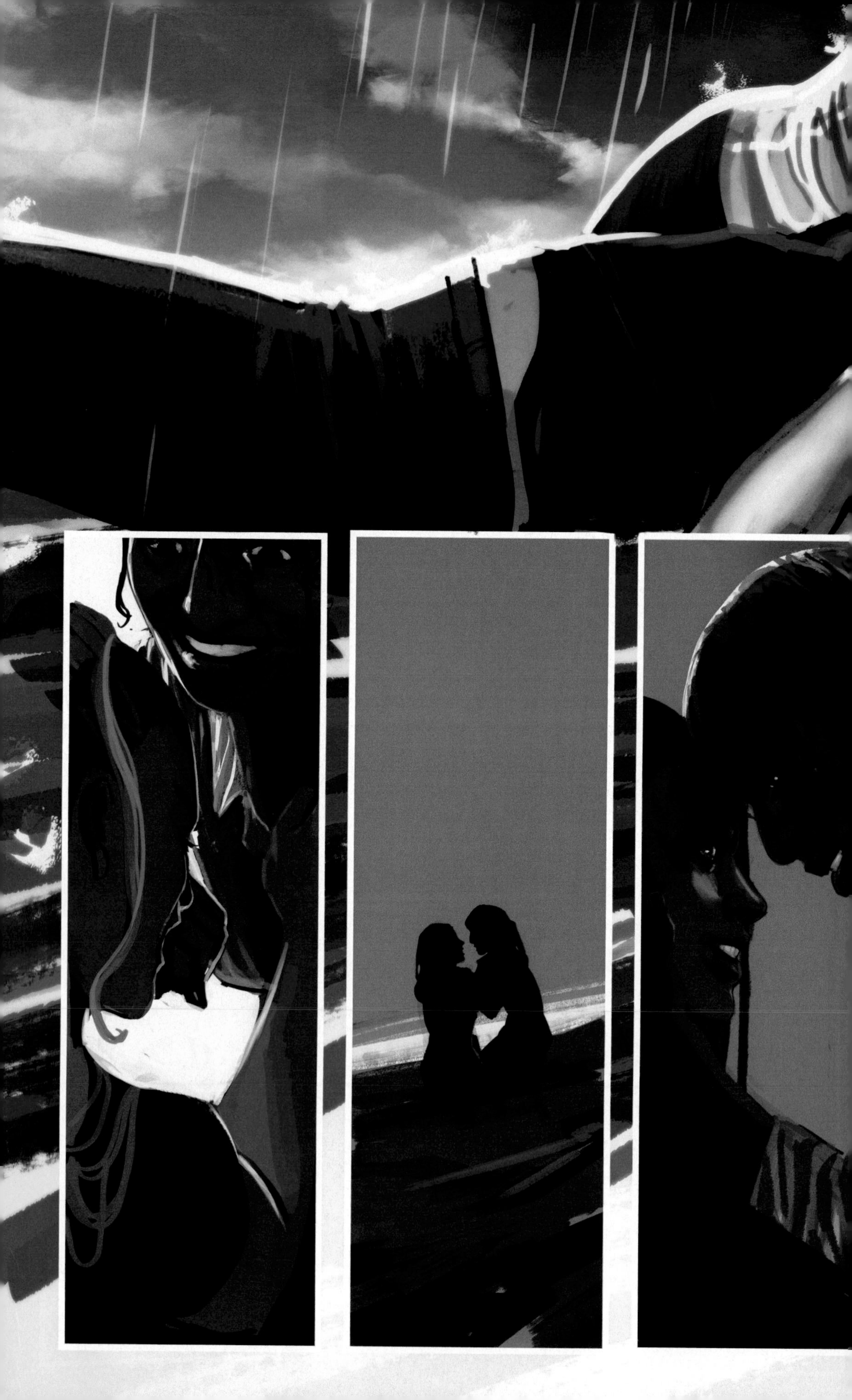

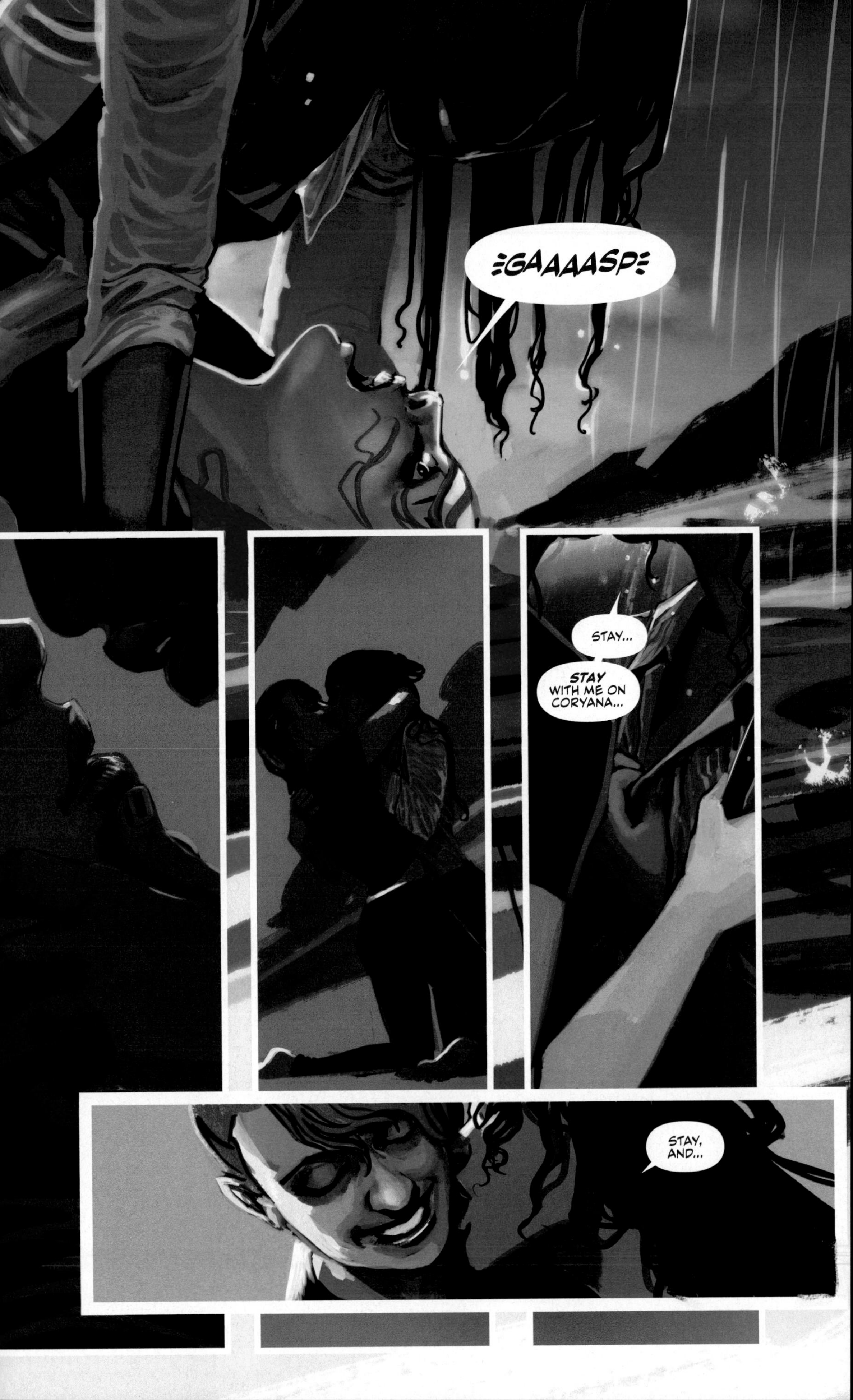
GAAAASP
STAY...
STAY WITH ME ON CORYANA...
STAY, AND...

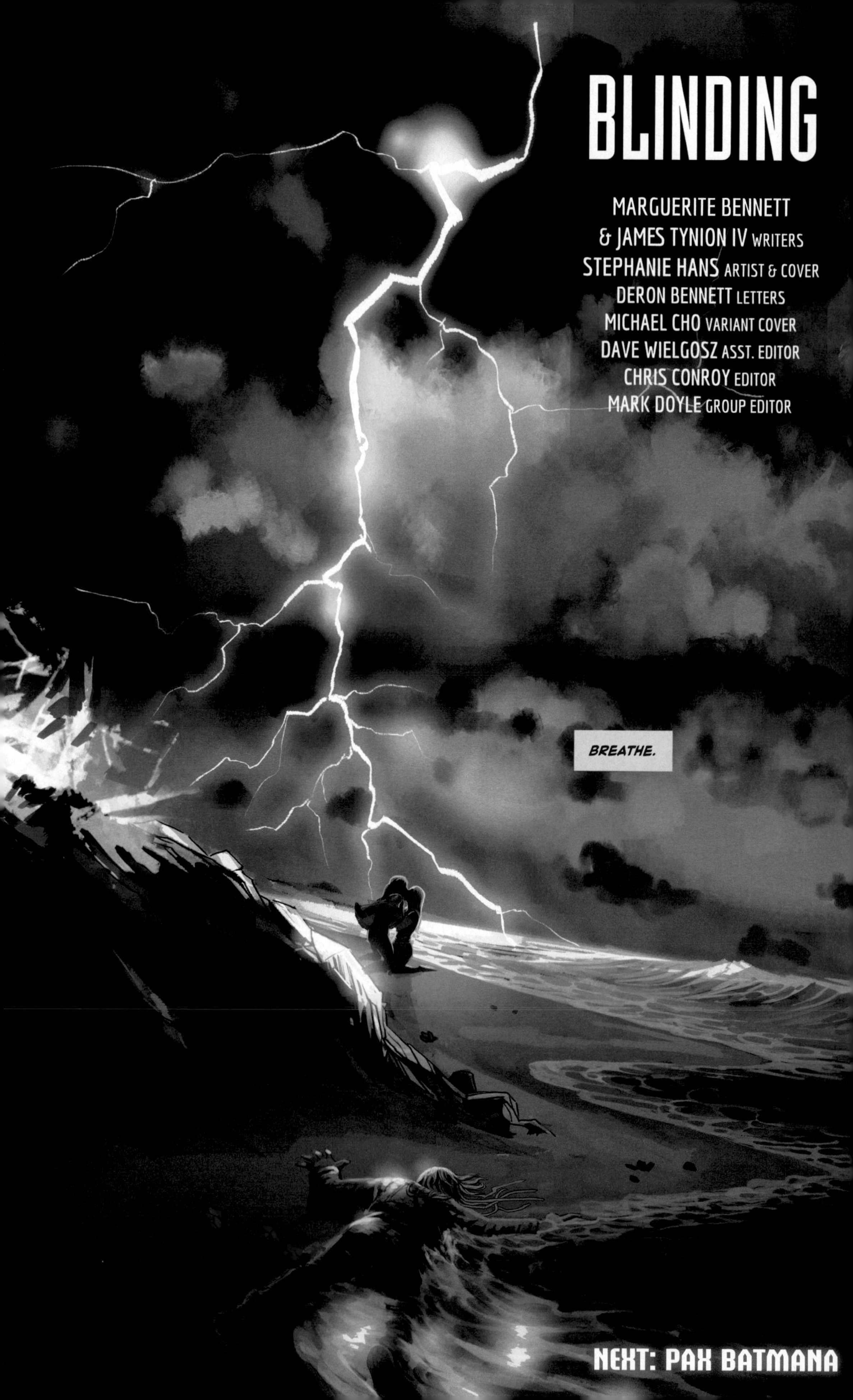
BLINDING
MARGUERITE BENNETT
& JAMES TYNION IV WRITERS
STEPHANIE HANS ARTIST & COVER
DERON BENNETT LETTERS
MICHAEL CHO VARIANT COVER
DAVE WIELGOSZ ASST. EDITOR
CHRIS CONROY EDITOR
MARK DOYLE GROUP EDITOR
BREATHE.
NEXT: PAX BATMANA

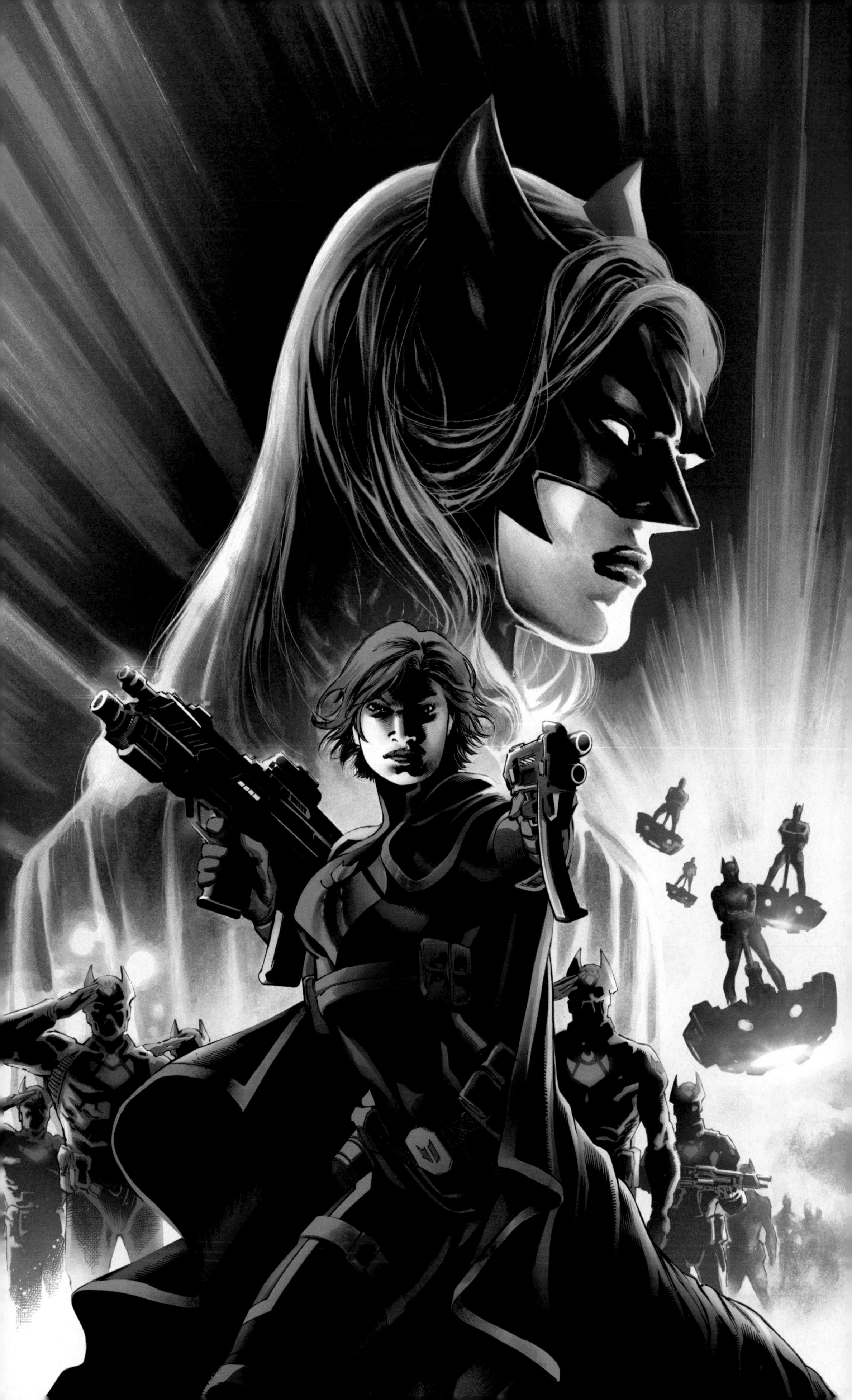

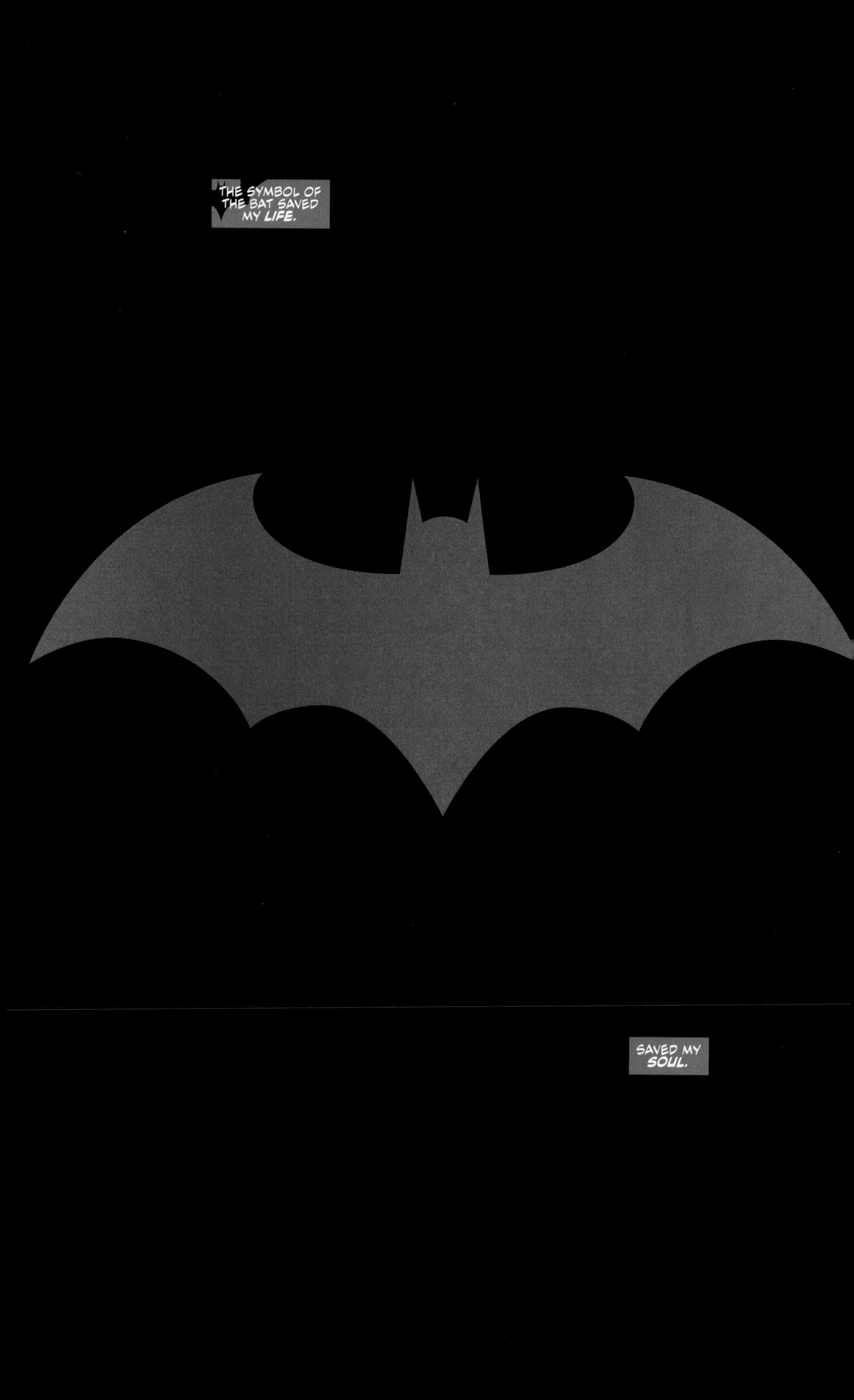
THE SYMBOL OF THE BAT SAVED MY LIFE.
SAVED MY SOUL.

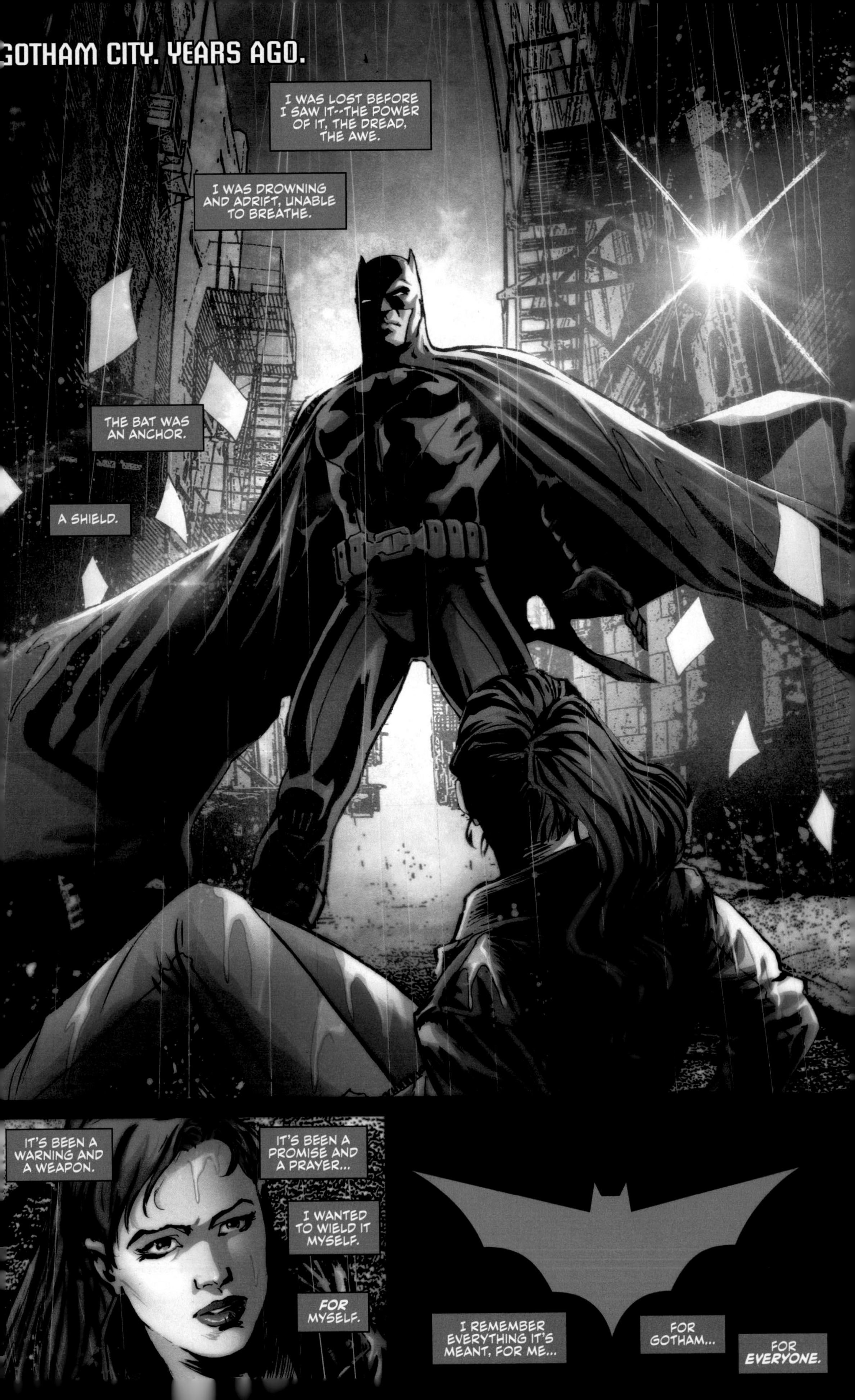
GOTHAM CITY. YEARS AGO.
I WAS LOST BEFORE I SAW IT--THE POWER OF IT, THE DREAD, THE AWE.
I WAS DROWNING AND ADRIFT, UNABLE TO BREATHE.
THE BAT WAS AN ANCHOR.
A SHIELD.
IT'S BEEN A WARNING AND A WEAPON.
IT'S BEEN A PROMISE AND A PRAYER...
I WANTED TO WIELD IT MYSELF.
FOR MYSELF.
I REMEMBER EVERYTHING IT'S MEANT, FOR ME...
FOR GOTHAM...
FOR EVERYONE.

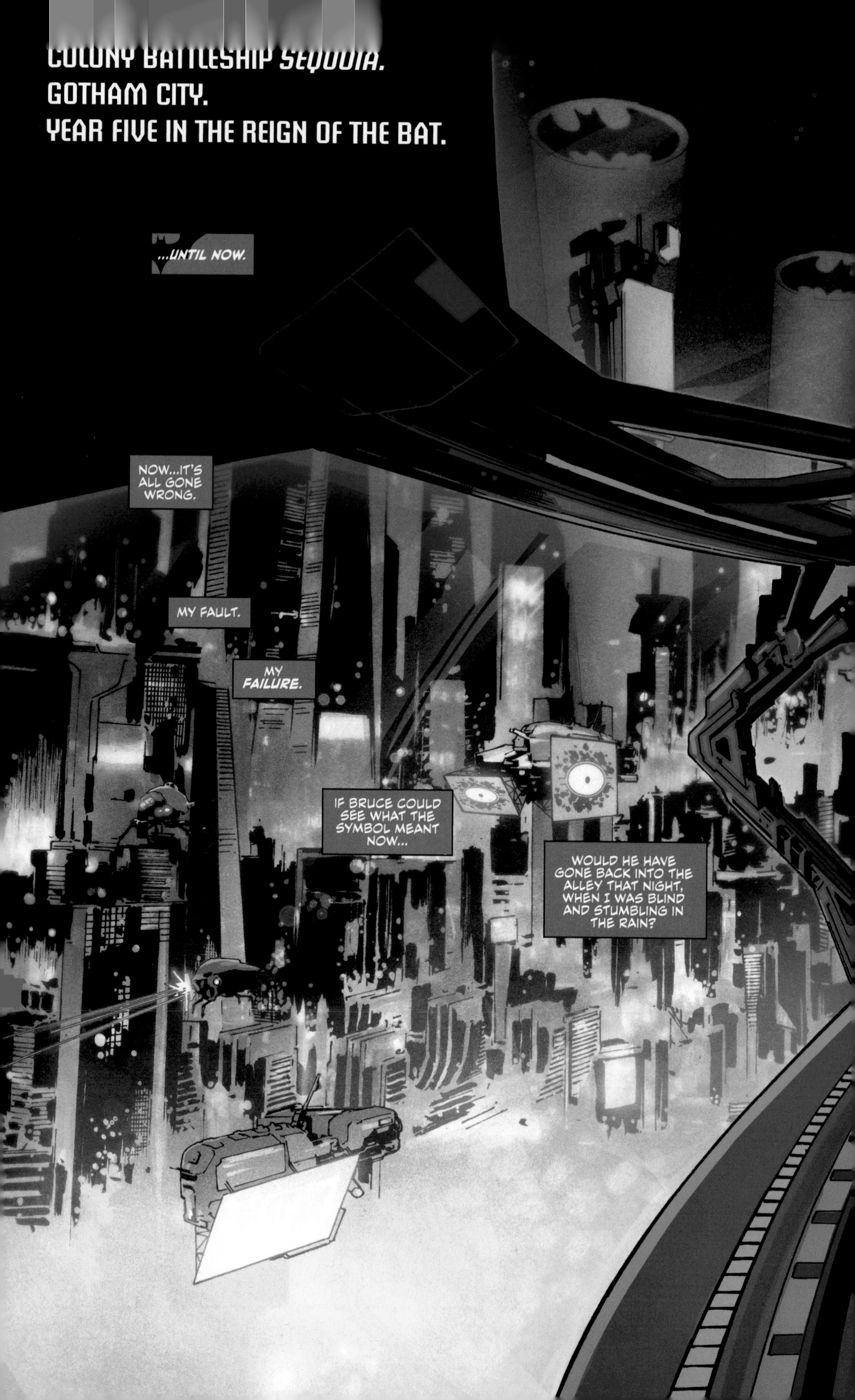
COLONY BATTLESHIP SEQUOIA.
GOTHAM CITY.
YEAR FIVE IN THE REIGN OF THE BAT.
...UNTIL NOW.
NOW...IT'S ALL GONE WRONG.
MY FAULT.
MY FAILURE.
IF BRUCE COULD SEE WHAT THE SYMBOL MEANT NOW...
WOULD HE HAVE GONE BACK INTO THE ALLEY THAT NIGHT, WHEN I WAS BLIND AND STUMBLING IN THE RAIN?

PAX BATMANA

MARGUERITE BENNETT & JAMES TYNION IV Writers RENATO ARLEM Artist
ADRIANO LUCAS Colors DERON BENNETT Letters
EDDY BARROWS, EBER FERREIRA & ADRIANO LUCAS Cover MICHAEL CHO Variant Cover
DAVE WIELGOSZ Asst. Editor CHRIS CONROY Editor MARK DOYLE Group Editor

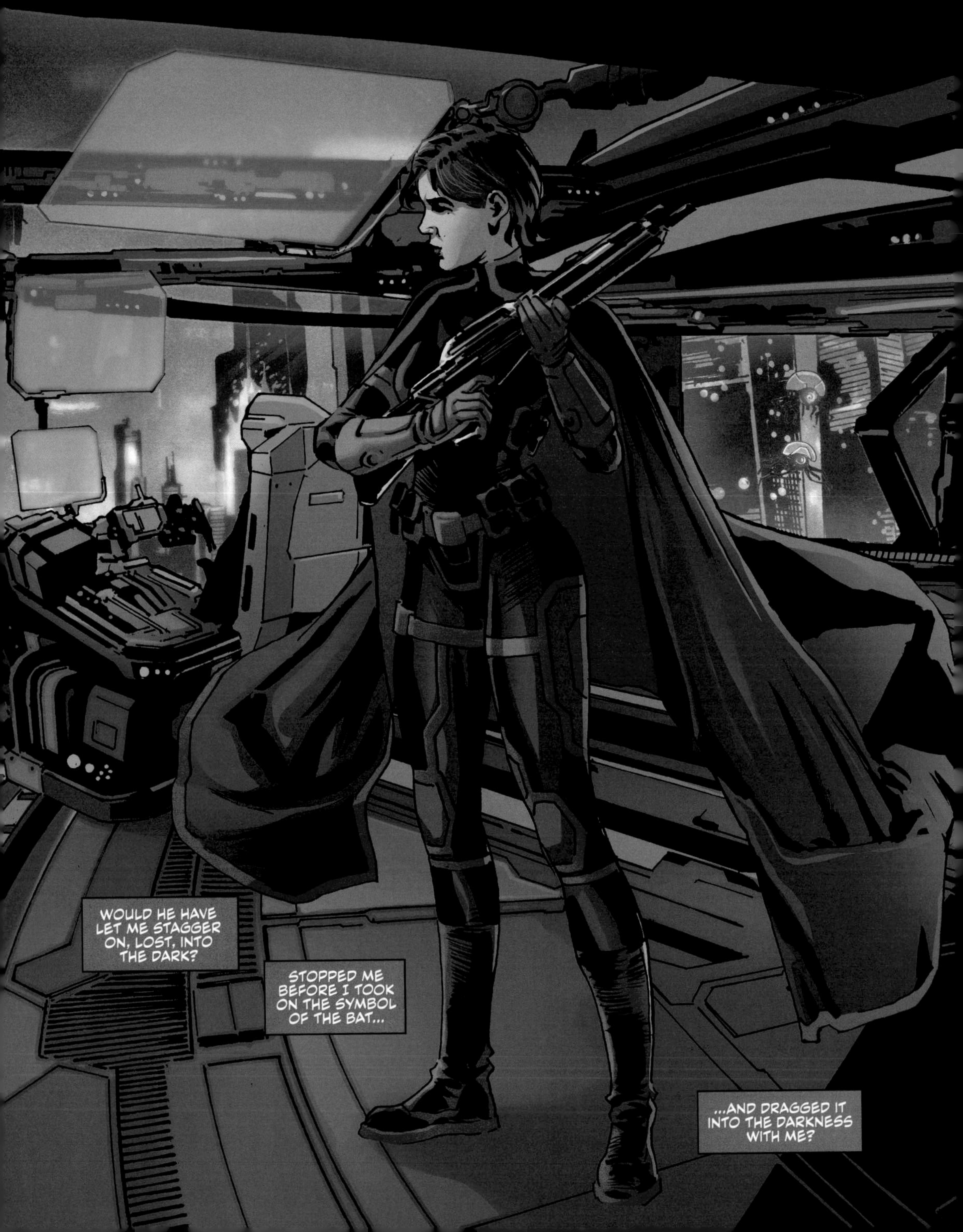
WOULD HE HAVE LET ME STAGGER ON, LOST, INTO THE DARK?
STOPPED ME BEFORE I TOOK ON THE SYMBOL OF THE BAT...
...AND DRAGGED IT INTO THE DARKNESS WITH ME?

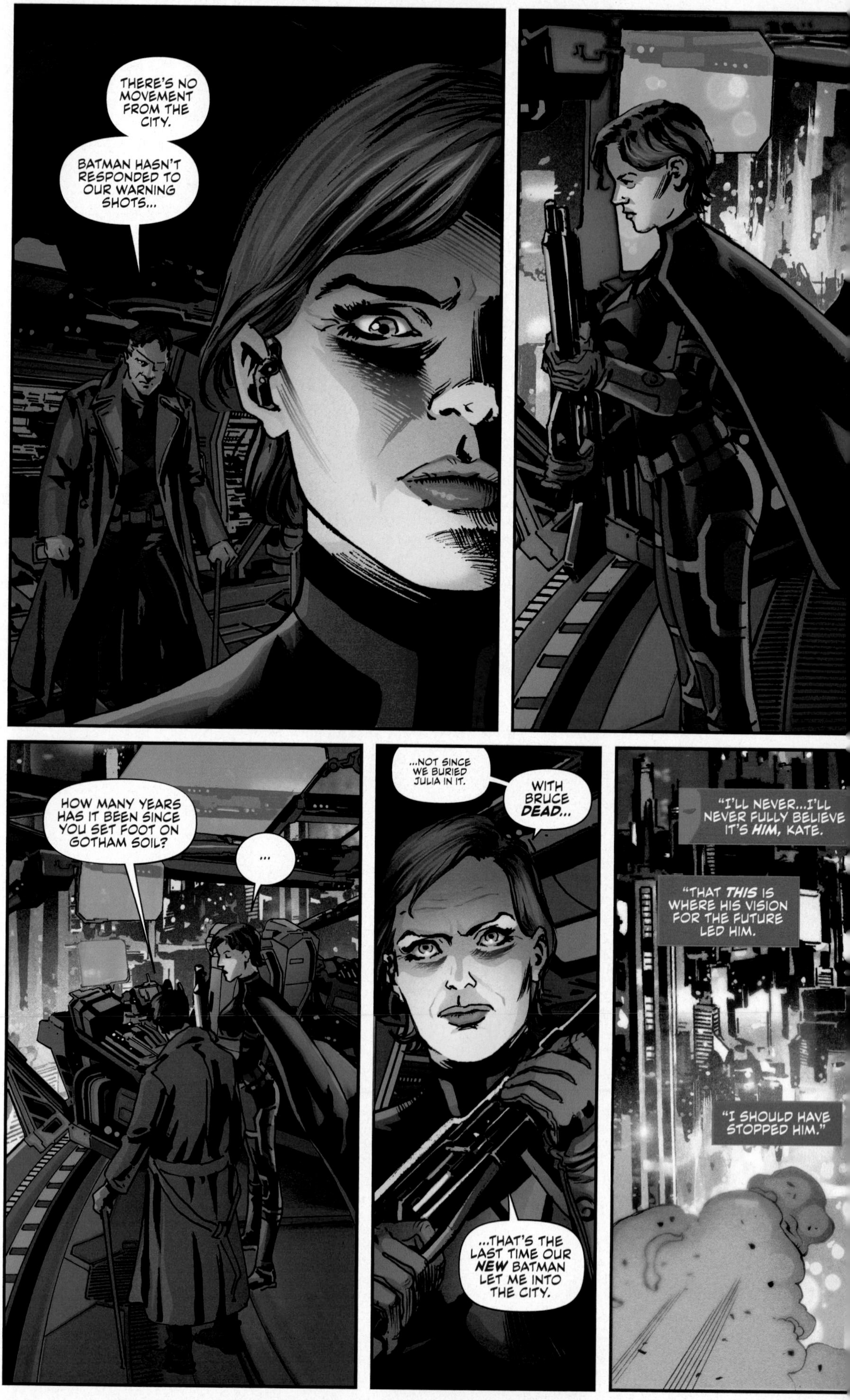
THERE'S NO MOVEMENT FROM THE CITY.
BATMAN HASN'T RESPONDED TO OUR WARNING SHOTS...
HOW MANY YEARS HAS IT BEEN SINCE YOU SET FOOT ON GOTHAM SOIL?
...
...NOT SINCE WE BURIED JULIA IN IT.
WITH BRUCE *DEAD...*
...THAT'S THE LAST TIME OUR *NEW* BATMAN LET ME INTO THE CITY.
"I'LL NEVER...I'LL NEVER FULLY BELIEVE IT'S *HIM*, KATE.
"THAT *THIS* IS WHERE HIS VISION FOR THE FUTURE LED HIM.
"I SHOULD HAVE STOPPED HIM."

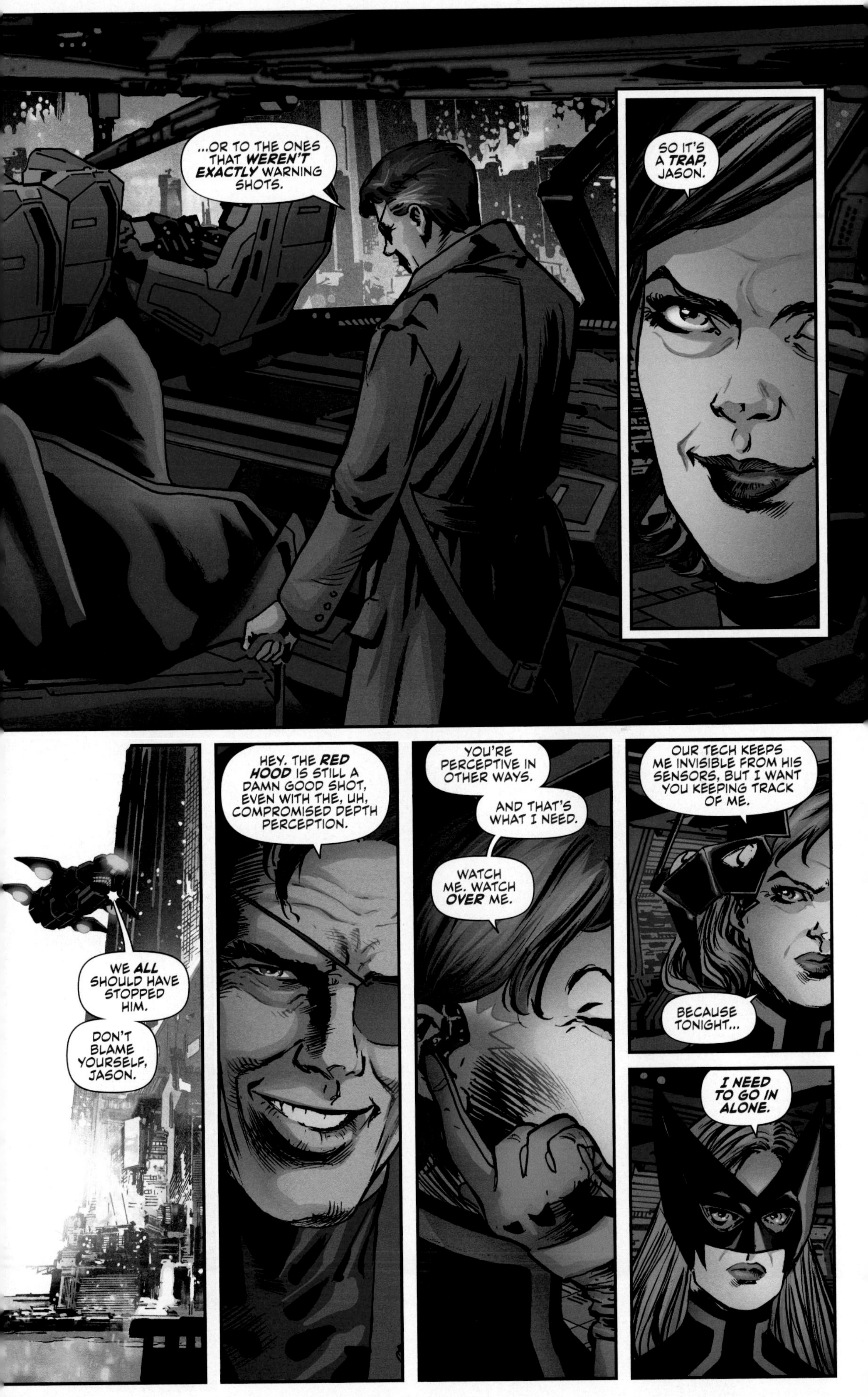
...OR TO THE ONES THAT WEREN'T EXACTLY WARNING SHOTS.
SO IT'S A TRAP, JASON.
WE ALL SHOULD HAVE STOPPED HIM.
DON'T BLAME YOURSELF, JASON.
HEY. THE RED HOOD IS STILL A DAMN GOOD SHOT, EVEN WITH THE, UH, COMPROMISED DEPTH PERCEPTION.
YOU'RE PERCEPTIVE IN OTHER WAYS.
AND THAT'S WHAT I NEED.
WATCH ME. WATCH OVER ME.
OUR TECH KEEPS ME INVISIBLE FROM HIS SENSORS, BUT I WANT YOU KEEPING TRACK OF ME.
BECAUSE TONIGHT...
I NEED TO GO IN ALONE.

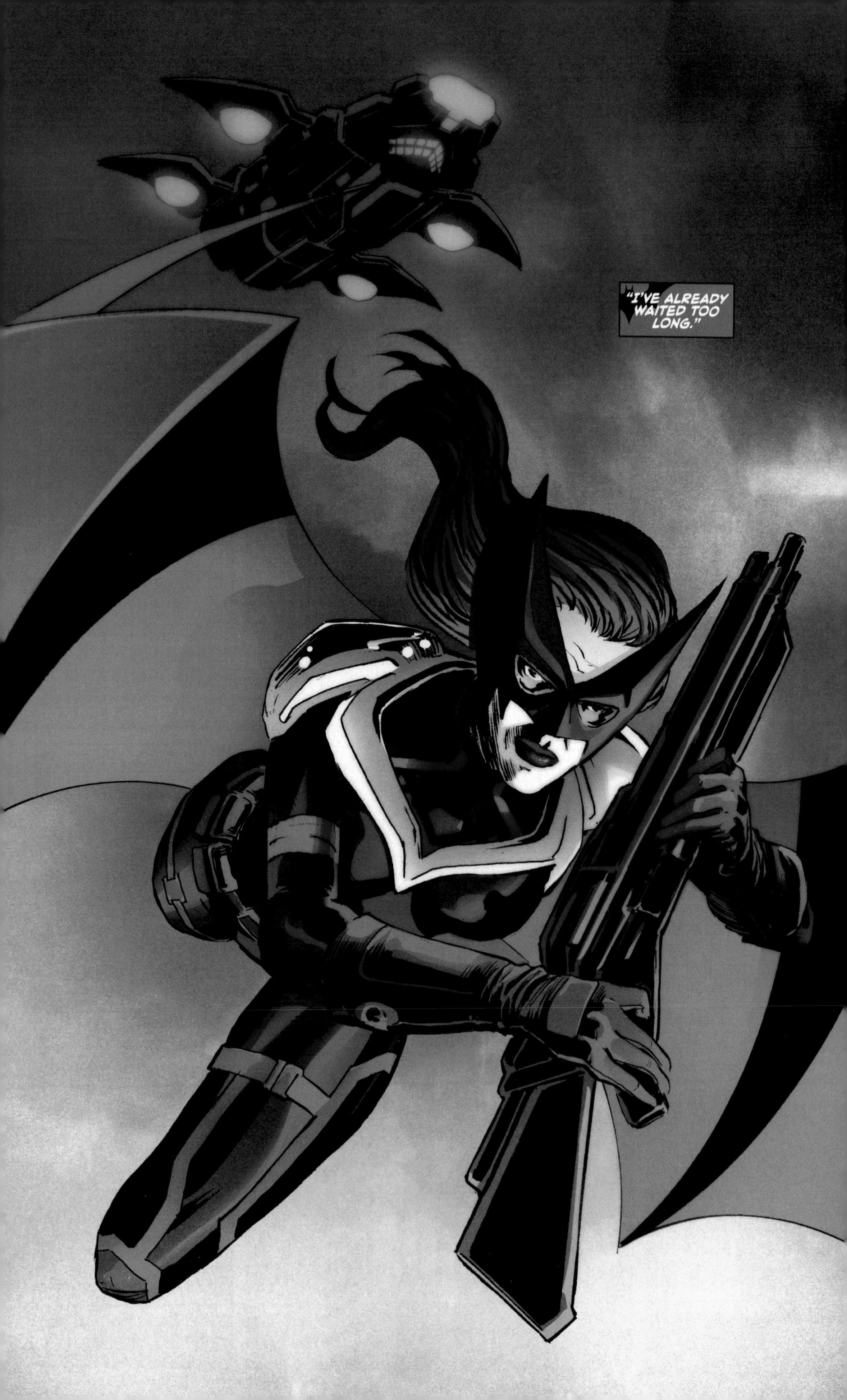
"I'VE ALREADY WAITED TOO LONG."

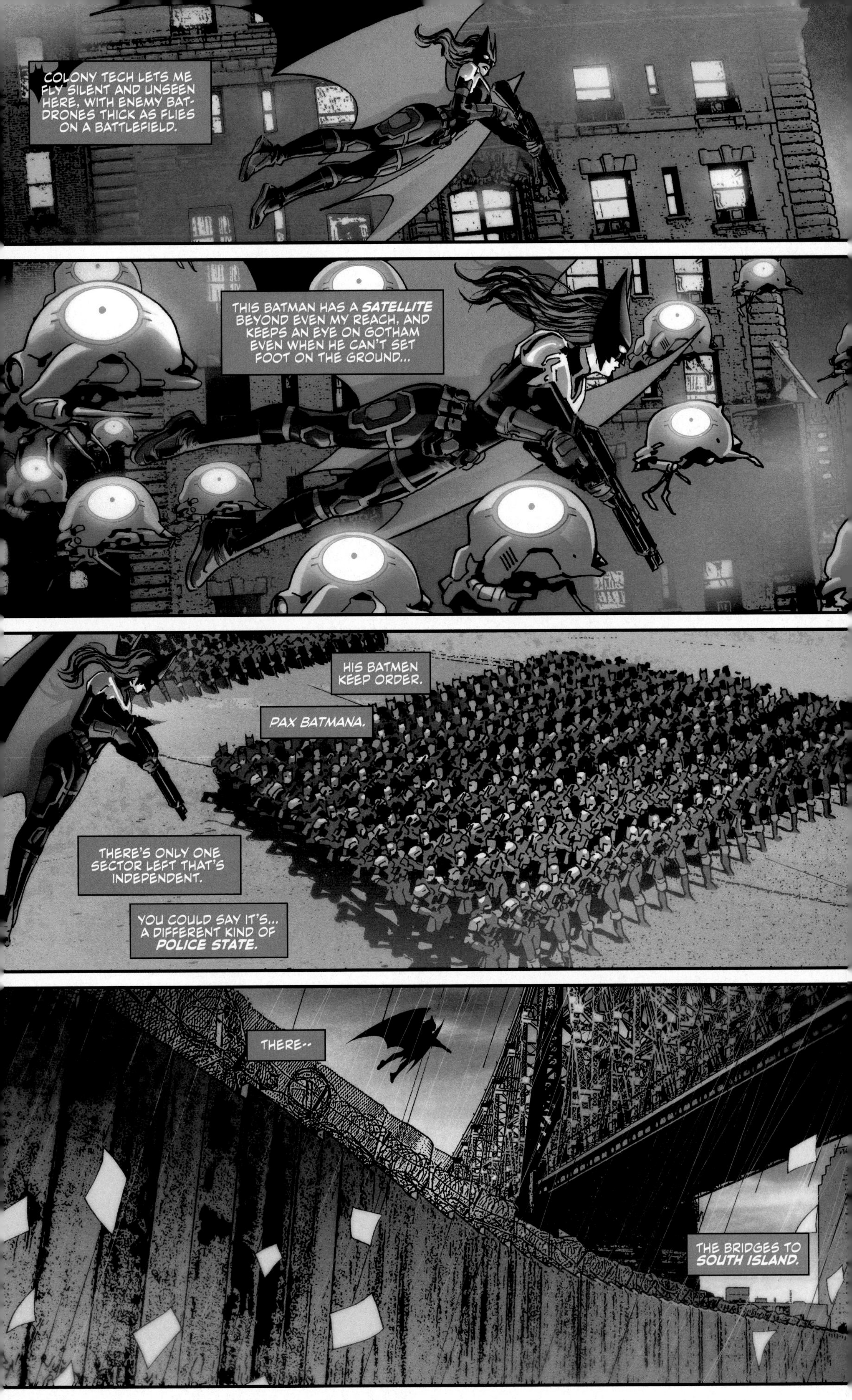
COLONY TECH LETS ME FLY SILENT AND UNSEEN HERE, WITH ENEMY BAT-DRONES THICK AS FLIES ON A BATTLEFIELD.
THIS BATMAN HAS A SATELLITE BEYOND EVEN MY REACH, AND KEEPS AN EYE ON GOTHAM EVEN WHEN HE CAN'T SET FOOT ON THE GROUND...
HIS BATMEN KEEP ORDER.
PAX BATMANA.
THERE'S ONLY ONE SECTOR LEFT THAT'S INDEPENDENT.
YOU COULD SAY IT'S... A DIFFERENT KIND OF POLICE STATE.
THERE--
THE BRIDGES TO SOUTH ISLAND.

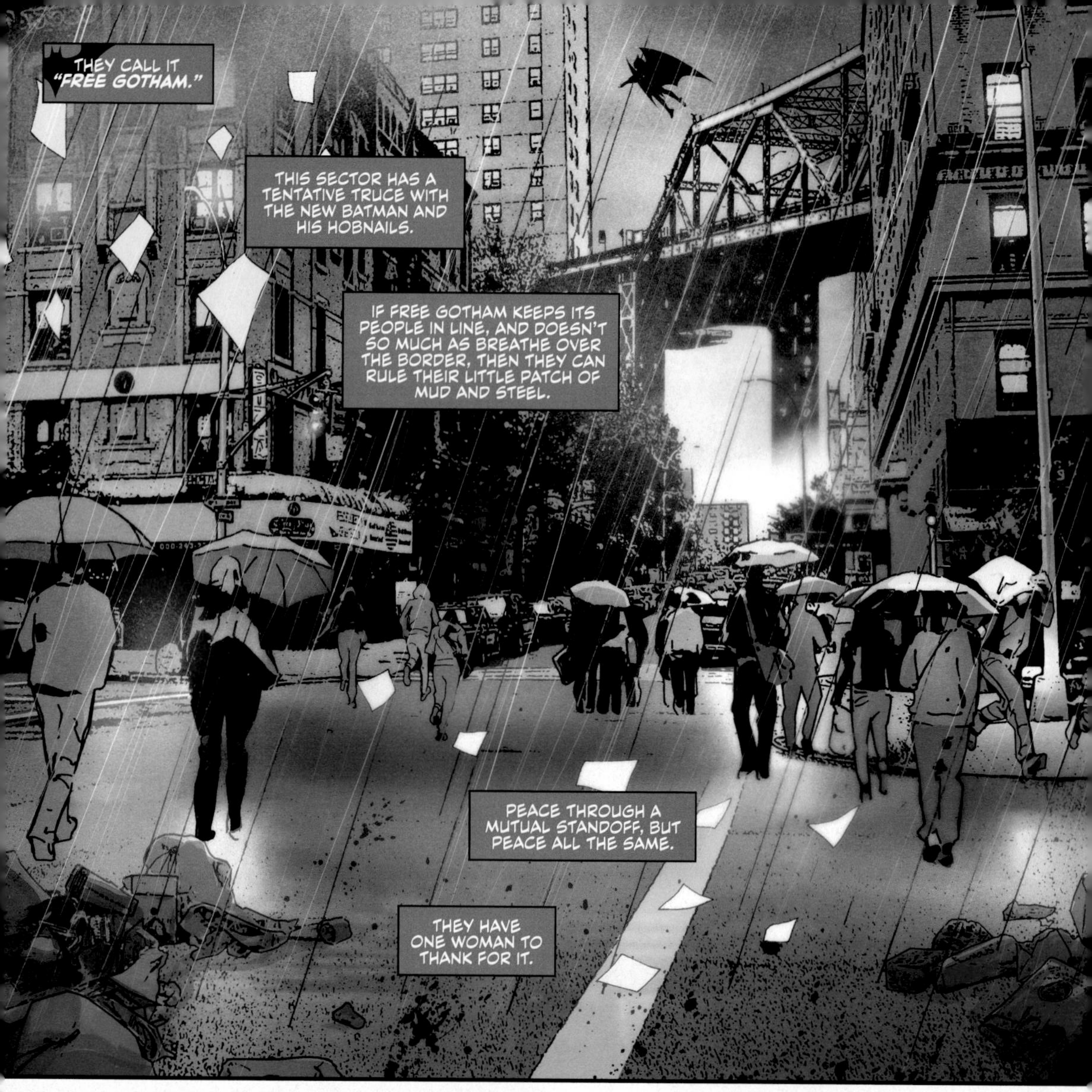
THEY CALL IT "FREE GOTHAM."
THIS SECTOR HAS A TENTATIVE TRUCE WITH THE NEW BATMAN AND HIS HOBNAILS.
IF FREE GOTHAM KEEPS ITS PEOPLE IN LINE, AND DOESN'T SO MUCH AS BREATHE OVER THE BORDER, THEN THEY CAN RULE THEIR LITTLE PATCH OF MUD AND STEEL.
PEACE THROUGH A MUTUAL STANDOFF, BUT PEACE ALL THE SAME.
THEY HAVE ONE WOMAN TO THANK FOR IT.

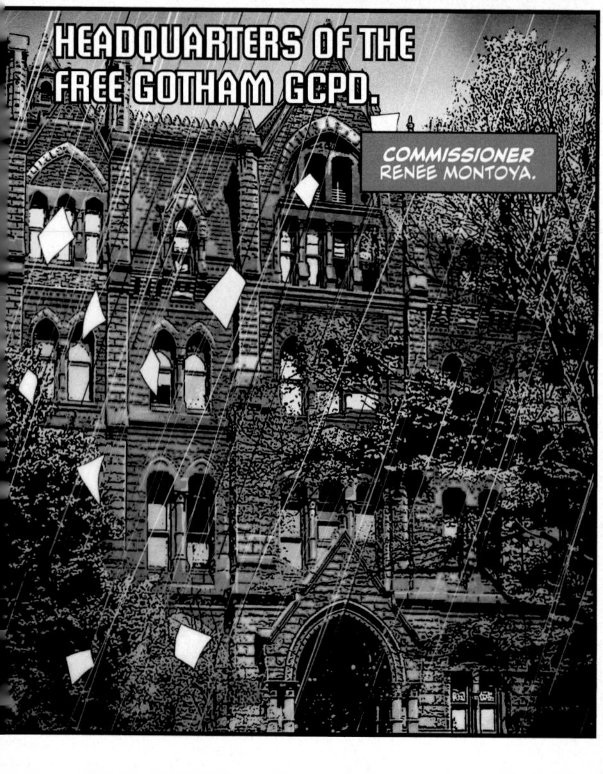
HEADQUARTERS OF THE FREE GOTHAM GCPD.
COMMISSIONER RENEE MONTOYA.

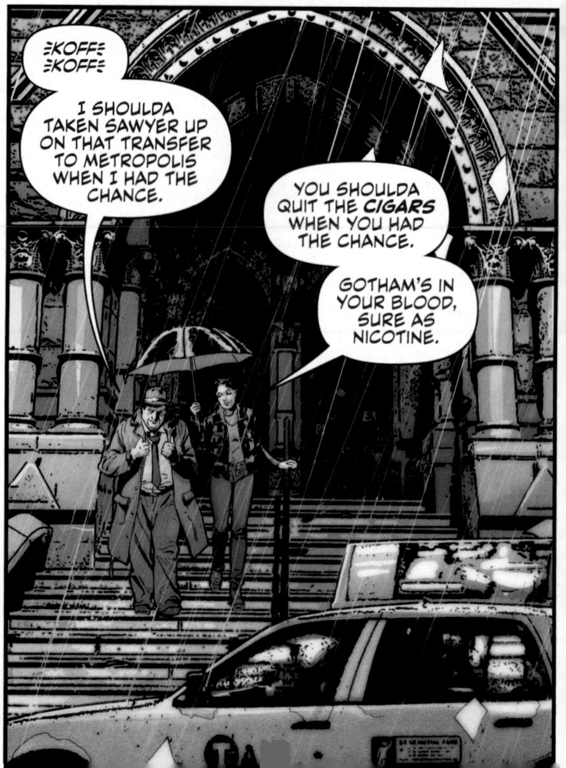
KOFF KOFF
I SHOULDA TAKEN SAWYER UP ON THAT TRANSFER TO METROPOLIS WHEN I HAD THE CHANCE.
YOU SHOULDA QUIT THE CIGARS WHEN YOU HAD THE CHANCE.
GOTHAM'S IN YOUR BLOOD, SURE AS NICOTINE.

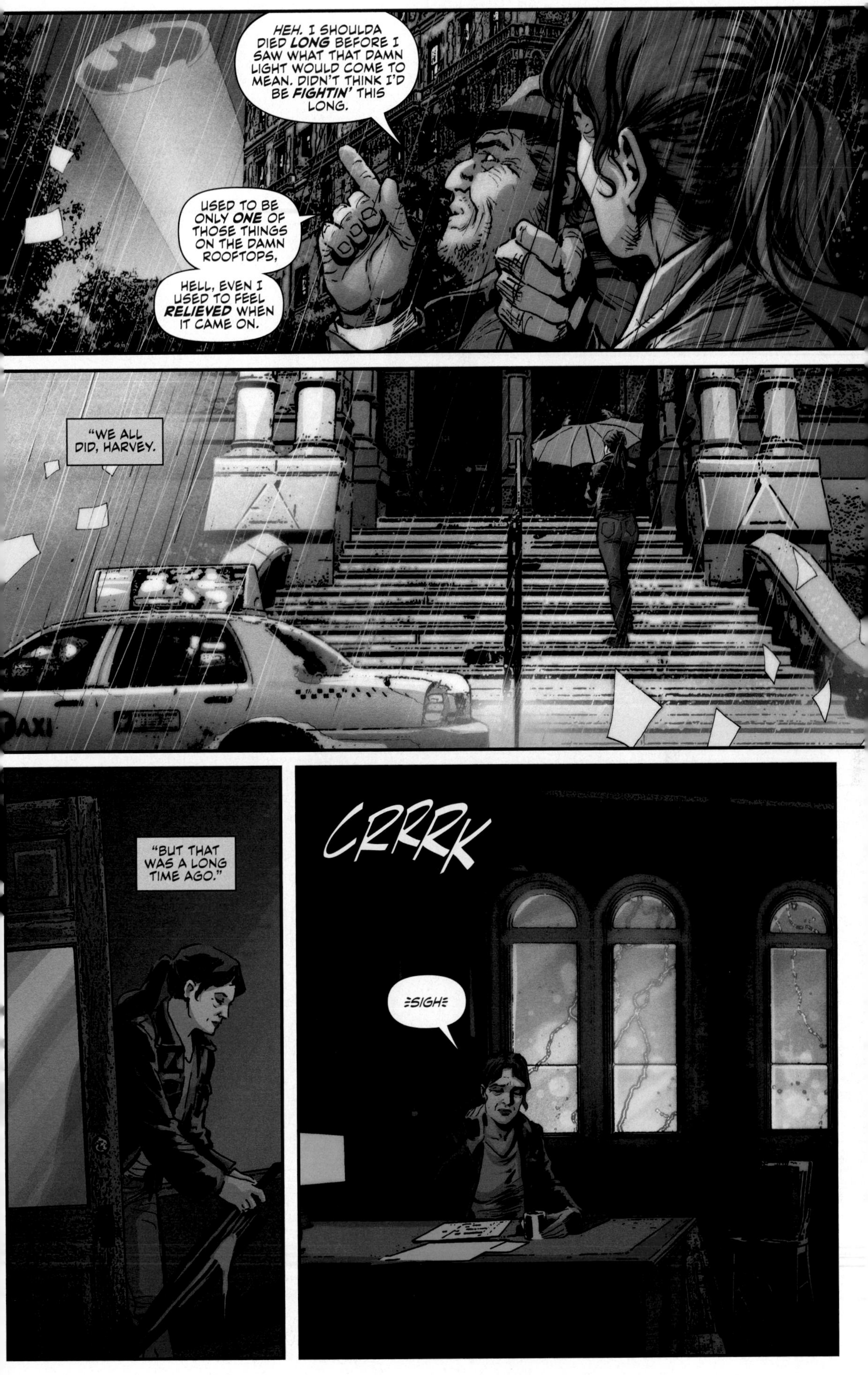
HEH. I SHOULDA DIED LONG BEFORE I SAW WHAT THAT DAMN LIGHT WOULD COME TO MEAN. DIDN'T THINK I'D BE FIGHTIN' THIS LONG.
USED TO BE ONLY ONE OF THOSE THINGS ON THE DAMN ROOFTOPS,
HELL, EVEN I USED TO FEEL RELIEVED WHEN IT CAME ON.
"WE ALL DID, HARVEY.
TAXI
"BUT THAT WAS A LONG TIME AGO."
CRRRK
SIGH

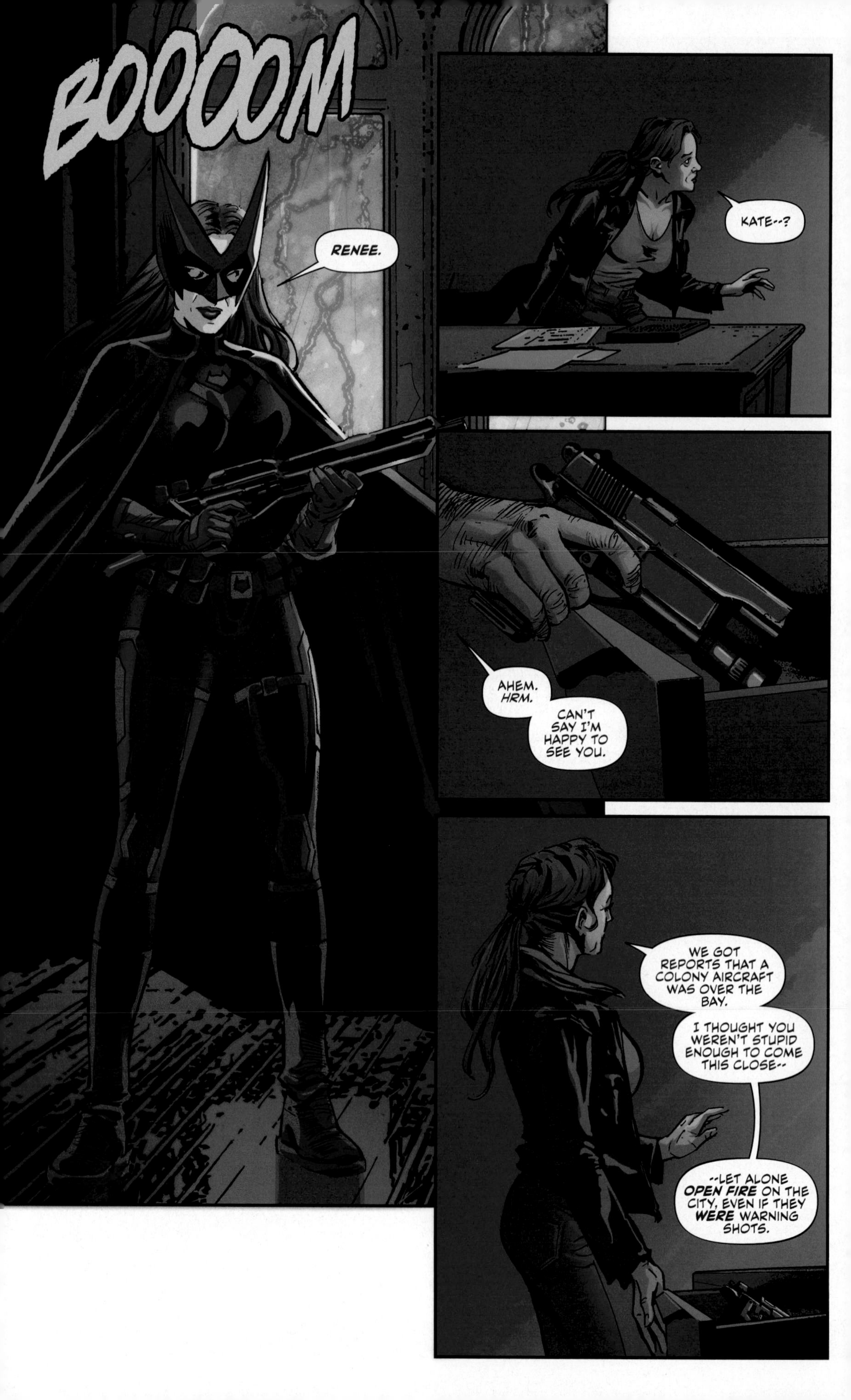
BOOOOM
RENEE.
KATE--?
AHEM. HRM.
CAN'T SAY I'M HAPPY TO SEE YOU.
WE GOT REPORTS THAT A COLONY AIRCRAFT WAS OVER THE BAY.
I THOUGHT YOU WEREN'T STUPID ENOUGH TO COME THIS CLOSE--
--LET ALONE OPEN FIRE ON THE CITY, EVEN IF THEY WERE WARNING SHOTS.

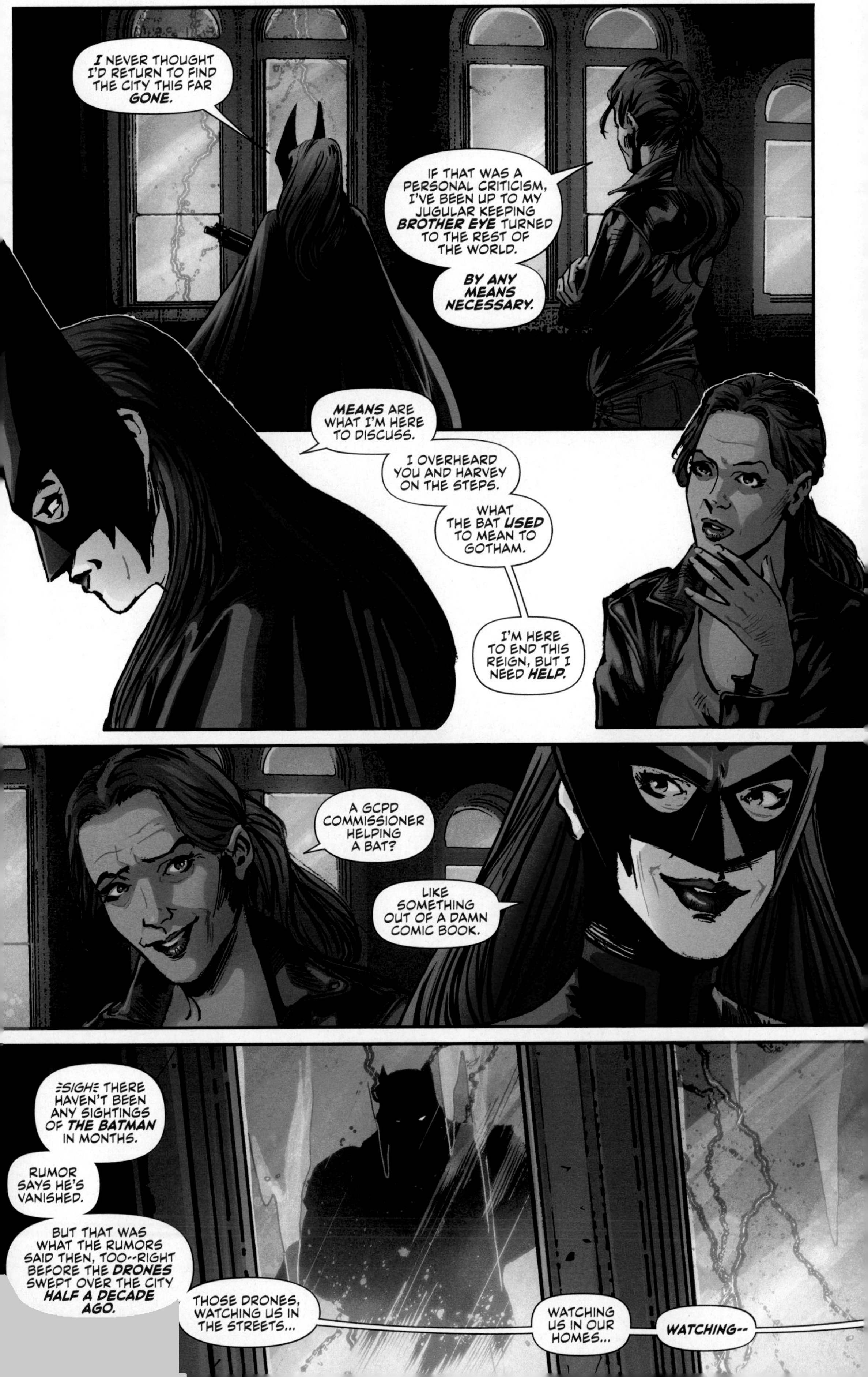
I NEVER THOUGHT I'D RETURN TO FIND THE CITY THIS FAR GONE.
IF THAT WAS A PERSONAL CRITICISM, I'VE BEEN UP TO MY JUGULAR KEEPING BROTHER EYE TURNED TO THE REST OF THE WORLD.
BY ANY MEANS NECESSARY.
MEANS ARE WHAT I'M HERE TO DISCUSS.
I OVERHEARD YOU AND HARVEY ON THE STEPS.
WHAT THE BAT USED TO MEAN TO GOTHAM.
I'M HERE TO END THIS REIGN, BUT I NEED HELP.
A GCPD COMMISSIONER HELPING A BAT?
LIKE SOMETHING OUT OF A DAMN COMIC BOOK.
=SIGH= THERE HAVEN'T BEEN ANY SIGHTINGS OF THE BATMAN IN MONTHS.
RUMOR SAYS HE'S VANISHED.
BUT THAT WAS WHAT THE RUMORS SAID THEN, TOO--RIGHT BEFORE THE DRONES SWEPT OVER THE CITY HALF A DECADE AGO.
THOSE DRONES, WATCHING US IN THE STREETS...
WATCHING US IN OUR HOMES...
WATCHING--

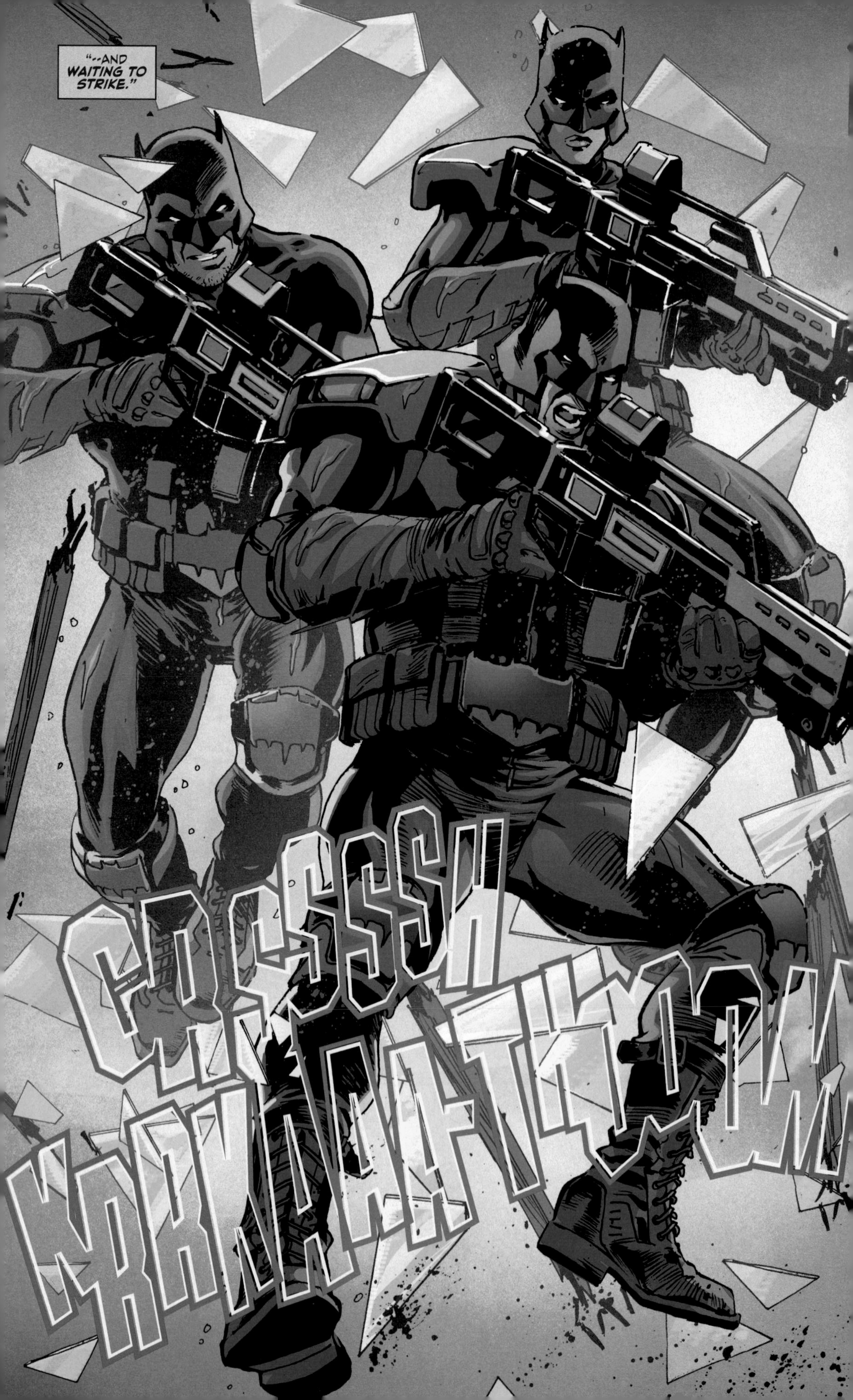
"--AND WAITING TO STRIKE."
CRSSSH

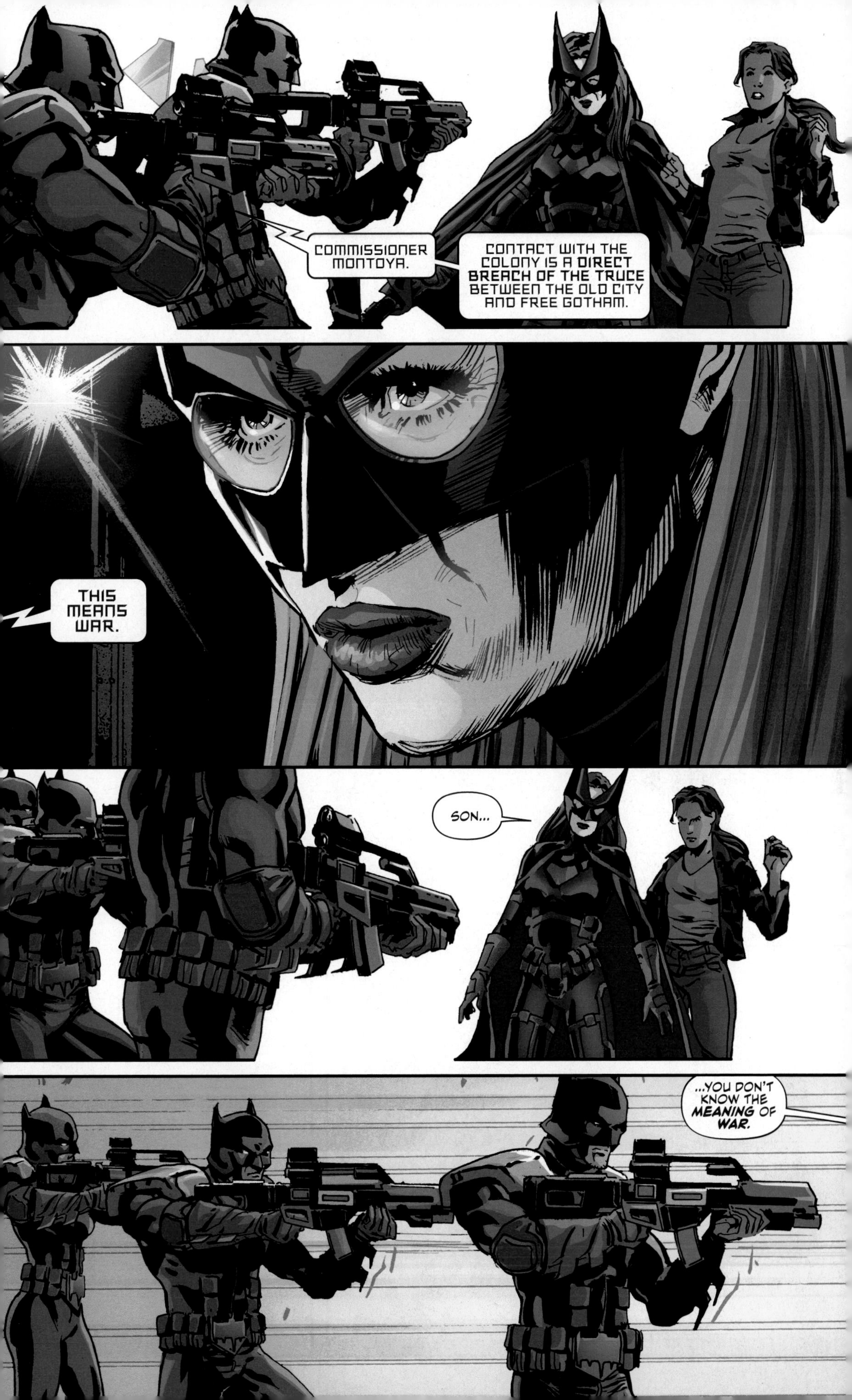

COMMISSIONER MONTOYA.
CONTACT WITH THE COLONY IS A **DIRECT BREACH OF THE TRUCE** BETWEEN THE OLD CITY AND FREE GOTHAM.
THIS MEANS WAR.
SON...
...YOU DON'T KNOW THE ***MEANING*** OF ***WAR.***

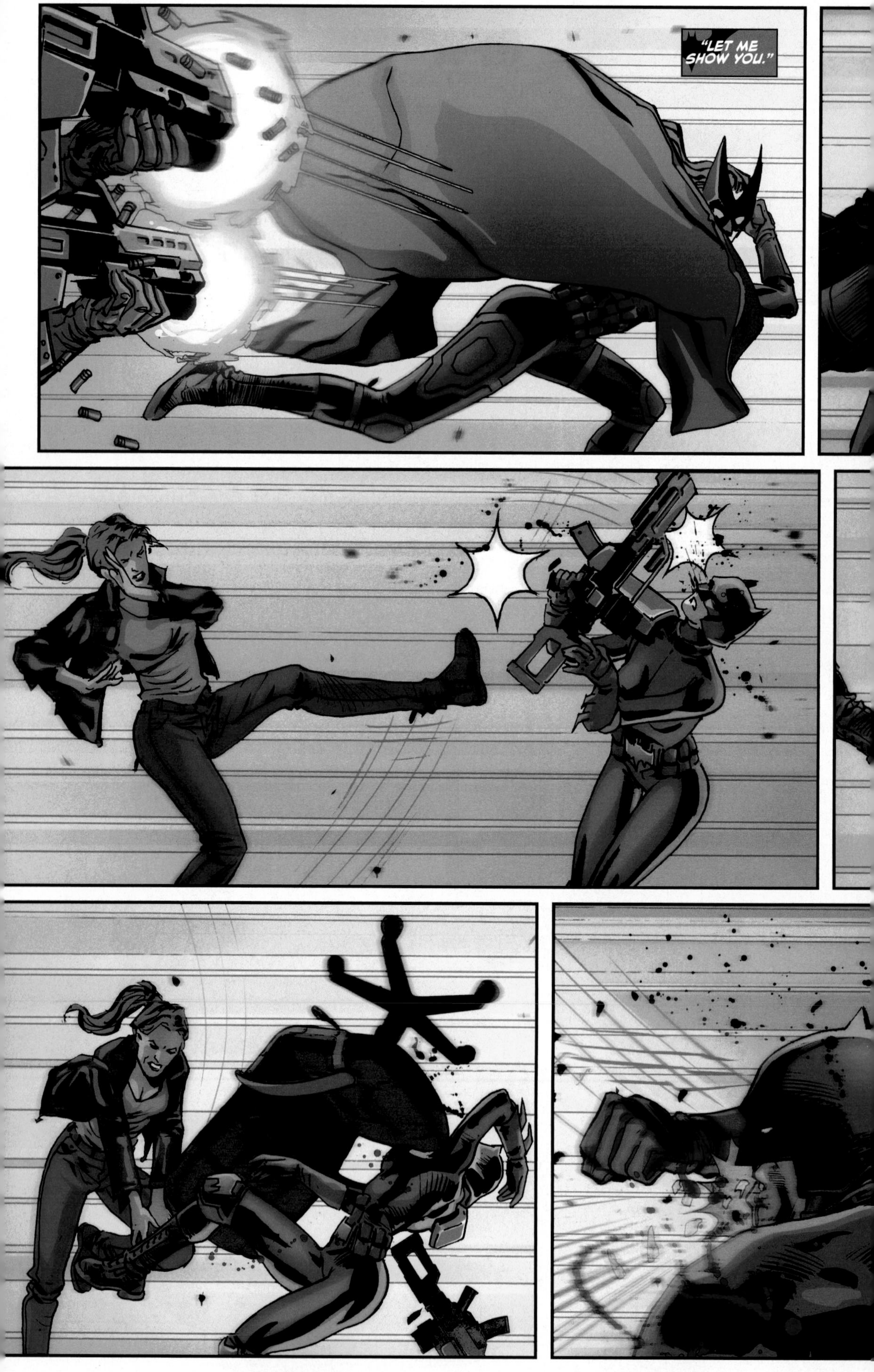
"LET ME SHOW YOU."

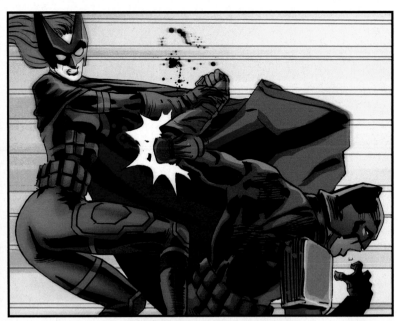

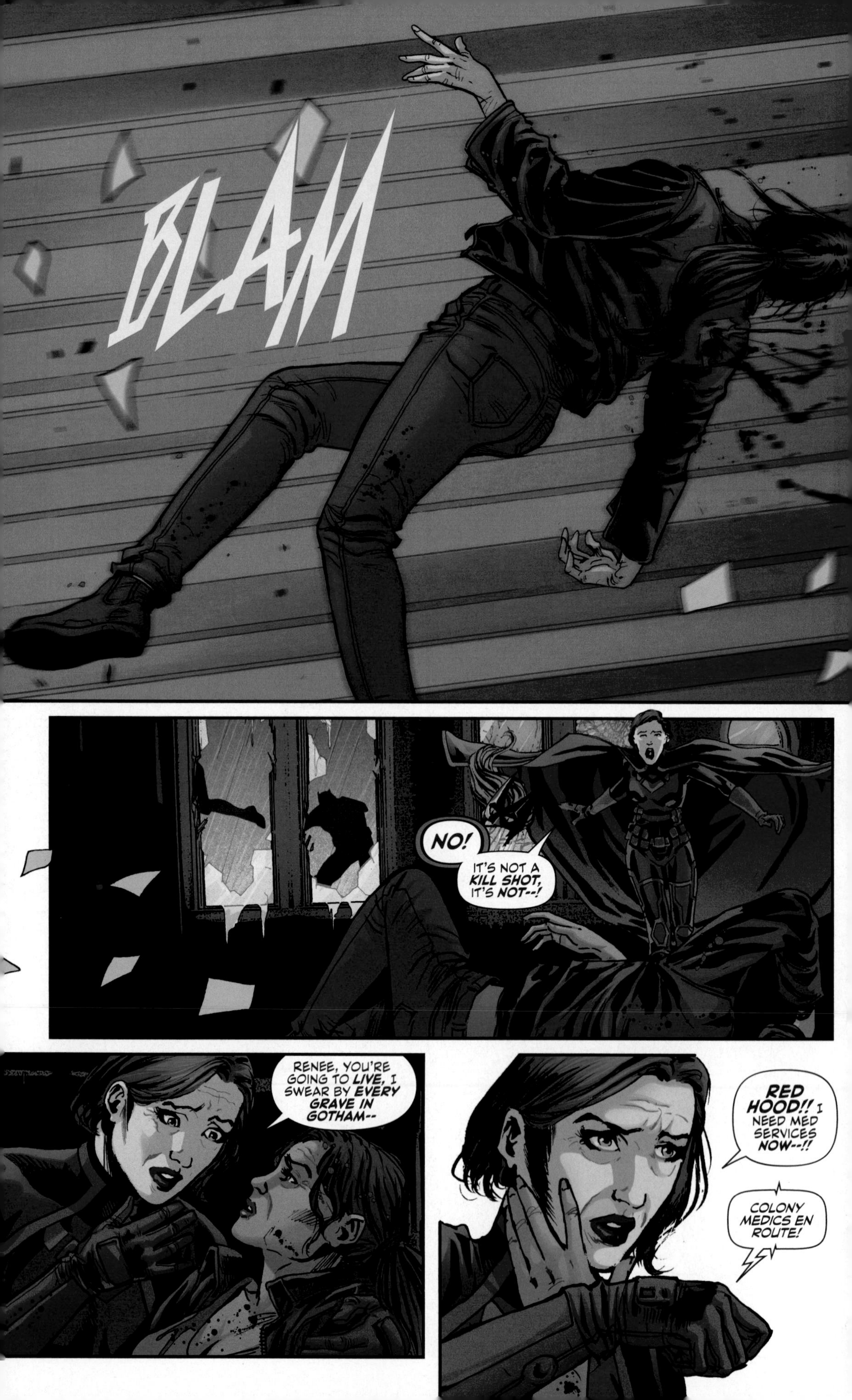
BLAM
NO!
IT'S NOT A KILL SHOT, IT'S NOT--!
RENEE, YOU'RE GOING TO LIVE, I SWEAR BY EVERY GRAVE IN GOTHAM--
RED HOOD!! I NEED MED SERVICES NOW--!!
COLONY MEDICS EN ROUTE!

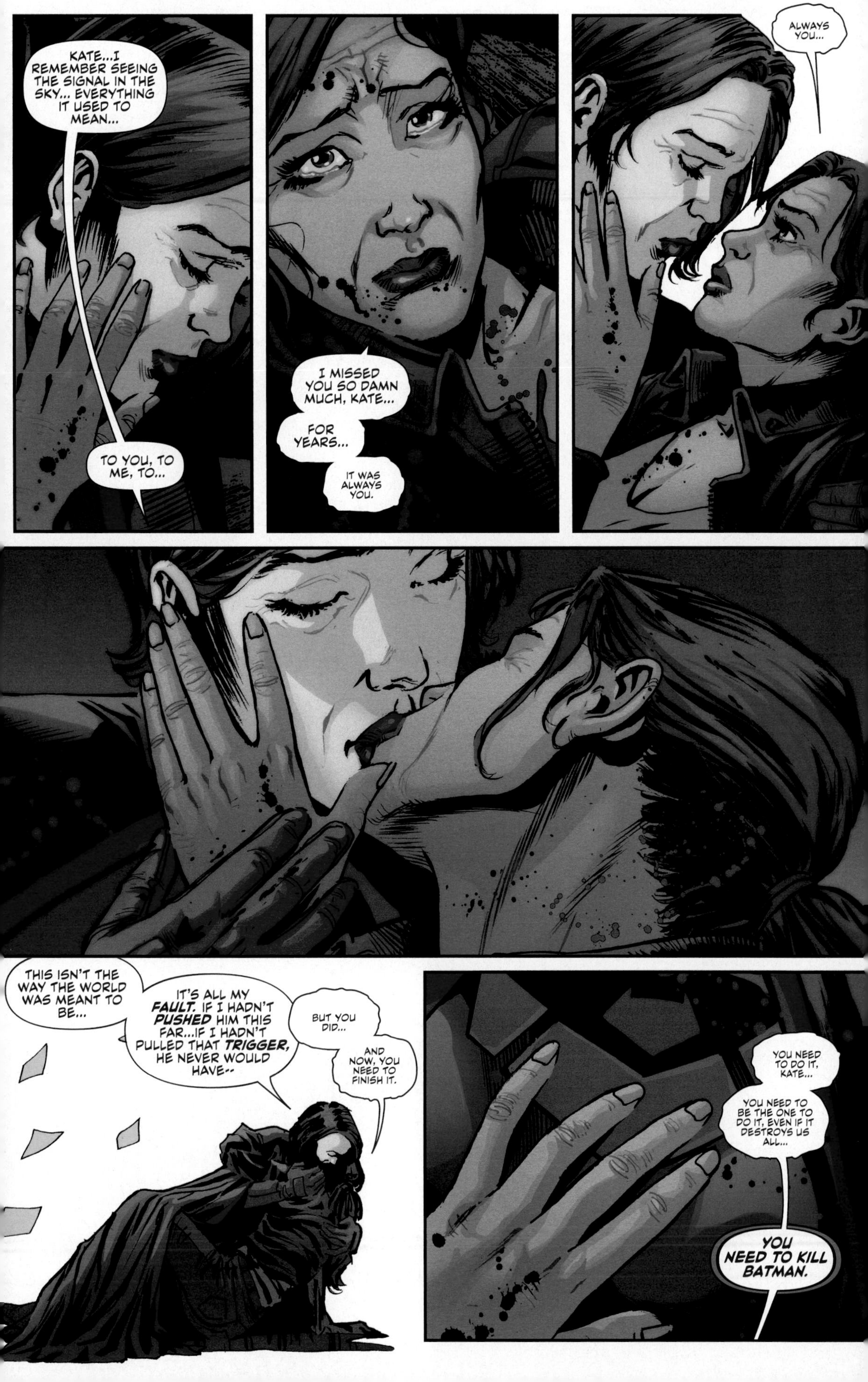
KATE...I REMEMBER SEEING THE SIGNAL IN THE SKY... EVERYTHING IT USED TO MEAN...
TO YOU, TO ME, TO...
I MISSED YOU SO DAMN MUCH, KATE...
FOR YEARS...
IT WAS ALWAYS YOU.
ALWAYS YOU...
THIS ISN'T THE WAY THE WORLD WAS MEANT TO BE...
IT'S ALL MY FAULT. IF I HADN'T PUSHED HIM THIS FAR...IF I HADN'T PULLED THAT TRIGGER, HE NEVER WOULD HAVE--
BUT YOU DID...
AND NOW, YOU NEED TO FINISH IT.
YOU NEED TO DO IT, KATE...
YOU NEED TO BE THE ONE TO DO IT, EVEN IF IT DESTROYS US ALL...
YOU NEED TO KILL BATMAN.

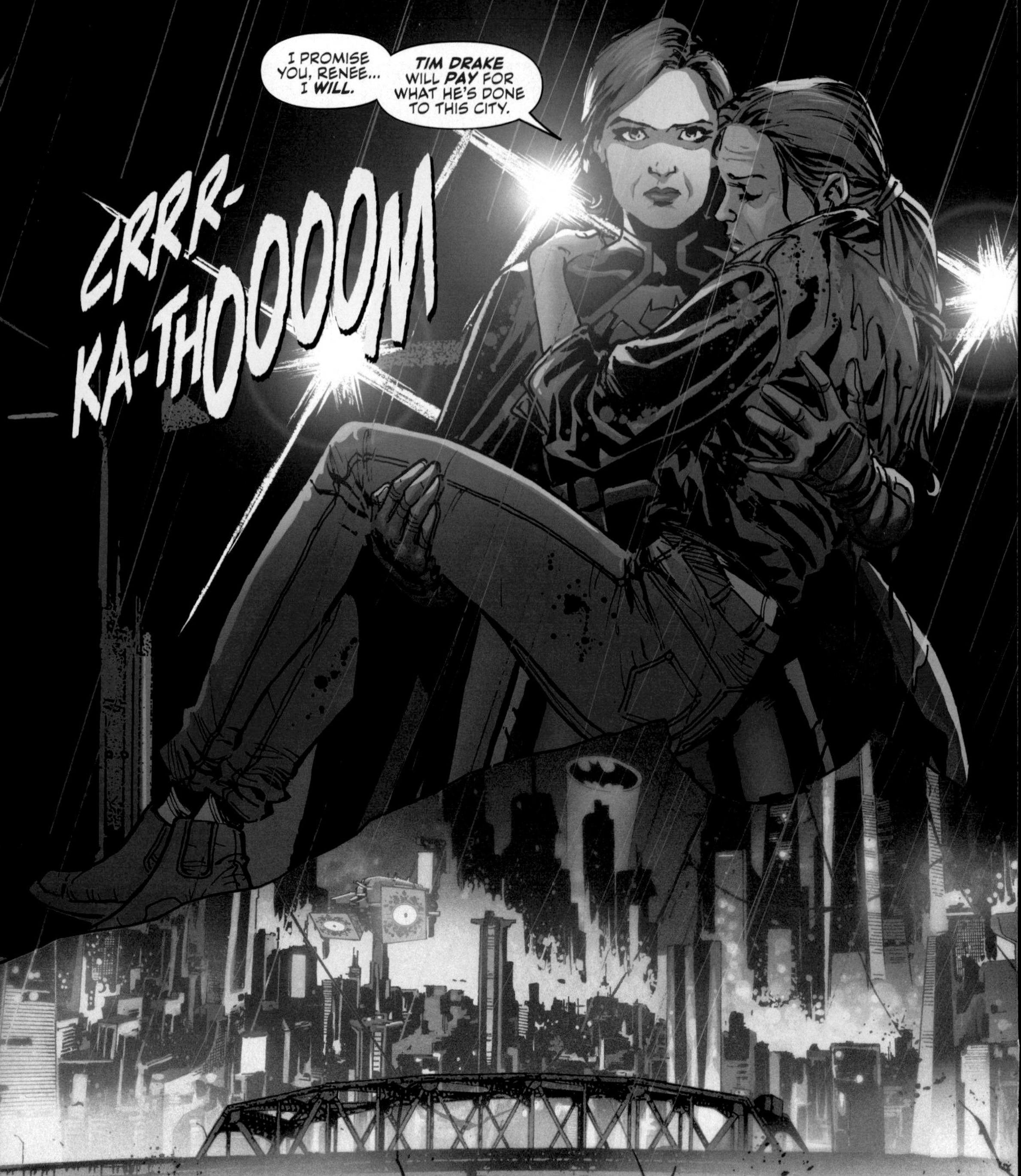
I PROMISE YOU, RENEE... I WILL.
TIM DRAKE WILL PAY FOR WHAT HE'S DONE TO THIS CITY.
CRRR-KA-THOOOOM
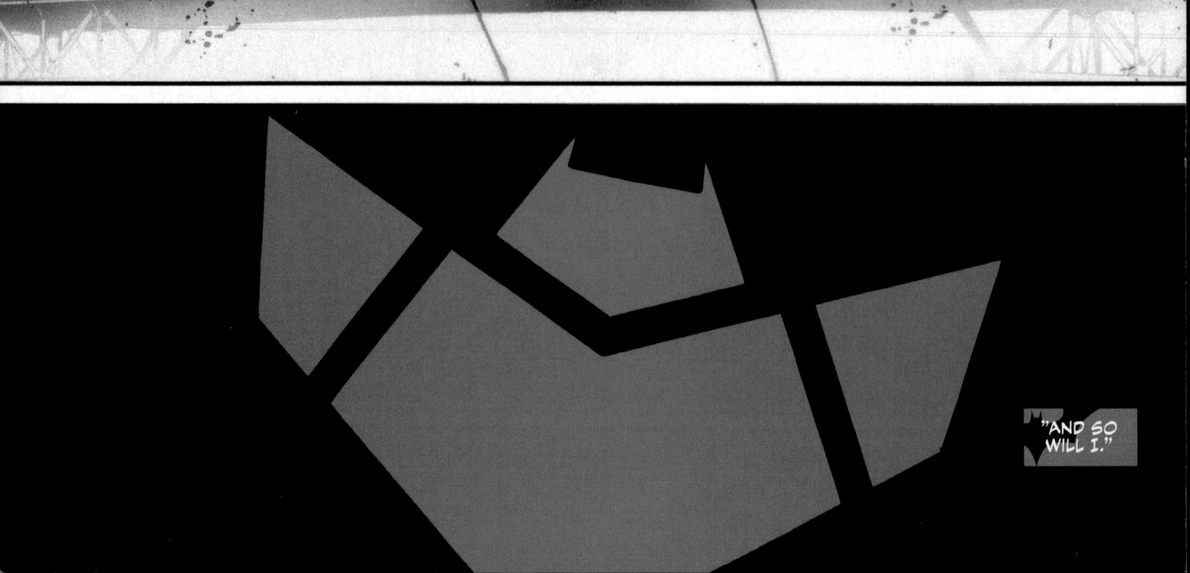
"AND SO WILL I."

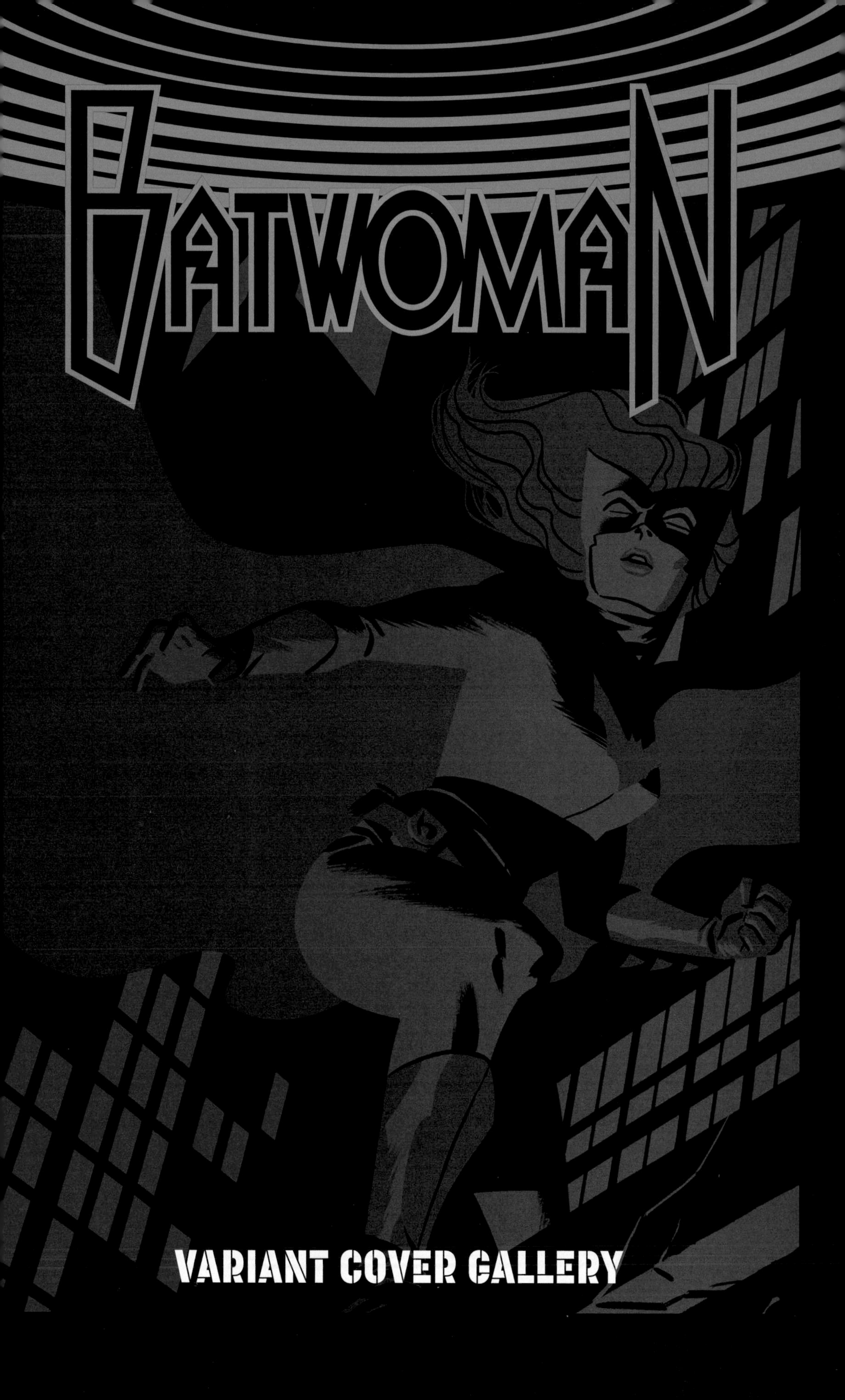
BATWOMAN
VARIANT COVER GALLERY

BATWOMAN: REBIRTH #1 by JAE LEE and JUNE CHUNG

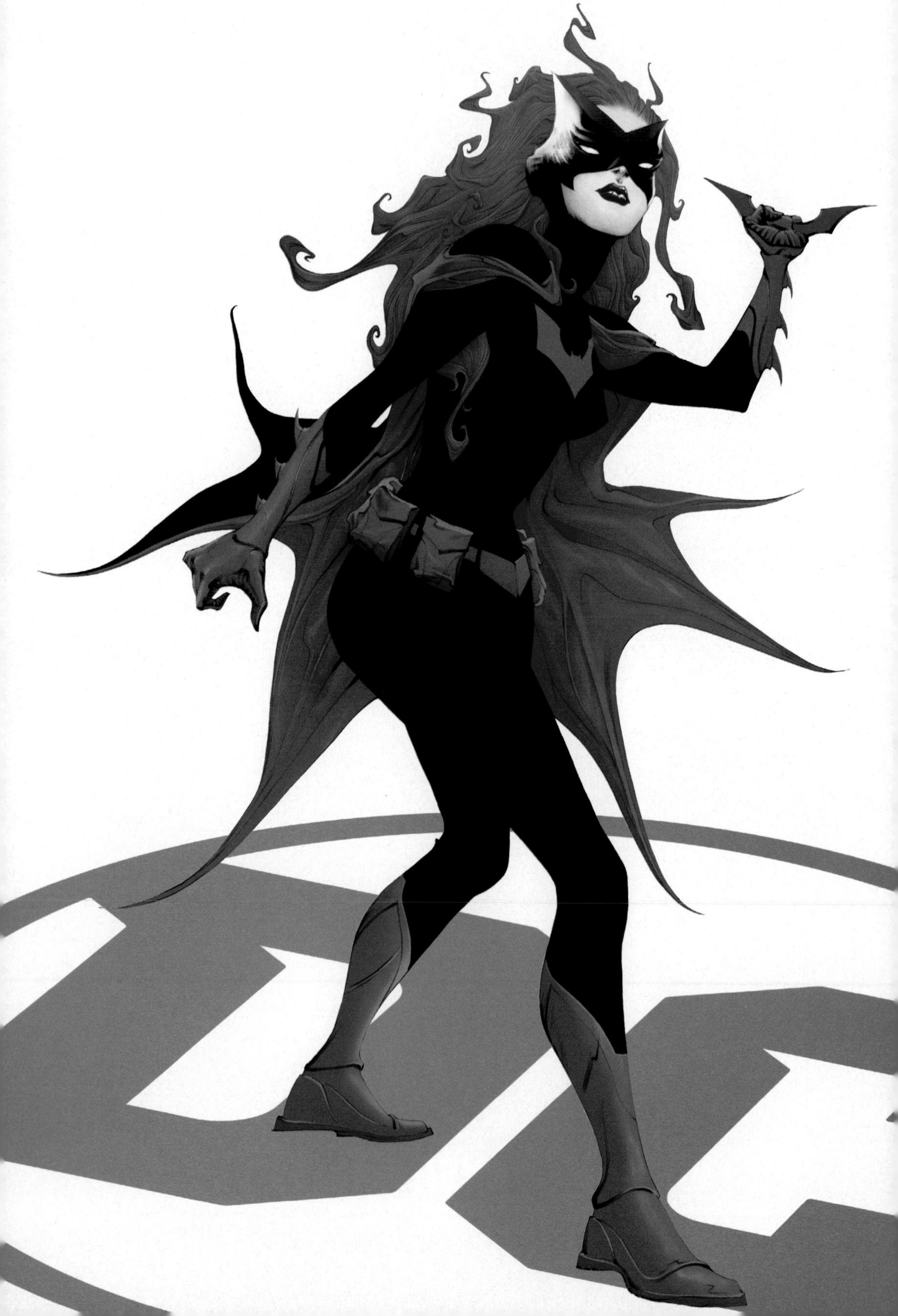

BATWOMAN #1 by J.G. JONES

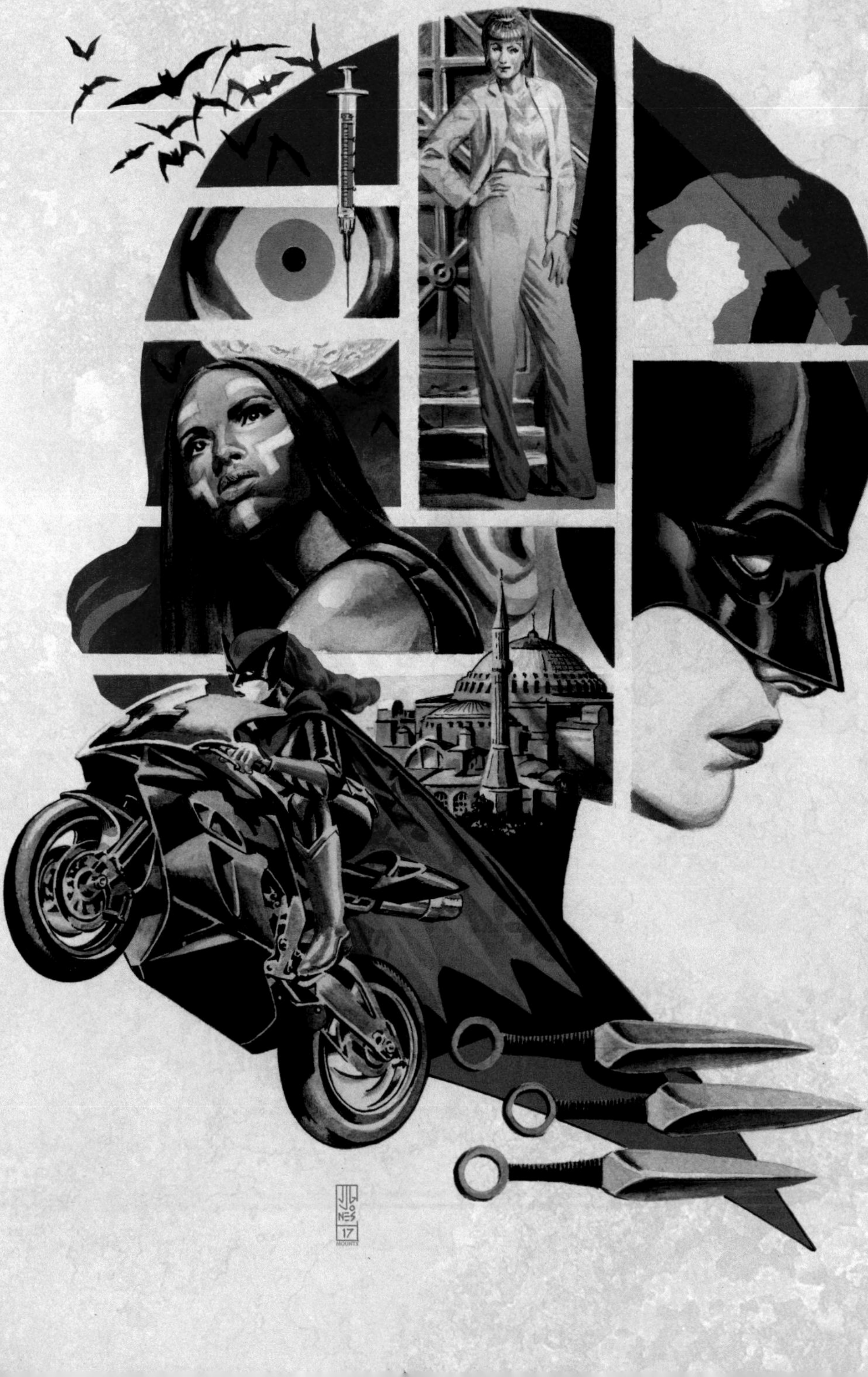

BATWOMAN #2 by J.G. JONES

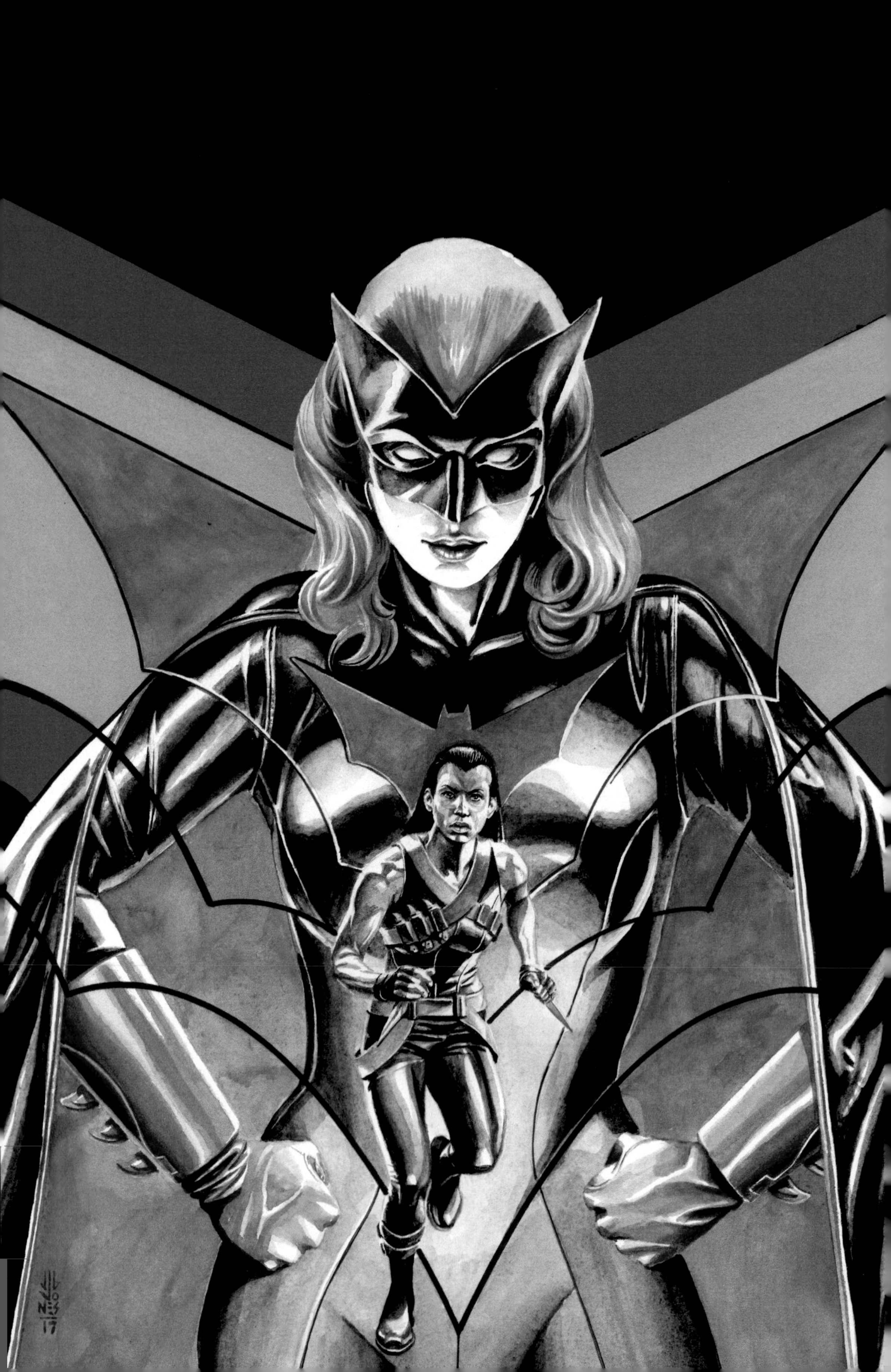

BATWOMAN #3 by J.G. JONES

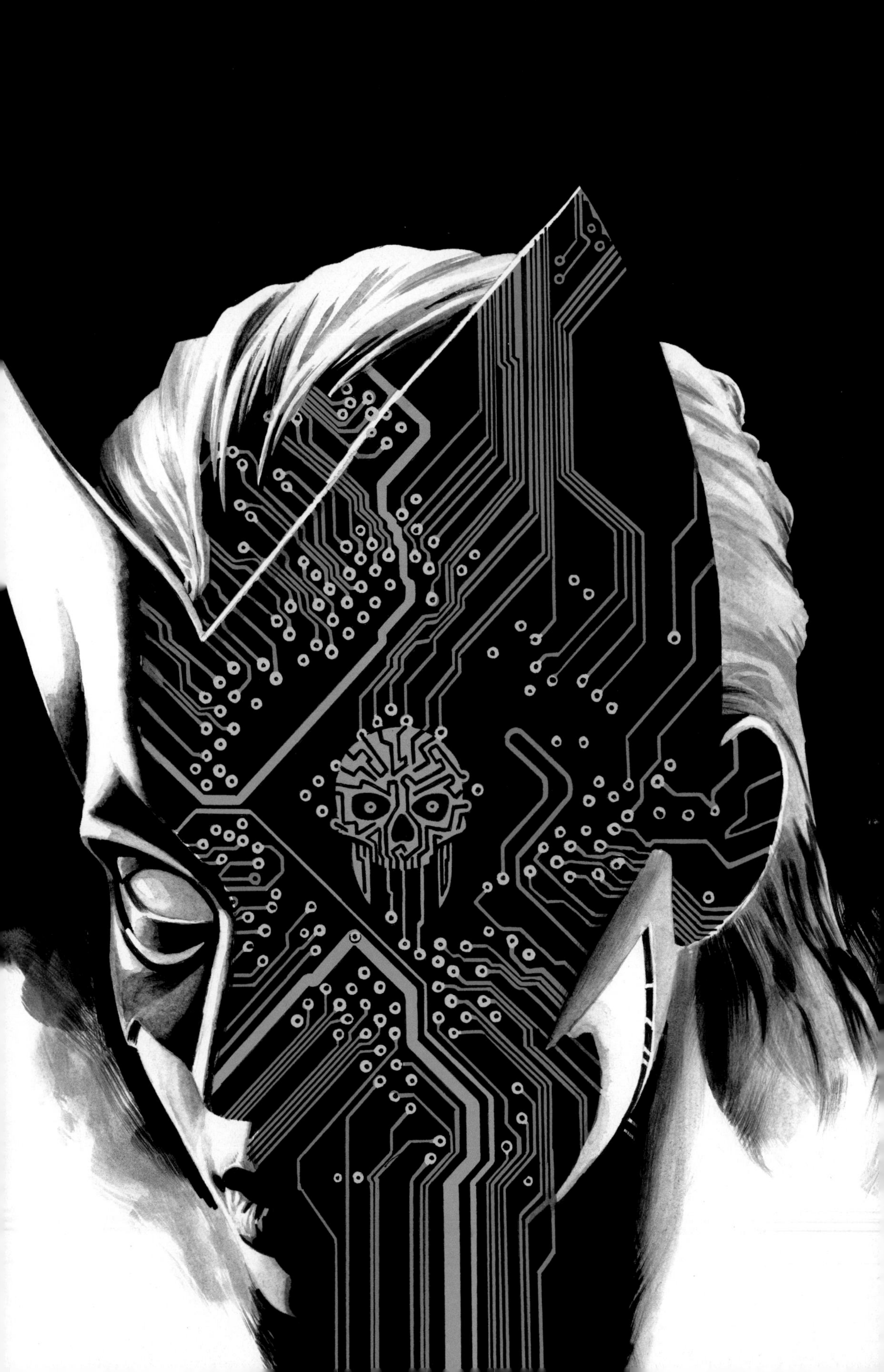

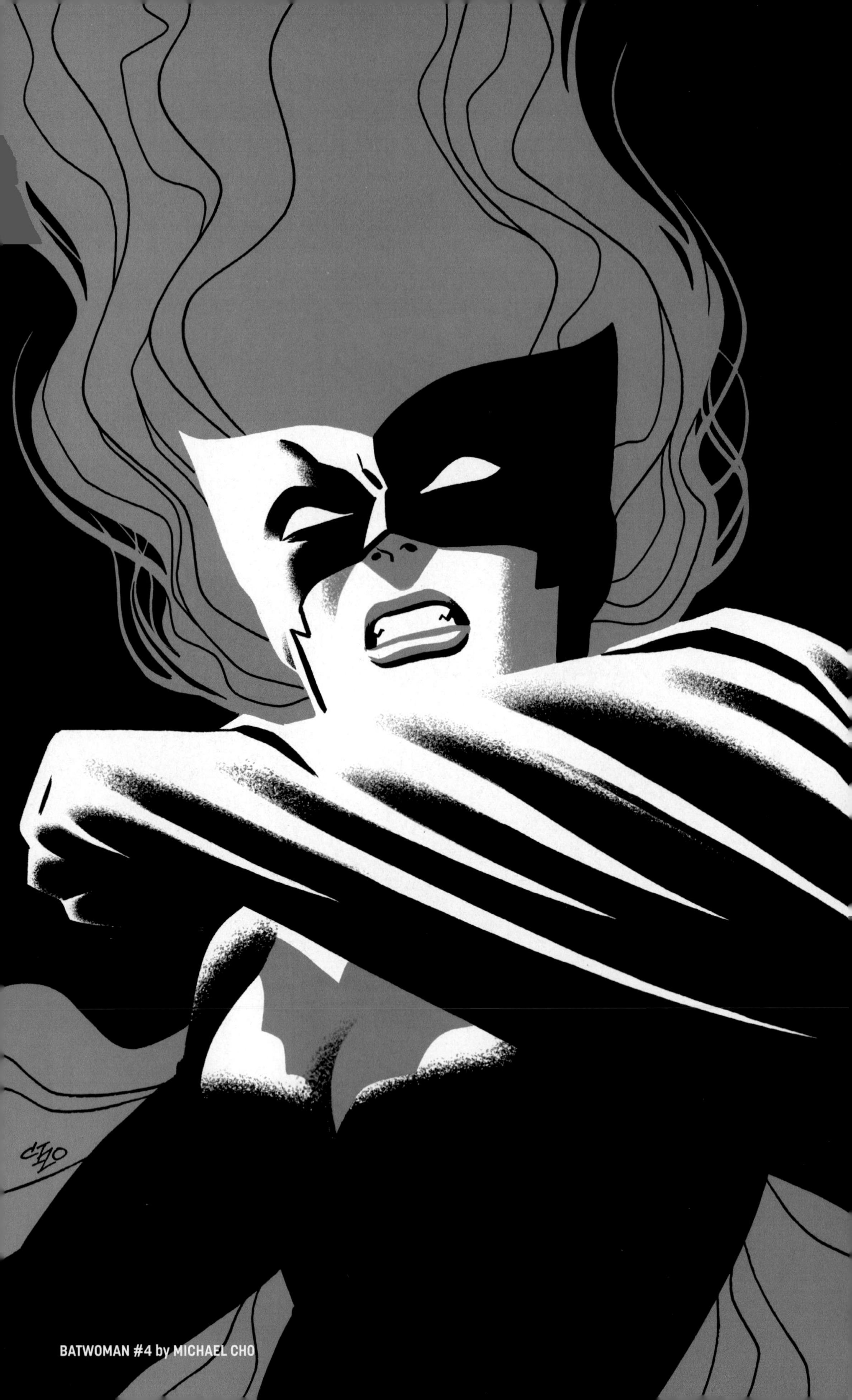

BATWOMAN #4 by MICHAEL CHO

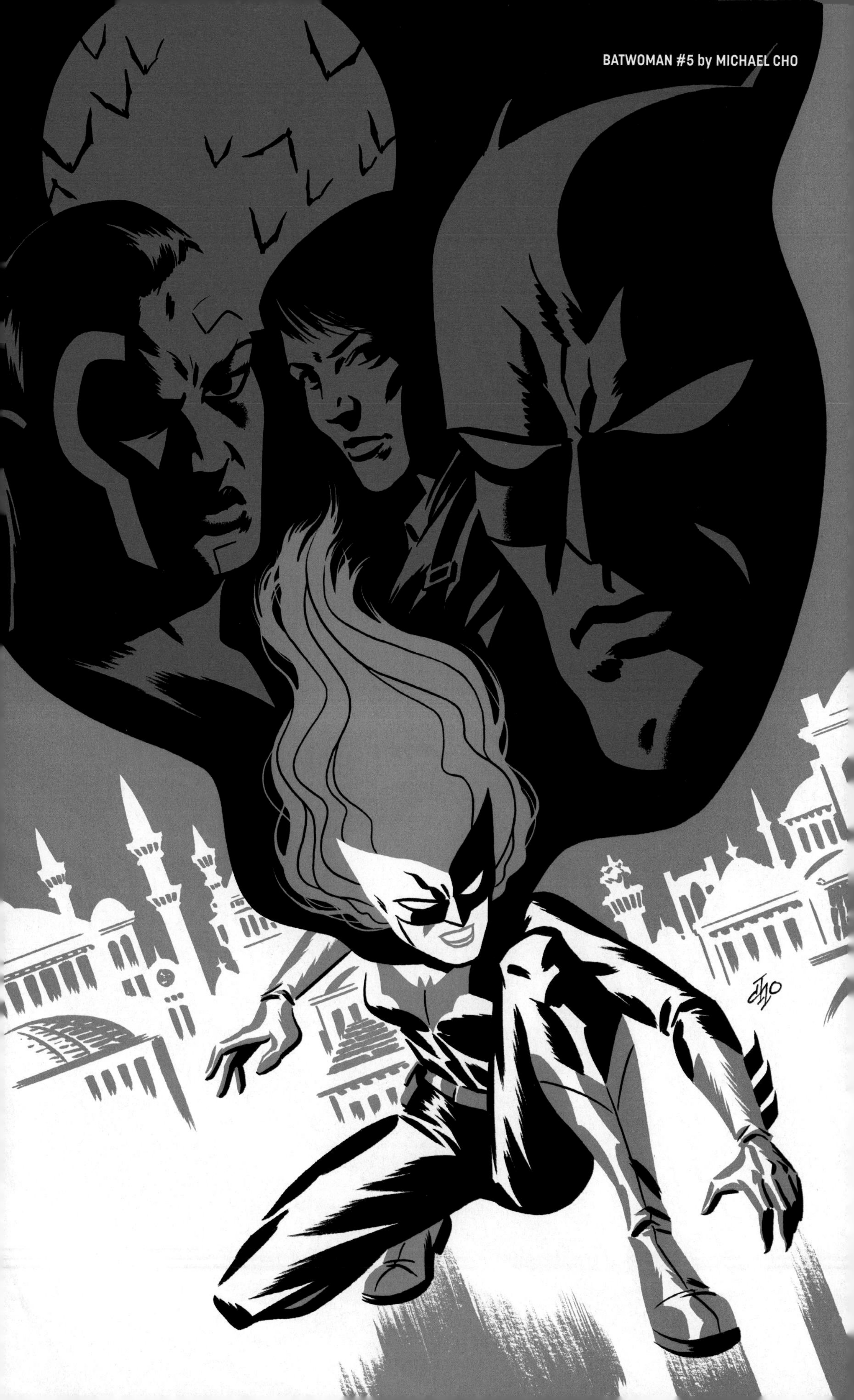

BATWOMAN #5 by MICHAEL CHO

BATWOMAN #6 by MICHAEL CHO

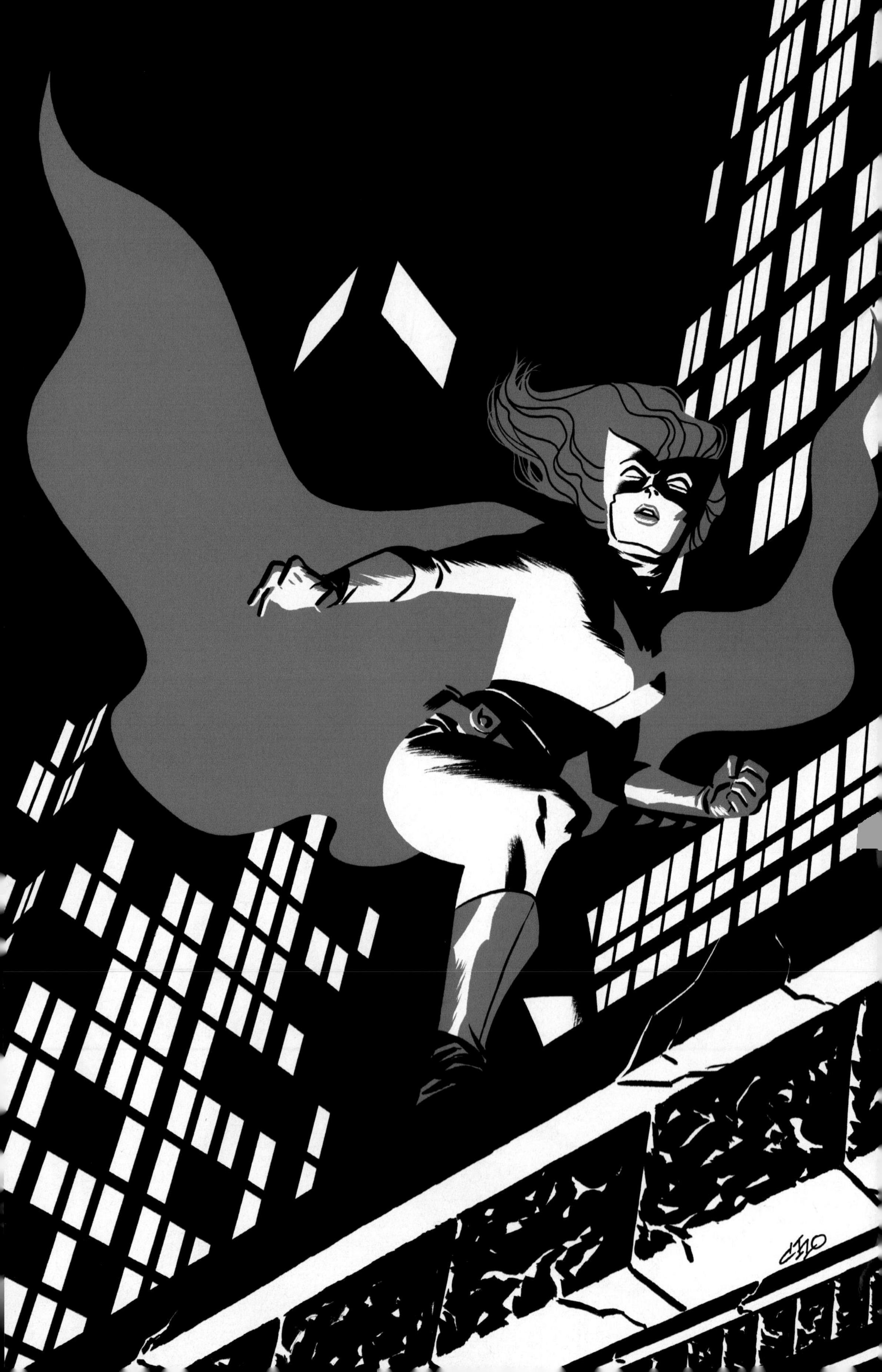

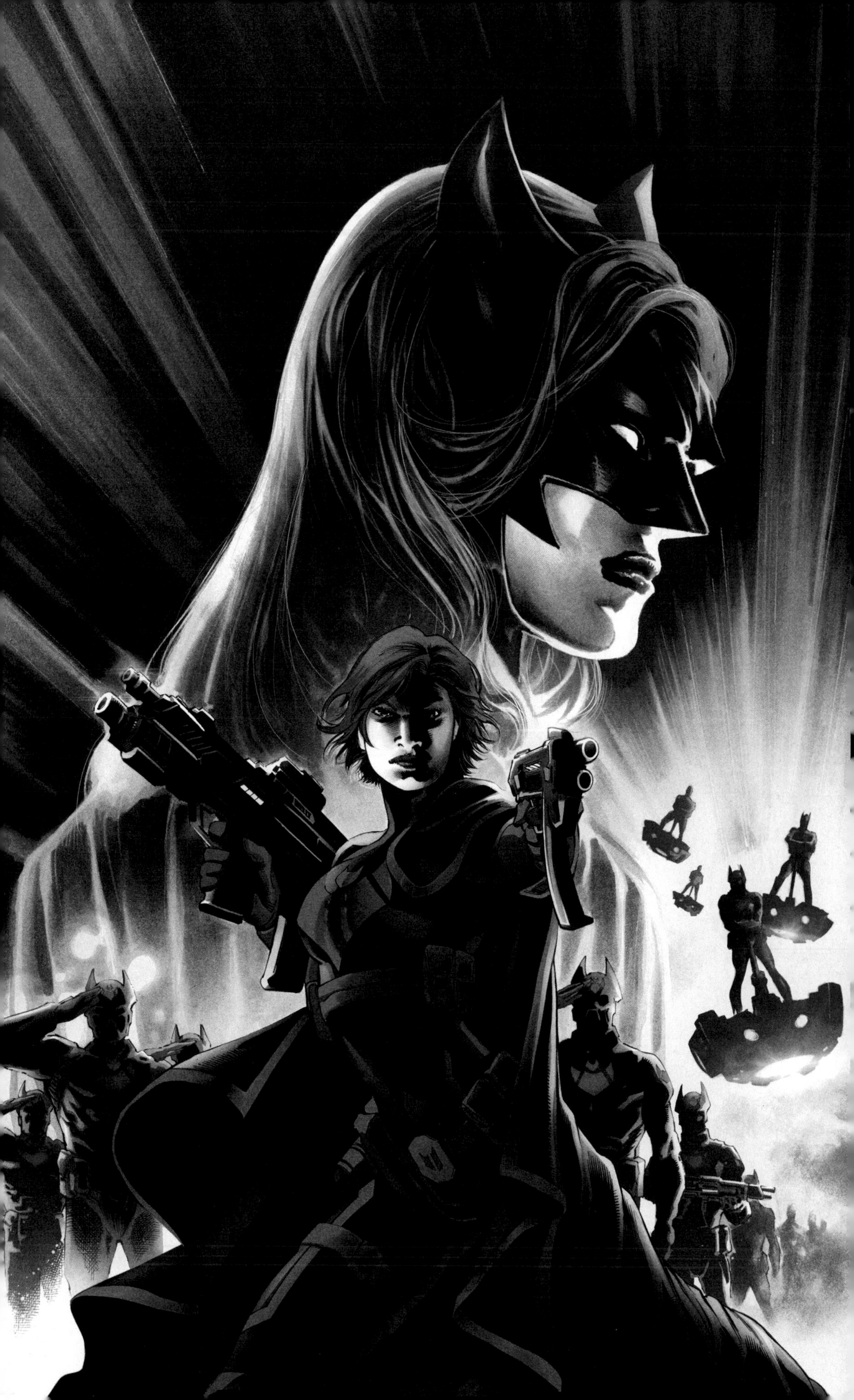

"One of the best writers for Wonder Woman in the modern era."
– **NERDIST**

WONDER WOMAN BY
GREG
RUCKA
with J.G. JONES
& DREW JOHNSON

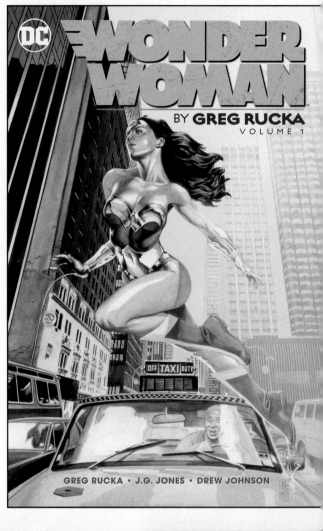

WONDER WOMAN BY GREG RUCKA
VOLUME 1

GREG RUCKA • J.G. JONES • DREW JOHNSON

BATWOMAN: ELEGY
with J.H. WILLIAMS III

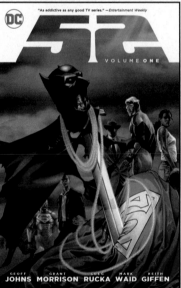

52 VOL. 1
with VARIOUS ARTISTS

GOTHAM CENTRAL BOOK ONE
with ED BRUBAKER
& MICHAEL LARK

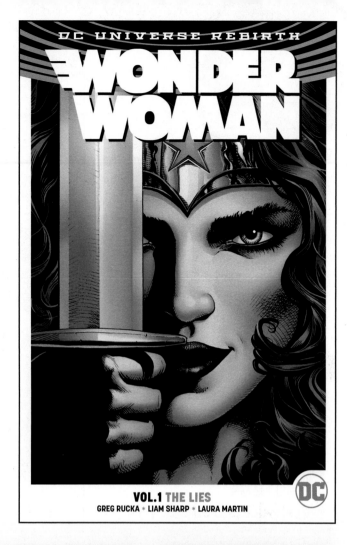

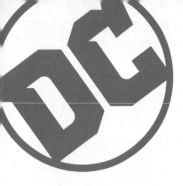

"It's nice to see one of the best comics of the late '80s return so strongly."
– Comic Book Resources

"It's high energy from page one through to the last page." **– BATMAN NEWS**

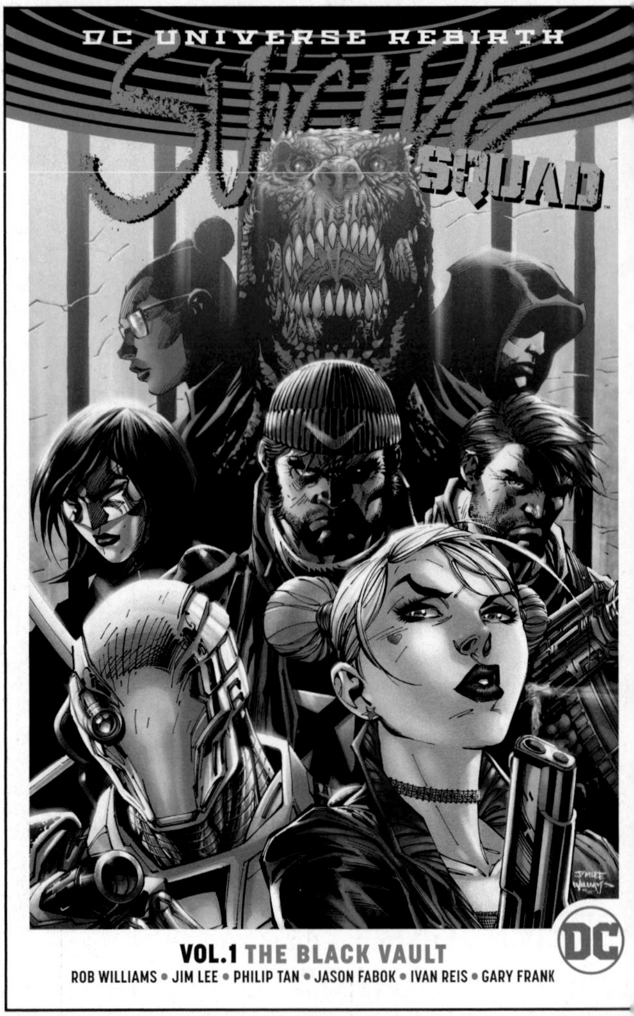
DC UNIVERSE REBIRTH
SUICIDE SQUAD
VOL.1 THE BLACK VAULT
ROB WILLIAMS • JIM LEE • PHILIP TAN • JASON FABOK • IVAN REIS • GARY FRANK

DC UNIVERSE REBIRTH

SUICIDE SQUAD

VOL. 1: THE BLACK VAULT

ROB WILLIAMS
with JIM LEE and others

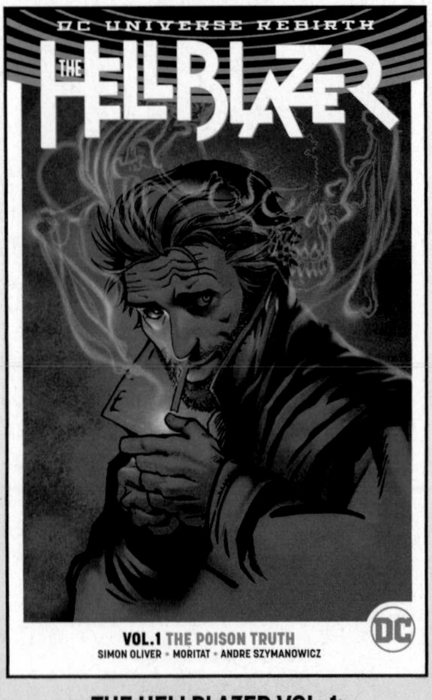
DC UNIVERSE REBIRTH
THE HELLBLAZER
VOL.1 THE POISON TRUTH
SIMON OLIVER • MORITAT • ANDRE SZYMANOWICZ

THE HELLBLAZER VOL. 1: THE POISON TRUTH

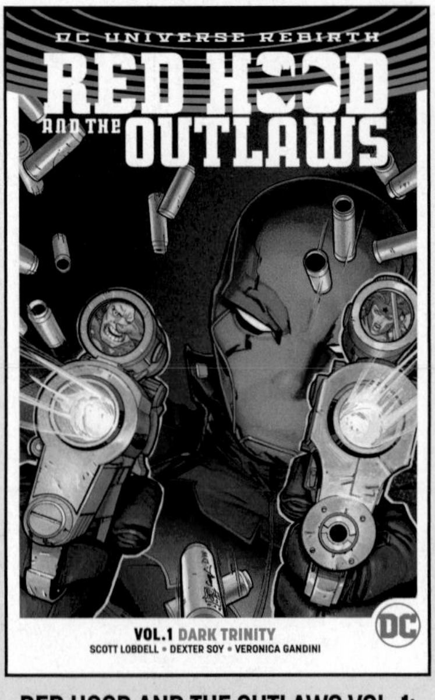
DC UNIVERSE REBIRTH
RED HOOD AND THE OUTLAWS
VOL.1 DARK TRINITY
SCOTT LOBDELL • DEXTER SOY • VERONICA GANDINI

RED HOOD AND THE OUTLAWS VOL. 1: DARK TRINITY

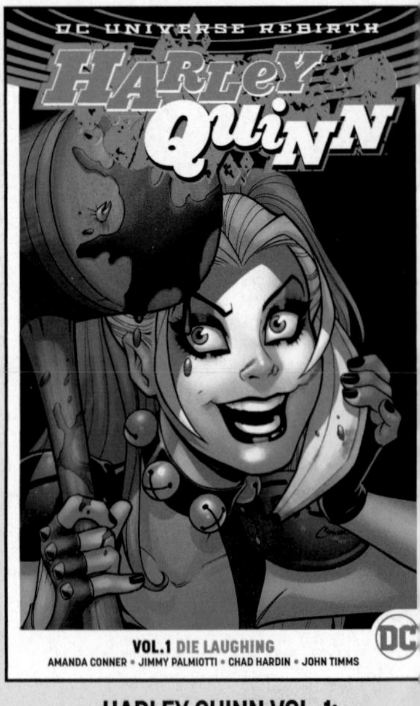
DC UNIVERSE REBIRTH
HARLEY QUINN
VOL.1 DIE LAUGHING
AMANDA CONNER • JIMMY PALMIOTTI • CHAD HARDIN • JOHN TIMMS

HARLEY QUINN VOL. 1: DIE LAUGHING

Get more DC graphic novels wherever comics and books are sold!